LUISE KAISH

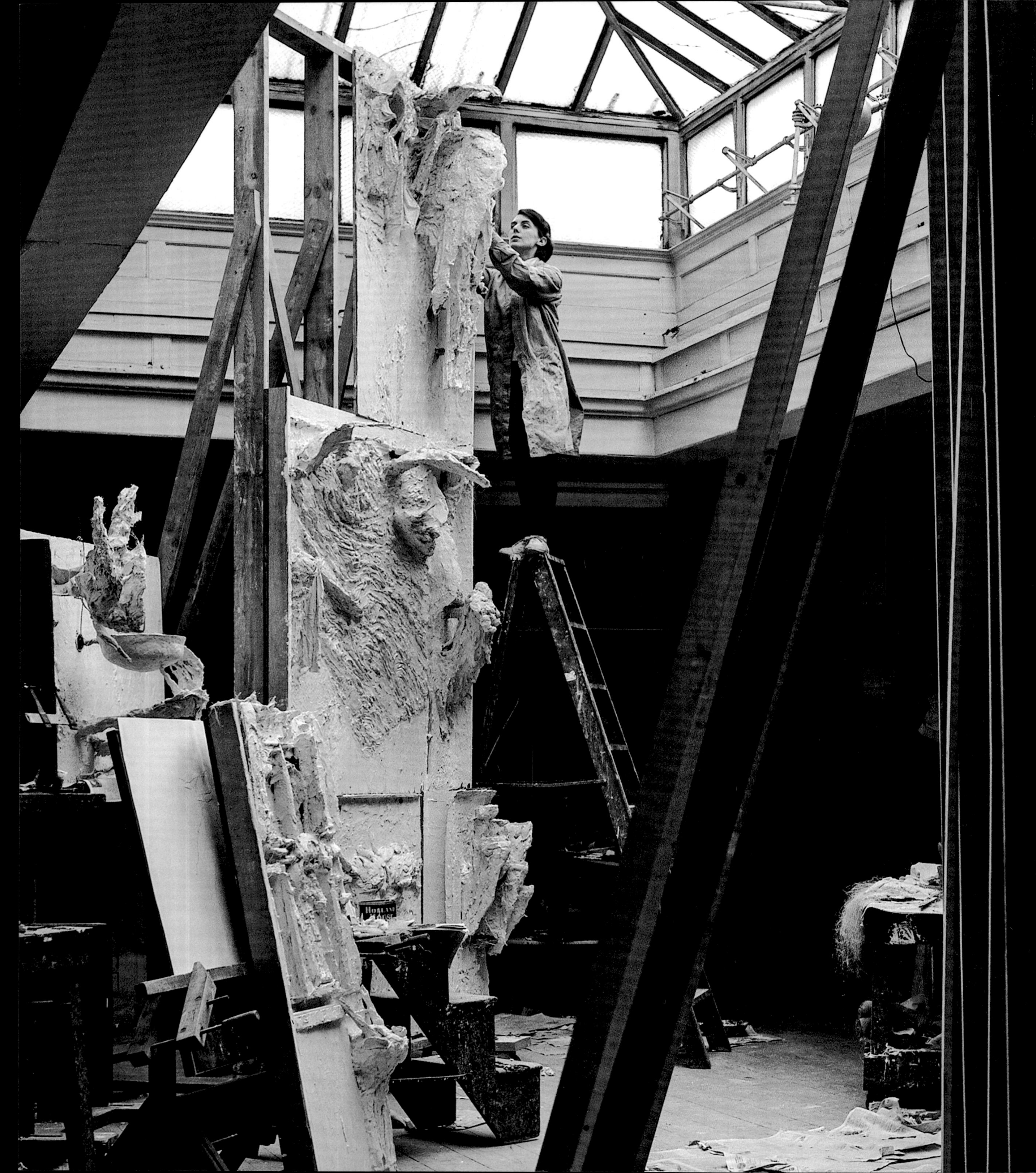

LUISE KAISH

An American Art Legacy

Edited by Maura Reilly

Essays by Daniel Belasco, Samuel D. Gruber, Eleanor Heartney,
Norman L. Kleeblatt, Gail Levin, and Roger Lipsey

D Giles Limited
In association with Kaish Family Art Project LLC, New York

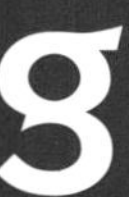

First published in the UK in 2020 by GILES
An imprint of D Giles Limited
66 High Street,
Lewes, BN7 1XG, UK
gilesltd.com

Library of Congress Control
Number: 2020943162

ISBN (hardcover): 978-1-911282-51-8

For the Kaish Family Art Project LLC:
Melissa Kaish, Managing Member
Maura Reilly, Editor

For D Giles Limited:
Produced by GILES, an imprint of D Giles Limited
Copy-edited and proofread by Jodi Simpson
Designed by Alfonso Iacurci
Printed and bound in China

All measurements are in inches and centimeters

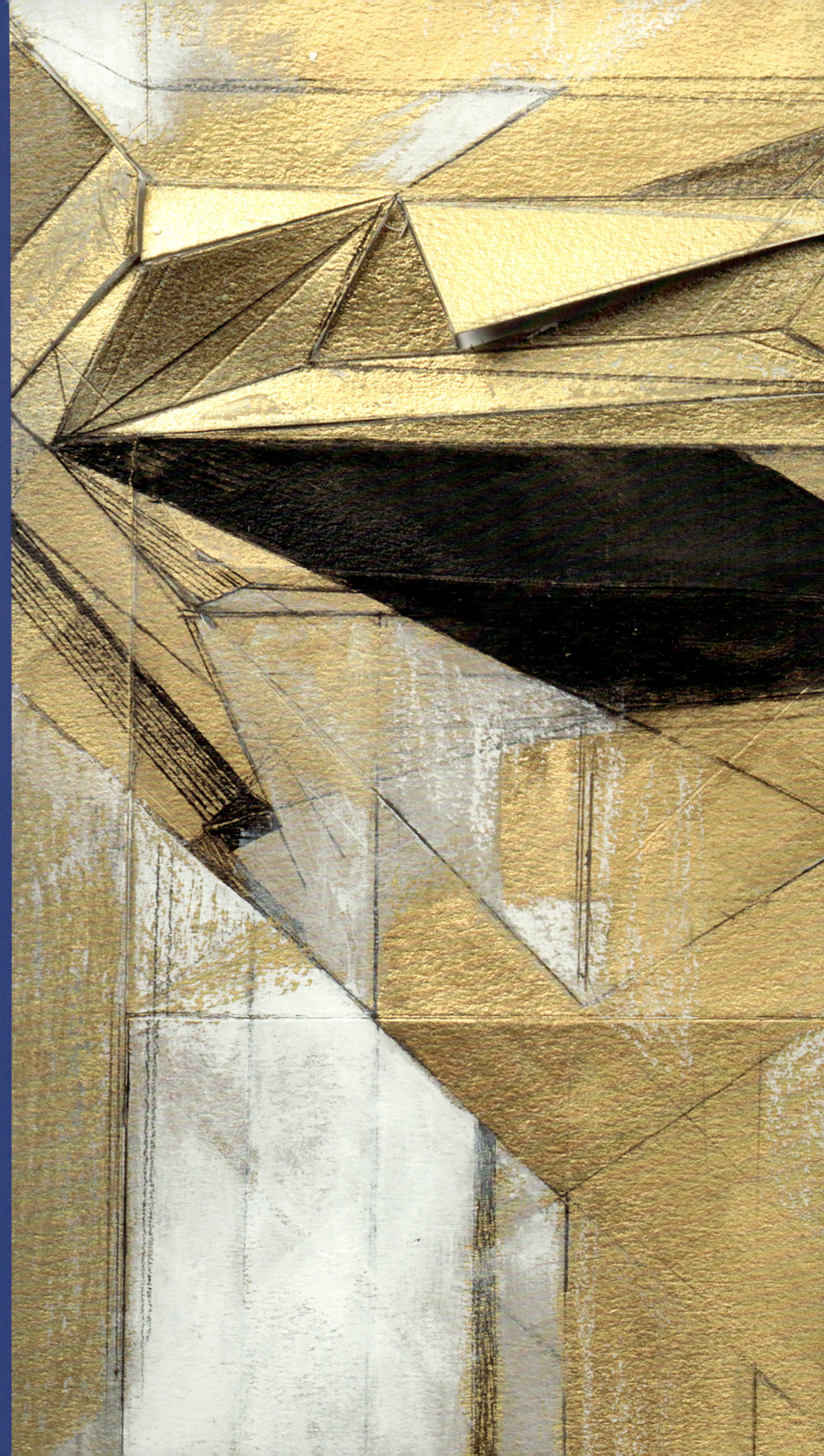

Front cover: Luise Kaish. *Poet in Two Worlds*
(*Deep Space*) (detail), 1975–78 (see Plate 62)

Back cover: Luise Kaish, American Academy in
Rome, 1972. Photo: Morton Kaish

Frontispiece: Luise Kaish, at work on the Ark of
Revelation, MacDougal Street studio, New York,
circa 1962

p. 4: Luise Kaish. *There II*, maquette for
axonometric bronze relief (detail), 2012
(see Plate 102)

pp. 6 & 7: Luise Kaish. *Rising Blue Tide* (detail),
circa 2007–11 (see Plate 99)

CONTENTS

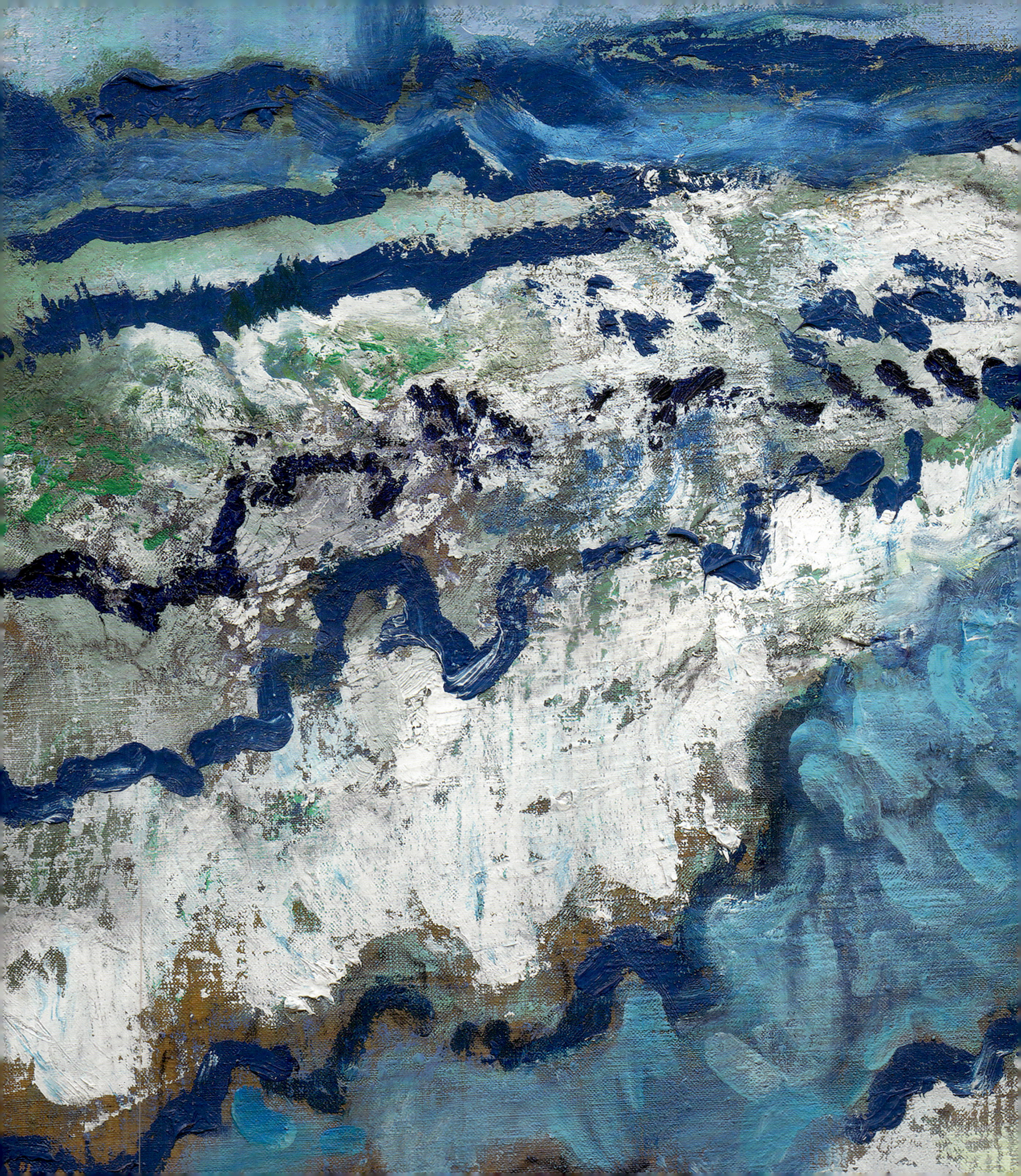

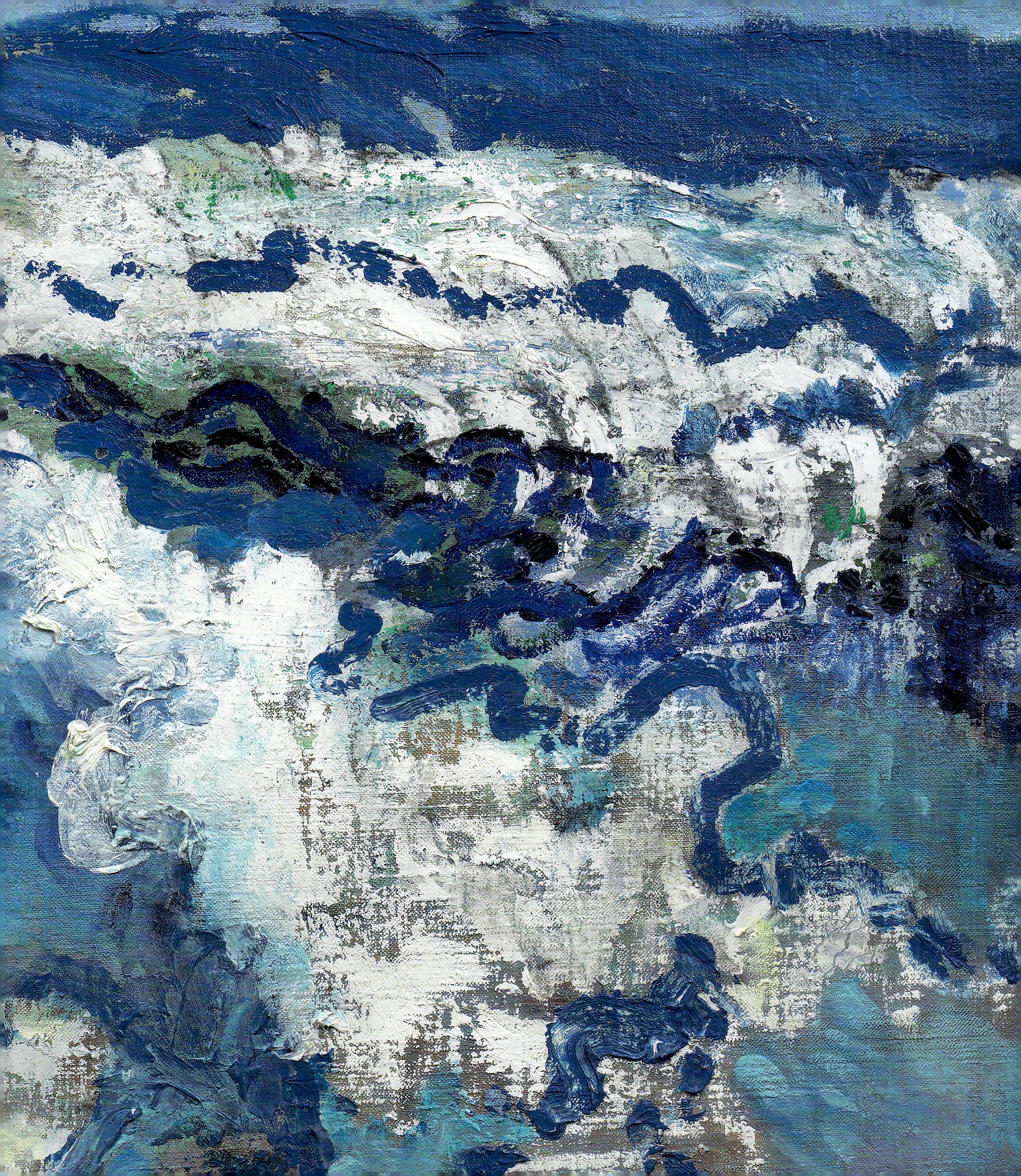

The first photograph I ever saw of Luise Kaish showed her in front of a model for the great *Ark of Revelation*, a work she was commissioned to create for the Congregation B'rith Kodesh in Rochester, New York. When the bronze Ark was installed it measured a monumental thirteen and a half feet high and fifteen and a half feet wide. This image of Kaish with the *Ark* left a lasting impact on me. I was in awe of the sheer scale and beauty of her artwork. Even in a photograph, I felt the *Ark* had an uncanny ability to transcend, to foster an emotional reaction, to move those that encounter it. I later learned of how Kaish had signed the contract for the commission for this monumental project when she was nine months pregnant—in fact, just one day before giving birth. Pondering this image, I realized its power to disrupt the traditional story of twentieth-century art, which all too often restricted its definition of success to men and overlooked the tremendous accomplishments of the women who worked alongside them.

For too long this limited narrative imposed a value system that made it exceptionally difficult for artists who did not conform to this model to succeed. Despite this, Luise Kaish did succeed. She was a central figure in the New York art scene in the second half of the twentieth century and was widely admired for her exploration of materiality, process, and multidisciplinary discourse. During her lifetime she garnered many prestigious awards and fellowships, including the Guggenheim Fellowship, Rome Prize Fellowship, and Louis Comfort Tiffany Foundation Grant, and her art was exhibited at such venerable institutions as the Museum of Modern Art in New York, the Metropolitan Museum of Art, and the Whitney Museum of American Art. She received many high-profile commissions and her art was sought out for private and corporate collections. In addition to her success as a practicing artist, Kaish mentored future generations of artists through her role as an educator. She chaired the graduate Painting and Sculpture division at Columbia University, where she was a professor of Visual Arts. She also lent her wisdom and support to numerous organizations that promoted the arts, acting as a trustee and then trustee emerita of the American Academy in Rome; a trustee and executive member of the Augustus Saint-Gaudens Memorial, National Park Service; a board member of the Sculptors Guild; and a member of the New York City Fine Arts Commission.

Today her work is represented in the most esteemed museum collections in the United States, including the Smithsonian American Art Museum, the Metropolitan Museum of Art, the Whitney Museum of American Art, and the Jewish Museum, and many other institutions, including the Syracuse University Art Museum, where I am director. I was given the honor of writing this foreword because of Kaish's strong ties with Syracuse University; anyone who visits the campus will feel her presence when they encounter her over-life-size sculpture *Saltine Warrior* in the central quad. Kaish completed both her undergraduate and graduate studies here, and studied under the renowned Croatian sculptor Ivan Meštrović while completing her MFA. As a testament to her sheer talent and initiative, Kaish was commissioned to create *Saltine Warrior* while she was still a graduate student. When creating the commission she sought out a Native American model, the son of a chief of the Onondaga Nation on whose land Syracuse University now stands, and asked him to pose for the sculpture. Soon after the sculpture was completed she was honored in the reservation's ceremony of the Green Corn, and years later received Syracuse University's highest honor, the George Arents Pioneer Medal.

Luise Kaish truly was a pioneer, a trailblazer who had a lasting impact on the development of the New York art scene. For too long the amazing accomplishments and contributions of women such as Kaish have been understudied. I am grateful that in recent years there has been an active effort by historians and museum professionals alike to reexamine the past and give greater voice to the women whose art shaped the twentieth century. I congratulate Maura Reilly and the Kaish Family Art Project, especially Melissa Kaish and Morton Kaish, for their vision and efforts in making this impressive book possible. By bringing together this remarkable selection of Luise Kaish's art with the writings of seven preeminent scholars, this book offers a new window into the life and work of this extraordinary artist. Through its wide reach it will ensure that her contributions to the art scene are told, and in doing so will help shape a more inclusive and accurate history of twentieth-century art.

Vanja Malloy, Ph.D.
Director and Chief Curator
Syracuse University Art Museum

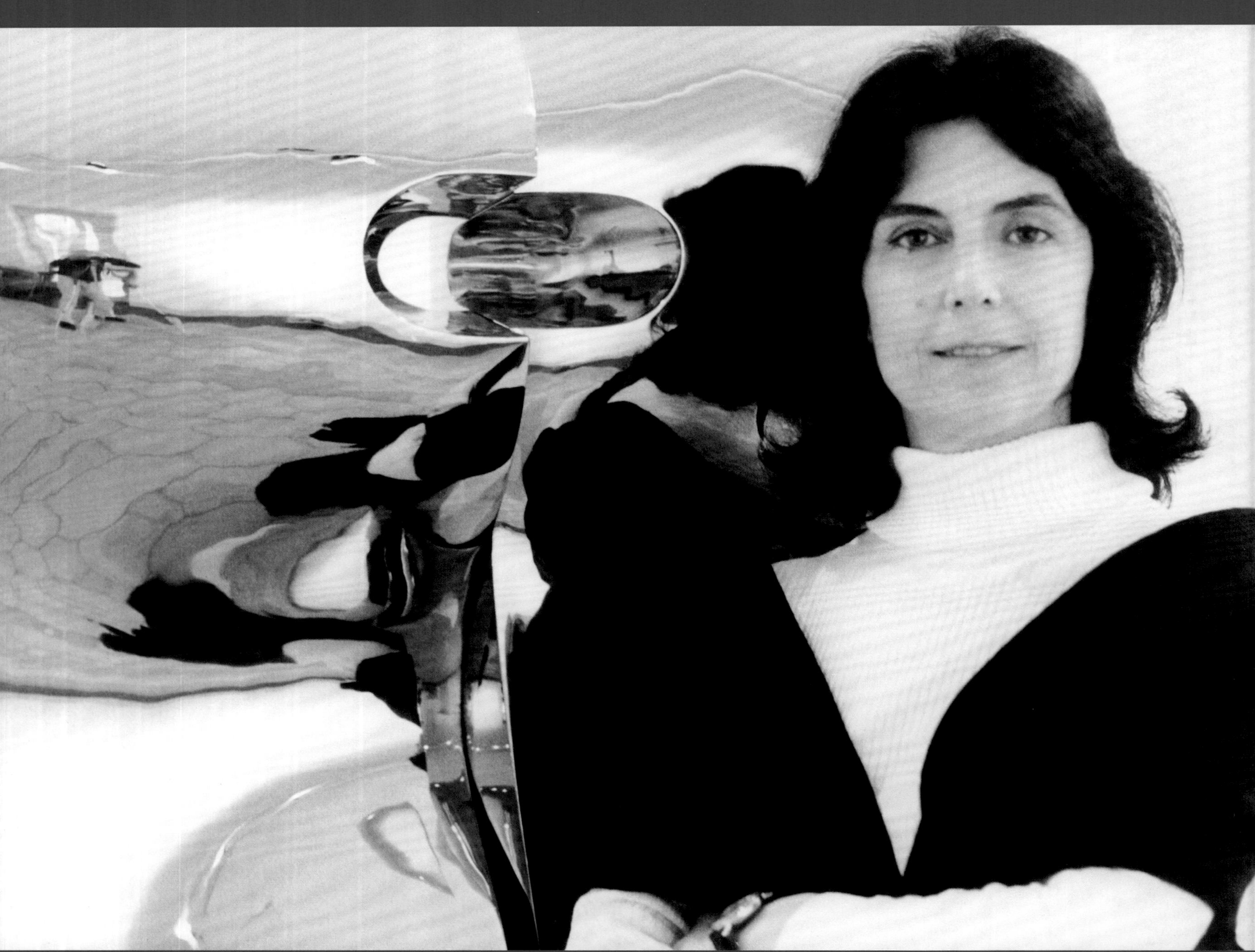

INTRODUCTION

Maura Reilly

Luise Kaish at the opening of her exhibition, American Academy in Rome, 1972

Luise Kaish was a major figure in American art of the mid- to late twentieth century. Over the course of her seven-decade-long career, Kaish produced an immense body of work in multiple mediums—including stone, bronze, stainless steel, collage, and acrylic—and in styles ranging from abstract to representational. She explored a wide range of subjects, from small- and large-scale biblical works to painterly collages and landscape paintings. She is widely known for her monumental commissions, epic, ambitious works using techniques like casting and welding that had historically been associated only with male artists. From the early 1950s until her death in 2013, Kaish exhibited regularly in museums and galleries, to great acclaim. She was one of few women to receive the most coveted artist awards of her day and her art was collected by the most important museums in the United States. She was also an educator. At a time when few women artists were getting hired in prominent art faculty positions, in 1980 Kaish was appointed chair of the Division of Painting and Sculpture at Columbia University in order to rebuild the department—a position she held until 1986.

Kaish was highly recognized in her heyday and lauded by all of the major American art critics. Irving Sandler praised the expanse of her sculptural works as representative of "the awesomeness of the breadth of God"; Robert M. Coates described her reliefs in bronze as possessing a "sweeping energy that parallels the turbulence of Turner in painting"; John Canaday described Kaish as "a rarity" whose sculpture had attained "a sense of power and authority leavened with a poetic innocence," and whose stylistic sources—Meštrović, Baskin, Pomodoro—though recognizable, were not imitative and avoided traditional clichés; and Harold Rosenberg singled out her work in a group show in 1967 as one of the "masterpieces," alongside George Segal, Elaine de Kooning, Robert Rauschenberg, Ben Shahn, and Red Grooms.[1]

A retrospective exhibition in 1973 at the Jewish Museum, which included work produced over two decades, further solidified Kaish's career as an artist of great importance. A contemporary review noted that the exhibition demonstrated her "continuing search for the sacred" and that "it is this spiritual sense which distinguishes her work from other sculptors of her generation."[2] At a time when post-minimalism and conceptual art were at their height, Kaish's interest in biblical themes and the sacred set her apart from the art world's reigning aesthetics. Yet curator Avram Kampf argued that her abstract works, which "derive from her deep mystical inclinations," were wholly contemporary insofar as they explored "untold regions and stages of an internal universe."[3]

Despite the fact that religion, spirituality, and the sacred have been vital wellsprings of Western art for two millennia, during Kaish's lifetime these subjects were decidedly out of fashion. This is not the case today, as the overthrowing of formalism and its narrow definition of modernism are bringing these subjects back into play. Thus, in order to contextualize Kaish's work fully, it is necessary to situate her within the context of an alternative modernism—one that posits a parallel history to formalism in which artists use abstraction to express spiritual explorations.

Charlene Spretnak's groundbreaking book *The Spiritual Dynamic in Modern Art* is critical to a rethinking of conventional histories that emphasize the formalist underpinnings of the emergence of abstraction in twentieth-century art.[4] Spretnak posits that spirituality, as seen in the works of Kazimir Malevich, Wassily Kandinsky, Henry Moore, Isamu Noguchi, Mark Rothko, Louise Nevelson, and others, was the driving force of modernism. This is a history that was largely suppressed by mid-century critics such as Clement Greenberg and Harold Rosenberg and is only recently gaining widespread recognition. It is within this context that Kaish's work gains renewed relevance. Eleanor Heartney's essay in this volume, "An Art of the Spirit," provides the context for Kaish's devotion to the spiritual in art, arguing that she moved from an exploration of themes from Jewish scripture to more mystical and abstract expressions based on her interest in Kabbalah, pantheism, and space exploration.

Kaish's early biography is fascinating. She received a bachelor and a master's degree in fine arts from Syracuse University, traveled extensively and internationally, studied art history with Diego Rivera and painting with Alfredo Zalce in Mexico City, sang with the Mexican national chorus, and rode with the Mexican Olympic riding team. In her essay "Becoming Luise Kaish, Sculptor of Spirit," Gail Levin examines Kaish's extraordinary biography of the 1940s–60s, including her childhood, religious upbringing, graduate years, marriage, first sculpture commission, and European travels, as well as her early monumental sculptural commissions, for which she partnered with leading architects. She underscores the gender bias in the art world at that time, and situates Kaish as one of a few women sculptors of her generation to gain professional success despite the odds, alongside Ruth Asawa, Jackie Ferrera, Yayoi Kusama, and Beverly Pepper. Public commissions by women artists were largely unheard of in Kaish's day, and her works serve as early reminders of monumental sculptural achievement by women in a male-dominated field.

Samuel Gruber explores Kaish's biography through the perspective of her religious art, from her biblical bronzes to her commissions, with special attention paid to the artist's ability to move from figurative to abstract to cerebral, based on the needs of each commission. He situates Kaish's work in relation to pre–World War II Jewish American sculptors such as William Zorach and Nathan Rapoport. Gruber delves into Kaish's role as a thinker as well as a sculptor, highlighting the key religious texts she consumed in preparation, which ranged from a close reading of the Bible and Louis Ginzberg's *Legends of the Jews*, and later the mystical text of the Zohar and writings on Jewish mysticism by Gershom Scholem. Gruber examines Kaish's commission for Temple B'rith Kodesh at length, presenting it as an important work in the context of synagogue history: first, because the commission was granted to a woman, which was unprecedented at that time, and second, because the commission represented human figures, which Gruber describes as "an exciting shock."[5]

In his essay "Voyages of Discovery," Daniel Belasco also examines Kaish's monumental bronze sculptures, which the artist produced between 1951 and 1976. Focusing on the religious commissions, Belasco describes how Kaish resolved technical challenges associated with large-scale sculptures, analyzing their production processes, materials used, and sensitivity to site as key indicators of her artistic brilliance as a sculptor. Belasco also offers a detailed history of the commissions themselves: how they came about, how decisions on content were made, and how Kaish ultimately produced them, collaborating with fabricators, riggers, shippers, installers, and architects.

While working on her large-scale sculptural commissions, Kaish continued throughout the late 1950s and 1960s to produce smaller sculptures that packed a dramatic punch, often with religious themes. She exhibited forty-six cast or welded bronzes, for instance, at her first solo show at the Sculpture Center in New York in 1958—a show that was favorably received by such major art critics as Dore Ashton, Irving Sandler, and Robert Dash, with the latter highlighting the "sudden sense of epiphany and the blistering pain of revelation that infused the works."[6] She was also simultaneously exhibiting her work in group shows at New York's Museum of Modern Art, Sculptors Guild, Whitney Museum of American Art, and Sculpture Center, as well as the Pennsylvania Academy of Fine Arts and other national venues. During this period, Kaish produced a series of desert-themed welded abstractions inspired by travels through the American West, and a series of welded figures, including a variety of animals and girls at play. In 1967, she produced her first overtly political work, *Equation*, for the important *Protest and Hope: An Exhibition of Contemporary American Art* at the New School for Social Research that featured works in response to the social turbulence of the 1960s.

In the mid-seventies, Kaish turned to the medium of collage, and she began layering, scarring, tearing, and burning her canvases—attacking them as a sculptor would to give them three-dimensionality. Norman Kleeblatt, in his essay "Abstraction/Frustration/Transformation," focuses on a specific group of works from the 1970s known as the "burntworks," tracing their origins and examining the formal and structural aspects of their creation. Kleeblatt connects Kaish's approach to the processes of assemblage and especially "femmage," which were being exhibited, articulated, and codified in the 1960s and 1970s. He also examines her approach in terms of destructive impulses in the practice of postwar American artists in general, and the kabbalistic concept of creation by destruction, which was being popularized for intellectual consumption through the writings of Gershom Scholem.

By the mid-1980s, Kaish was producing rip-and-spot painterly collages. About her collages, Kaish explained, "I re-entered painting through the medium of collage which enabled me to still work tactically with materials on a two-dimensional surface while satisfying some of my craving for color as an expressive experience."[7] In a review of her 1981 exhibition of collages at Staempfli Gallery in New York, Roger Lipsey describes how the new works

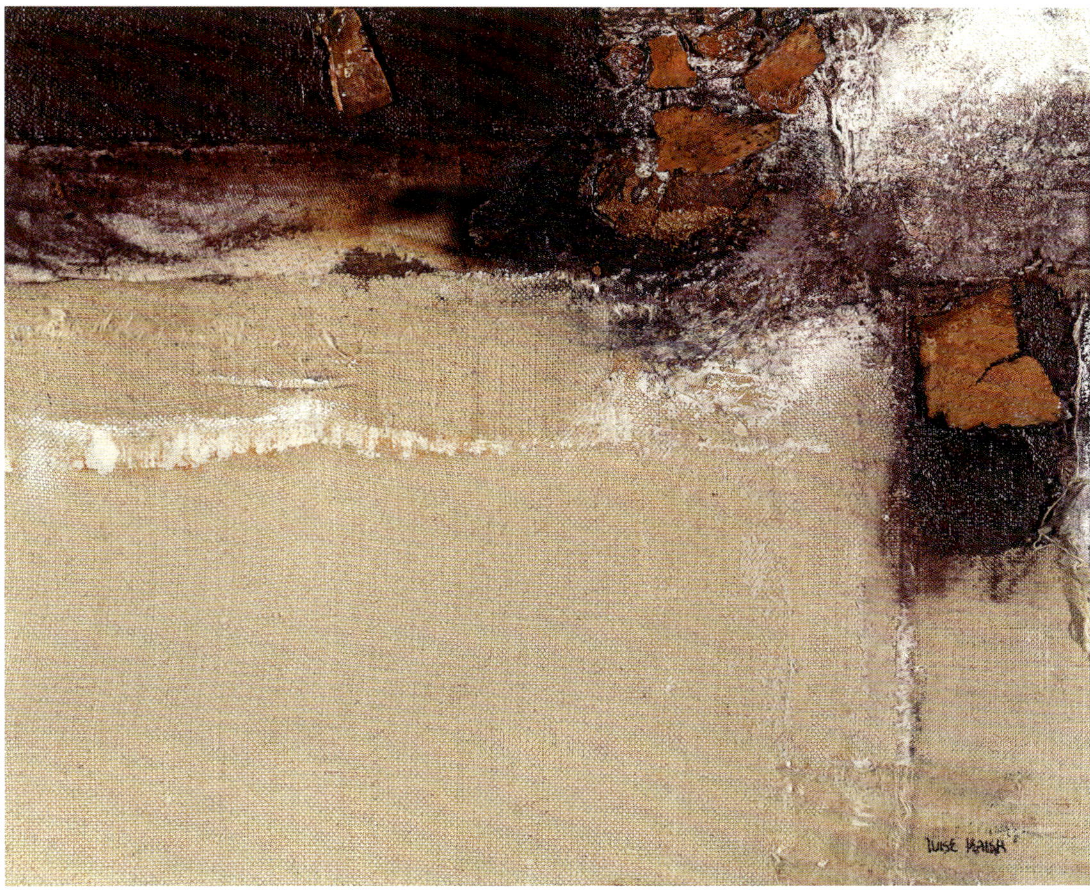

Fig. 1 Luise Kaish, *Storm Sitka No. 1*, 1980, mixed media on canvas, 8 × 9 ½ in. (20.3 × 24.1 cm)

revealed "a sculptor's sensibility in its architectonic structure of overlapping planes, ambiguous spaces, and sensitivity to the mass of thin canvas stripping."[8] As Kaish said at the time, "I build, layer, tear, and rebuild my canvas reliefs, at times contemplatively, at times in a frenzy of energy."[9] This shift in Kaish's practice represents a movement from her minimalism aesthetic of the early to mid-1970s towards an increasingly painterly post-minimalist style in which the hand of the artist is everywhere apparent (Fig. 1).

Kaish continued producing experimental paintings into the late 1980s, exhibiting many of them in her 1988 solo show *New Paintings* at Staempfli Gallery. Reviewing the exhibition for *Arts Magazine*, critic Gerrit Henry described the works as "simultaneously handsome and rambunctious."[10] He isolated one work as a particular favorite: *New York Heart* (1986–87), which he described as a "zanily disfigured figure" with a corrugated cardboard house and inset heart with purple and red perpendiculars for arms—"a painted and collaged pictorial

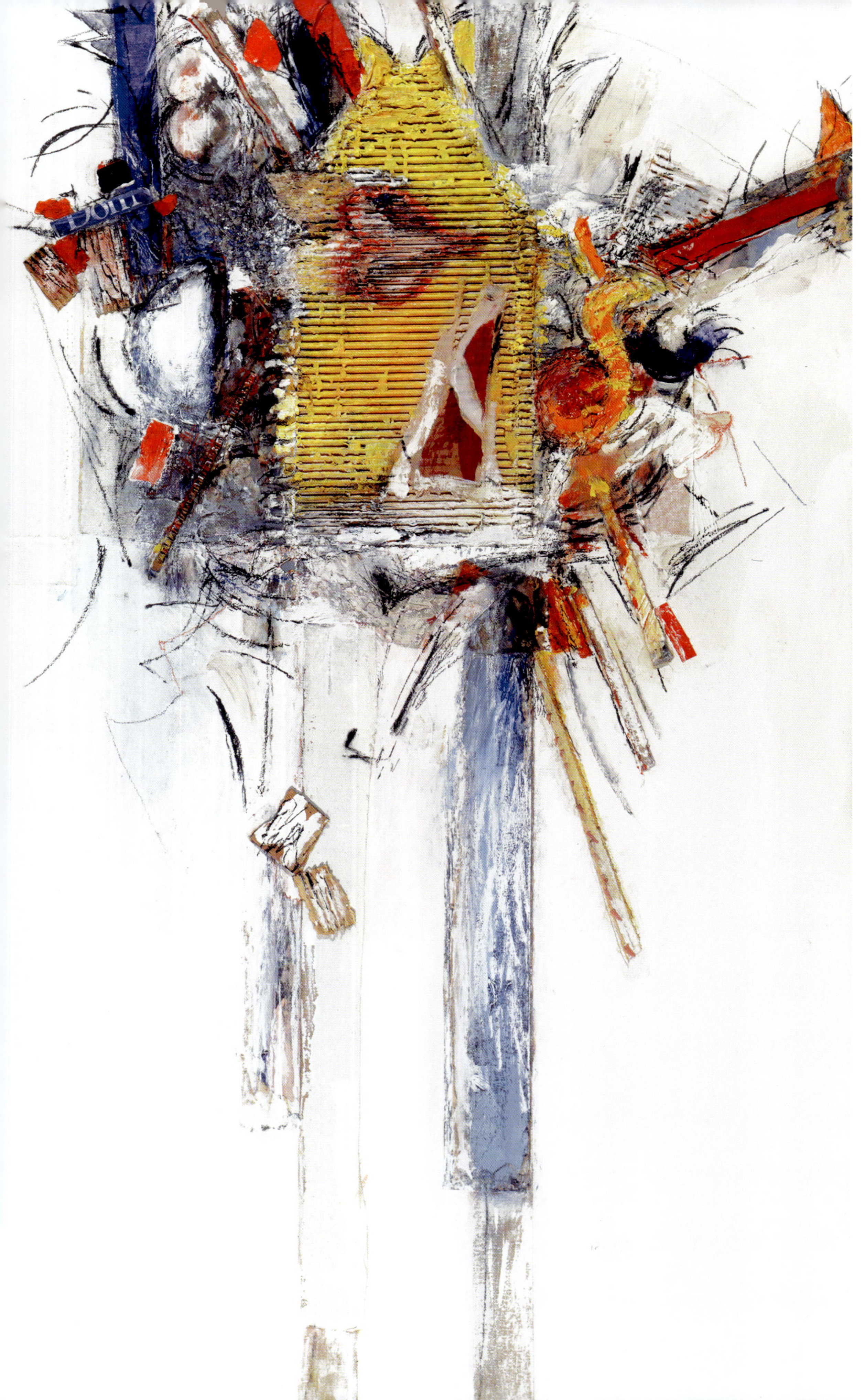

Fig. 2 Luise Kaish, *New York Heart*, 1986–87, mixed media on canvas, 55 × 33 ¾ in. (139.7 × 85.7 cm)

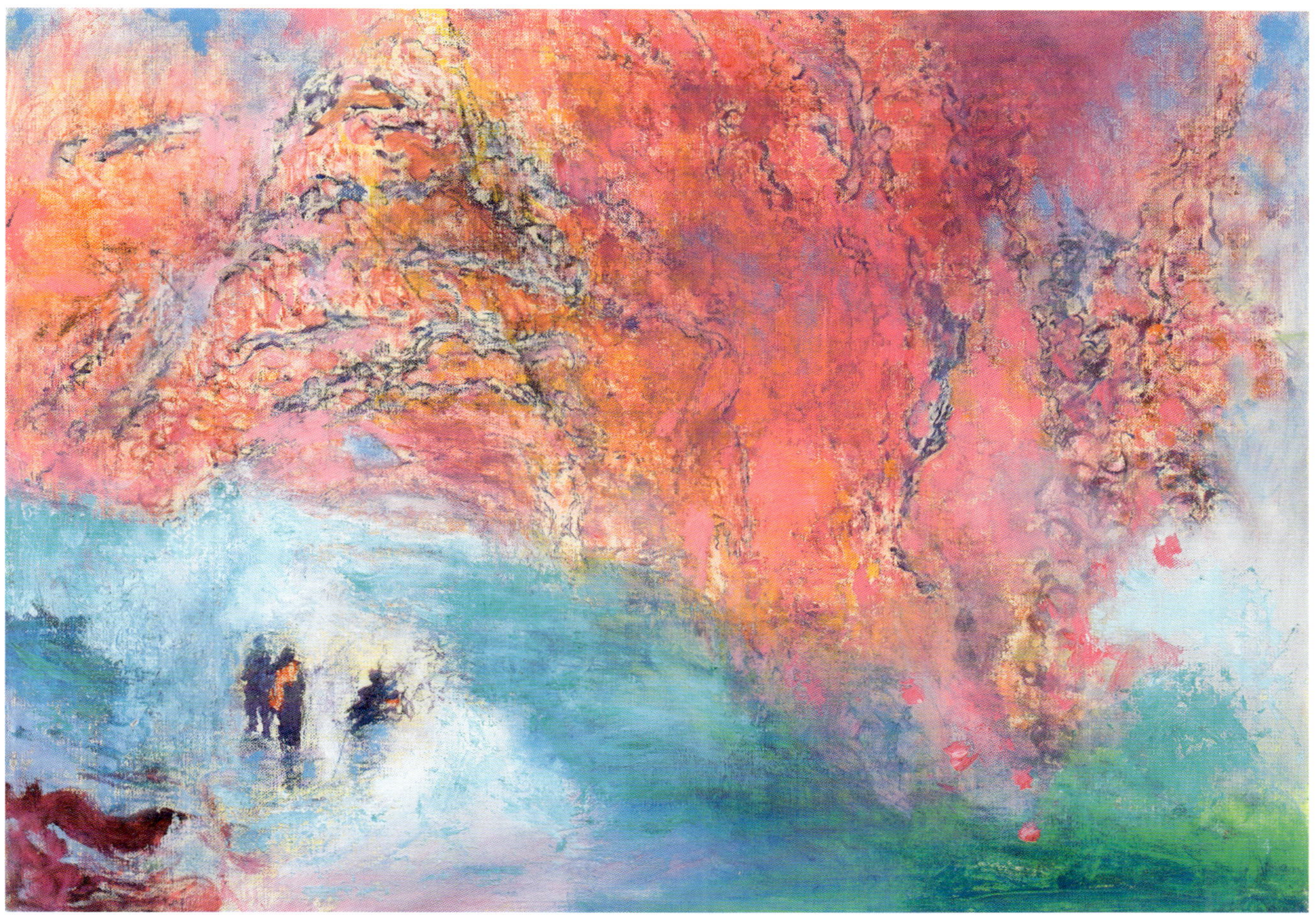

Fig. 3 Luise Kaish, *Blossom Allée*, circa 1993–98, oil on linen, 16 × 22 in. (40.6 × 55.9 cm)

chaos for a body" (Fig. 2).[11] Other compositions from this period were quasi-geometric, like *New York Blue* (1985–87), a multihued orb-with-triangle resting lightly on little cream and horizontal blue stripes—a composition Henry argued "could out-geo Neo-Geo."[12]

Roger Lipsey's essay in this volume, "Place and Journey: The Later Art of Luise Kaish," explores Kaish's painterly production of the 1980s, with special attention paid to her series of paintings and collages titled *Lovers Houses* (1983–90) and *Portals* (mid-1980s), which reveal her preference at the time for contrasting colors, asymmetry, and architectonic elements. Lipsey describes how Kaish donned the sensibility of the modernist tradition that she had studied during her travels, comparing her work to the French group Les Nabis and such artists as Kasimir Malevich, Wassily Kandinsky, and Robert Rauschenberg. Yet, despite Kaish's nods to these great modernist masters, her works were altogether her own, "masterful rather than imitative." As a maker of icons, Kaish developed her own visual language, filling her paintings with "energy, inventiveness, vitality, celebration." Kaish's works invite us to linger, Lipsey argues.

In the 1990s, until her death in 2013, Kaish moved away from abstraction, producing innumerable painted landscapes. These works are remarkable in that Kaish began utilizing ultra-bright, Fauve-like colors for the first time in her long career. She was inspired by the high skies over the Hudson River, the Long Island Hamptons, and southern Florida. Her favorite point of inspiration at this time was an off-the-path secluded grove of very old flowering trees in Central Park, a place she called her "allée," where she returned again and again (Fig. 3). Kaish presented the land- and skyscape paintings in a solo exhibition at the Century Association in New York in 1998, and throughout the 1990s and 2000s at the National Academy of Design, where she was a member.

Throughout her career, Kaish was an exceptional chronicler of her creative process. Toward the end of her life, she summed up her thoughts on art:

> "Who knoweth the spirit of man?" In this search, and with the fundamental earth, the artist strives after the spirit. In the series of shapes and forms he creates, he expresses his feelings towards his fellow man and the world he knows. Form without content is a pleasing diversion. Man has many faces and many cultures and in his innate drive to express himself and to re-create, his art has taken on many different aspects. When stripped of the superficial, the timely aspect, the great art of all ages remains to us as a monumental entity, the soaring of man's contention with the finite, his search for the infinite, his identification with God.[13]

Like Nicolas Poussin before her, Kaish aimed to "paint the passions." She did just that during her extraordinarily prolific and celebrated career. She will be remembered for her immense talent, highly individual point of view, pursuit of the sublime, keen execution, and passion for life, which, despite the tides of changing tastes, will remain forever significant.

Endnotes

1. Irving Sandler, "Luise Kaish," *Art News* 57 (April 1958); Robert M. Coates, "The Art Galleries: Whither, Whither?" *The New Yorker*, December 19, 1964, 152–55; John Canaday, "10 Studio Exhibitions Are Summarized," *New York Times*, April 27, 1968; Harold Rosenberg, "Art of Bad Conscience," *Artworks and Packages* (London: Thames & Hudson, 1969).

2. "Kaish Exhibit Opens at Jewish Museum," review of the exhibition *Luise Kaish Sculpture* at the Jewish Museum, New York, unknown publication, c. October 1973, clipping, Luise Kaish archives, New York.

3. Avram Kampf, "Introduction," *Luise Kaish Sculpture*, exh. cat. (New York: Jewish Museum, 1973), 5.

4. Charlene Spretnak, *The Spiritual Dynamic in Modern Art: Art History Reconsidered, 1800 to the Present* (Basingstoke, UK: Palgrave Macmillan, 2014).

5. Samuel Gruber, *American Synagogues: A Century of Architecture and Jewish Community* (New York: Rizzoli, 2003), 124.

6. Robert Dash, "Luise Kaish," *Arts Magazine* 32, no. 7 (April 1958): 63.

7. "Luise Writings," Luise Kaish archives.

8. Roger Lipsey, "Luise Kaish's Small Worlds," *Arts Magazine* 56, no. 3 (November 1981): 160.

9. *Luise Kaish: Recent Collages*, exh. cat. (New York: Staempfli Gallery, 1981).

10. Gerrit Henry, "Luise Kaish: A Lyrical Essay," *Arts Magazine* 62, no. 7 (March 1988): 88.

11. Ibid.

12. Ibid.

13. Luise Kaish, preparatory notes for *Luise Kaish*, exh. cat. (New York: Sculpture Center, 1958), Luise Kaish archives.

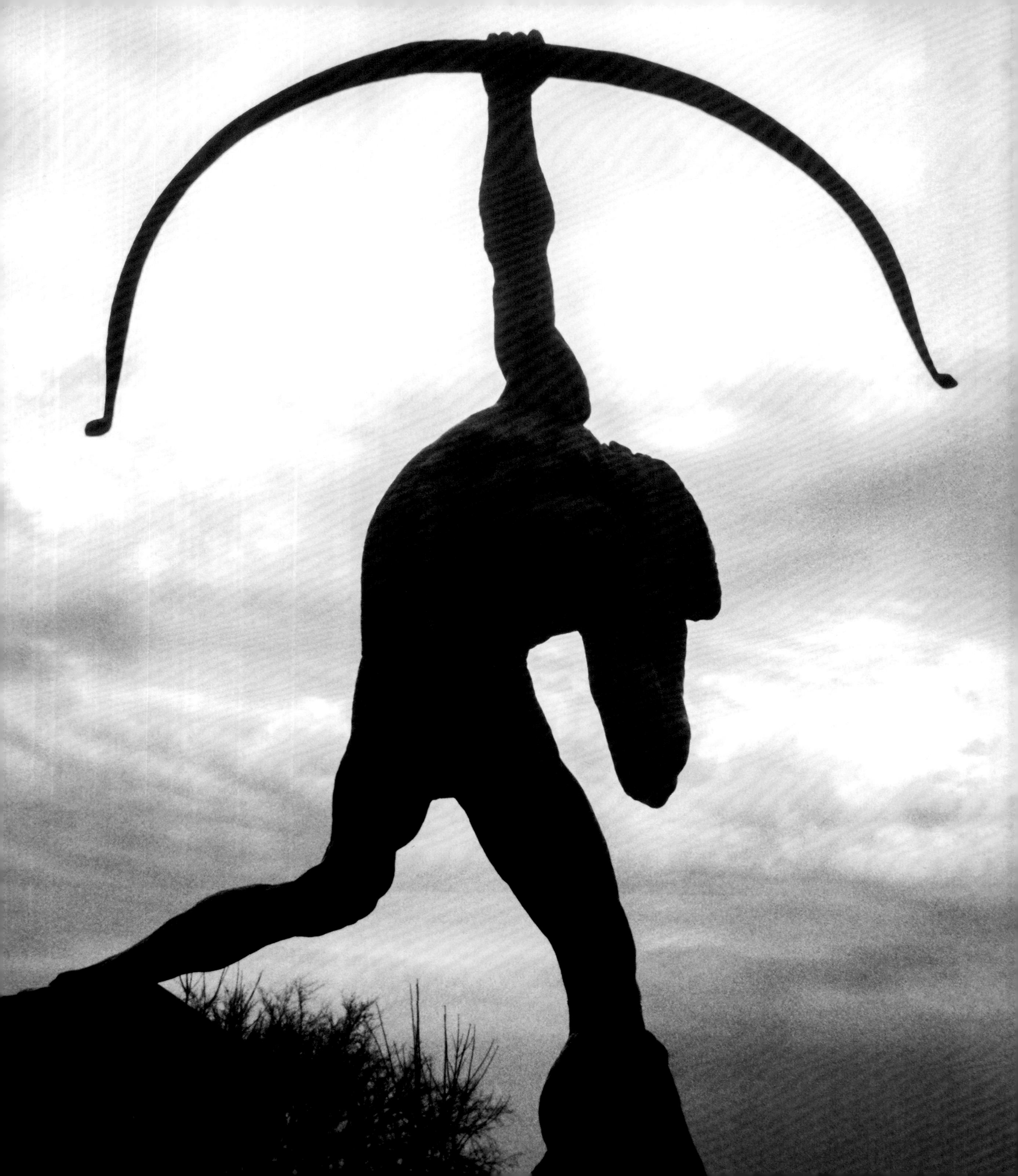

BECOMING LUISE KAISH, SCULPTOR OF SPIRIT

Gail Levin

For me art is re-creation. It is the putting into form and substance of the visions of the soul and the spirit and the mind of man. It transcends the visual and in the poetry of creation expresses the striving of man after God, his desire to form a continuous pattern of identification with the source of all being.[1]

–Luise Kaish

For most women in the generation of Luise Clayborn Meyers Kaish, the way to success as a visual artist was by no means clear. In the world of fine art, gender bias reigned, if anything, more strongly among sculptors. Against a woman, Kaish once observed, "I think there is prejudice in only one sense, and that is to be taken seriously."[2] Women were often relegated to crafts such as quilts, needlework, and mosaics, once called "minor arts"; it was said by feminist artists in the 1970s that "Anonymous was a woman."[3] Professional art schools were often out of reach for women, as were prestigious galleries to sell their art. Men, who had the funds to build art collections, most often sought out work by male artists. Though few art teachers, collectors, or museum personnel of the time took women artists seriously, Kaish was to win teachers and patrons who appreciated her dedication and talent.

Despite the predominant gender bias, Kaish achieved professional success and recognition as an artist, as did a small group of women who were born, like her, in the 1920s: sculptors Ruth Asawa, Lila Katzen, Jackie Ferrara, Yayoi Kusama, and Beverly Pepper come to mind, as do painters such as Helen Frankenthaler, Grace Hartigan, Joan Mitchell, and Miriam Schapiro.[4] While some of these contemporaries managed to attain greater fame, Kaish produced memorable work not only in sculpture, but also in painting and collage. She received important sculptural commissions and her work entered the permanent collections of major museums, including the Metropolitan Museum of Art and the Smithsonian American Art Museum. At the same time, she forged a distinguished career as an educator, becoming professor of Visual Arts at Columbia University, where she chaired the graduate Painting and Sculpture division.[5] She also enjoyed a long marriage to a fellow artist, the painter Morton Kaish, with whom she produced a devoted daughter, Melissa Kaish Dorfman, which led to the pleasures of grandchildren.

None of this would merit notice were it not so rare among women artists of her generation. Kusama, for instance, having attempted suicide more than once, checked herself

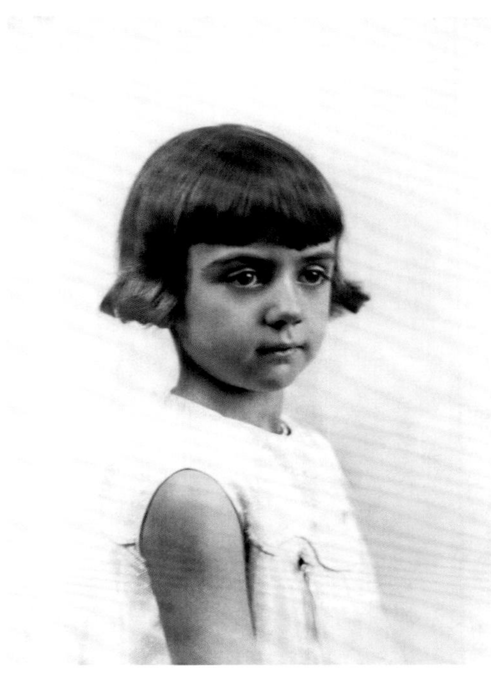

Fig. 4   Luise Meyers, age four years, 1929

into a hospital for the mentally ill, where, it is said, she still chooses to reside.[6] Some other contemporary women artists, who also married artists, were forced to take sole responsibility for child care, while their husbands focused on pursuing their own careers. Some of the children in such marriages came to resent their mothers, who yearned for creative time in the studio and recognition of their own work. Other women artists succumbed to imbibing an excess of alcohol, encouraged by the social settings of the art world, especially from the 1950s, in meeting places such as New York's Cedar Tavern, just down the block from the Kaishes' own MacDougal Street studio in Greenwich Village. In contrast to the multiple vicissitudes suffered by many other women artists, however, Kaish's story was happier.

The middle child of Elsa Brown and Harry Meyers, Luise was born in the Deep South, though her place of birth was not to prove significant; her parents soon moved with her and her older sister from Atlanta to Flushing, Queens, then a small town in New York City, where her younger brother was born (Fig. 4). Her father's family had been in the United States since the early nineteenth century. Harry's grandfather, Solomon Clayborn, was a Jewish religious scholar who had emigrated from Russia and lived in Cincinnati, Ohio, where his daughter, Annie, married Louis Meyers. The couple initially lived in Cincinnati, then moved to Cripple Creek, Colorado, where Harry was born, before moving back east to Louisville, Kentucky.

Young Harry Meyers studied music and was so talented that he was sent to live with an uncle in Cincinnati, in order to study with the Belgian violinist, composer, and conductor Eugène-Auguste Ysaÿe, who taught in Cincinnati from 1918 to 1922. Once Ysaÿe left to return to Belgium, Harry, then a successful violinist in the Cincinnati Symphony, lost hope that he would achieve a career as a soloist. He decided to give up performance and go into the business of manufacturing musical instruments, "traveling the world to do it."[7] He saw to it that his three children had serious musical training. From before she turned five, Luise had to spend two hours a day practicing the violin. This continued until she turned fourteen and was allowed to begin piano lessons.[8] Such early ingrained discipline proved useful for the visual arts as well.

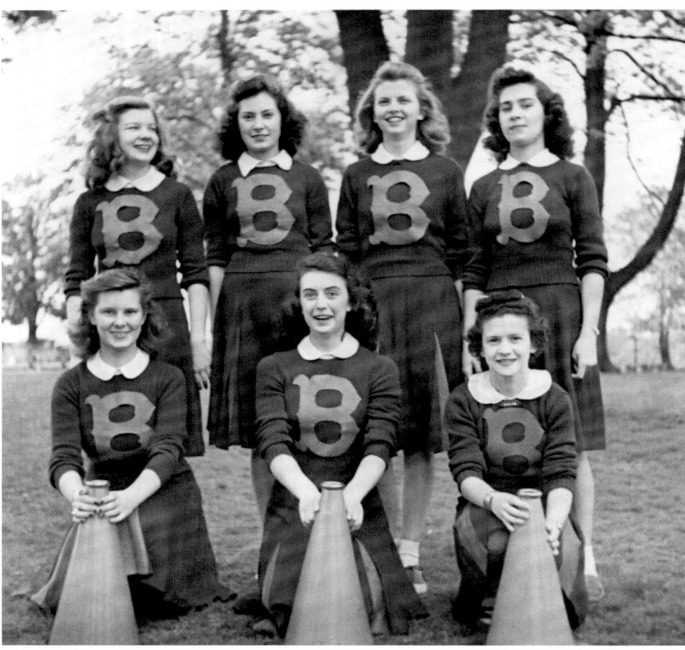

Fig. 5 Luise Meyers (first row, center), captain of the cheerleaders at Bayside High School, Queens, New York, circa 1940

Fig. 6 Luise in Mexico, 1946–47

Luise's mother, Elsa Brown, from a Polish Catholic family in Detroit, converted to Judaism when she married Harry. When Luise was just ten, the couple separated, yet Elsa, a strong matriarchal figure, continued her devotion to the Jewish religion.[9] Despite having only a high school education, she was very cultured and saw to it that her children were well educated and regularly attended concerts, the theater, and dance performances. She and Luise sang and played piano together and shared a love of flowers, birds, and other animals, as well a profound devotion to one another. Elsa fostered a lifelong sense of independence in Luise.

Luise already excelled at Bayside High School in Queens. At sixteen, she was the art editor of the yearbook and captain of the cheerleaders (Fig. 5). She recalled, "I honestly can't remember when I began to draw. If the mood really took me, I used to conveniently become ill and my mother would let me stay home and draw: people, flowers, animals—almost anything."[10] The Shakepearean words she chose to accompany her yearbook photograph suggest that she had already decided upon her destiny: "In framing an artist, art has thus decreed; To make some good but others to exceed."[11] While some of her female classmates imagined becoming teachers or secretaries, and some of her male classmates saw themselves as future certified public accountants or aeronautical engineers, Luise wanted to be an illustrator. With that goal in mind, she competed for a Certificate of Merit for "Advertising Art," from R. H. Macy & Co., and her work was included in the 1942 Greater New York Regional Competition for the National High School Art Exhibition at the Carnegie Institute in Pittsburgh.

From the fall of 1942 until her graduation with honors in 1946, Luise attended the College of Fine Arts at Syracuse University in upstate New York. To pay for her college expenses, she worked in New York City during the summers as a draftsperson for naval architects Cox & Stevens. She felt the discipline and expertise required in those wartime summers were to become increasingly important over the years.[12] Had World War II not

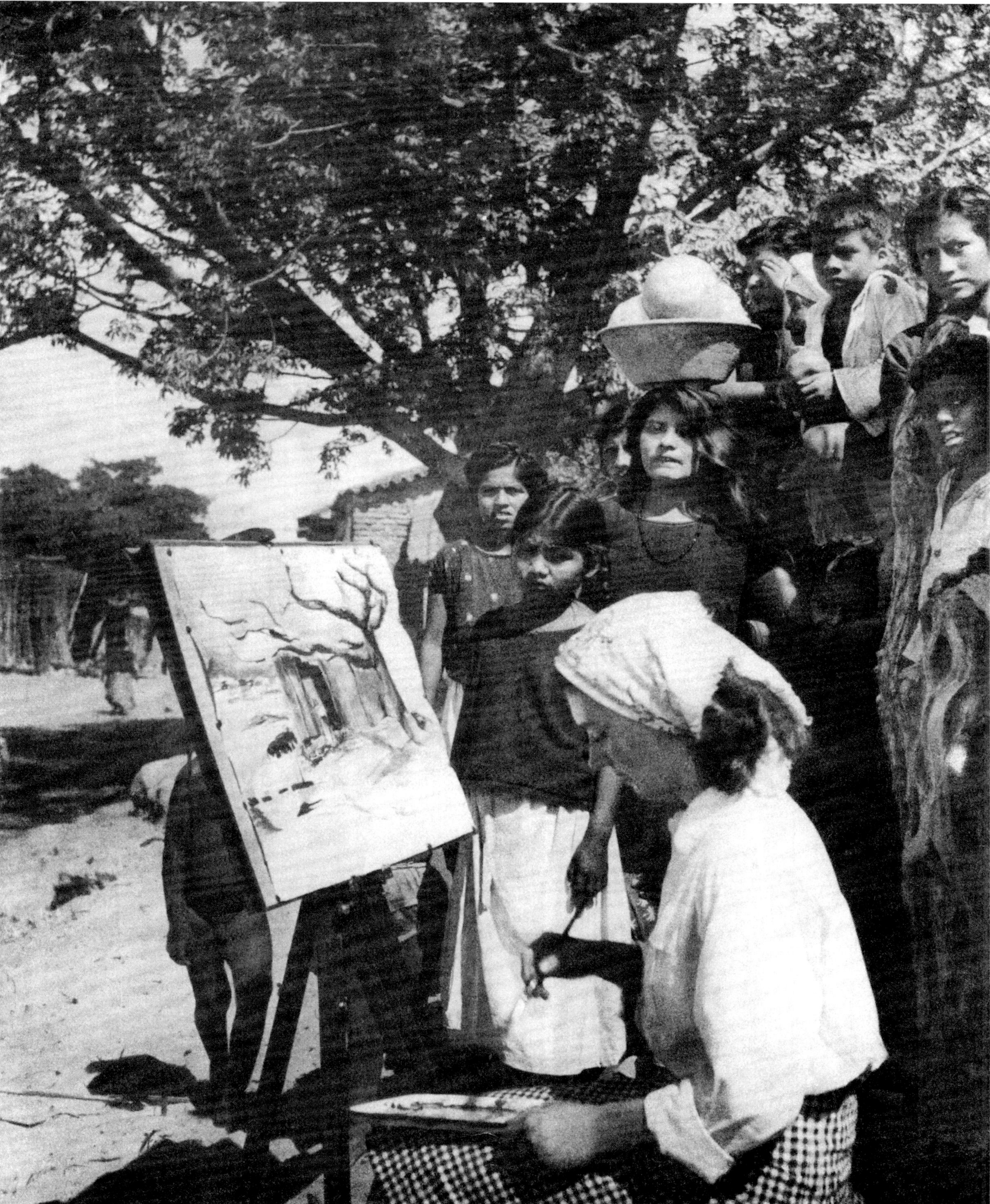

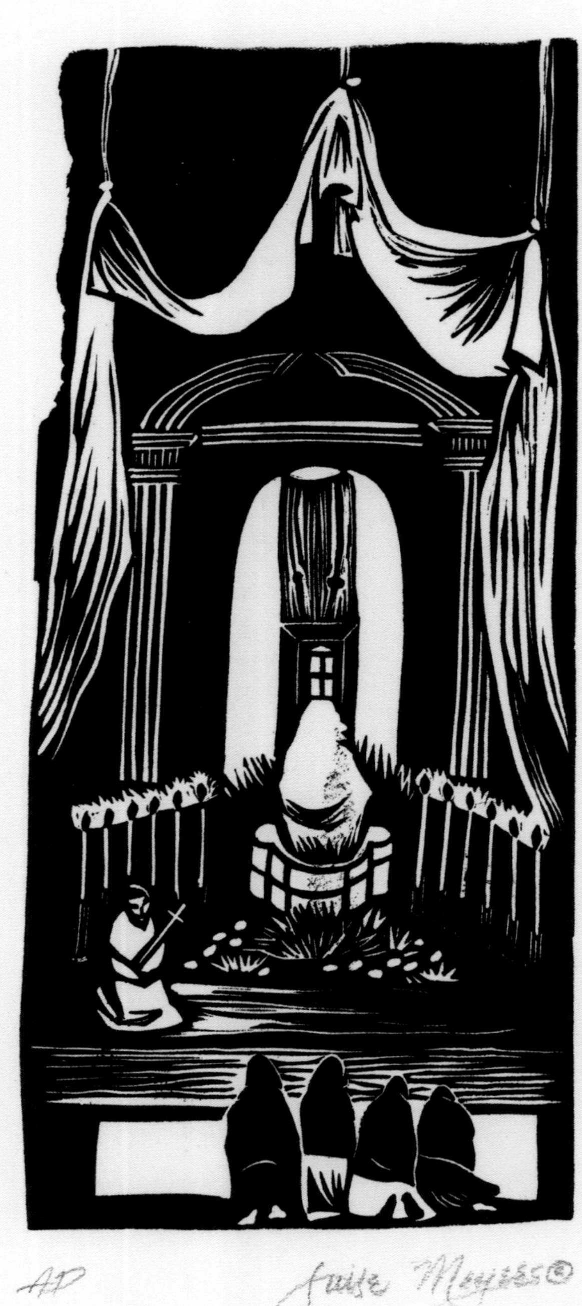

Fig. 7 Luise Kaish, *Church at Guadalupe*, 1947, linocut, 13 ½ × 9 in. (34.3 × 22.9 cm)

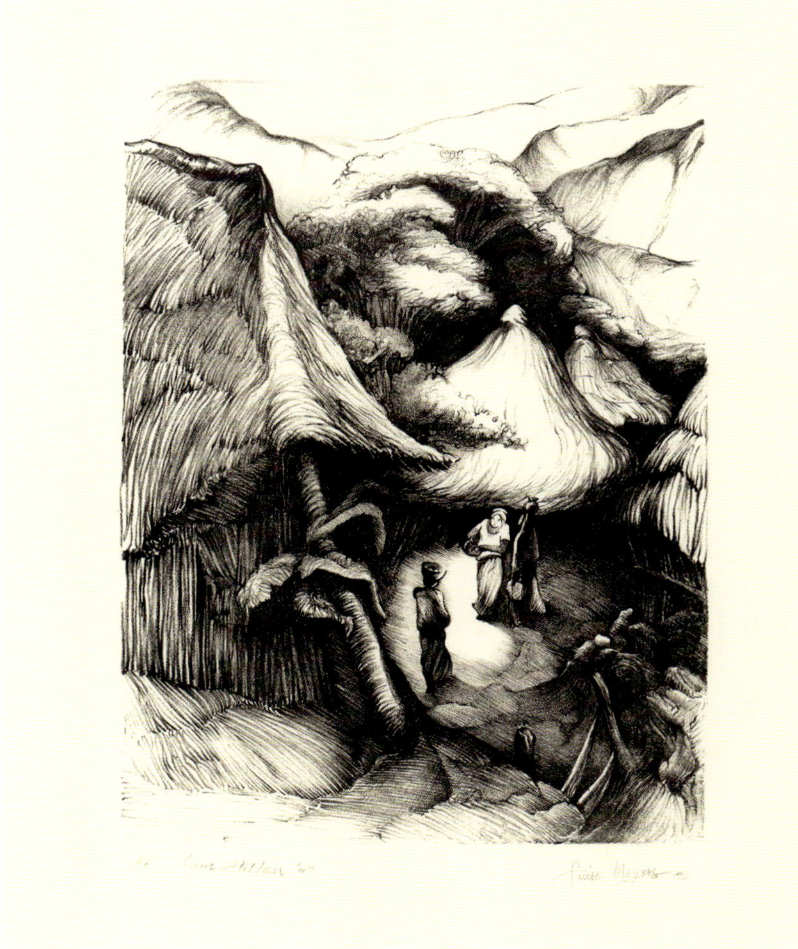

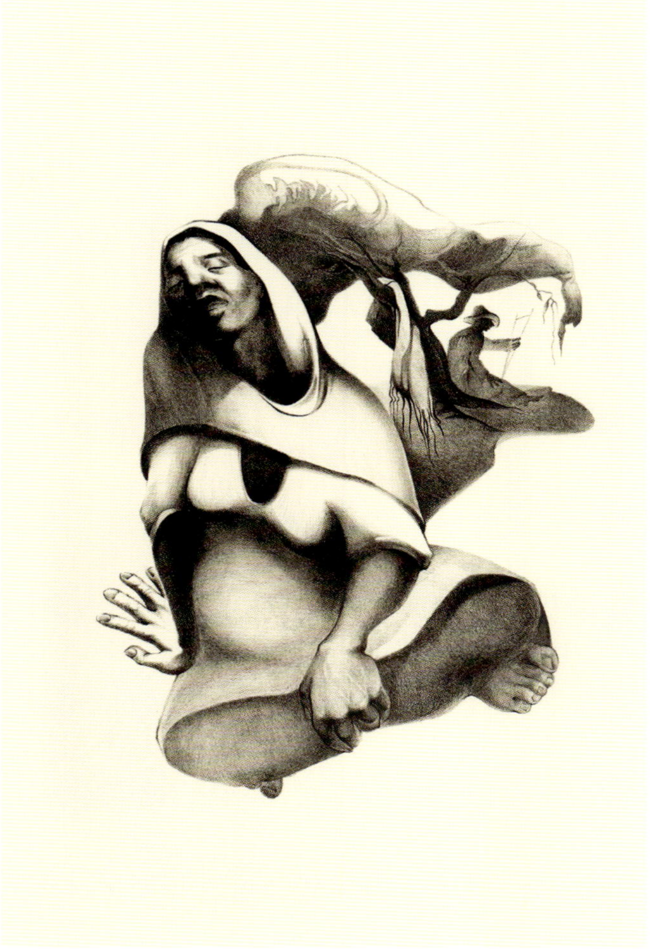

Fig. 8 Luise Kaish, *Lake Atitlan*, 1947, lithograph, 21 × 17 in. (53.3 × 43.2 cm)

Fig. 9 Luise Kaish, *Mexican Woman*, 1947, lithograph, 24 × 19 in. (60.9 × 48.3 cm)

coincided with her college years, Luise, who had won a traveling fellowship, would have gone on a grand tour of Europe, visiting the great works of Western art. Instead, postponing the graduate fellowship that she was also awarded, she elected to travel alone to Mexico and study there—early evidence of her lifelong gusto for adventure, for foreign travel, and for seeing art in other cultural settings (Fig. 6). To prepare, Luise determined to learn Spanish, taking first in an intensive language program at Columbia University.[13]

In Mexico City, Luise enrolled in the Escuela de las Artes del Libro (now the Escuela Nacional de Artes Gráficas), and began to study etching, woodwork, and lithography. During the evenings, she worked further on lithography in the cooperative workshop of the Taller de Gráfica Popular, a print collective founded in 1937 by artists Leopoldo Méndez, Pablo O'Higgins, and Luis Arenal, who sought to use art to promote revolutionary social causes. Their printshop became a base of political activity and artistic production, and attracted Mexicans such as Diego Rivera, with whom Luise studied, as well as many foreigners, including fellow Americans Elizabeth Catlett and Charles White.

Luise's prints from her time in Mexico—both woodcuts and lithographs— attest to her ability and originality. Her small linocut *Church at Guadalupe* of 1947 is bold and expressive in its depiction of the interior of a chapel with women praying (Fig. 7). In the same period, her lithograph *Lake Atitlan* features a dramatic bird's-eye view of a few figures in a shadowy environment (Fig. 8). Another lithograph, *Mexican Woman,* expresses the suffering of the poor; the sense of agony is magnified by the distant view of a crippled man holding out his crutch (Fig. 9). Her figurative subjects, such as the 1947 *Young Girl,* reveal a level of empathy that makes these images especially compelling (Fig. 10).

Luise also studied drawing with Guerrero Galván and painting with Alfredo Zalce at the Escuela Nacional de Pintura, Escultura y Grabado, known as La Esmeralda, in Mexico City. Soon she added a life-modeling class, and supplemented this with a sculpture and wood-carving school in the Exconvento de la Merced, in the historic city center.[14] Since Syracuse had not offered any courses in sculpture, this was her first such experience, and she focused on modeling figures in clay. While she studied visual arts, she also built on her musical background, auditioning with Luis Sandi and being accepted for the Coro Nacional de Mexico. She sang with the choir for their 1947 concert season and was able to earn enough income to stay longer in Mexico. While her parents accepted her decision, at least one of her friends was motivated to encourage her to come home.

Luise had met a fellow art student at Syracuse, Morton Kaish, who had grown up in Maplewood, New Jersey, the son of Jewish immigrants from Russia and Romania. He recalls an occasion when he and Luise were both in a group, ice skating: "The stars were out. The night sky purple. I thought her beautiful beyond compare."[15] He was eighteen; Luise was just over a year older, and a year ahead in school. They corresponded while she was in Mexico and he was in the Merchant Marines. He wrote to her with exciting news: the eminent sculptor Ivan Meštrović, the Croatian modernist who had been imprisoned in Yugoslavia, had been brought to the United States by William P. Tolley, the chancellor of Syracuse University, and would teach a limited number of advanced students there.[16]

Responding to Morton Kaish's tip proved significant on several levels. It prompted Luise to come back to study for a master's degree at Syracuse, which gave her a fellow-ship, while she concurrently taught undergraduate courses in life drawing and lithogra-phy. Above all, she began working with Meštrović, known for both his carving and cast bronze work. He would inspire and shape Luise's future in sculpture: "He was one of the most magnificent people I ever met, a truly great man, and a great artist. I think the thing about him was that he was only interested in working."[17] For Luise, Meštrović was not only an inspiration, but "an aesthetic relevation and role model. I was to expe-rience again and again this way of seeing: this concept of the constantly evolving series of silhouettes of the precise and individual expression of forms and the manipulation of light."[18] In Meštrović's studio, she studied modeling, plaster casting, and stone and wood carving in the round and in relief (Fig. 11). Luise was one of only eight graduate students and Meštrović was quick to recognize and appreciate her talent.

Luise married Morton Kaish in 1948. The union took place only after Luise had answered Morton's proposal with a warning: "Well, you really have to know. If it's the white picket

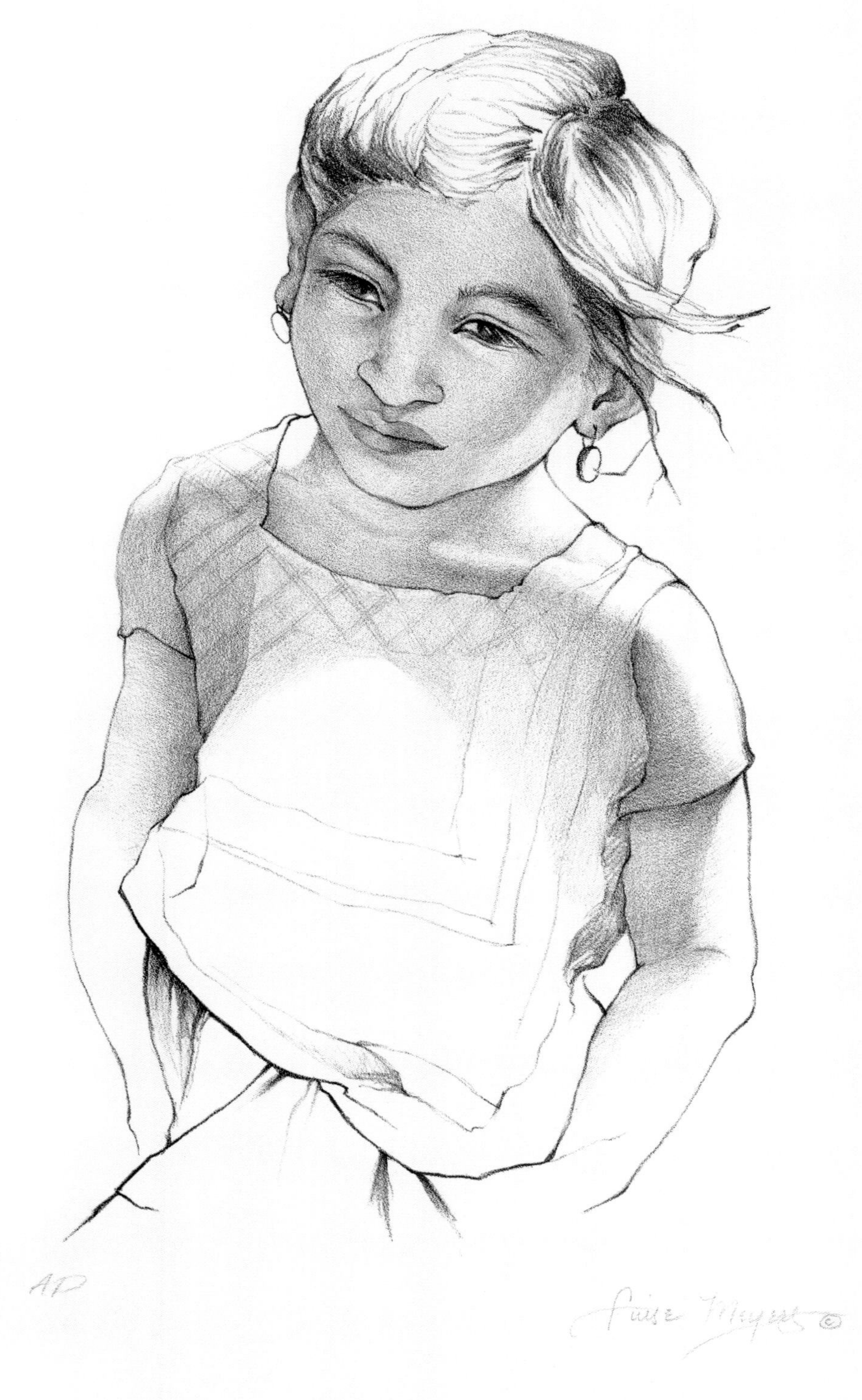

Fig. 10   Luise Kaish, *Young Girl*, 1947, lithograph, 18 ½ × 12 in. (47 × 30.5 cm)

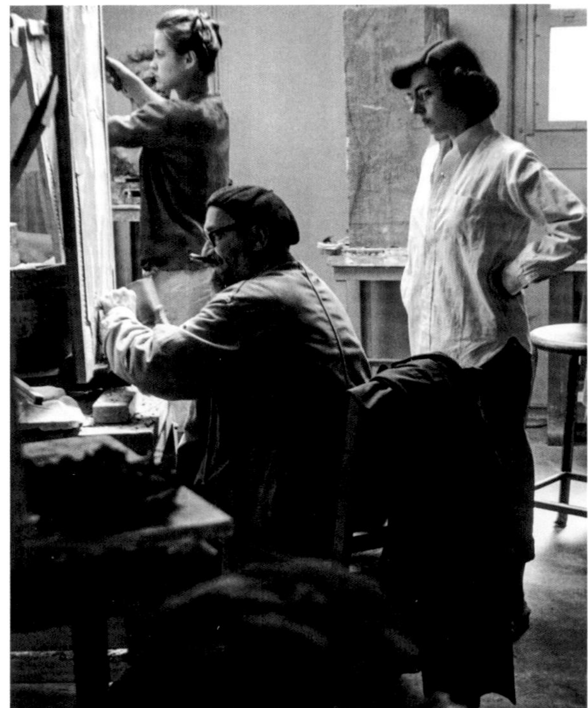

Fig. 11   Luise with Ivan Meštrović, Syracuse University, 1947–49

fence life that interests you, I'm not the girl for you."[19] He recalls with admiration her "immense curiosity," her "sense of wonder about traveling the world" (Fig. 12).[20] Morton Kaish would prove remarkably adaptable, adjusting his life to fit Luise's wishes and drive. He remembers when Luise passed by the demolition site of the old Syracuse post office and saw large blocks of Onondaga bluestone being hauled away. Her enthusiasm earned a mention in the local newspaper: "It made my mouth water . . . It's almost as hard as granite . . . and it works up into a beautiful finish. It's native to New York, but all the quarries have been deserted and you can't get it any more. I wanted some of that stuff awfully bad."[21] From the four tons of stone she had delivered to the sculpture studio's backyard for just twelve dollars, she carved *Mother and Child*, a sculpture twenty inches high, which got her into the *American Sculpture 1951* show at the Metropolitan Museum of Art, chosen from 1,066 entries in a national competition (Pl. 2).[22] Depicting a mother tenderly cradling her child's head against her cheek, in the style of Byzantine icons, was as close as the young sculptor had come to thinking about motherhood.

The first challenge to Luise and Morton's marriage came when Meštrović was approached by the seniors of the class of 1951 to create a monumental figure in bronze to represent the mascot of the Syracuse University athletic teams. Meštrović was too busy with other commissions; instead, he held a competition among his students, each of whom was to submit a model of the proposed sculpture. When Meštrović chose Luise's entry, Morton recalled, he changed the couple's "structure of living."[23] Morton referred not only to the university-owned studio assigned to Luise for the project, but also to her part-time work making fashion drawings for newspaper ads for E. W. Edwards, a local department store, for which she earned three dollars per drawing. She had produced these drawings late at night, after returning home from school, but now, under the pressure of the commission, she couldn't continue. She turned to Morton, who told her, "No way I can do it." To which she responded, "You can. Why don't you try!" He took over the assignment, assuring this part of their modest income.[24] This set up a pattern of working in fashion illustration that would sustain the couple for many years.

Luise, thrilled to win her first commission, threw herself into the project with great energy and imagination. She sought out the perfect model and eventually arranged for a member of the Onondaga Nation to pose for her sculpture, which was ten feet high. For accuracy, she studied anatomy at the medical college, dissecting an arm and a leg.[25] Her *Saltine Warrior*,

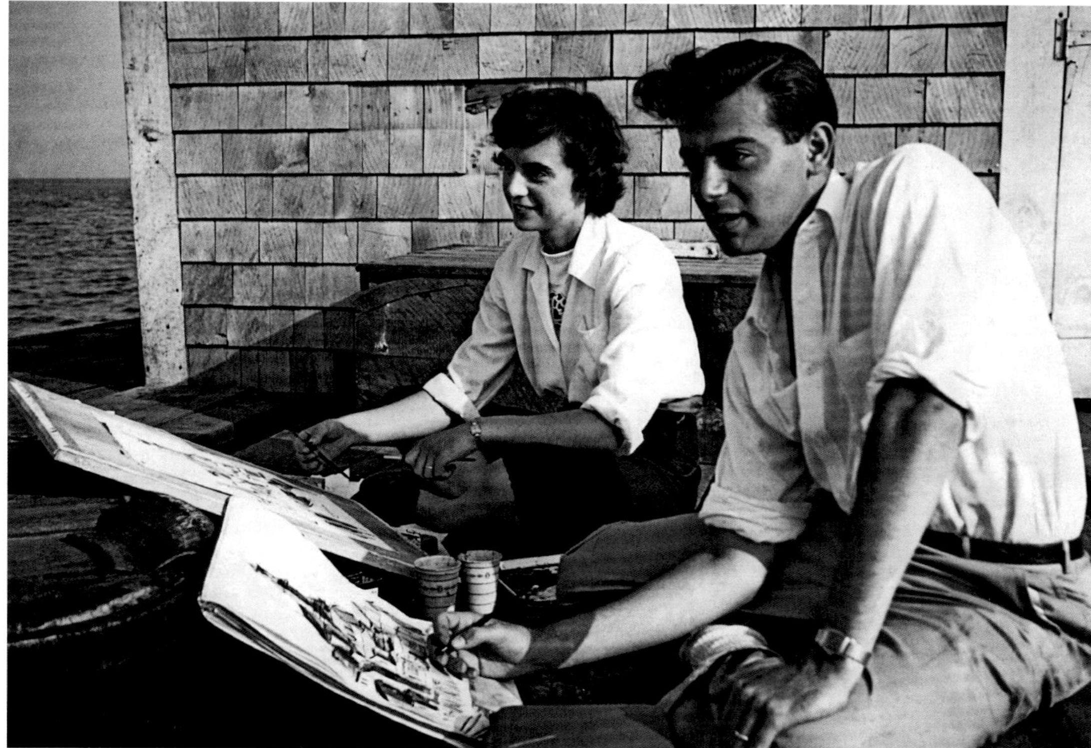

Fig. 12 Luise and Morton Kaish, Provincetown, Massachusetts, 1949

cast in bronze, depicting a brave archer, was honored at the ceremony of the Green Corn in the Native American reservation's Long House.[26] Years later, her sculpture, no longer symbolizing the school's mascot, was moved around the campus, at last finding a prominent resting place in front of the main staircase to Carnegie Library (Fig. 14).[27]

As Morton was about to graduate, his fashion drawings were spotted by Sibley's department store in Rochester, about ninety miles west of Syracuse, which offered him a regular job. The store, informed that "Kaish" was not one but two artists, offered to hire them both. And so the couple moved to Rochester in 1950, with the idea that they could live on one salary and save the other to travel to Europe. In Rochester, seeking the kind of Jewish community that she had known growing up in Flushing, Luise sought out the Reform congregation of Temple B'rith Kodesh. The "eloquent, brilliant" rabbi Philip Bernstein, who had worked for the Eisenhower administration, helping to settle hundreds of thousands of dislocated victims of the Holocaust, did not disappoint. The friendship formed there would last well beyond the two years that the Kaishes stayed in Rochester.[28]

In the autumn of 1951, the *Mother and Child* that Luise had carved out of Onondaga bluestone was selected for inclusion in the Metropolitan Museum of Art's *American Sculpture 1951* show and she was awarded a grant of $2,000 from the Louis Comfort Tiffany Foundation, allowing her to travel and study sculpture in France and Italy. The couple stopped on the way to visit London, since Luise was eager to see the Greek and Assyrian sculpture collections in the British Museum. She also telephoned and was invited to tea with the American-born sculptor Jacob Epstein (1880–1959), whose controversial work she admired.

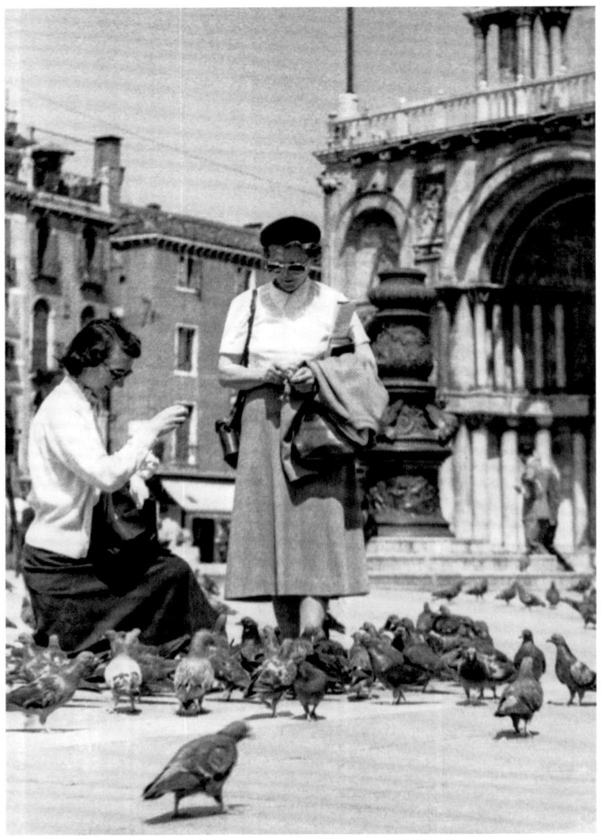

Fig. 13   Luise with her mother, Elsa, Venice, circa 1952

But postwar London was still bleak, so the Kaishes quickly moved on to the Netherlands, Belgium, and then France. They spent the fall in Paris, where Morton enrolled at the Académie de la Grande Chaumière, making prints. Luise sought out and met the contemporary Russian-born sculptor Ossip Zadkine and studied the sculpture in the Rodin and Cluny museums. Luise's obsession with Romanesque sculpture led her and Morton to explore many Romanesque and Gothic churches, especially Vézelay Abbey and Autun Cathedral in France. After several months they both fell ill with the flu and decided to go south in search of warmer weather. They headed for Italy, with only a brief stop along the way in Switzerland.

Settling in Florence, which she called "intoxicating," Luise carved in stone at the Istituto Statale d'Arte and made some castings in bronze at the Bearzi Foundry, which was known for saving the renowned Baptistery doors by Lorenzo Ghiberti. She reported to the Tiffany Foundation: "My work in Italy was divided between a creative work period in Florence and the study of sculpture and its encompassing relationships to the other arts of that country. Sculpturally it is the most profound."[29] She also singled out for praise "the great Michelangelo," as well as "some of the Greek and Roman masterpieces to be seen in Rome and in the National Museum in Naples."[30]

In late spring 1952, the Kaishes left for Rome in an old car purchased from another sculptor, Sahl Swarz, who had also been working in Florence but was then co-director of the Sculpture Center in New York. Morton agreed to Luise's wish to invite her mother to travel with them (Fig. 13). They met Elsa's ship in Genoa and proceeded to drive across southern France to Spain, from Andalusia, through Madrid, to the caves of Altamira, sharing their excitement at seeing the prehistoric artworks. They drove back via Paris, sailing home from Le Havre.

The next item on the couple's agenda was to prepare for what they thought of as a "joint one-man show," actually a dual show, at the Memorial Art Gallery at the University of Rochester, attained when the first prize of the Juror's Show Award was bestowed on them as a couple. Luise's winning entry was her *Mother and Child*. That the honor was shared suggests that the couple as partners were more harmonious than competitive.

Back in New York City, Luise could not afford to continue casting bronze. She began to consider the possibilities of welding and took a course at the Sculpture Center, renewing her acquaintance with Sahl Swarz, whom they had met in Florence. She explored working with steel, iron, bronze, copper, and experimented with enamels and the plat-ing of metals. In a 1953 feature on women welders, a journalist noticed "Luise Kaish, a delicate-looking girl, who turns out massive-appearing abstract pieces."[31] In 1954, the couple took a ten-thousand-mile road trip through the American West, where national parks and deserts suggested new themes for Luise's sculpture.

Despite their Western adventure, Rome still beckoned. In 1956–57, Luise and Morton spent two years working there. They found an unheated walk-up studio near the Trevi Fountain, whose stone floors enabled Luise to weld—though oxygen and acetylene tanks had to be carried up seven stories to the studio. After visits to the Great Synagogue of Rome, Luise began a group of sculptures inspired by the literature of the Old Testament. She exhibited some of these forty-seven biblical bronzes in January 1958 at the Memorial Art Gallery in Rochester, which acquired one of the pieces, *Abraham, Abraham,* for its permanent collection; Temple B'rith Kodesh acquired two small pieces, through patronage from the community of their rabbi from Rochester, Philip Bernstein.

Rabbi Bernstein and his wife, on the way home from a trip to Israel, stopped by to visit the Kaishes in Rome, where Luise's biblical sculptures caught the rabbi's eye. His visit coincided with the imminent move of his temple to a new sanctuary designed by the Italian-born modernist architect Pietro Belluschi, who from 1951 to 1965 was dean of the School of Architecture at the Massachusetts Institute of Technology. The rabbi arranged for Luise to meet with Belluschi. She brought her wax maquettes to the meeting and was commissioned to create a monumental bronze *The Ark of Revelation* for the synagogue's main sanctuary, the contract for which was signed in the office of New York lawyers, in May 1961, just one day before Luise gave birth to her daughter Melissa. Years later, Luise would recall: "Summing up agreement on the remaining contractual points, not a word was said by the three men, regarding me from across the room, to include a provision for the condition, so apparent . . . that I was nine months pregnant. We were to celebrate not only the beginning of the *Ark*, but the birth the very next day of our daughter, Melissa."[32]

This was a productive time for Luise, whose 1957 bronze figurative sculpture *The Blessing (Two)* (Pl. 14) was one of seventy-nine works selected by Dorothy C. Miller and James Thrall Soby from more than seven hundred works submitted for inclusion in the Museum of Modern Arts's 1959 show *Recent Sculpture U.S.A.*, which also traveled to muse-ums in Denver, Los Angeles, St. Louis, and Boston.

Luise, while taking care of her newborn daughter, produced *The Ark of Revelation* in their skylit MacDougal Street studio, surrounded by the raucous counterculture life of the 1960s (see Pls. 17, 18).[33] The *Ark*, measuring fourteen feet high by fifteen wide and composed of eighteen panels, would be installed in the sanctuary and dedicated in 1964. Luise had already won a Guggenheim Foundation grant to create a pair of bronze doors on the biblical themes of Revelation, a project that would eventually feature twelve high

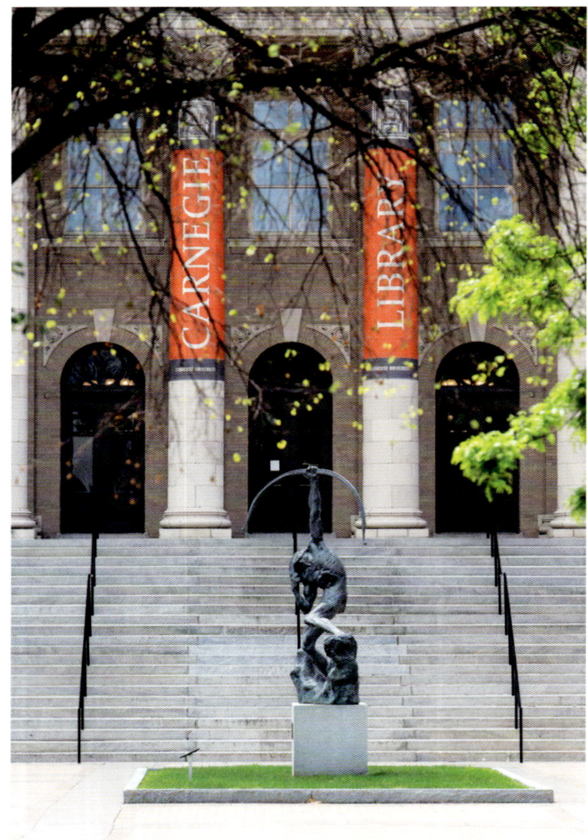

Fig. 14 *Saltine Warrior* in front of Carnegie Library, Syracuse University, Syracuse, New York, 2018

reliefs. "As a sculptor," she explained, "the Bible and the Zohar have been sources of poetic and symbolic imagery and inspiration."[34]

The Ark of Revelation features Moses and the Ten Commandments, part of an overall theme of God's communication to Man; Luise selected the biblical references herself and recalled that Rabbi Bernstein was "totally supportive." She noted that "he understood the 'figural aspect' of depicting the Hebrew prophets to be a vehicle for the expression of the historical Covenant between God and Israel, and the interpretations as expressive of spiritual revelations in the Bible."[35] She drew inspiration from the excavations at the Dura-Europos synagogue in Syria, which revealed third-century figurative wall paintings of biblical scenes.

Luise followed this work with another monumental bronze, the *Christ in Glory* (1965–66), weighing more than three tons and measuring over thirteen feet in height, commissioned for the Holy Trinity Mission Seminary in Silver Spring, Maryland, by architect James T. Canizaro, who had admired the Rochester *Ark* (see Pls. 19, 20). The committee of Catholic priests, evidently appreciating her spiritual commitment, approved the project.

Another major synagogue sculpture followed in 1967–68, when Temple Beth Shalom, a congregation of the Conservative movement, located in Wilmington, Delaware, commissioned *Ark Doors* for its new building designed by the architect Richard D. Chalfant (see Pls. 21, 22). In line with Orthodox Jewish tradition, the temple wanted doors without any figuration. Using high and low relief and script borrowed from the Dead Sea Scrolls for kabbalistic symbols and the Ten Commandments, Luise produced an abstract design seven feet high in polished reflective bronze with a huge circle symbolizing *Ein Sof* or "Unending Light," a concept from a thirteenth-century kabbalistic text, referring to "the Entire Plan of the Universe."[36]

It is clear that spirituality played a large role in shaping Luise Kaish's work as a sculptor. About spirit, she said, "For me that is what creativity stems from. Art is a celebration of God, of the spirit within us, of what we discover in ourselves."[37] The alacrity and insouciance with which she traveled alone to study for a year in Mexico show how fearless she was. Later she would remark, "If you have a work of art, you should have a corresponding spiritual experience. Most things reveal themselves very slowly."[38]

Endnotes

1. Luise Kaish, quoted in *Luise Kaish*, exh. cat. (New York: Sculpture Center, 1958), n.p.

2. Emery Grossman, "Interview with Luise Kaish, Sculptor," *Temple Israel Light* 8, no. 3 (November–December 1966): 6.

3. See Virginia Woolf's 1929 essay, *A Room of One's Own*, in which Woolf notes, "For most of history, Anonymous was a woman." Her essay was based on a series of lectures delivered the previous year at Newnham College and Girton College, two women's colleges of the University of Cambridge, England. This phrase was later adapted by feminist artists such as Miriam Schapiro (1923–2015).

4. Luise Clayborn Meyers Kaish lived from September 8, 1925, to March 7, 2013. She sometimes exhibited in group shows with Ruth Asawa (1926–2013), Helen Frankenthaler (1928–2011), Grace Hartigan (1922–2008), and Miriam Schapiro (1923–2015): for example, *American Women: Twentieth Century*, Lakeview Center for the Arts and Sciences, Peoria, Illinois, September 15–October 29, 1972.

5. Luise Kaish was recruited by Columbia University's Dean Schuyler Chapin as chair of the Division of Painting and Sculpture, as well as professor of Visual Arts.

6. Ashley Chappo, "The Stunning Story of the Woman Who is the World's Most Popular Artist," *Observer*, April 6, 2015, https://observer.com/2015/04/the-stunning-story-of-the-woma n-who-is-the-worlds-most-popular-artist/.

7. Morton Kaish, interview by author, June 4, 2019, New York, transcript, 1. Harry became the founder and president of the Carl Fischer Musical Instrument Company.

8. Luise Kaish, manuscript written before her eightieth birthday, 2005, Luise Kaish archives, New York.

9. Morton Kaish, oral history with Liza Zapol, July 31, 2015, New York, transcript, 3, Luise Kaish archives.

10. Grossman, "Interview with Luise Kaish, Sculptor," 6.

11. *Triangle*, Bayside High School Yearbook, Bayside, New York, 1942, 30. The quotation is from a Jacobean play, *Pericles, Prince of Tyre*, attributed at least in part to William Shakespeare and included in modern editions of his collected works despite questions over its authorship.

12. Her late axonometric drawings reflect a striking resolution of these sentiments. See Luise Kaish, "Thoughts and Comments on Century Exhibition: Luise Kaish 2012," Luise Kaish archives.

13. Morton Kaish, interview by author, 7.

14. The former convent became certified by the government as an art school only in 1943; among the notable teachers on its faculty at this time were Frida Kahlo (1907–1954), María Izquierdo (1902–1955), and Diego Rivera (1886–1957).

15. Morton Kaish, quoted in "Luise Clayborn Kaish, 1925–2013," *The Century Yearbook 2014* (New York: Century Association, 2014), 353.

16. President Franklin D. Roosevelt asked Syracuse University Chancellor William Tolley to help create what would ultimately become the Servicemen's Readjustment Act of 1944 (the GI Bill), which became significant in positioning the future of the United States. Ivan Meštrović (1883–1962) was imprisoned for political reasons. There was an "increasing rift between him and the Yugoslav idea . . . augmented by his political hatred of communism." See Vinko Srhoj, "Ivan Meštrović and Politics as an Arena for Ahistorical Idealism," *Ars Adriatica*, no. 4 (2014): 369–384, https://hrcak.srce.hr/index.php?id_clanak_jezik=193438&show=clanak.

17. Grossman, "Interview with Luise Kaish, Sculptor," 6.

18. Grossman, "Interview with Luise Kaish, Sculptor," 6.

19. Morton Kaish, interview by author, 7.

20. Ibid.

21. Luise Kaish, quoted in Pat Barry, "About Women: Post Office Stone Pays Sculptor Dividends," *Democrat and Chronicle* (Rochester), May 30, 1951, 7.

22. "'Stone Ruins' Carved: Sculptor Uses Old P.O. Rock," *Democrat and Chronicle* (Rochester), June 3, 1951. *American Sculpture 1951: A National Competitive Exhibition* was on show at the Metropolitan Museum of Art from December 7, 1951, to February 24, 1952. Members of Jury of Admission included Robert Beverly Hale, Donald Hord, Cecil Howard, Robert Laurent, Hugo Robus, David Smith, and William Zorach.

23. Morton Kaish, interview by author, 13.

24. Ibid., 14

25. Ibid., 15.

26. Morton Kaish recalls that the *Saltine Warrior* was honored at a gala opening presided over by Chancellor William Tolley. Morton Kaish, oral history with Liza Zapol, 10.

27. By 1978, changing notions of respect for Native Americans caused university officials to curtail the tradition of students dressing in Native American costumes for pep rallies and, not long afterwards, to drop the Native American figure as the university mascot. When first installed in 1951, the *Saltine Warrior* was placed at the main gate of the university. Then, in August of 1967, the sculpture was moved in front of Carnegie Library to make way for the construction of a new engineering building. It has remained in this location since that time. While the Saltine warrior was no longer in use as a mascot after 1978, Kaish's sculpture has remained on view.

28. Morton Kaish, interview by author, 17.

29. Luise Kaish to Henry Hobart Nichols, July 10, 1952, Luise Kaish archives.

30. Ibid.

31. "Sculptresses Turn to Welder's Torch," *New York Times*, November 7, 1953, 23.

32. Luise Kaish, "Maquette to Monument," (lecture, Temple B'rith Kodesh, Rochester, New York, October 15, 2010).

33. The couple's MacDougal Street studios were located above the Rienzi coffee shop where Allen Ginsberg read his Beat poetry.

34. Luise Kaish, American Jewish Congress F-10 (149), 1973, Luise Kaish archives. The Zohar, a collection of commentaries on the Torah (the five books of Moses), is the foundation of Jewish mystical thought known as Kabbalah.

35. Luise Kaish, unidentified typescript, n.d., Luise Kaish archives.

36. Luise Kaish, typescript of lecture, mid-1970s, Luise Kaish archives.

37. Luise Kaish, American Jewish Congress F-10 (149), 1973, Luise Kaish archives.

38. Grossman, "Interview with Luise Kaish, Sculptor," 6.

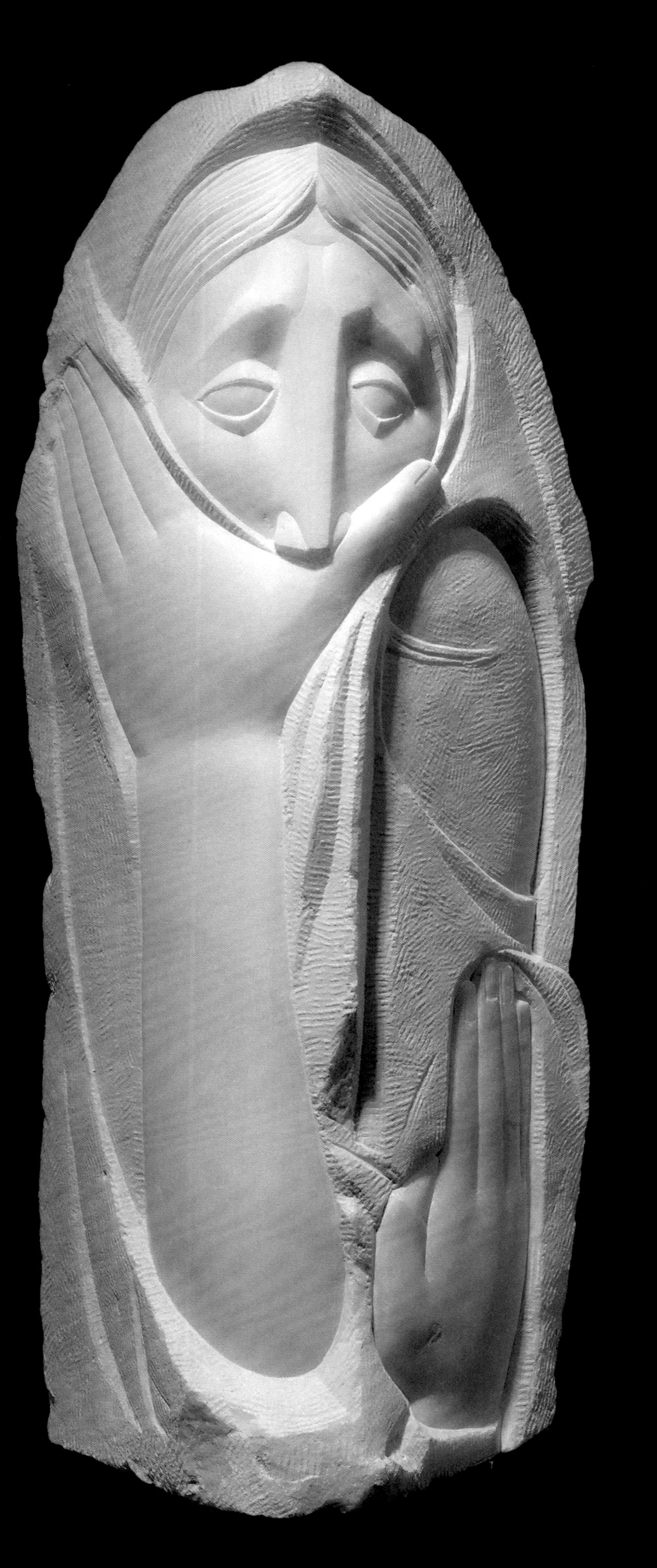

Plate 1
Luise Kaish. *Birth*,
circa 1948–50, carrara marble,
23 × 10 in. (58.4 × 25.4 cm)

Plate 2
Luise Kaish. *Mother and
Child*, 1950, bluestone,
20 × 14 ½ × 13 ½ in.
(50.8 × 36.8 × 34.3 cm)

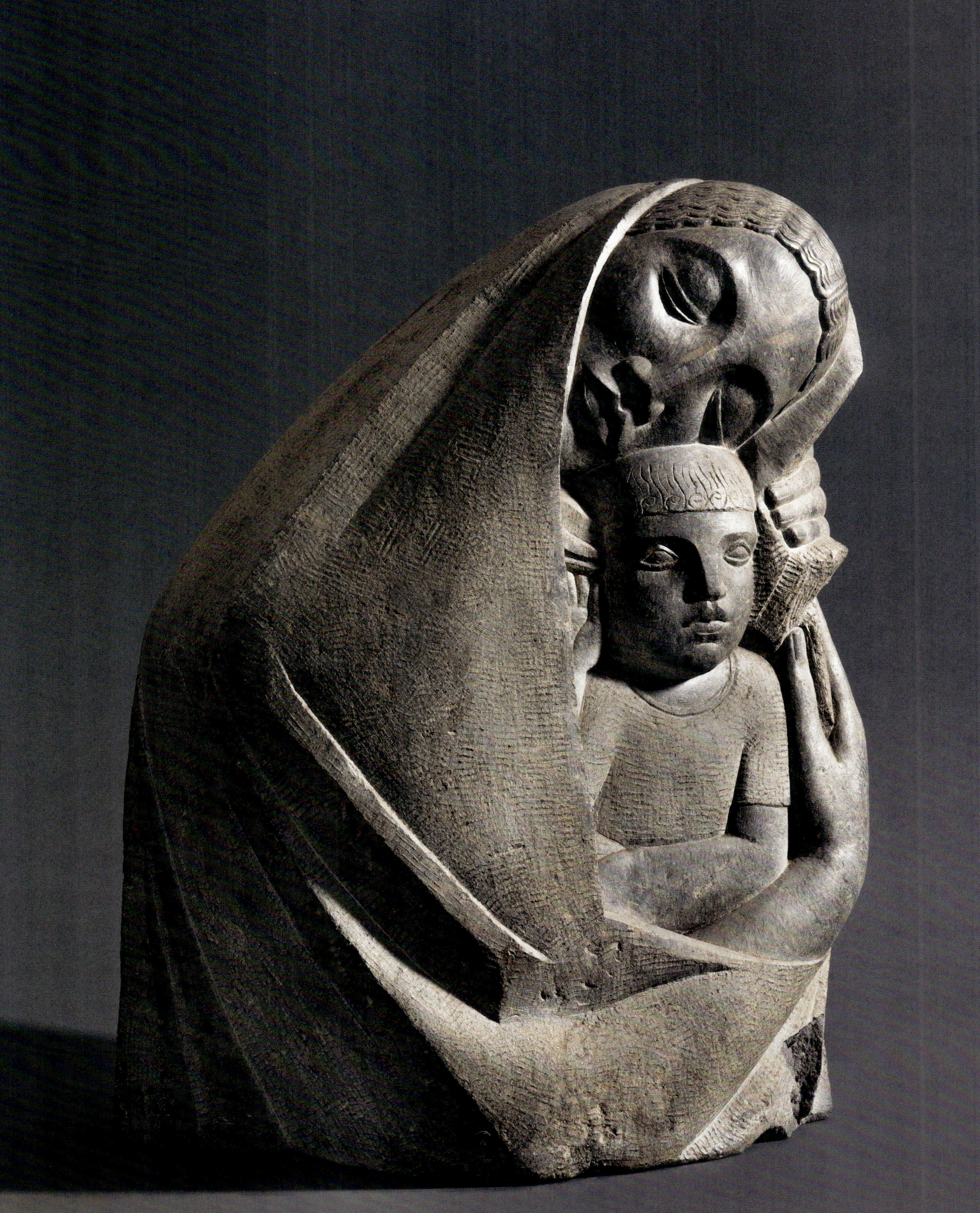

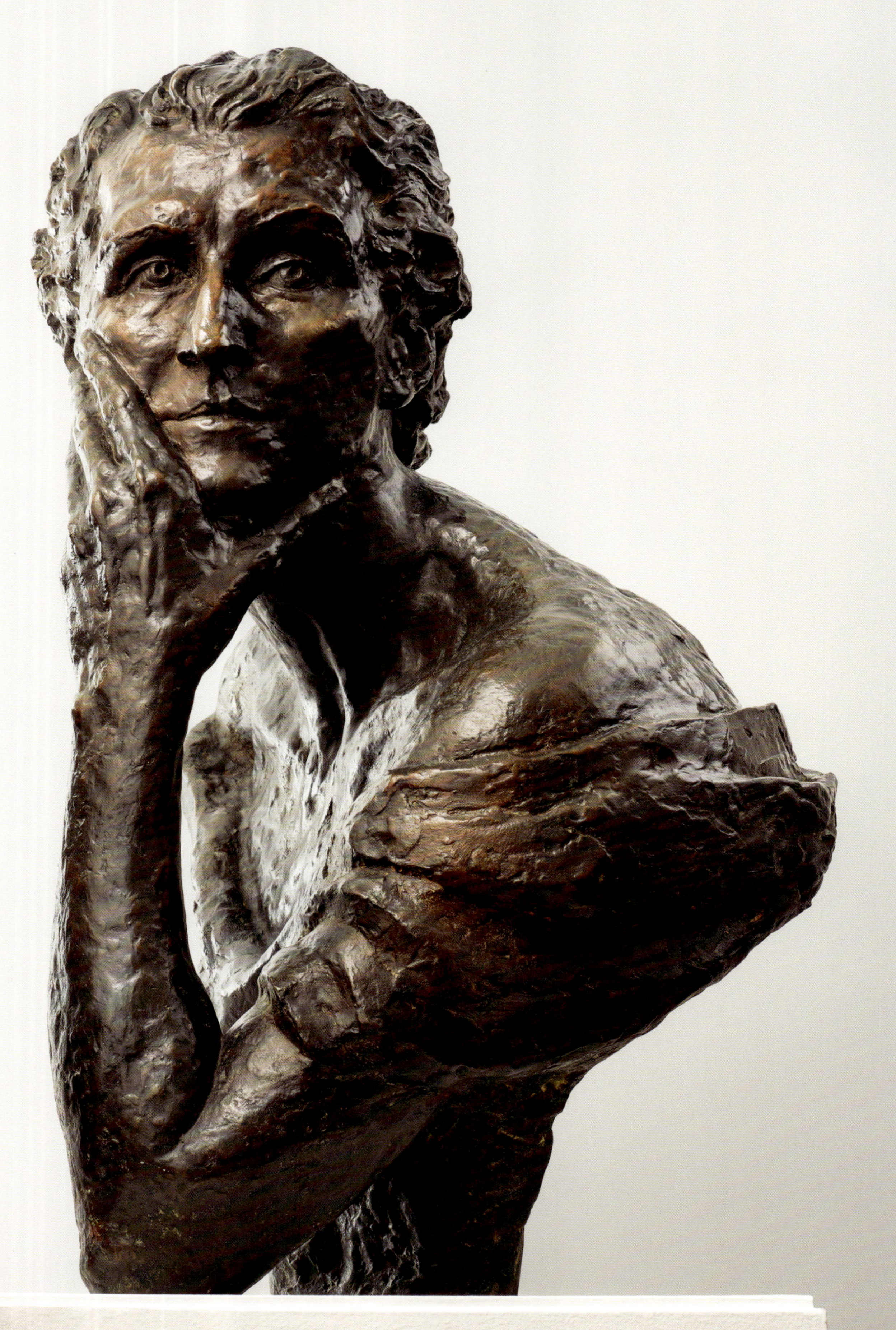

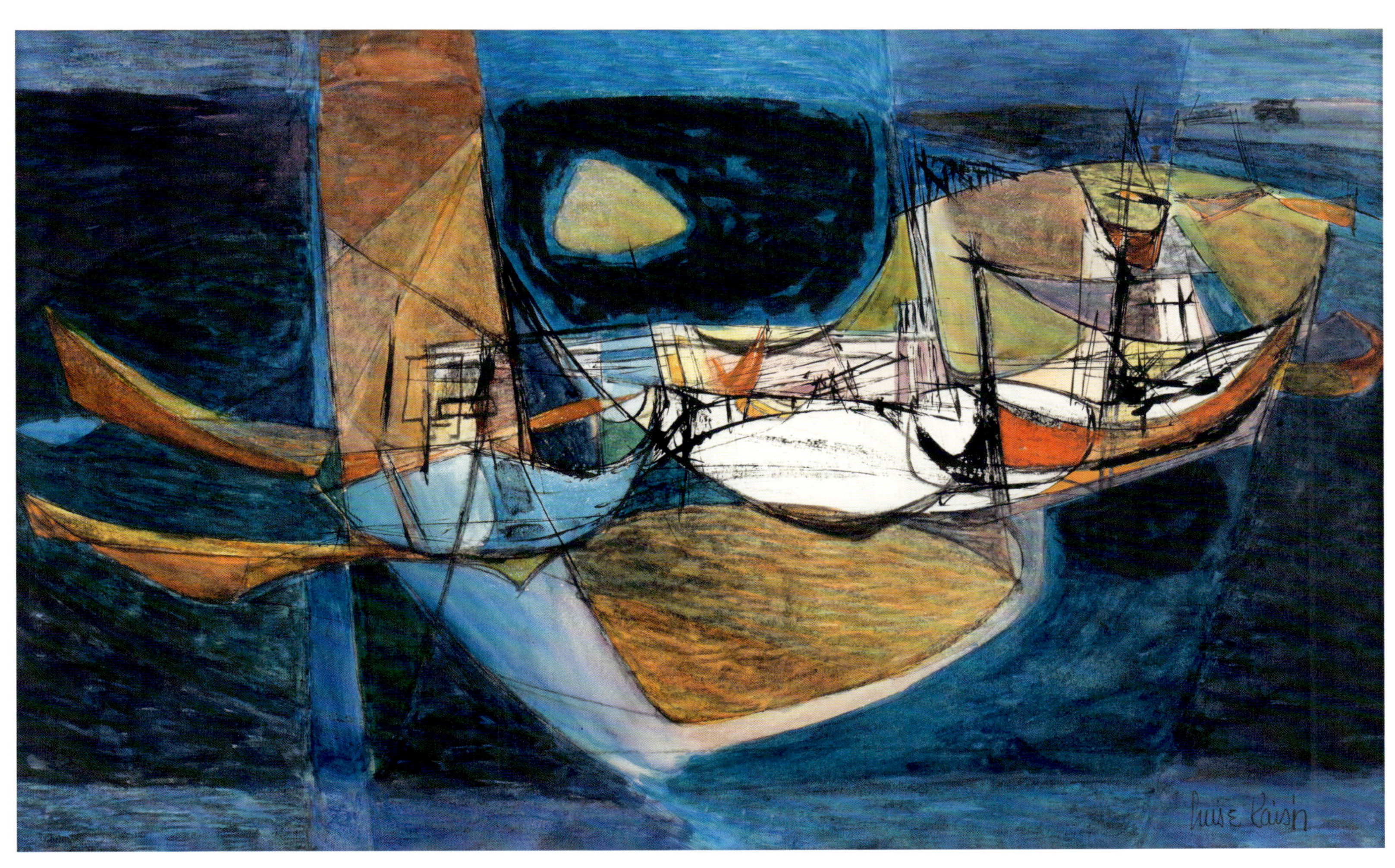

Plate 3
Luise Kaish. *Portrait of the Artist's Mother, Elsa*,
1950, bronze, 25 × 18 in. (63.5 × 45.7 cm)

Plate 4
Luise Kaish. *Dawn at Mememsha*,
circa 1952–55, watercolor and ink,
14 ¼ × 22 ½ in. (36.2 × 57.2 cm)

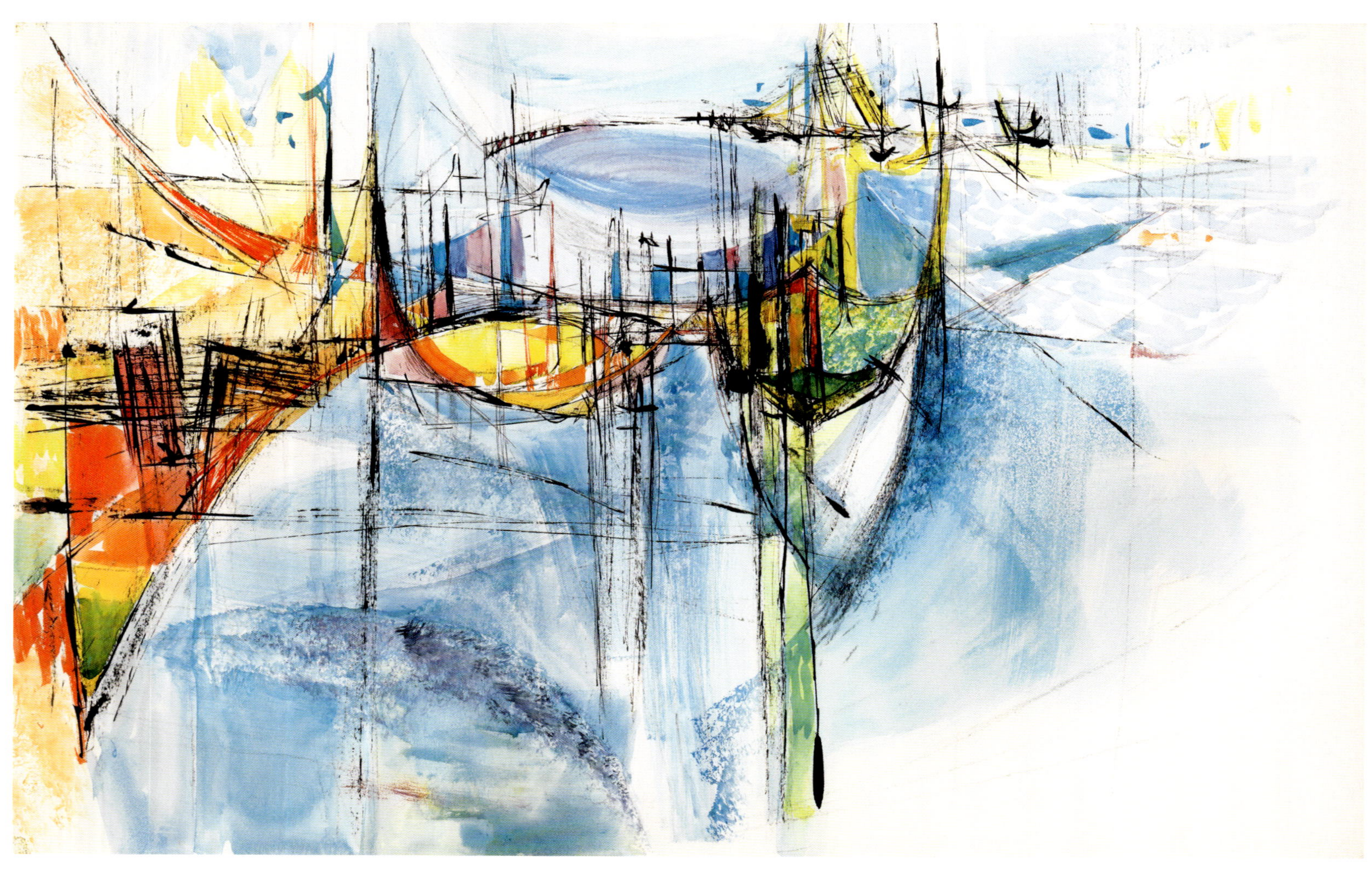

Plate 5
Luise Kaish. *Untitled Dawn at Mememsha, Series III*, circa 1952–55,
watercolor and ink, 14 ¼ × 22 ½ in. (36.2 × 57.2 cm)

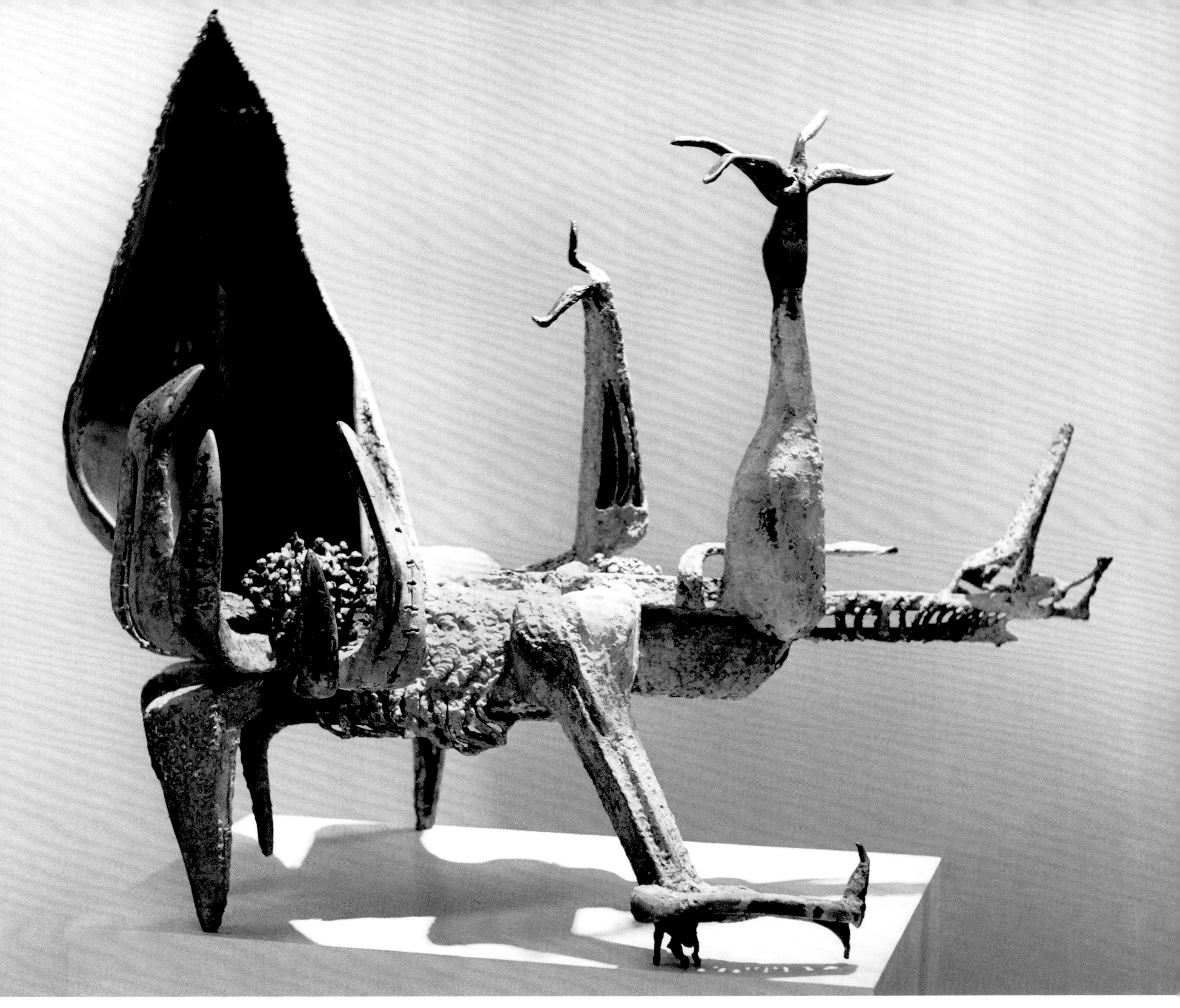

Luise Kaish. *Desert Spectre*, 1954, welded steel, 30 × 36 × 21 in.
(76.2 × 91.4 × 53.5 cm)

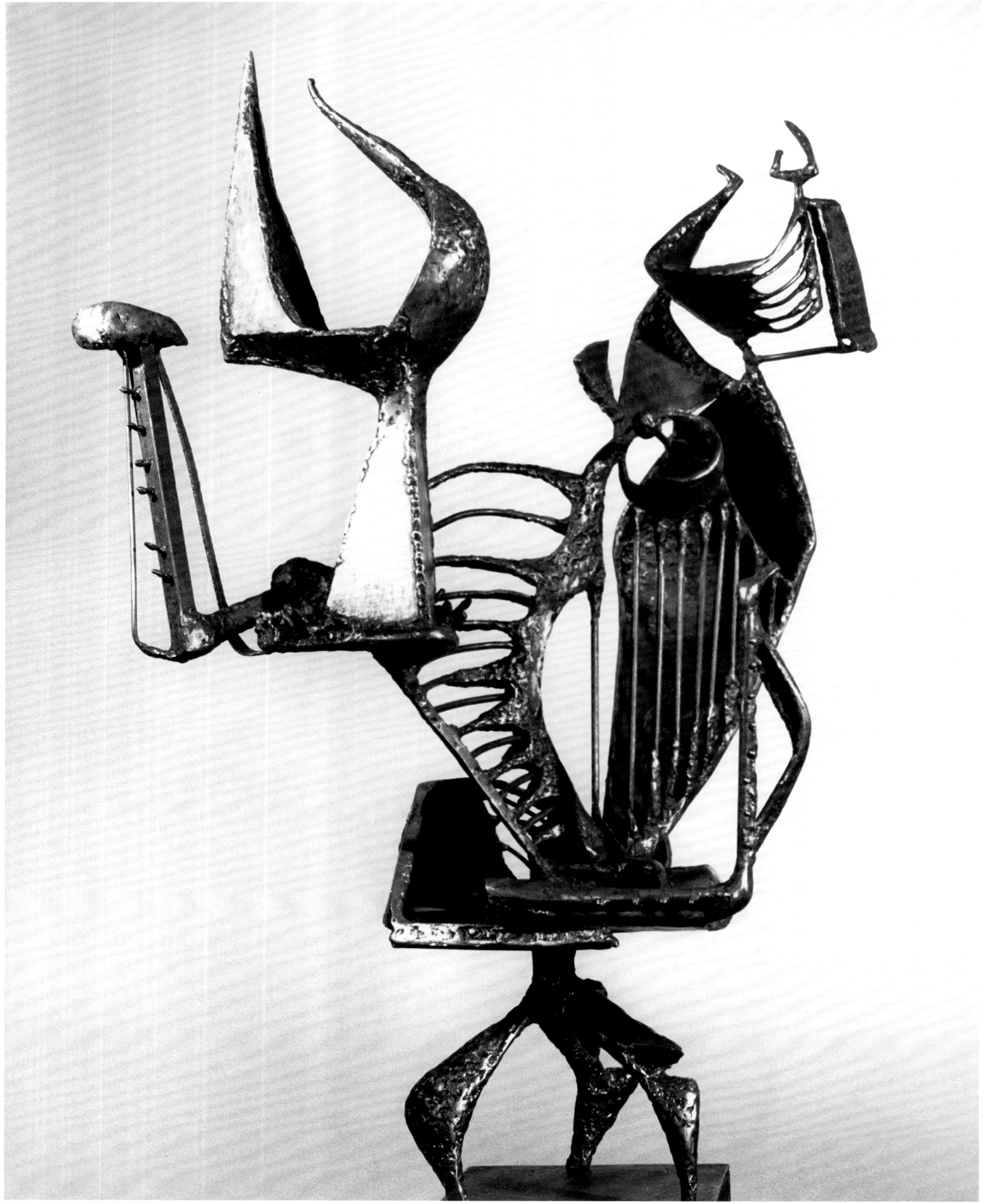

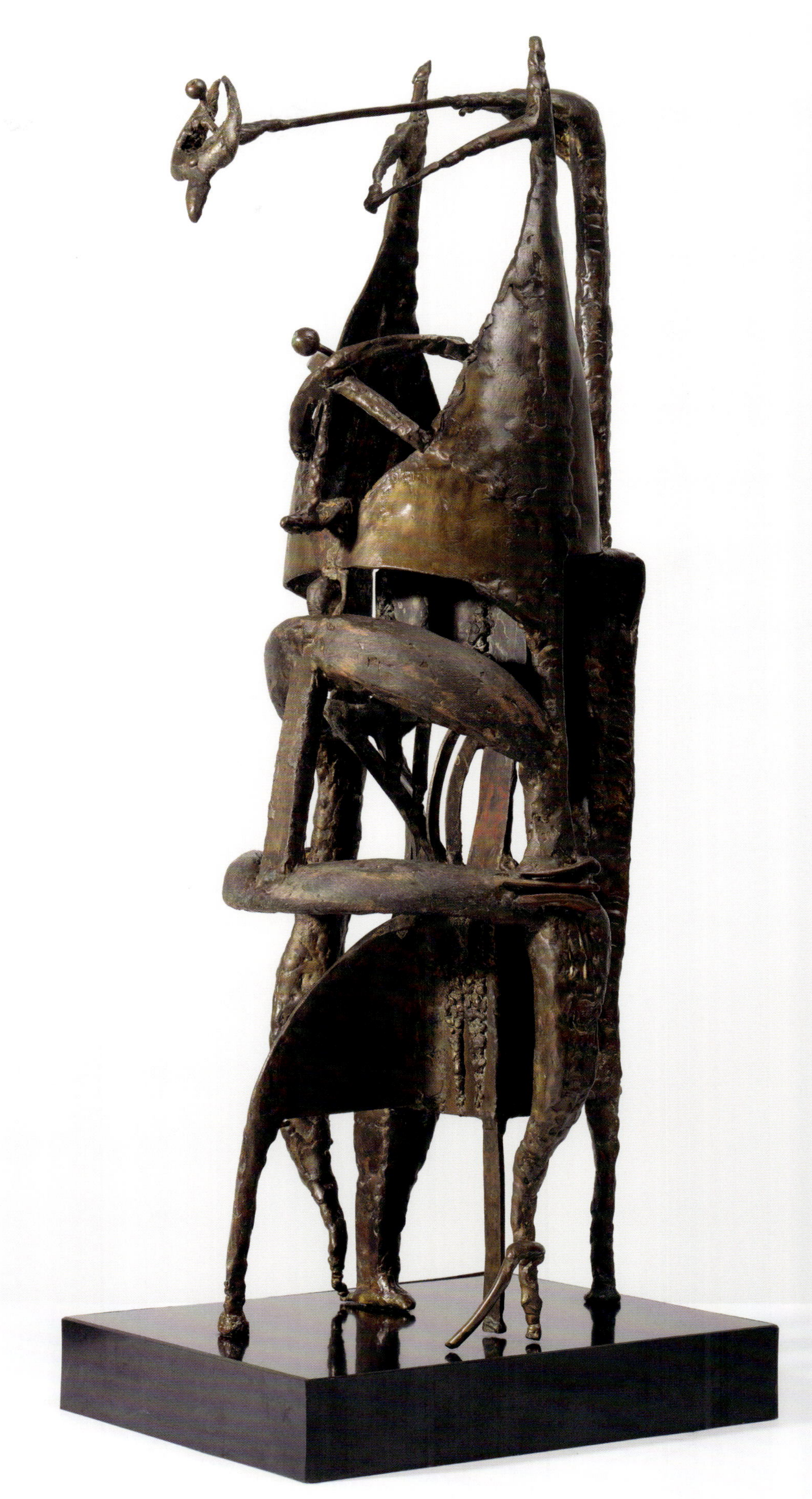

Plate 7
Luise Kaish. *And Behold a Ladder*, 1954, welded steel, 30 in. (76.2 cm) high

Plate 8
Luise Kaish. *New Ireland*, 1954, bronze, 24 × 9 × 7 in. (60.9 × 22.9 × 17.8 cm)

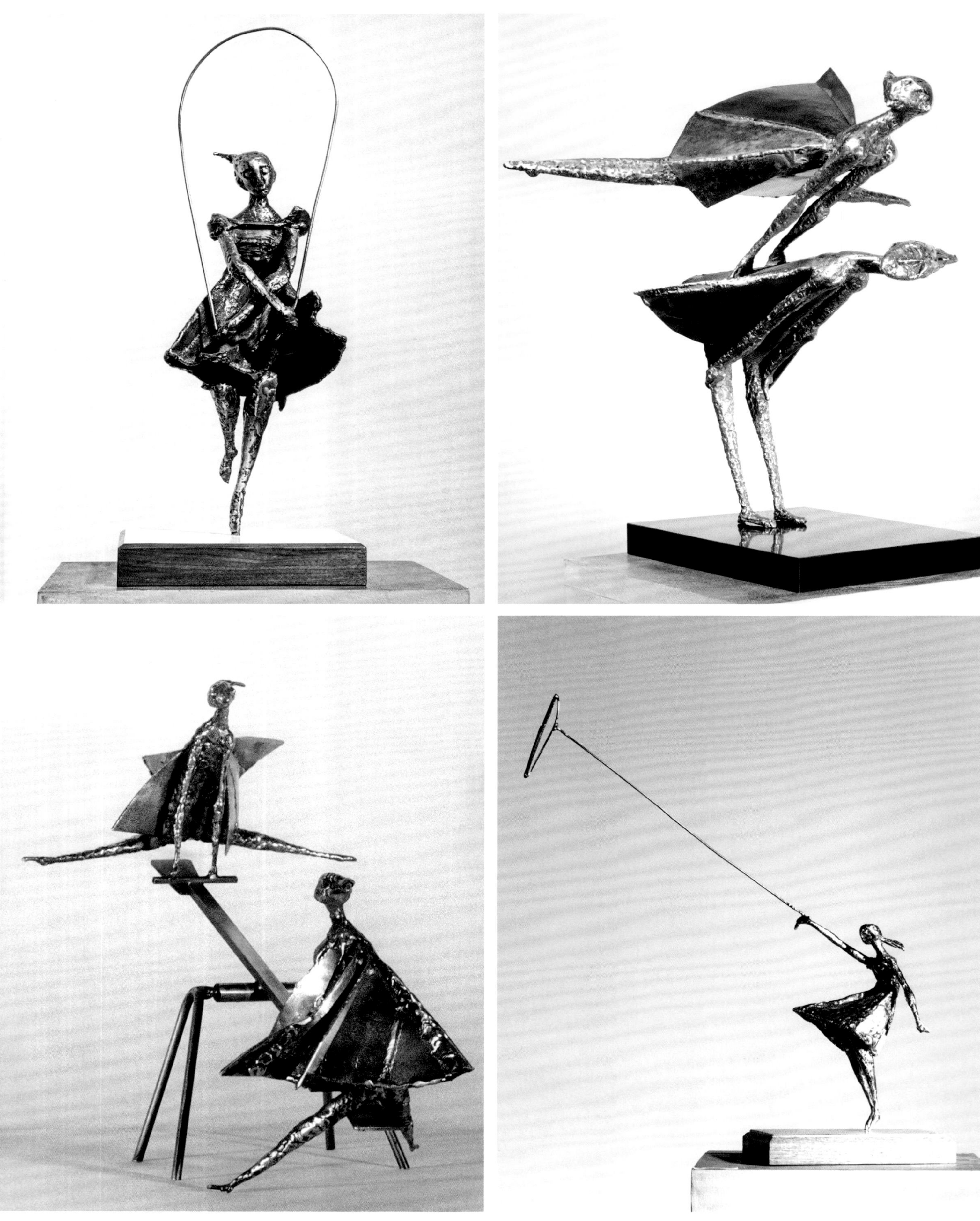

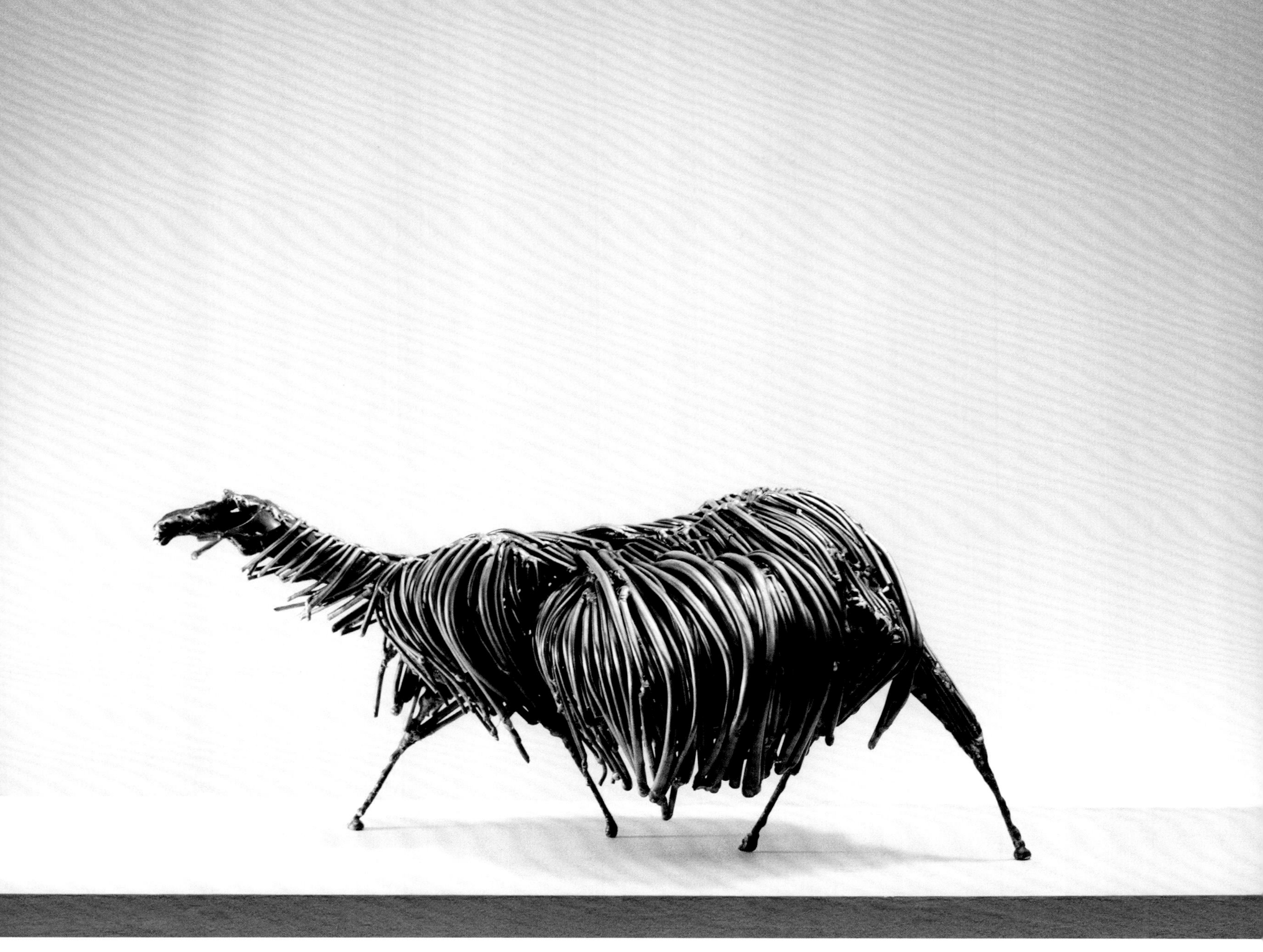

Plate 9
Luise Kaish.

Double Dutch, 1955, welded steel, 10 in. (25.4 cm) high

Leap Frog, 1955, welded steel, 11 in. (27.9 cm) high

See Saw, 1955, welded steel, 11 in. (27.9 cm) high

Flying the Kite, 1955, welded steel, 16 in. (40.6 cm) high

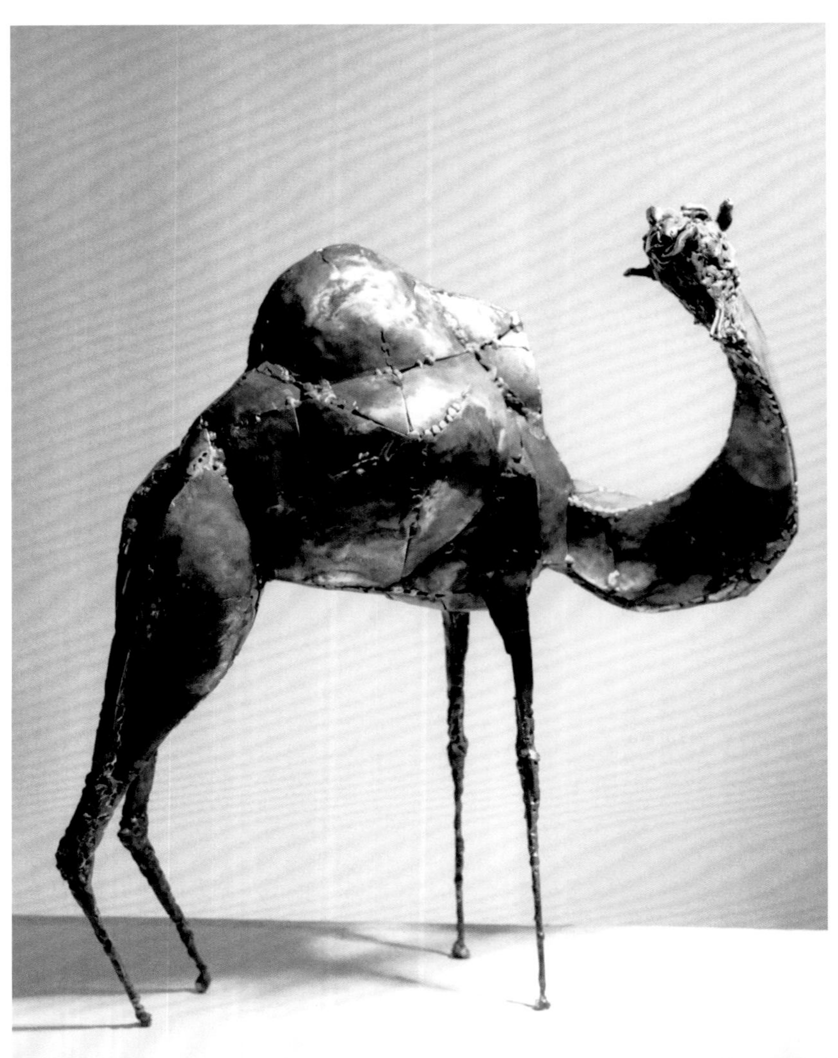

Plate 11
Luise Kaish. *Laughing Camel*, 1957, welded bronze, 18 in. (45.7 cm) high

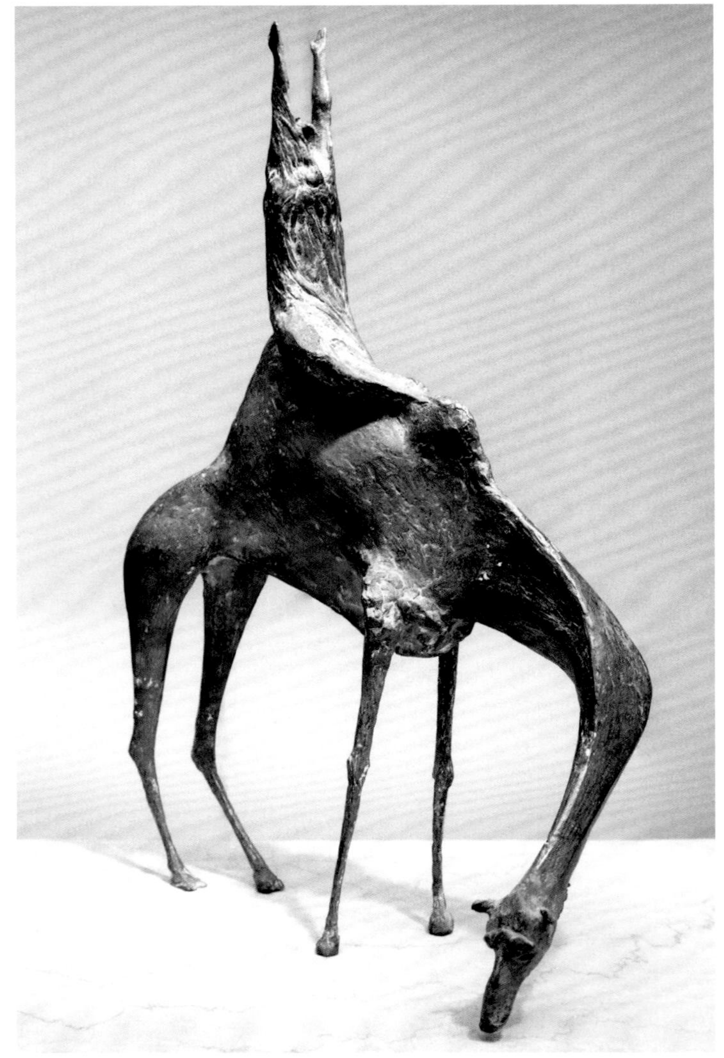

Plate 12
Luise Kaish. *Prophet*, 1957, bronze, 22 × 18 × 7 in.
(55.9 × 45.7 × 17.8 cm)

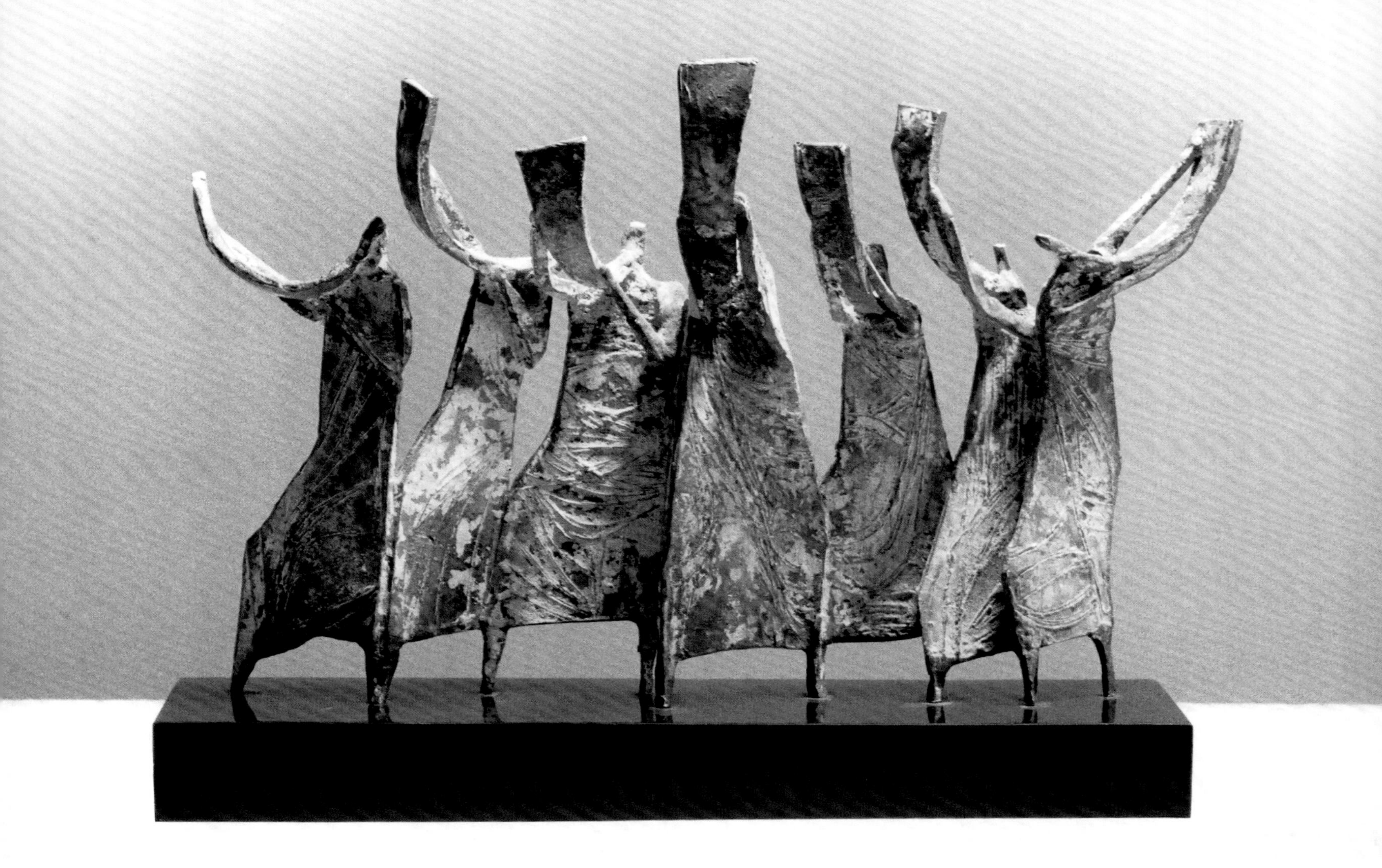

Plate 13
Luise Kaish. *Trumpeters of Jericho*, 1957, bronze, 6 × 10 in. (15.2 × 25.4 cm)

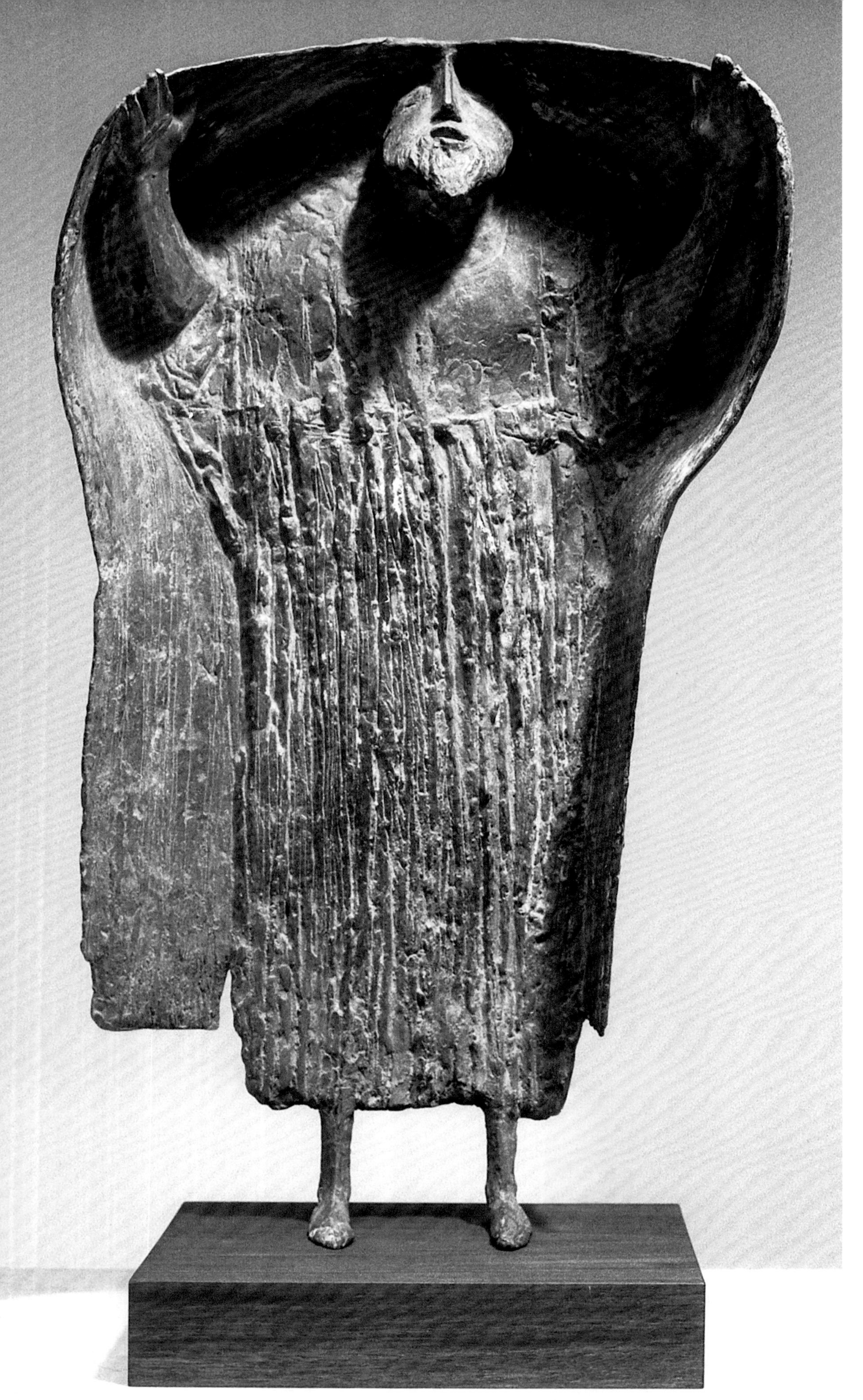

Plate 14
Luise Kaish. *The Blessing (Two)*,
1957, bronze, 19 × 14 in.
(48.3 × 35.6 cm)

Plate 15
Luise Kaish. *Angel of Joshua*, 1957,
bronze, 61 in. (154.9 cm) high

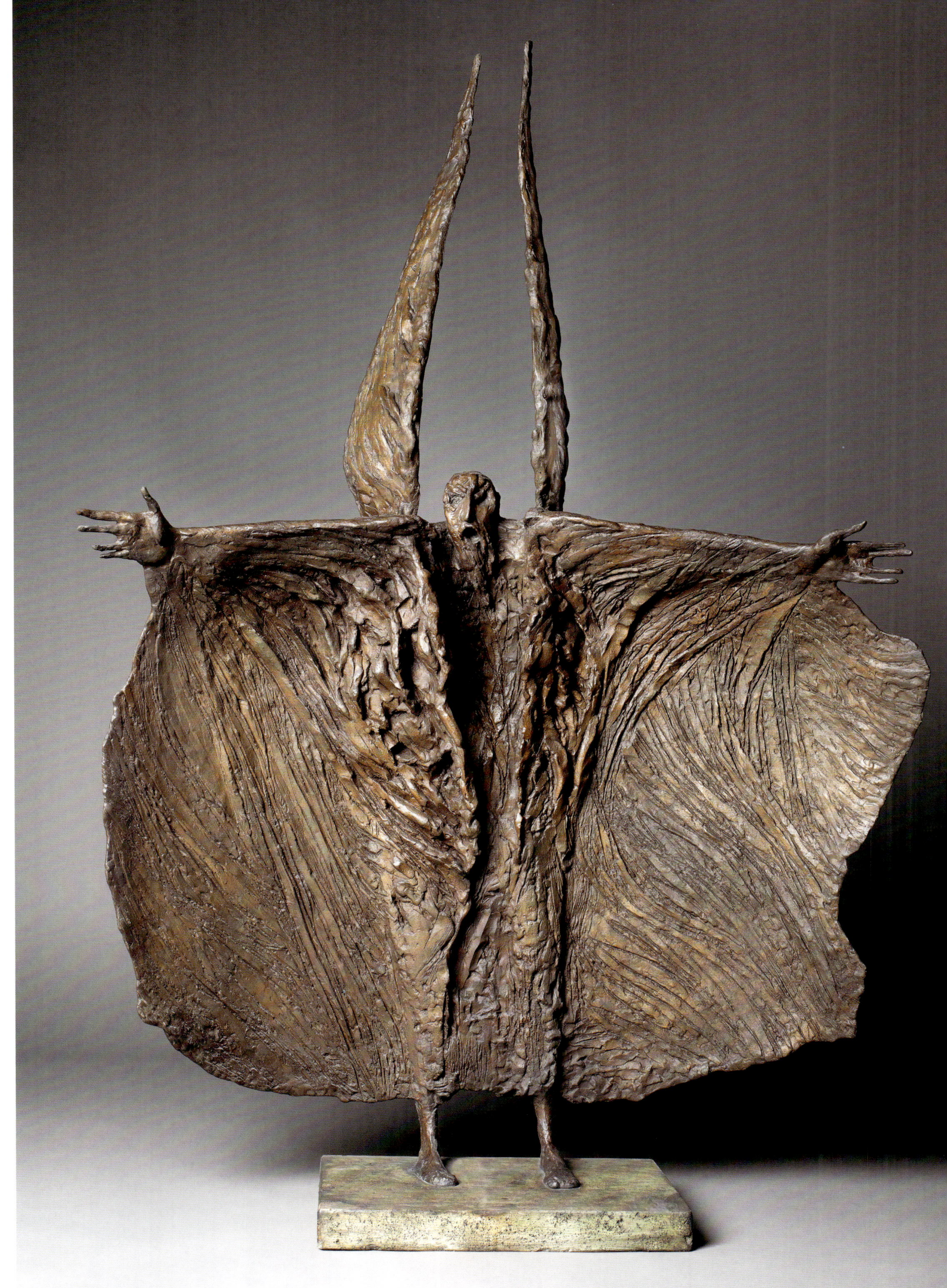

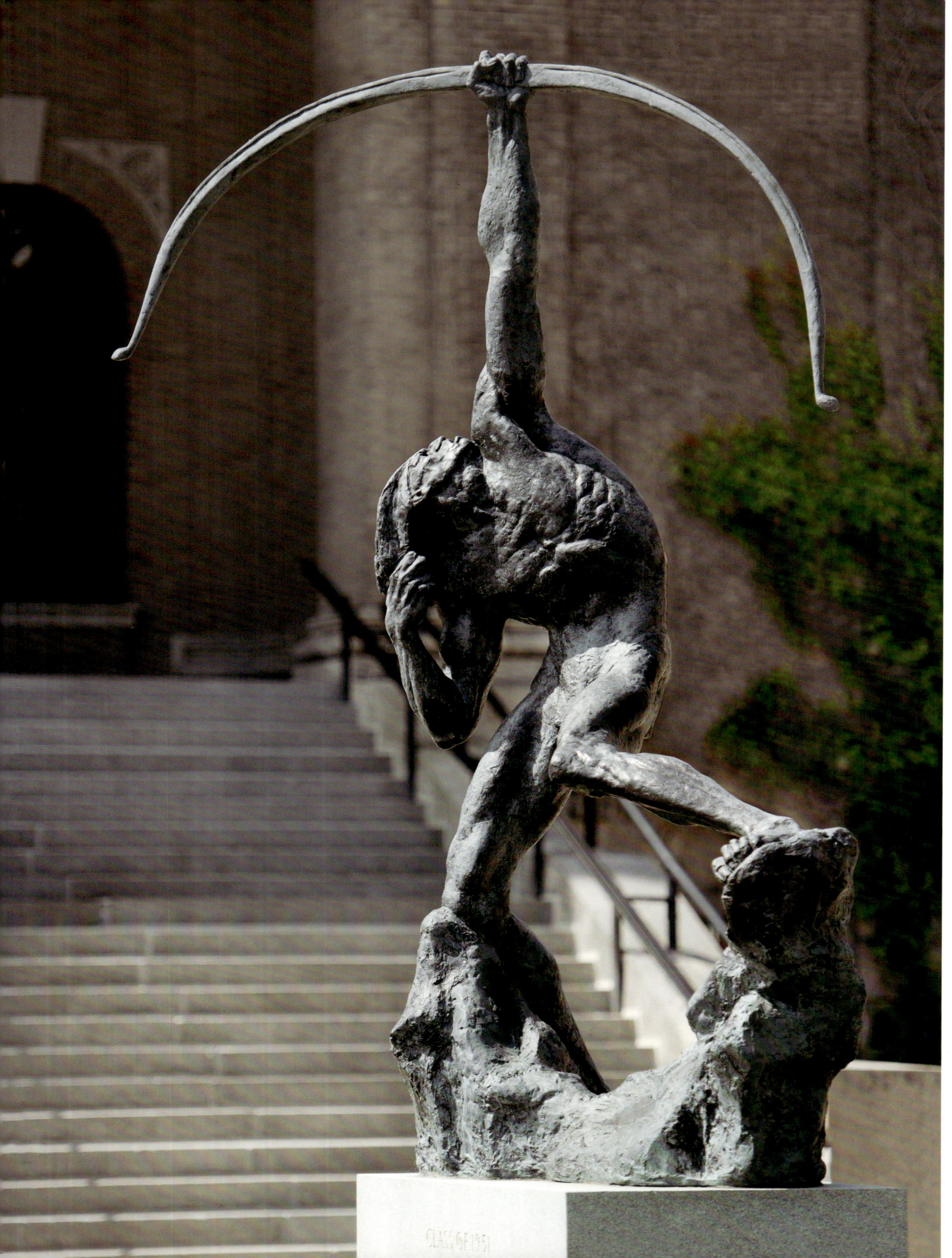

The sculptor speaks
through idea and presence.
I perceive — masses, curves, planes meeting
and intersecting.
The body, the land, the flower —
all molecules of energy,
continually changing, reshaped —
revealed to the senses —
by the mysteries of light.

–Luise Kaish

Plate 16
Luise Kaish. *Saltine Warrior*, 1951, bronze,
10 ft. (3.04 m) high. Collection, Syracuse
University, Syracuse, New York

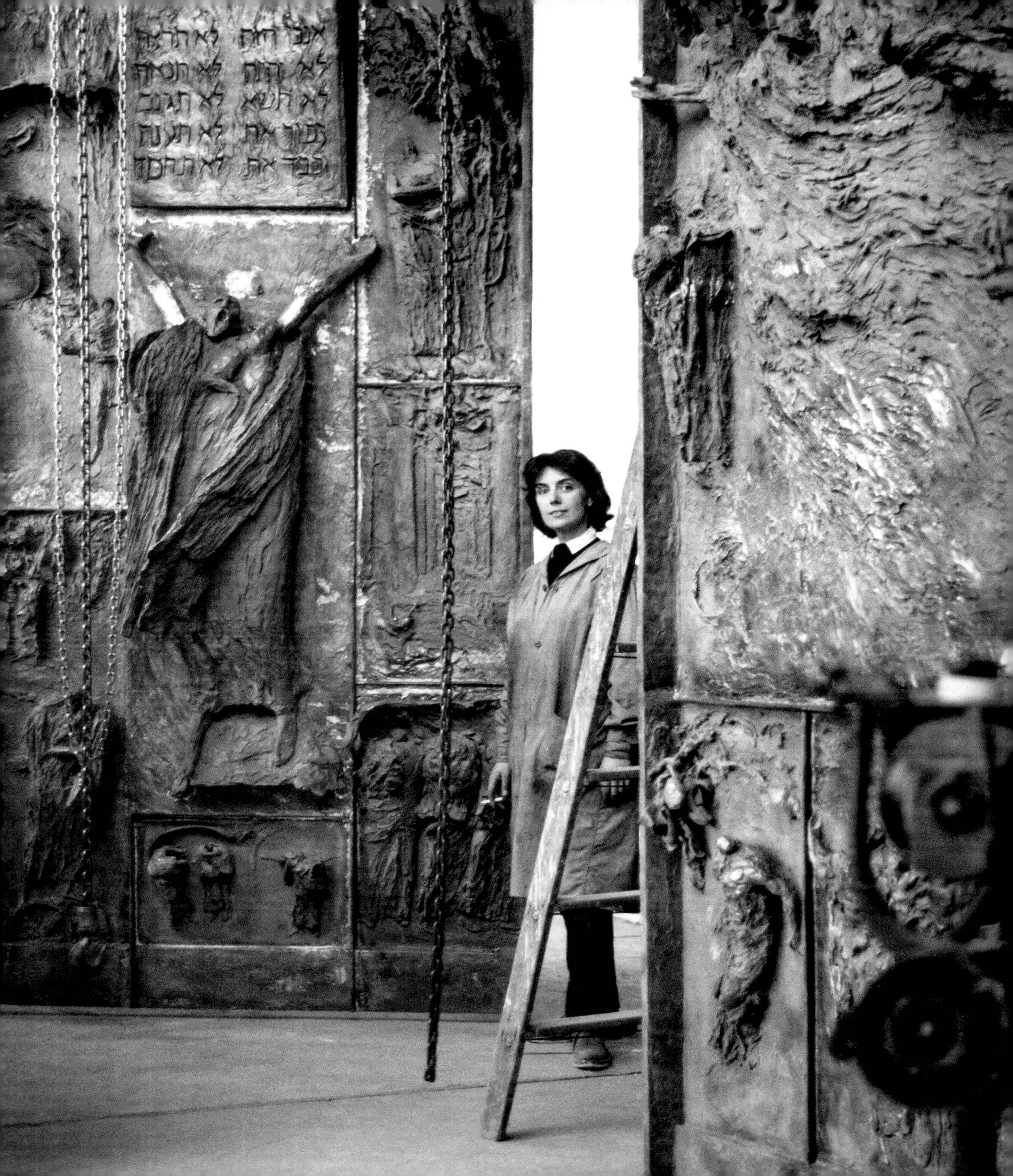

VOYAGES OF DISCOVERY

LUISE KAISH'S MONUMENTAL BRONZES

Daniel Belasco

Luise Kaish with bronze castings of *The Ark of Revelation* at the Modern Art Foundry, Queens, New York, 1962–63

For me art and religion are bridges in a voyage of discovery.[1]

–Luise Kaish

Luise Kaish's three decades of large-scale bronzes realized her quest for a sculpture of conse-quence—a didactic visual art in the tradition of the Parthenon frieze and Giotto's Scrovegni Chapel, incorporating the abstract symbolism of cross-cultural values. Most large-scale metal sculptures have their own unique set of technical challenges to be resolved in a collaborative way between the artist, fabricator, rigger, shipper, installer, and architect. Kaish embraced the new demands for stylistic experimentation and technological know-how in postwar American sculpture. The following essay surveys her monumental sculptures created between 1951 and 1976, and examines their creation and commissioning histories, analyzing their production processes, materials, and techniques. Kaish's mastery of craftsmanship, sensitivity to site, and consummate professionalism resulted in an exceptional body of work.

Education of a Sculptor

Making sculpture was as much a creative as a methodological undertaking for Kaish. In her studies with Ivan Meštrović at Syracuse University, where she earned a master of fine arts in 1951, she excelled in carving and modeling, and won a commission to create a monumen-tal sculpture of the university's mascot. She cast the ten-foot-high bronze *Saltine Warrior* at the Modern Art Foundry in Queens, New York, known for old-world craftsmanship and traditional practices (Fig. 15). Hungry for more experience, she spent a good deal of the 1950s in "the gathering of technical information."[2]

Sponsored by a Tiffany Foundation fellowship, Kaish lived in Florence in 1951–52, stud-ying the procedures of lost-wax bronze casting with Bruno Bearzi, a scholar and artist who conserved and cast replicas of the Ghiberti doors. She also carved stone in Florence's Instituto Statale d'Arte and practiced clay modeling in her studio. Kaish gained exposure to wax modeling, which became her favored working method, allowing her to clearly record her thinking and reduce the steps in bronze casting.[3] Working in wax gives bronze sculpture the "freshness of surface" that she observed in the work of sixteenth-century Mannerist artist Giambologna.[4] Kaish continued to develop professional networks and artisanal skills during her return to Italy in 1956–57, living in Rome and becoming fluent in Italian. Kaish cast forty-seven sculptures of prophets and other religious subjects at the venerable Nicci and Bruni foundries. Through her tenacity and expertise, she cultivated mutual trust and respectful connections with foundry craftsmen.

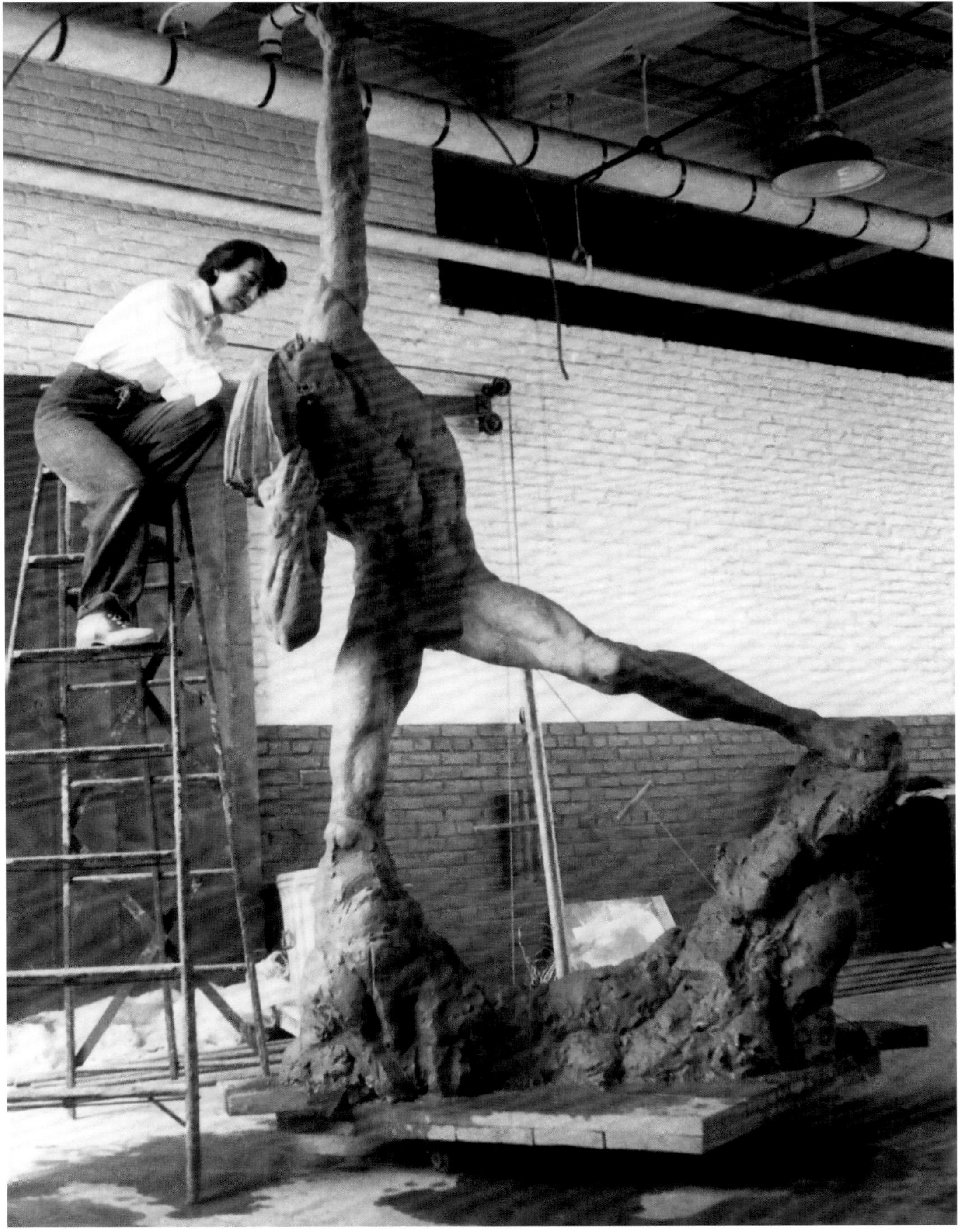

Fig. 15 Luise at work on her first commission, the *Saltine Warrior*, 1950

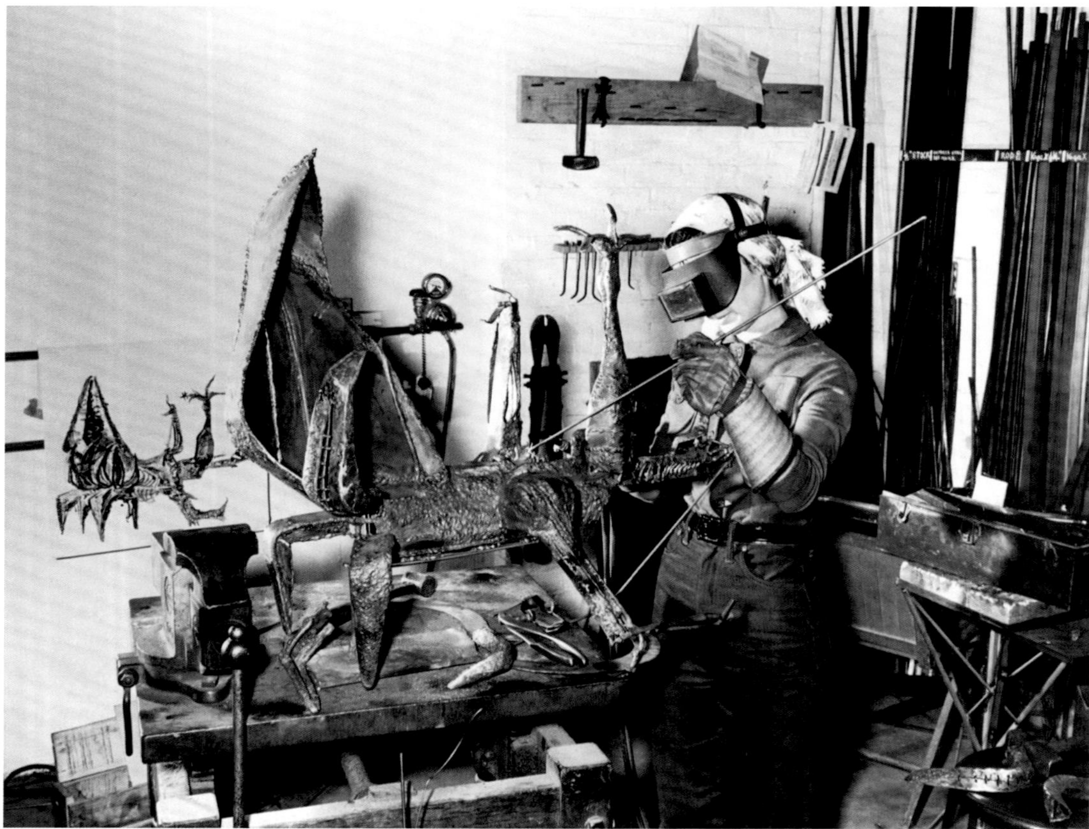

Fig. 16 Luise welding *Desert Spectre*, Sculpture Center, New York, circa 1954

Kaish also developed proficiency in the welding and fabrication of metal. In the early and mid-1950s she participated in a vibrant community of avant-garde artists at the Sculpture Center in New York, then co-directed by Sahl Swarz (Fig. 16). To make direct metal sculpture, considered the most advanced medium for contemporary sculpture at the time, she learned the properties of copper, iron, steel, and other metals and acquired the techniques of welding, enameling, plating, and patinating. A quick study, she participated in the pioneering 1953 exhibition *Women Welders*, which challenged stereotypes about "women's work." In a *New York Times* photograph, Kaish can be seen wearing a welder's mask, working on *Desert Spectre* (see Pl. 6).[5] This figure, though just thirty-six inches high, possesses mythopoetic subject matter and scale, providing a hint at her future ambitions, with intricate forms counterbalancing large masses.

The Ark of Revelation

Kaish's spiritual pursuits dovetailed with the expanded role of individual expression in new synagogue and Jewish center construction in suburban areas across the United States. Jewish communities, especially those affiliated with the Reform and Conservative movements, looked to modern art and architecture to address major social issues of the day, from the trauma of the Holocaust to the mixed blessing of assimilation. Kaish revered the narrative

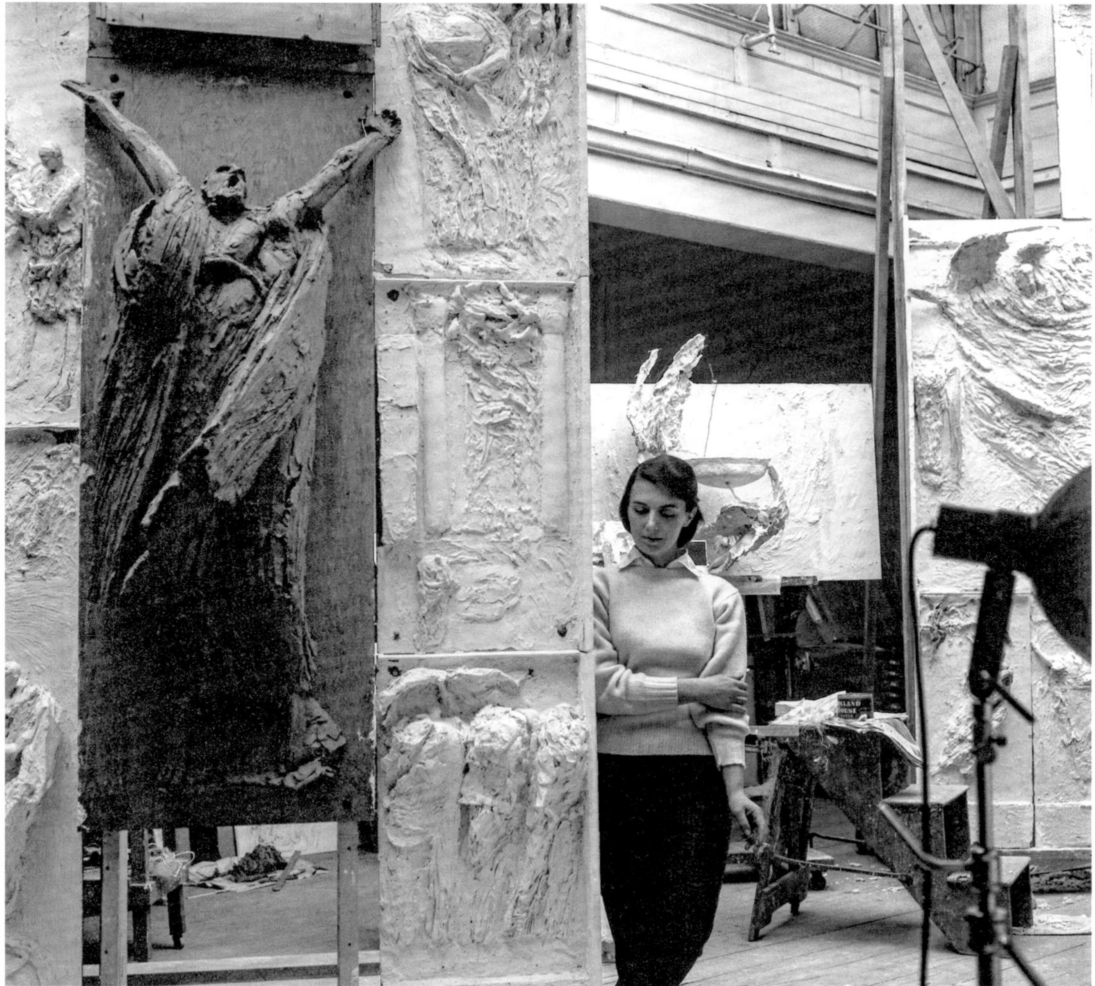

Fig. 17   Luise with *The Ark of Revelation*, MacDougal Street studio, New York, circa 1962

power of figural vignettes in the great bronze doors of European churches and believed that they could be adapted for a modern American spirit. She won a Guggenheim Fellowship in 1959 to materialize her dream of creating monumental bronze doors to greet synagogue visitors "with sculpture reliefs drawn from the great Hebraic figures and episodes of the Bible."[6] The group of wax models in her studio mapped a monument without a context.

Part of the modern architecture renaissance, Temple B'rith Kodesh, the largest Reform temple in Rochester, New York, planned to relocate in the early 1960s from its historical downtown building to a new fifteen-acre suburban campus designed by architect Pietro Belluschi.[7] Kaish had a close relationship with the temple's socially engaged senior rabbi Philip Bernstein, previously attending Friday-night services when she lived in Rochester. Bernstein introduced Kaish to Belluschi to advise on modern sculpture with Jewish themes.[8] Enthusiastic about adding Kaish to the design team, Belluschi wrote, "she is a most gifted artist with a deep spiritual quality, and I am very happy at the prospect of working with her."[9] In 1960 Kaish received the commission to create a monumental ark, or Torah cabinet, the focal point of the main sanctuary—an object of perhaps greater significance in Jewish ritual than her proposed grand entry doors.

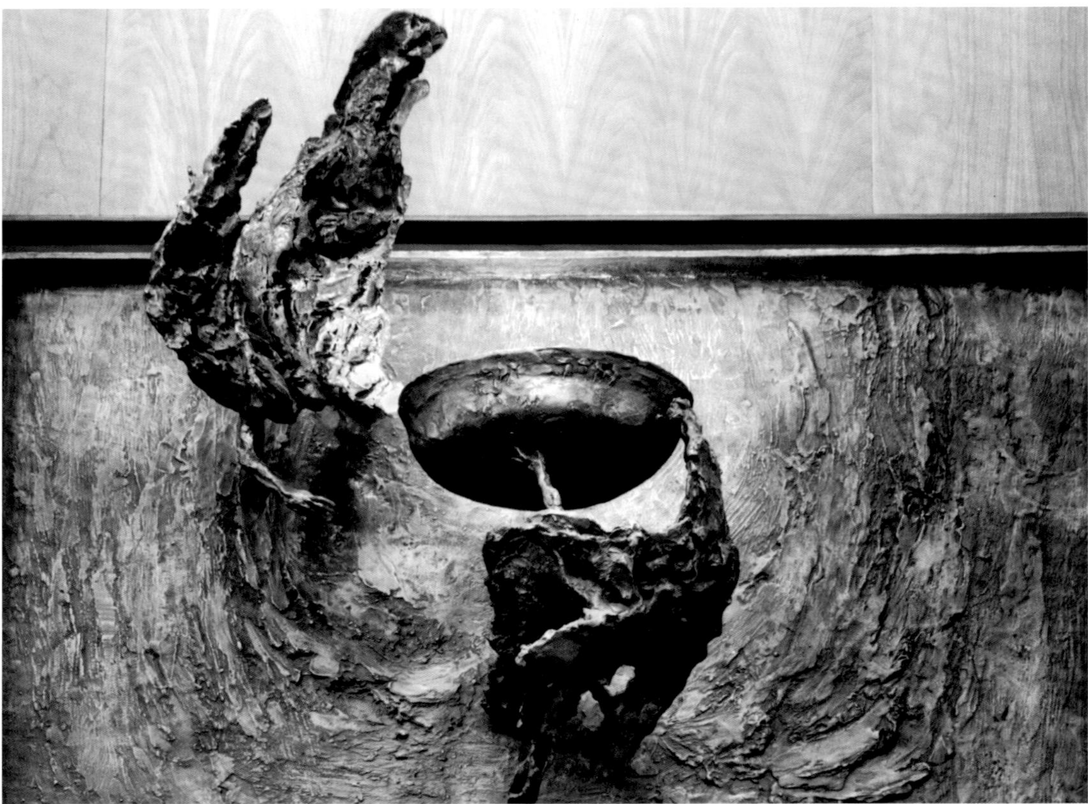

Fig. 18 Luise Kaish, *The Ark of Revelation* (detail of *ner tamid* [eternal light]), 1960–64 (see Plate 17)

The contract with B'rith Kodesh included a proviso that Kaish would negotiate with foundries on behalf of the temple to ensure that the final product would meet her exacting standards. Kaish preferred to know all the technical specifications in order to make the most accurate design possible. She asked Belluschi for schematic drawings of the ark, including the location and dimensions of the curtain track, and asked Bernstein for the measurements of the Torah scrolls, including ornaments, so her assistant Gene Leofanti could build the full-size wooden armature to scale. Once Bernstein and Belluschi approved her wax sketches, she sculpted the models in plaster, a quick-drying medium that required decisive handling. Kaish supervised the molding and casting of *The Ark of Revelation* at Modern Art Foundry, retouching the bronze until achieving an opulent finish.

The *Ark* realized Kaish's aspiration to find visual form for "an unremitting dialogue with God."[10] The *Ark,* measuring fourteen by fifteen feet, consists of eighteen rectangular panels of irregular size, each depicting a moment of revelation (Pls. 17, 18). The dominant figure is Moses, on the left side, seeming to spring forward with arms outstretched in divine encounter (Fig. 17). Other figures include the patriarchs Abraham and Jacob, the kings David and Solomon, and the prophets Isaiah and Ezekiel. The elongated heads, flowing garments, and feathery wings are stylistic motifs that Kaish developed in her small bronzes. In addition to the narrative panels, Kaish incorporated symbolic imagery and ritual objects into her *Ark,* such as the representation of the Ten Commandments at left, as well as the *ner tamid* (eternal light) on top (Fig. 18) and menorah (seven-branch candelabrum) on the right. Kaish imbued her monumental style with the sense of flux, inspired by narrative

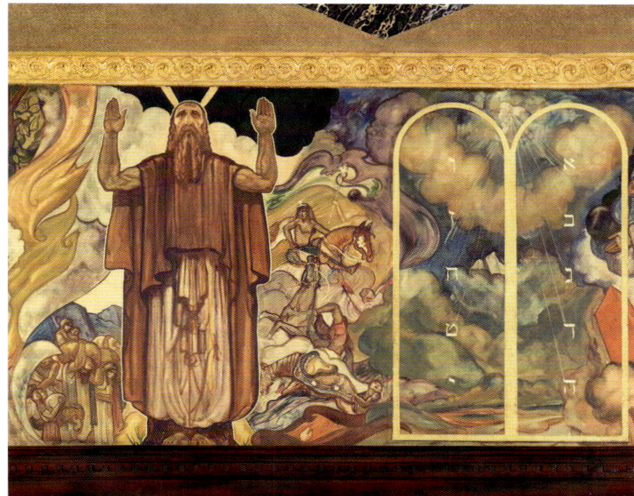

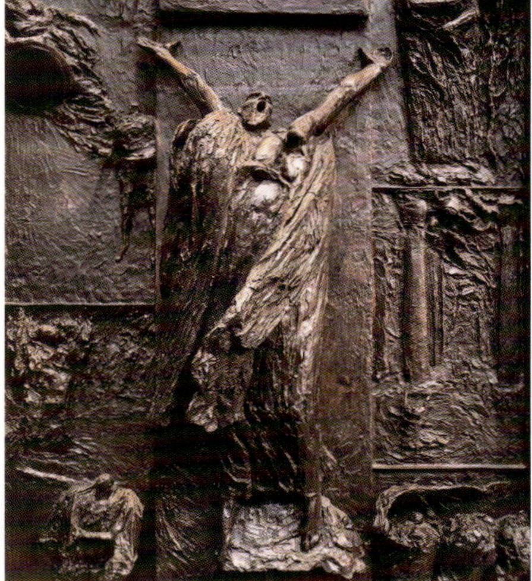

Fig. 19   Hugo Ballin, Warner Murals (detail of Moses), 1929, oil on canvas, 15 panels, 320 × 7 ft. (97.5 × 2.1 m), plus three lunettes, each approx. 18 × 36 ft. (5.5 × 11 m), Wilshire Boulevard Temple Sanctuary, Los Angeles, 1929

Fig. 20   Luise Kaish, *The Ark of Revelation* (detail of Moses), 1960–64 (see Plate 17)

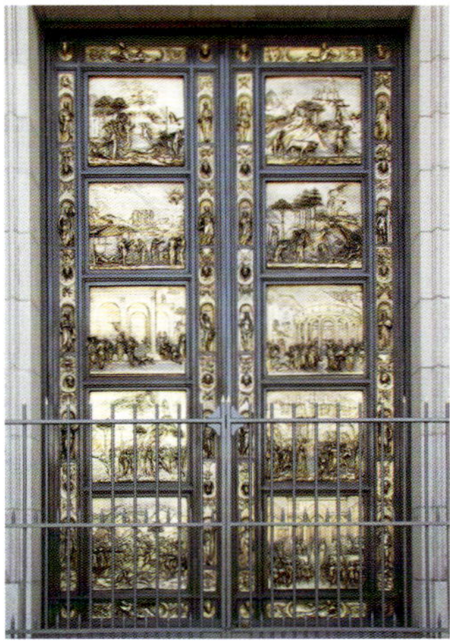

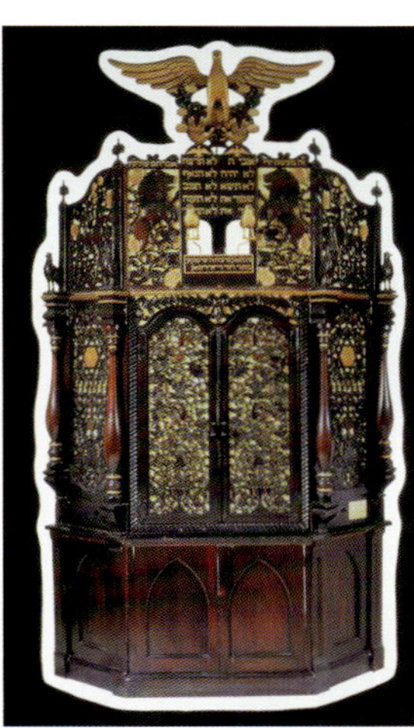

Fig. 21   Gothic-revival portal with the Doors of Paradise (replicas of Lorenzo Ghiberti's doors for the Baptistery of Florence Cathedral, 1425–52, gilded bronze), each approx. 16 ft. (4.8 m) high, Grace Cathedral, San Francisco

Fig. 22   Abraham Shulkin, Torah Ark, 1899, pinewood: hand-carved, openwork, stained, and painted, 125 × 96 × 30 in. (317.5 × 243.9 × 76.2 cm), Adath Yeshurun Synagogue, Sioux City, Iowa

low-relief sculpture in art history, especially the Romanesque and Gothic periods, as well as the animated sculpture of nineteenth-century French masters Jean-Baptiste Carpeaux and Auguste Rodin, specifically Rodin's *Gates of Hell* (1880–1917).

Because of the taboo-breaking figural imagery, Bernstein reviewed her wax sketches during multiple studio visits and consulted with other rabbis. Over the course of the project Kaish made some adjustments to avoid "Christological association."[11] The thrusting upwards movement of Kaish's Moses verges on ecstatic revelation, out of step with classical Reform decorum, such as the restrained symmetry of Moses in Hugo Ballin's mural in the sanctuary of the Wilshire Boulevard Temple, Los Angeles (Figs. 19, 20). To reconcile the contrasting traditions of European church sculpture and American synagogue art and make an original statement, she established the principle of asymmetry. This format rejects both the grid-like arrangement of church doors, such as Ghiberti's (Fig. 21), and the symmetrical decoration customary in American synagogues, such as Abraham Shulkin's Torah ark from Adath Yeshurun, Sioux City, Iowa (Fig. 22). *The Ark of Revelation*'s mix of high and low relief,

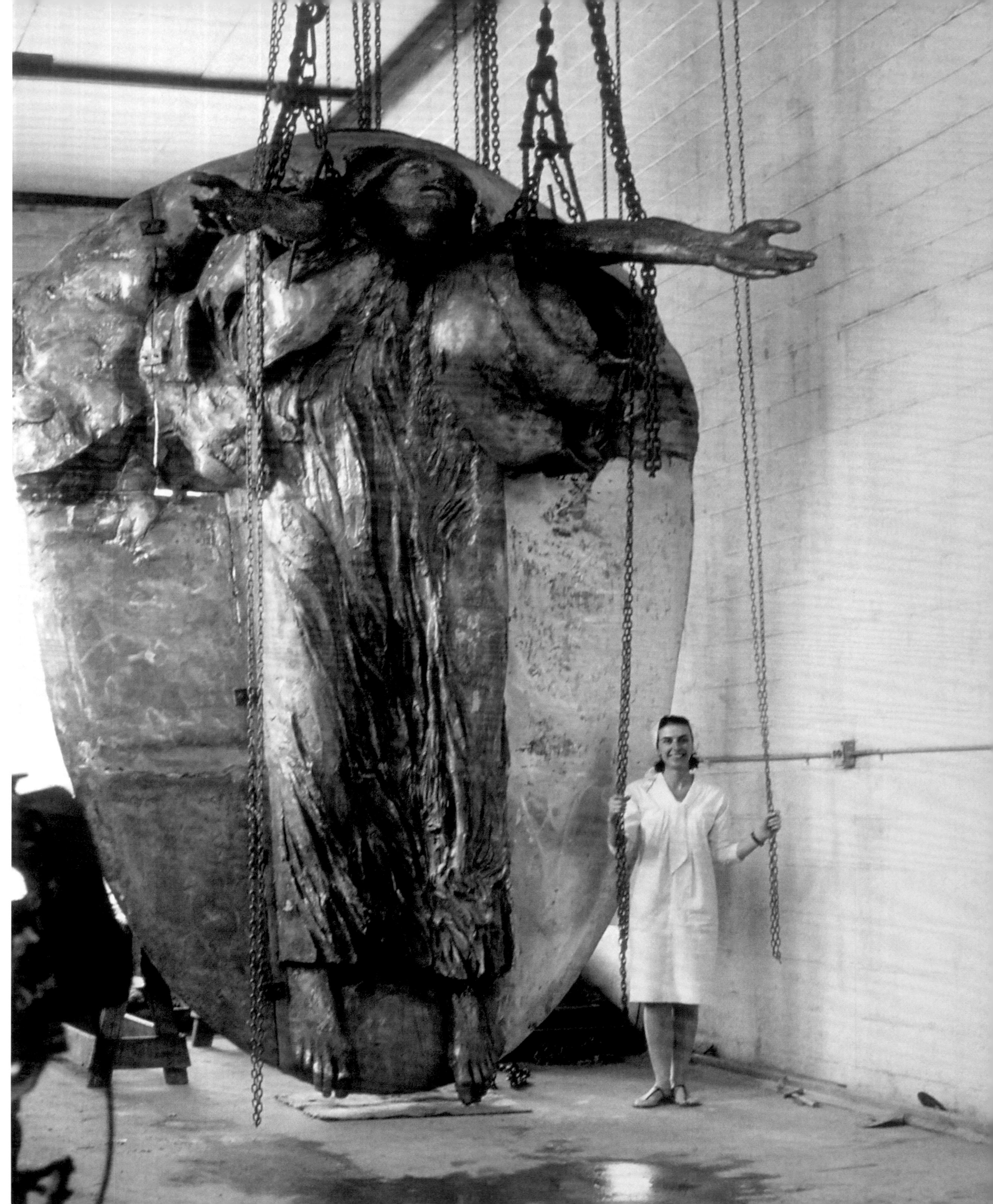

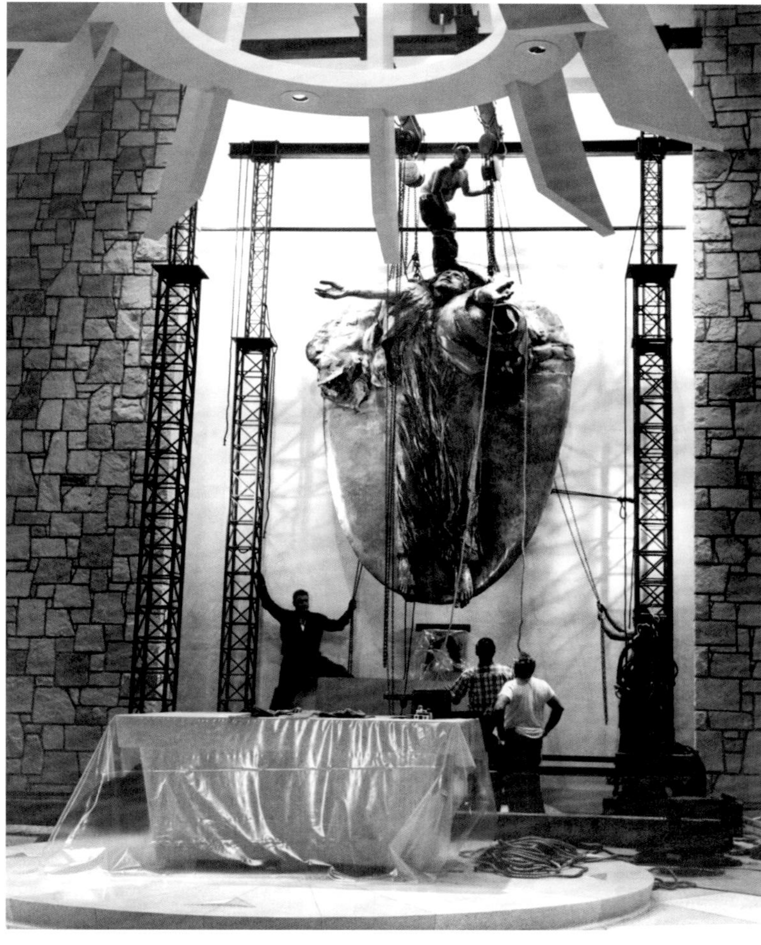

Fig. 24   Installing *Christ in Glory*, 1967

with some imagery lightly carved into the background and some figures nearly in the round, realized Kaish's principle of asymmetry, which, she wrote, would allow the *Ark* to "embody that feeling of richness and intrinsic value which I feel is so often lacking in modern synagogue decor."[12] The asymmetry of the arrangement of the panels and depth of the figures reflects the human relationship with God, which is essentially imbalanced.

Even before the installation of the two-ton sculpture in March 1964, thought leaders heralded Kaish's *Ark* as a masterpiece. Balfour Brickner, an influential Reform rabbi, said that the sight of the *Ark* at the foundry gave him goose pimples, calling it "the greatest piece of synagogue art in America today."[13] An *Architectural Digest* article about the synagogue included two photographs of the

Ark. Art historian Avram Kampf, in his still-authoritative book *Contemporary Synagogue Art* (1966), devoted twice as many pages to Kaish's *Ark* than to any other work.[14] This regard has stood the test of time. In 2003, scholar Samuel Gruber deemed the *Ark* one of "the major works of Judaica in the last half century."[15] Kaish's expressive figural gestures could be said to predict the Jewish renewal movement of the later 1960s and the new expression of joy through song and dance in American religion. The *Ark* became the definitive sculpture of her career and led to other major commissions.

Christ in Glory

The Ark of Revelation crossed denominational boundaries and resonated beyond the Jewish community. The *Times-Union*, Rochester's afternoon newspaper, published a diagram of the sculpture with the biblical sources for each panel (see Appendix A). Father Peter Sheehan, an accomplished liturgical composer affiliated with St. John Fisher College in Rochester, praised the *Ark* as in the tradition of Michelangelo and Ghiberti. Mississippi-based architect James T. Canizaro, on seeing an image of Kaish's *Moses*, commissioned her to make a "very

Fig. 23   Luise with *Christ in Glory* at the
Modern Art Foundry, circa 1965–67

devotional and powerful" bronze figure of Christ for the Holy Trinity Mission Seminary Church he designed in Silver Spring, Maryland.[16] This unexpected opportunity inspired one of her largest works (Fig. 23).

Kaish threw herself into the project, marshaling extensive research into Christian iconography to figure out how, as a Jew, she could sculpt a reverential Christ. Her wax sketches evolved from a conventional figure on a cross to her final design of a high-relief deity with outstretched arms enclosed by a mandorla (almond-shaped aureole). The Very Reverend Gerard P. Fredericks visited her studio to review the wax sketches and provided feedback, asking at one point that Christ be more upright and project farther from wall. A half year later he returned to Kaish's studio to review the one-third-size scale model. "We all approved the work enthusiastically," Fredericks wrote Canizaro.[17] Kaish hired craftsman Arthur Bruce Hoheb to enlarge her fourteen-inch wax model into the full-scale plaster, which she reassembled at Modern Art Foundry to inspect it from all angles. Kaish knew she had achieved success when one of the workers, an African American gate-cutter, pronounced, "come unto me ye little children."[18]

Perhaps the most problematic aspect of the commission was the installation. The full-size figure could not be moved in one piece through the double doors from the vestibule into the chapel. Kaish and the foundry team decided to cast the arms separately and use Roman joints to attach them on site without welding, thus avoiding seams and discoloration. Kaish mitigated the extra expenses as much as possible. "I am sure you have done a very diligent and thorough job," Canizaro wrote.[19] A crew from the foundry installed the twelve-foot-high, three-ton bronze *Christ in Glory* in 1967 (Fig. 24; Pls. 19, 20). The *Washington Post* printed a photograph of the complex rigging used for mounting, with a quote from Kaish that her sculpture expressed "the ecstasy of the spiritual oneness of man with God."[20] Belluschi also recognized this inclusive interpretation of Christ, praising the work as the "literary side of church art."[21]

Abstract Symbolism: *The Beth Shalom Ark Doors*

Sensitive curators and patrons considered *The Ark of Revelation* to be on the forefront of the shift in American culture from centralized religion to individual engagement with spirituality. Architect Richard D. Chalfant responded to Kaish's radical new aesthetic. In late 1966, he invited Kaish to create the ark, eternal light, and menorah for the new building he had designed for Congregation Beth Shalom in Wilmington, Delaware (Pls. 21, 22). She accepted the commission, but the Conservative congregation, which observed more traditional Jewish customs, presented some limitations. Their stricter interpretation of the Second Commandment prohibiting idolatry meant that she could not work with figural

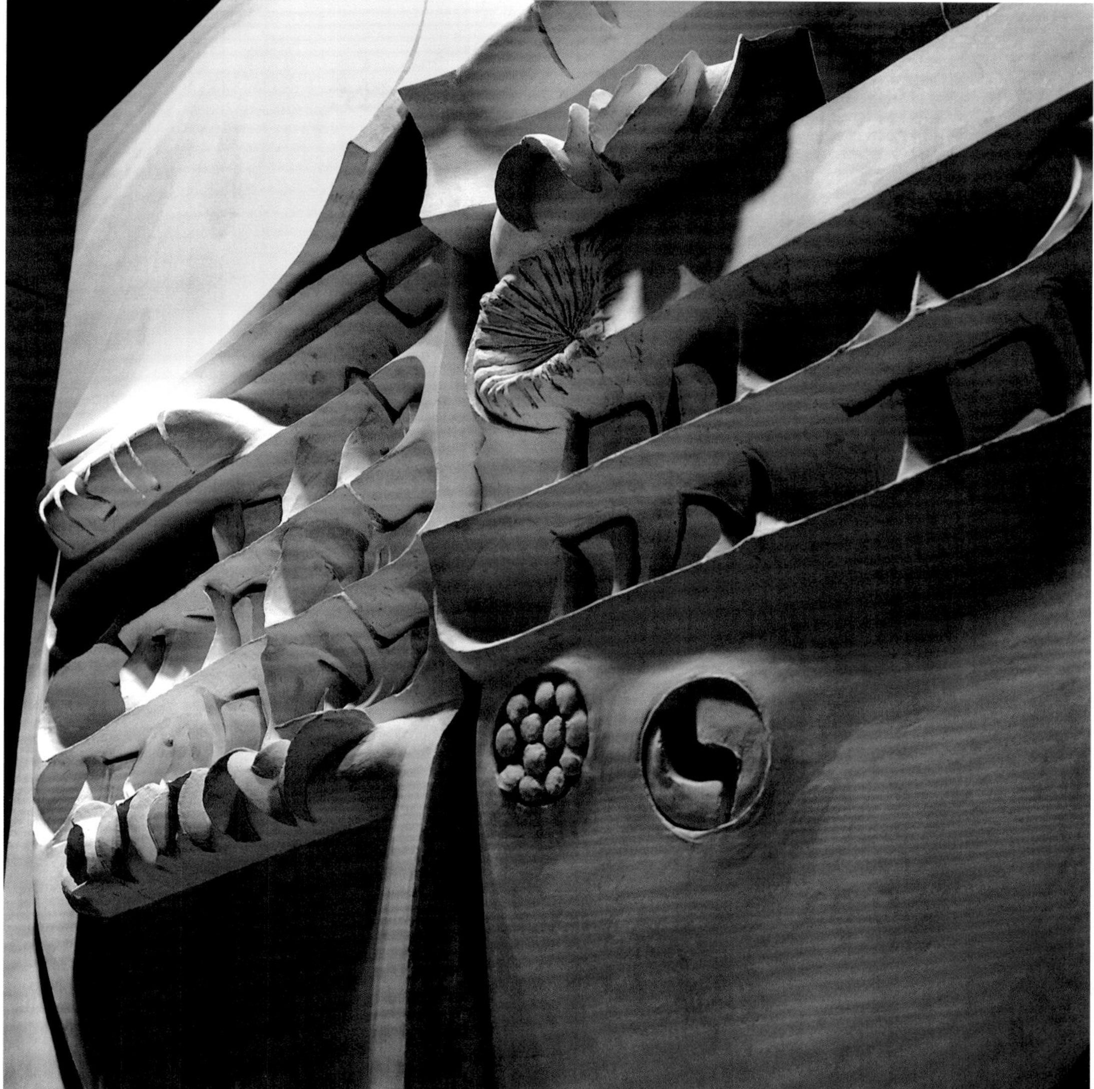

Fig. 25   Luise Kaish, *The Beth Shalom Ark Doors* (full scale plaster model), 1966–68 (see Plate 21)

imagery. Further, their observance of Sabbath labor restrictions meant that an electric motor could not be used to slide open the two ark door panels.

Kaish's reading of Kabbalah, or Jewish mysticism, furnished her with a new reservoir of abstract symbolism. The polished bronze ark doors interpret the Ten Commandments as an emotional source of spiritual connection to a profound power. The circular shapes represent the mystical concept of God as *Ein Sof* (without end), or the infinite. To counter this ineffable concept, she took a physical approach to rendering Hebrew letters and symbols, carving the words of the commandments (Fig. 25). Kaish placed five lines of text on each door at varying levels, applying her principles of asymmetry and high and low relief. Other symbols derived from Kabbalah, including a cluster of twelve circles representing the twelve tribes, the letter *yud* (the first letter in the tetragrammaton, the Hebrew name for God), and seven grooves that represent the *Sefiroth* (the Kabbalistic diagram of life forces), further energize the overall composition.

Kaish first sculpted in wax, then hired Hoheb to enlarge the sketches in plastiline. Kaish continued to refine the full-size model before Hoheb cast it in plaster to prepare the sculpture for bronze casting at Modern Art Foundry. Kaish discussed with Chalfant the options for mounting her sculptures on the wooden doors. They conferred over a mechanism that would allow the heavy doors to glide open simultaneously, determined the locations of holes and bolts to secure the sculpture to the doors, and approved neoprene gaskets to avoid electrolytic action between the bronze mounted to the steel frame. She helped the architect calculate the load the doors would bear, based on the average weight of bronze per square foot (Fig. 26). Even after installation, Kaish and Chalfant continued to cooperate on the lighting, as she requested additional spotlights to illuminate the polished finish. While many sculptors would have left these myriad details to the foundry and engineer to resolve, Kaish, ever the perfectionist, kept herself in the middle of the conversation to fulfill her vision.

Kaish exhibited a maquette of the doors in *Luise Kaish, Recent Sculpture*, her first solo exhibition at Staempfli Gallery in 1968. The *New York Times* critic John Canaday deemed Kaish one of the few artists "capable of producing satisfactory ecclesiastical sculpture today."[22] The ark doors were installed later that year. Though seven feet tall and weighing more than one thousand pounds each, they seem to float in front of the travertine wall behind the bimah. The congregation's rabbi, Jacob Kraft, wrote in an explanatory brochure that the doors possess "inscrutable power" (see Appendix B).[23] An aesthetic achievement within strict doctrinal and structural parameters, the *Ark Doors* freshly interpreted an archetypal Jewish symbol, the tablets of the law. Kaish later said the doors advanced her development of a series of spherical abstract sculptures with moveable components.[24]

Fastidious Fabrication: Temple B'nai Abraham and *La Lumière*

By the mid-1960s most advanced sculptors preferred the industrial look of fabricated work machined from stock materials (sheet metal, for example). Kaish adopted this practice to attain greater precision in her fine-tuned abstract forms, returning to Italy to explore new processes of making sculpture. From 1970 to 1972 she lived in Rome as a fellow of the American Academy, dialoguing with Buckminster Fuller about the relationship of intuition and creation. Kaish explored the spiritual symbolism of abstract forms in a series of kinetic orbs in cast and polished bronze, titled *In the Beginning* (see Pls. 48, 52). Around the same time Kaish also hired a lone practitioner to fabricate her series of stainless-steel *Voyages*, hammered and welded into undulating solids with a mirror finish (see Pls. 49, 50). Upon her return to New York, Kaish transferred the production of her monumental abstract work from foundries to fabricators.

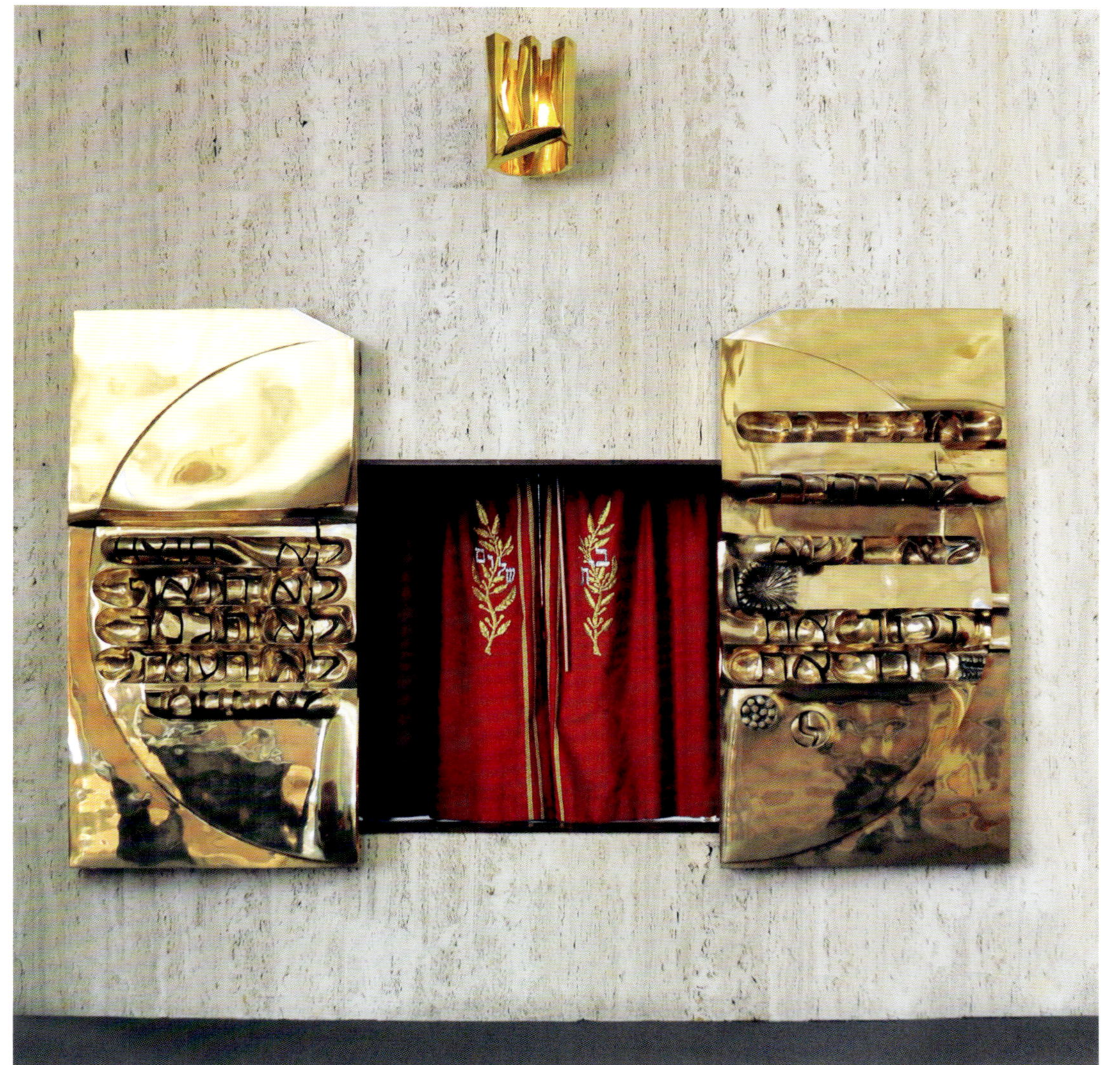

Fig. 26   Luise Kaish, *The Beth Shalom Ark Doors* (with doors open), 1968 (see Plate 22)

Temple B'nai Abraham, in Livingston, New Jersey, commissioned Kaish's first large-scale fabricated sculpture for its new building, designed by architect Edward Rothe, an associate of Gruzen & Partners. In 1973, Milgo Art Systems of Brooklyn fabricated the eternal light and menorah from sheets of Everdur bronze, a silicon alloy used for creative and industrial applications (Fig. 27). Its uniform consistency and surface quality made it an ideal material for polished fabricated jobs. Referencing its function as illumination, Kaish said the eternal light symbolized "spirit as light" and the menorah represented "power and simplicity."[25] The eight-by-eight-foot, eight-hundred-pound menorah's rectangular and triangle-chevron-shaped structure resembled contemporaneous minimalist sculptures (Pls. 23, 24). But the curved eternal light contained no straight lines, with bent triangular elements pointing towards the center, each cut in a unique shape, symbolizing the twelve tribes of Israel (Pls. 25, 26). The Jewish Museum's 1973 retrospective *Luise Kaish Sculpture* included Kaish's eternal light *Twelve Tribes A* (see Pl. 55), which led to the commission of a smaller version for the Hebrew Union College chapel in Jerusalem (Pl. 28).[26]

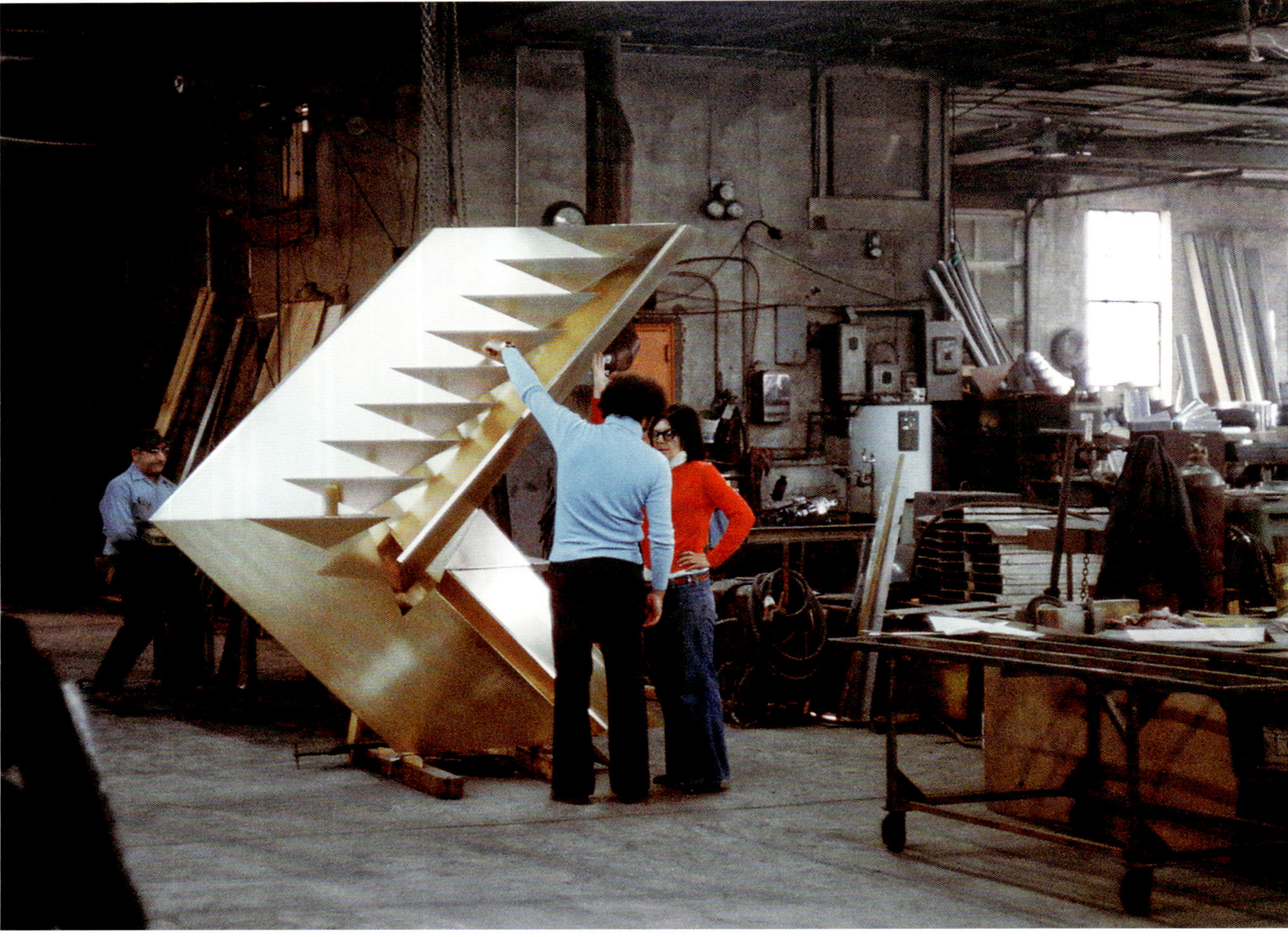

Fig. 27   Luise with Bruce Gitlin and the B'Nai Abraham *Menorah* at Milgo Art Systems, Brooklyn, New York, 1973

Kaish created her last major sculpture for the Continental Grain company's New York offices, designed by Davis Allen, senior designer at Skidmore, Owings & Merrill. *La Lumière* has a reflective surface to engage its environment—the fiftieth-floor reception area of a modern Park Avenue skyscraper. In this project Kaish articulated her new philosophy, positioning herself as a conceptual artist removing her hand from the creation of her sculpture without sacrificing attention to detail. "This is to be treated as a machined part and not as a sculpture," she wrote to potential fabricators.[27] Her technical notes called for the six-inch-high model to be scaled up to two bronze disks, three-quarters of an inch thick and four feet in diameter, joined at a right angle (Fig. 28). The plan called for thin grooves to be cut from the edge to close to the center. After some false starts with other shops, Kaish hired Milgo to complete the job by October 1976. Proprietor Bruce Gitlin recalled Kaish as a meticulous and knowledgeable perfectionist who demanded that her work be executed to the highest of standards.[28] Gitlin and Kaish searched for months to find thick sheets of bronze and a one-sixteenth-inch blade to mill a thin cut. She would visit the shop to inspect progress and view the sculpture from every vantage point, making a few tweaks. Kaish's work in monumental commissions culminated with the suspension of the 850-pound *La Lumière* at a forty-five-degree angle on a steel cable, an optimistic statement of the postmodern age (see Pl. 57).

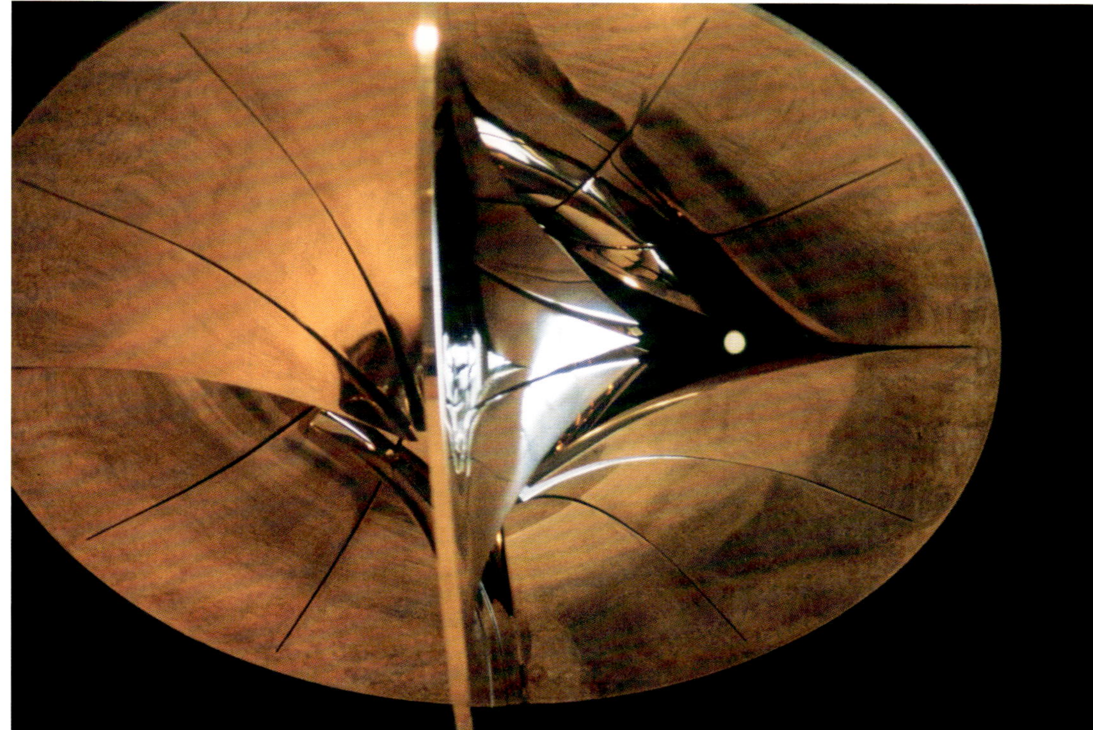

Fig. 28 *La Lumière* (detail), 1975–76 (see Plate 57)

The Wall of Martyrs and *the Holocaust Memorial*

Because of the renown of *The Ark of Revelation*, Kaish remained in demand for figural sculpture even as her personal practice evolved to abstract forms and symbols. While residing at the American Academy in Rome and producing *Voyages* and *In the Beginning*, Kaish received a visit from Stanley I. Batkin, the chair of the building committee of Beth El Synagogue Center in New Rochelle, New York. The Conservative temple selected her to make a monumental bronze frieze in their new center, designed by Edgar Tafel, a former apprentice of Frank Lloyd Wright, to educate children and congregants about Jewish history. Kaish accepted the assignment and dove into research. She focused her ideas of martyrdom around *kiddush hashem*, or personal sacrifice in the name of God to not break holy commandments. She created wax maquettes and shipped them to New York for approval. Then she hired a local artisan to make full-size plasters for casting by Bruni in Rome with her supervision. She arranged for the overseas shipments of the bronze panels in two large crates, which arrived in New York via Egypt, a historical irony not lost on the artist.

The Wall of Martyrs features eight discrete low-relief panels arranged in a staggered sequence, seventeen feet long and seven and a half feet high (Pl. 27; Appendix C).[29] Some panels appear highly realistic, like *The Crusades* (panel 5), and others more abstract, like *The Ten Martyrs* (panel 3) with its swirling circular form memorializing a rabbi wrapped in a Torah being burned alive. In the sinuous movement of one panel to another, one can see Kaish's central vision of Jewish history as unending, "like an unfolding flower filled with the heights of a poetic delight, exultation and despair—at once intensely human and ennobling, a mystical voyage."[30] Again, Kaish employed asymmetry as a visual structure to guide the eye through the imagery. The work appeared in her 1973 retrospective at the Jewish Museum before being installed in the synagogue in 1974. Soon after, Kaish's long-time patron Vera List commissioned her to make a Holocaust memorial to be installed in the Fifth Avenue outdoor courtyard entry of the museum (Pl. 29). Adapted from the final panel of *The Wall of Martyrs*, the memorial's imagery contrasts the horror of a crematorium and the beauty of flowers, articulating the agonizing paradoxes of Jewish life and history.

Luise Kaish sculpted from the heart for the public. Her ability to combine form and narrative to engage the viewer, using both figural and abstract imagery in a wide range of media, aligns her art with that of contemporaries such as Ruth Asawa, Ida Kohlmeyer, and Louise Nevelson. Standing at the intersection of sacred space, modernist sculpture, and Western art history, Kaish's monumental sculptures demonstrate that the essential form of revelation is asymmetrical, and that a voyage of discovery begins with the open-minded confrontation of imbalances.

Endnotes

1. *The First Estate: Religion in Review*, segment "Faith and Form," WNBC-TV, New York, January 6, 1974, video courtesy Kaish Family Art Project, New York.

2. Luise Kaish to Henry Hobart Nichols, July 10, 1952, Luise Kaish archives, New York.

3. The wax model eliminates the need for the creation of a wax replica of an original clay model. Jeffrey Spring, third-generation director of the Modern Art Foundry, helped my understanding of the significance of Kaish's modeling in wax. Jeffrey Spring, interview by Sarah McCollum Williams and the author, July 18, 2019.

4. Kaish to Nichols, July 10, 1952.

5. "Sculptresses Turn to Welder's Torch," *New York Times*, November 7, 1953, 23.

6. Luise Kaish to Rabbi Philip Bernstein, October 23, 1959, Luise Kaish archives. Additional correspondence between Kaish and Bernstein can be found in the Philip S. Bernstein Papers, D.269, Rare Books, Special Collections, and Preservation, River Campus Libraries, University of Rochester.

7. "A Major Synagogue by Belluschi," *Architectural Record* 134 (November 1963): 143–48. For more on Belluschi (1899–1994), see Meredith L. Clausen, *Spiritual Space: The Religious Architecture of Pietro Belluschi* (Seattle: University of Washington Press, 1992); Temple B'rith Kodesh is illustrated and discussed on pages 108–11. Temple B'rith Kodesh is also illustrated in the exhibition catalogue *Recent American Synagogue Architecture* (New York: Jewish Museum, 1963), though it was photographed before Kaish's *Ark* was installed.

8. Kaish suggested the temple consider acquiring Meštrović's limestone sculpture *Prophet Jeremiah* (1952) for the new building. She also created a large free-standing bronze menorah for the new synagogue, commissioned by a congregant.

9. Belluschi to Bernstein, November 17, 1959, Luise Kaish archives.

10. Luise Kaish, "The Ark," n.d., typescript, Luise Kaish archives.

11. Bernstein to Kaish, March 27, 1963, Luise Kaish archives. In this same letter Bernstein worried about the panel of Isaiah as the "suffering servant." He sent her some sources to read for inspiration, and made the astute observation that by removing the second figure she would make the panel less relational and Christian. Bernstein finally approved casting a week later. Bernstein to Kaish, April 4, 1963, Luise Kaish archives.

12. Kaish to Bernstein, October 23, 1959, Luise Kaish archives.

13. Balfour Brickner to Myron Schoen, memorandum, March 3, 1964, Luise Kaish archives.

14. Avram Kampf, *Contemporary Synagogue Art: Developments in the United States, 1945–1965* (New York: Union of American Hebrew Congregations, 1966), 227–37.

15. Samuel Gruber, *American Synagogues: A Century of Architecture and Jewish Community* (New York: Rizzoli, 2003), 124.

16. James T. Canizaro to Luise Kaish, September 24, 1965, Luise Kaish archives.

17. Gerald P. Fredericks to James T. Canizaro, June 4, 1966, Luise Kaish archives.

18. Kaish, "Notes on Commissions," c. 1960s, Luise Kaish archives.

19. Canizaro to Kaish, June 27, 1967, Luise Kaish archives.

20. Kaish quoted in *Washington Post*, August 5, 1967, Luise Kaish archives.

21. Belluschi to Kaish, August 30, 1968, Luise Kaish archives. He recalled seeing the wax sketch in her studio of "a beautiful figure of Christ."

22. John Canaday, "10 Studio Exhibitions Are Summarized," *New York Times*, April 27, 1968, 35.

23. Rabbi Jacob Kraft, *The Beth Shalom Ark Doors*, brochure (Wilmington, DE: Temple Beth Shalom, 1968), Luise Kaish archives.

24. Luise Kaish, "Sculpture: A Poetic Force" (lecture, University of Washington School of Art, presented in conjunction with Battelle Research Center, Seattle, July 10, 1979), typescript, Luise Kaish archives.

25. Luise Kaish, untitled statement, c. 1973, Luise Kaish archives.

26. Richard J. Scheuer to Luise Kaish, December 12, 1973, Luise Kaish archives.

27. Luise Kaish to Donald Gratz, November 17, 1975, Luise Kaish archives.

28. In this regard, Gitlin compared Kaish to Jeff Koons. Bruce Gitlin, interview by Melissa Kaish and the author, August 5, 2019.

29. The brochure printed for the dedication lists the eight scenes: *The Eternal Martyr*, *The Flight from Jerusalem*, *The Ten Martyrs*, *Masada*, *The Crusades*, *The Spanish Inquisition*, *The Chmielnitzki Massacre*, and *The Holocaust*. Thanks to Maura Reilly for sharing her photographs of the sculpture in situ.

30. Luise Kaish, untitled remarks, c. 1974, Luise Kaish archives.

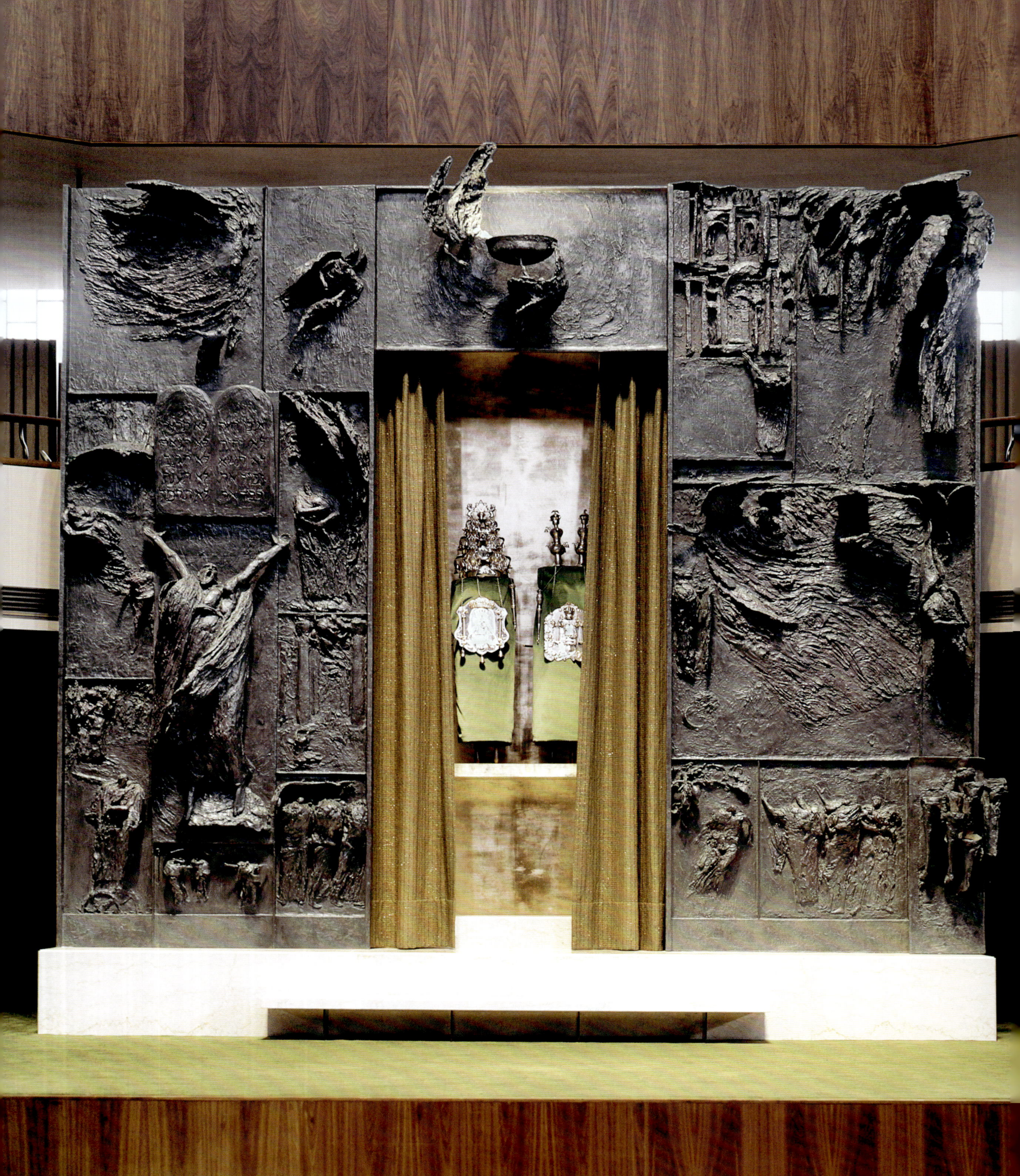

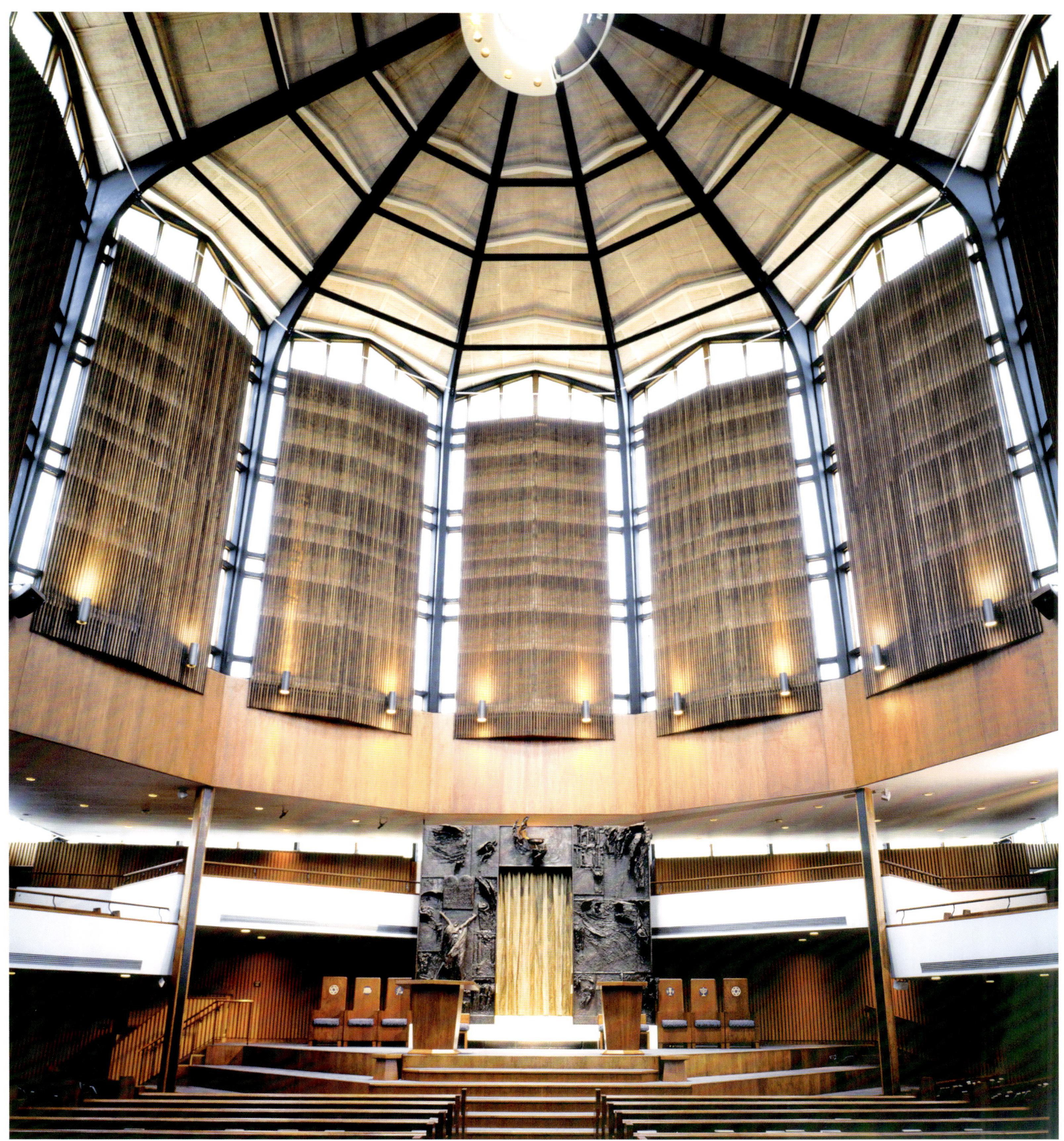

Plates 17 and 18
Luise Kaish. *The Ark of Revelation*,
1960–64, bronze, 14 × 15 ft. (4.3 × 4.6 m).
Temple B'rith Kodesh, Rochester, New York

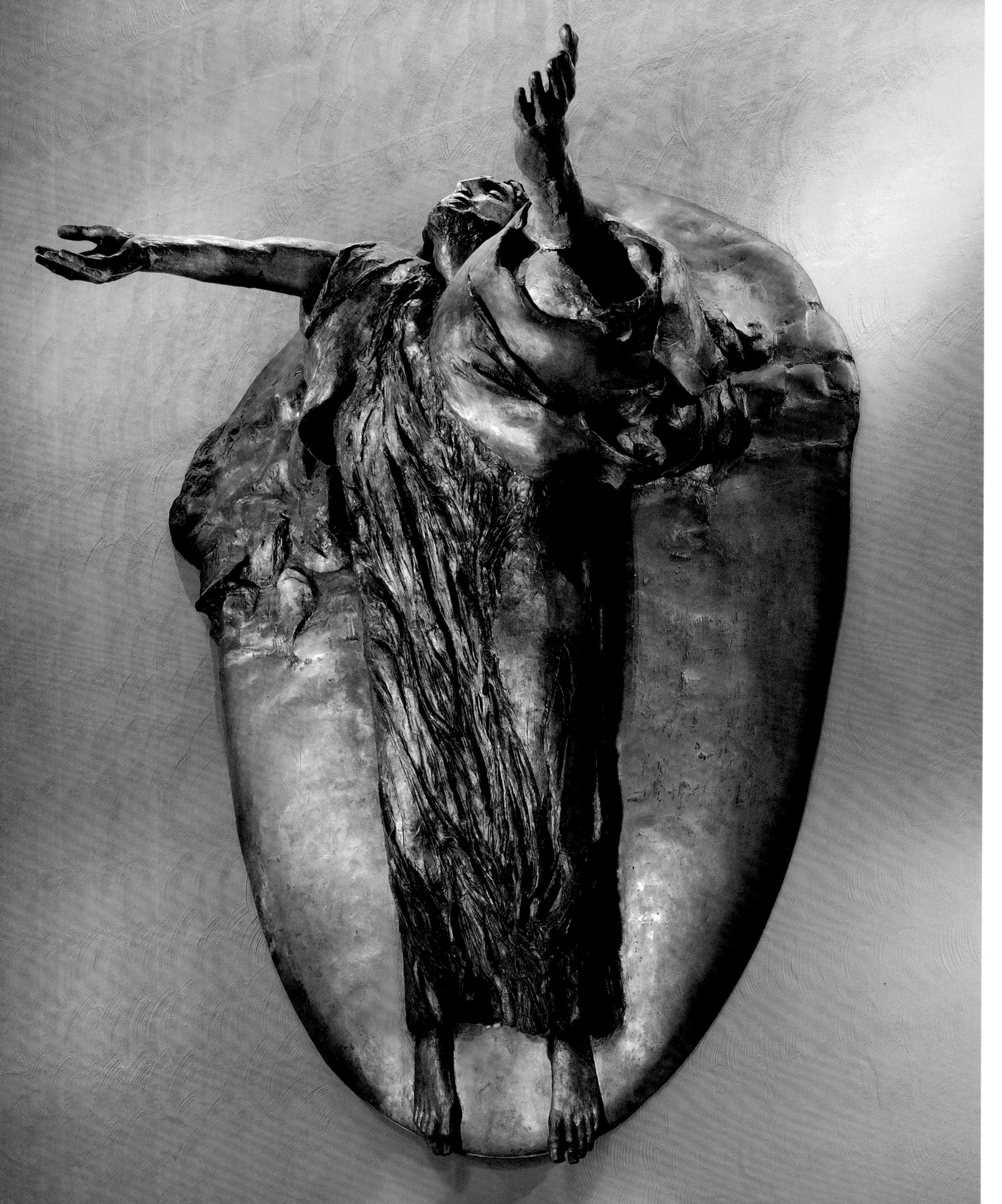

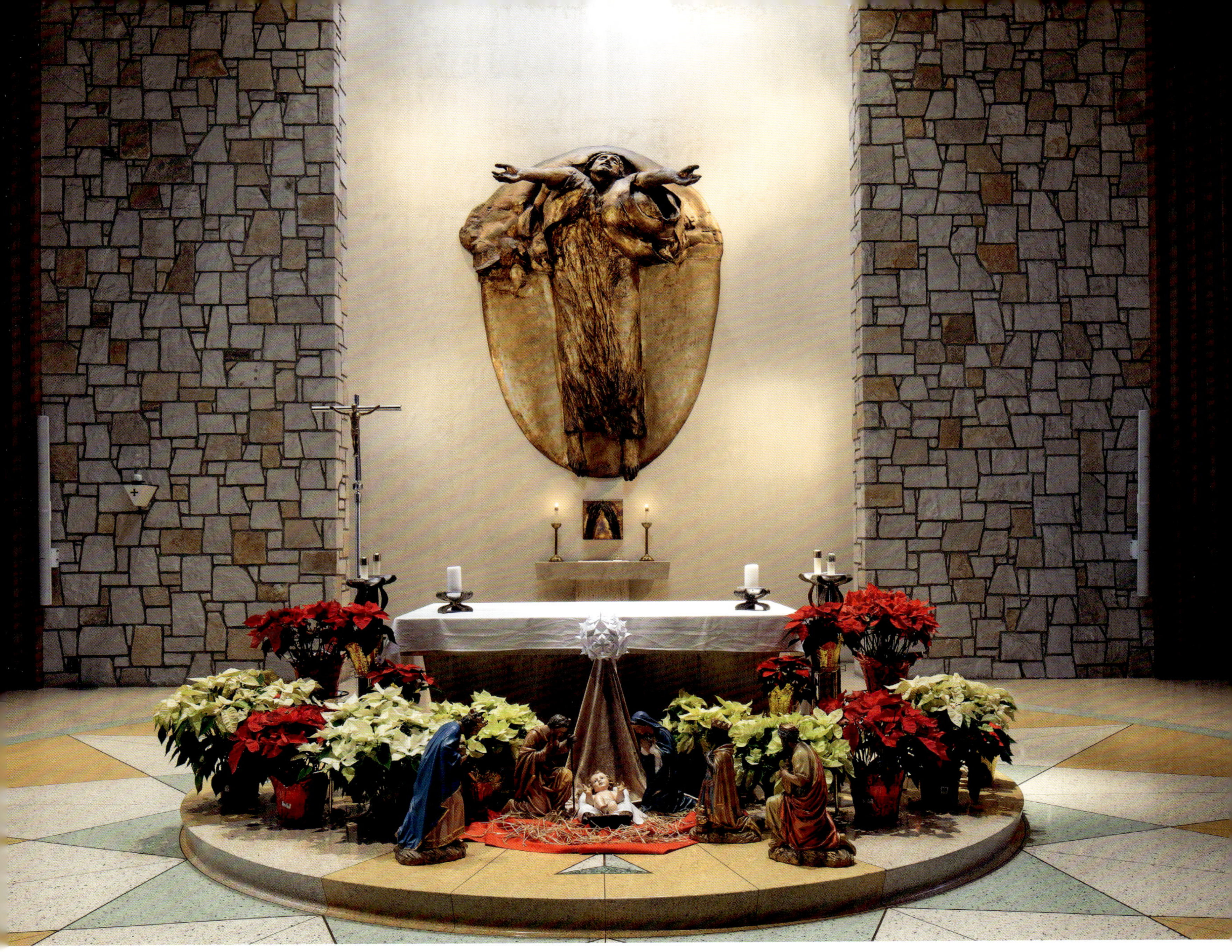

Plates 19 and 20
Luise Kaish. *Christ in Glory*, 1965–67, bronze,
13 ½ × 10 ft. (4.1 × 3 m). Holy Trinity
Mission Seminary, Silver Spring, Maryland

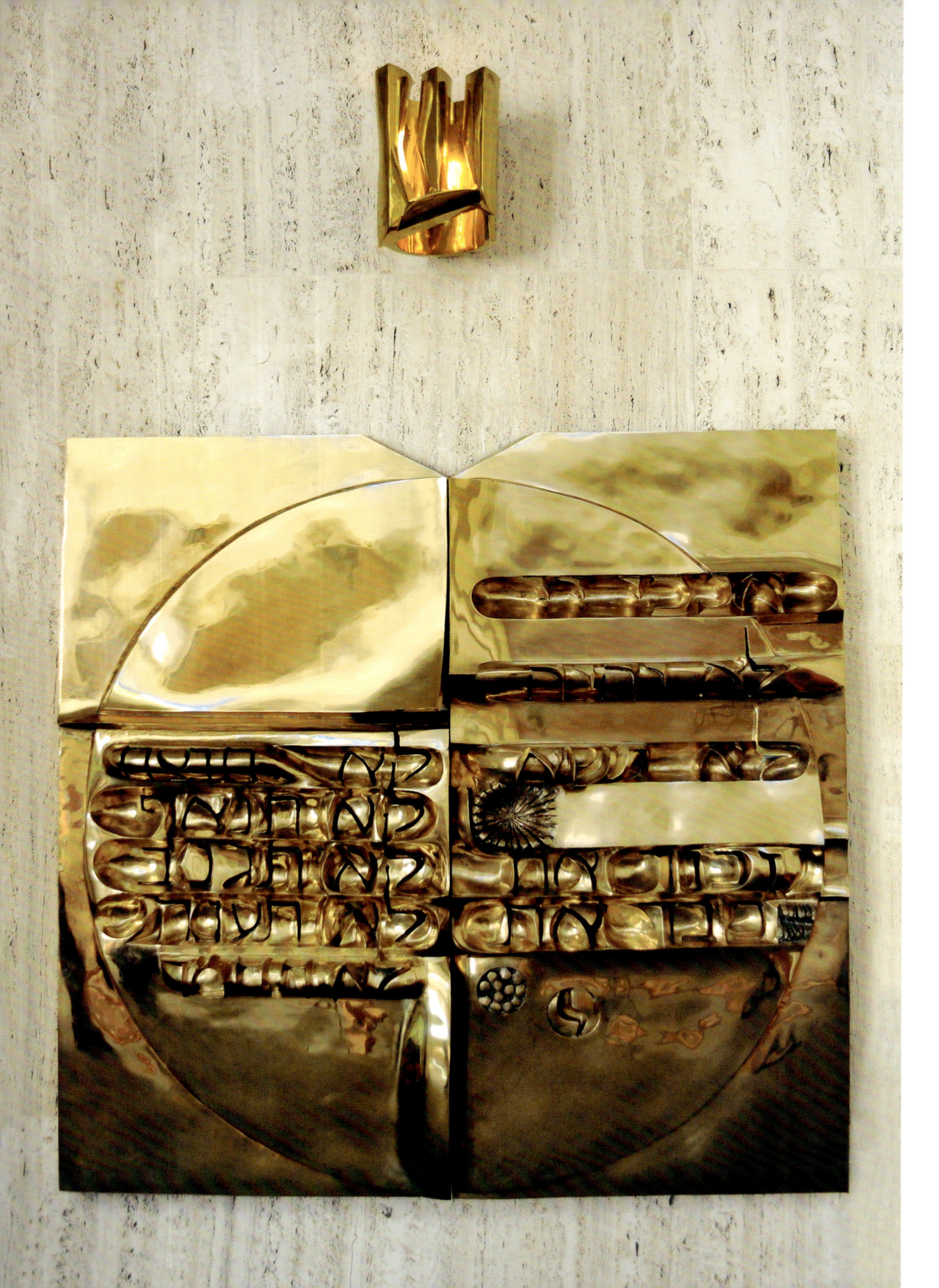

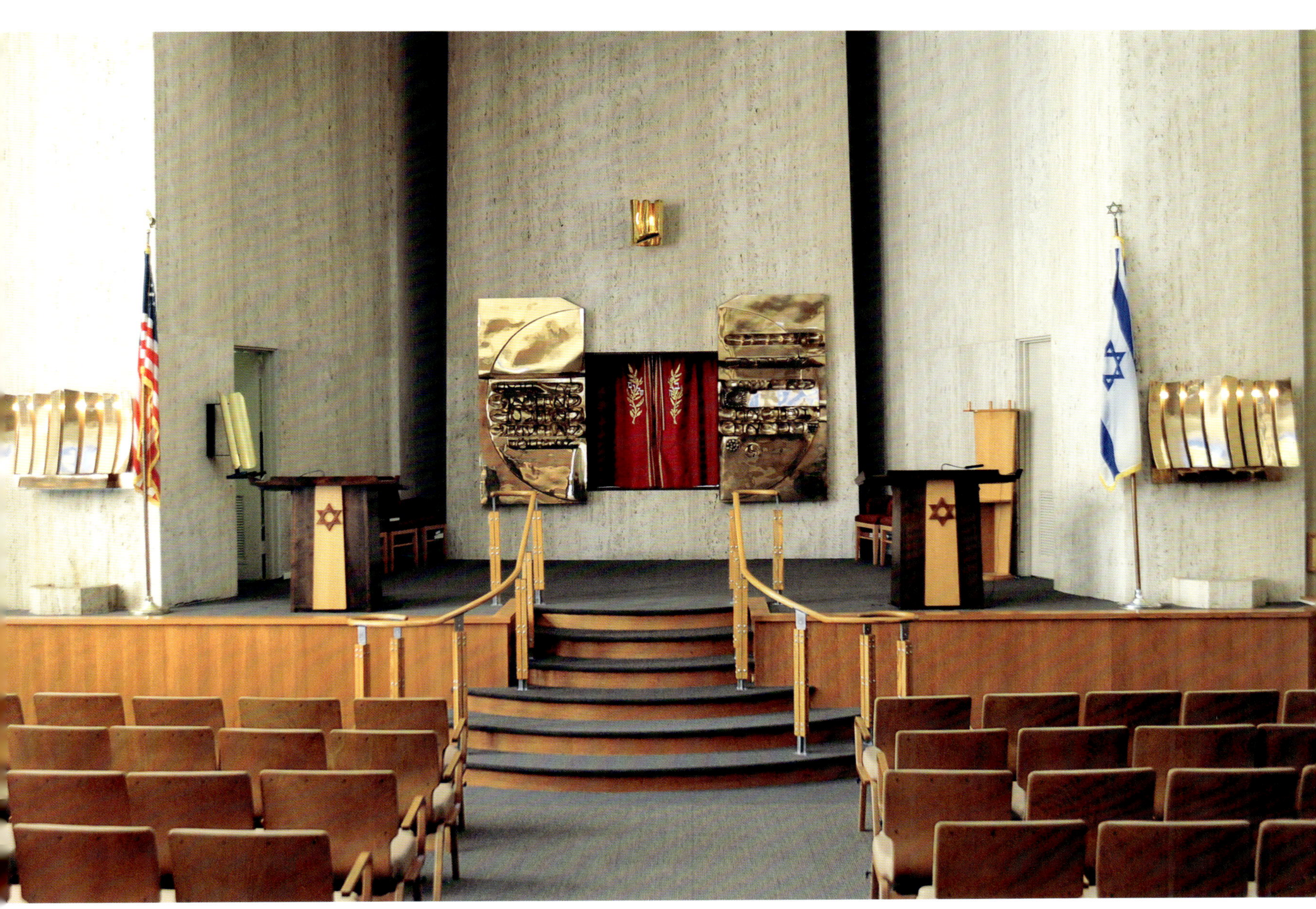

Plates 21 and 22
Luise Kaish. *The Beth Shalom Ark Doors*,
1967–68, bronze, 7 × 7 ft. (2.1 × 2.1 m).
Temple Beth Shalom, Wilmington, Delaware

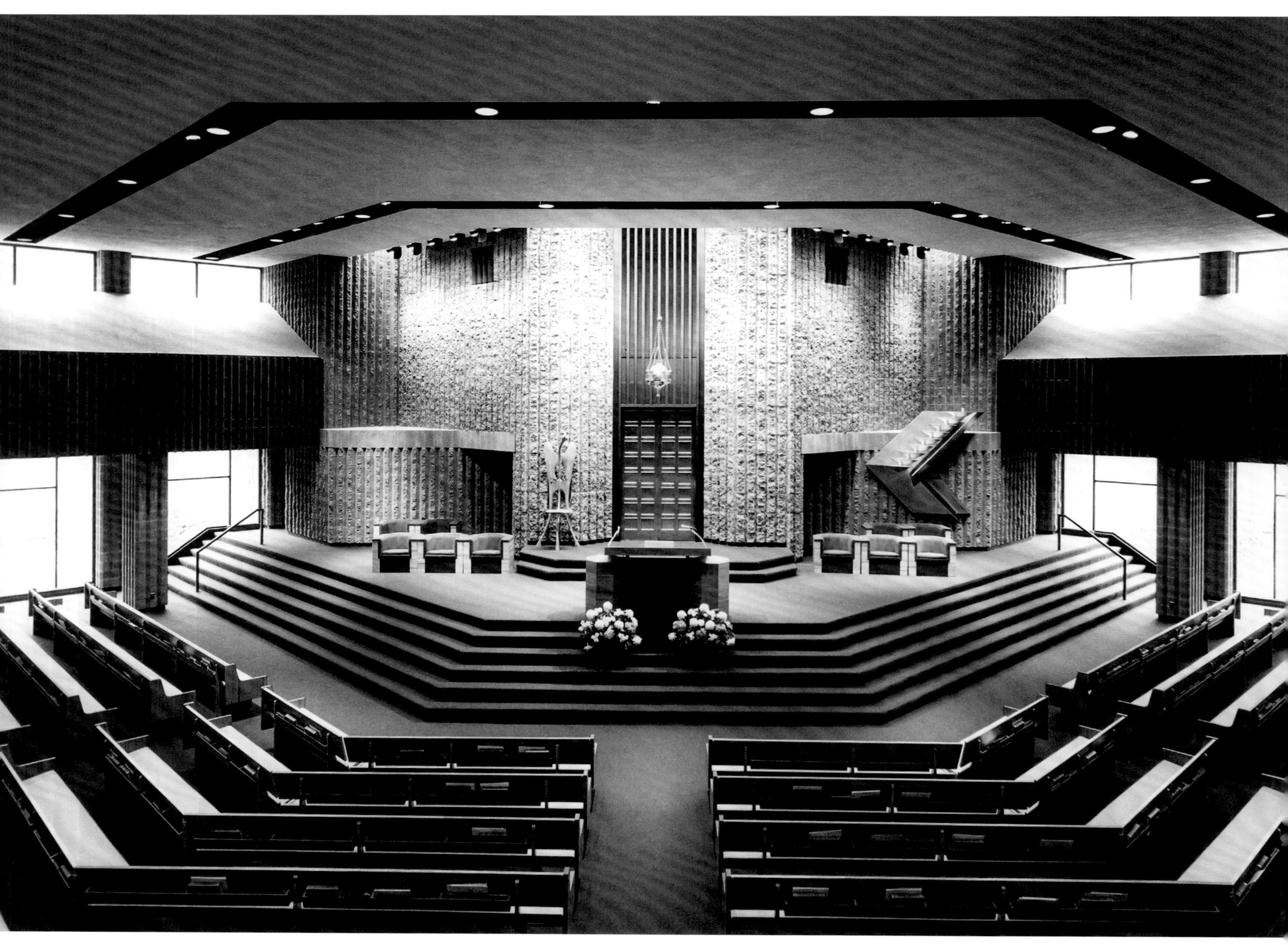

Plates 23 and 24
Luise Kaish. *Menorah*, 1973, Everdur bronze, 8 × 8 ft. (2.4 × 2.4 m).
B'Nai Abraham, Livingston, New Jersey

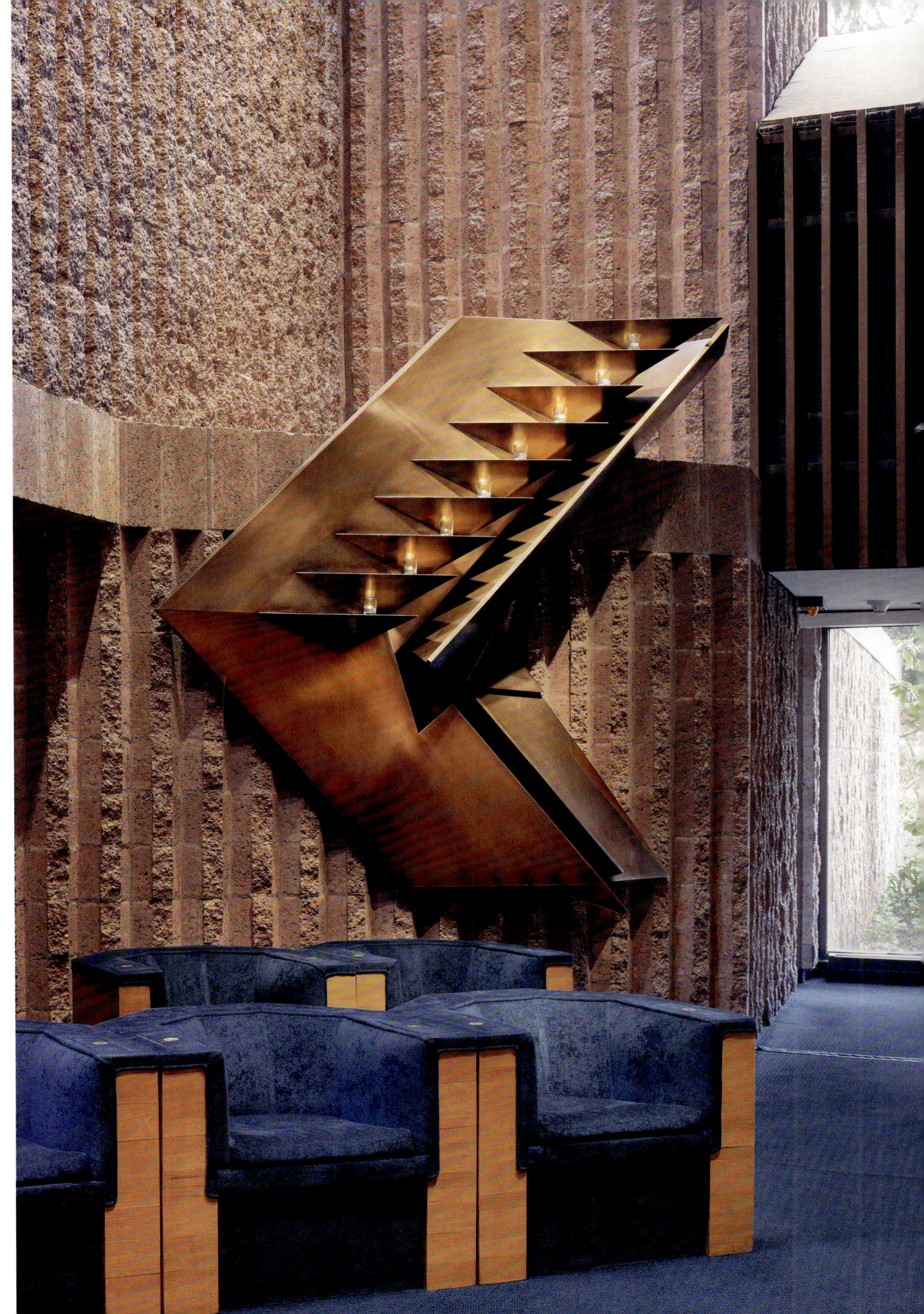

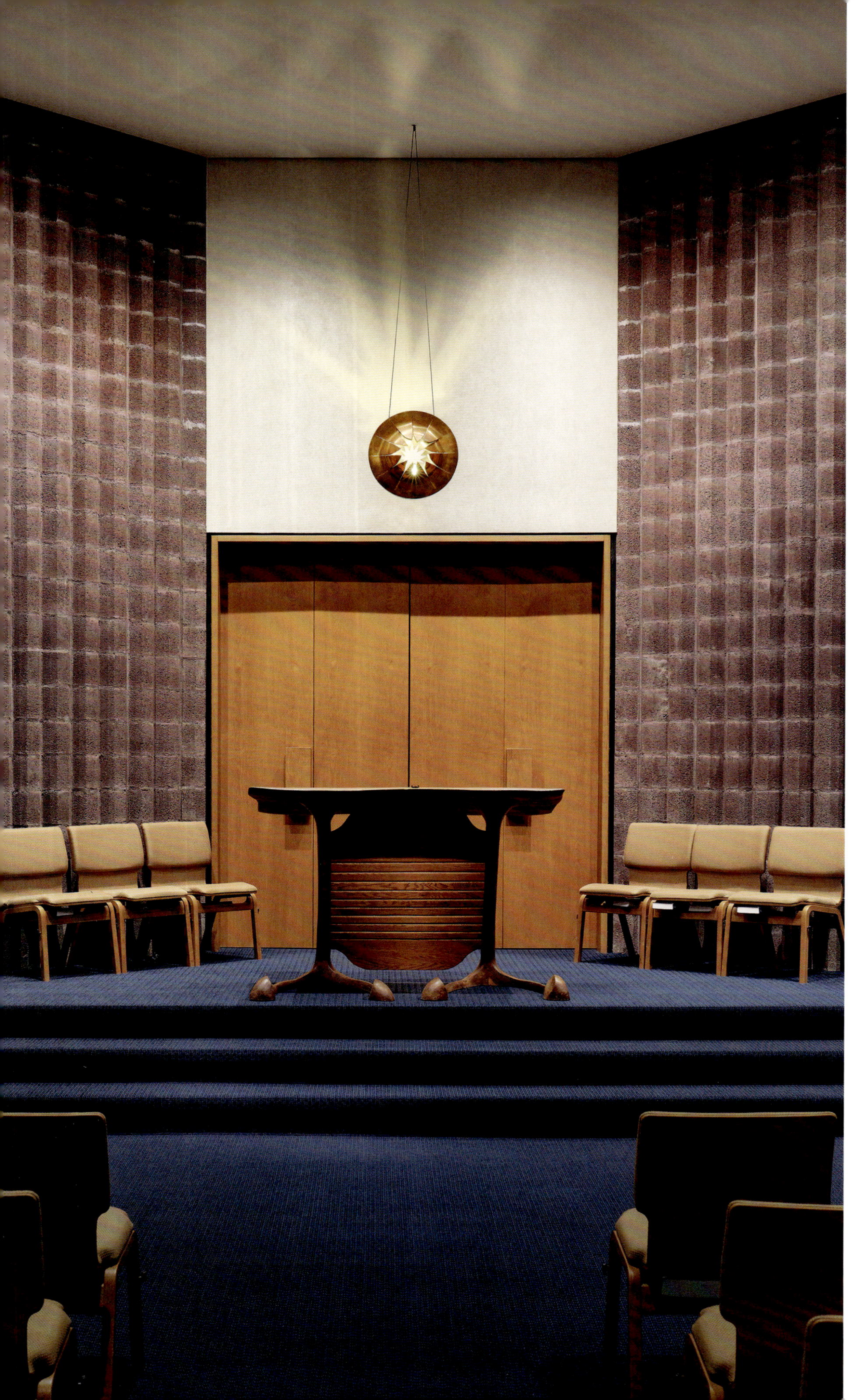

Plates 25 and 26
Luise Kaish. *Eternal Light*, 1973, Everdur bronze, 20 in. (50.8 cm) diameter. B'Nai Abraham, Livingston, New Jersey

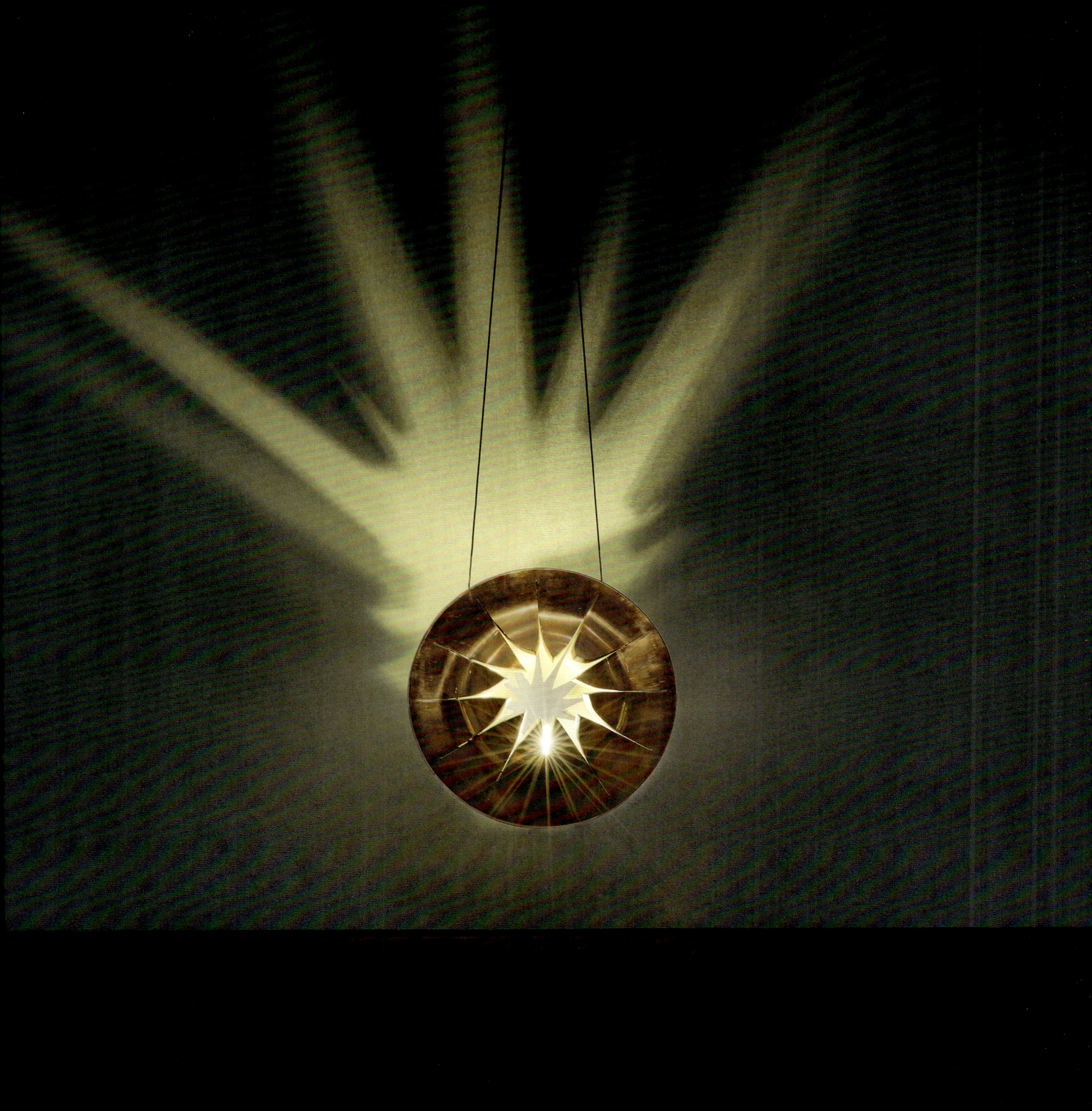

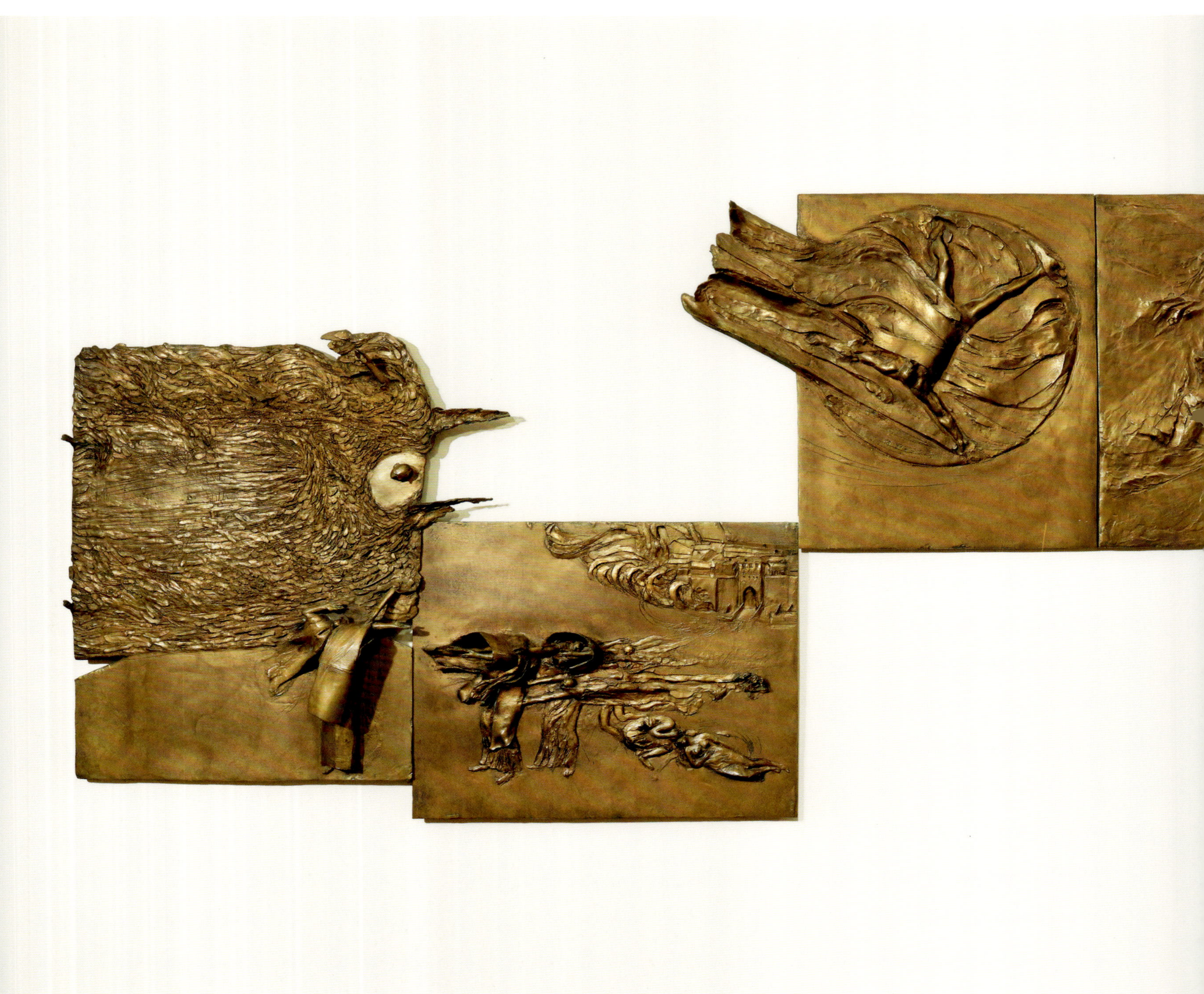

Plate 27
Luise Kaish. *The Wall of Martyrs*, 1972–74, bronze, 4 ¼ × 17 ft. (1.3 × 5.2 m).
Beth El Synagogue Center, New Rochelle, New York

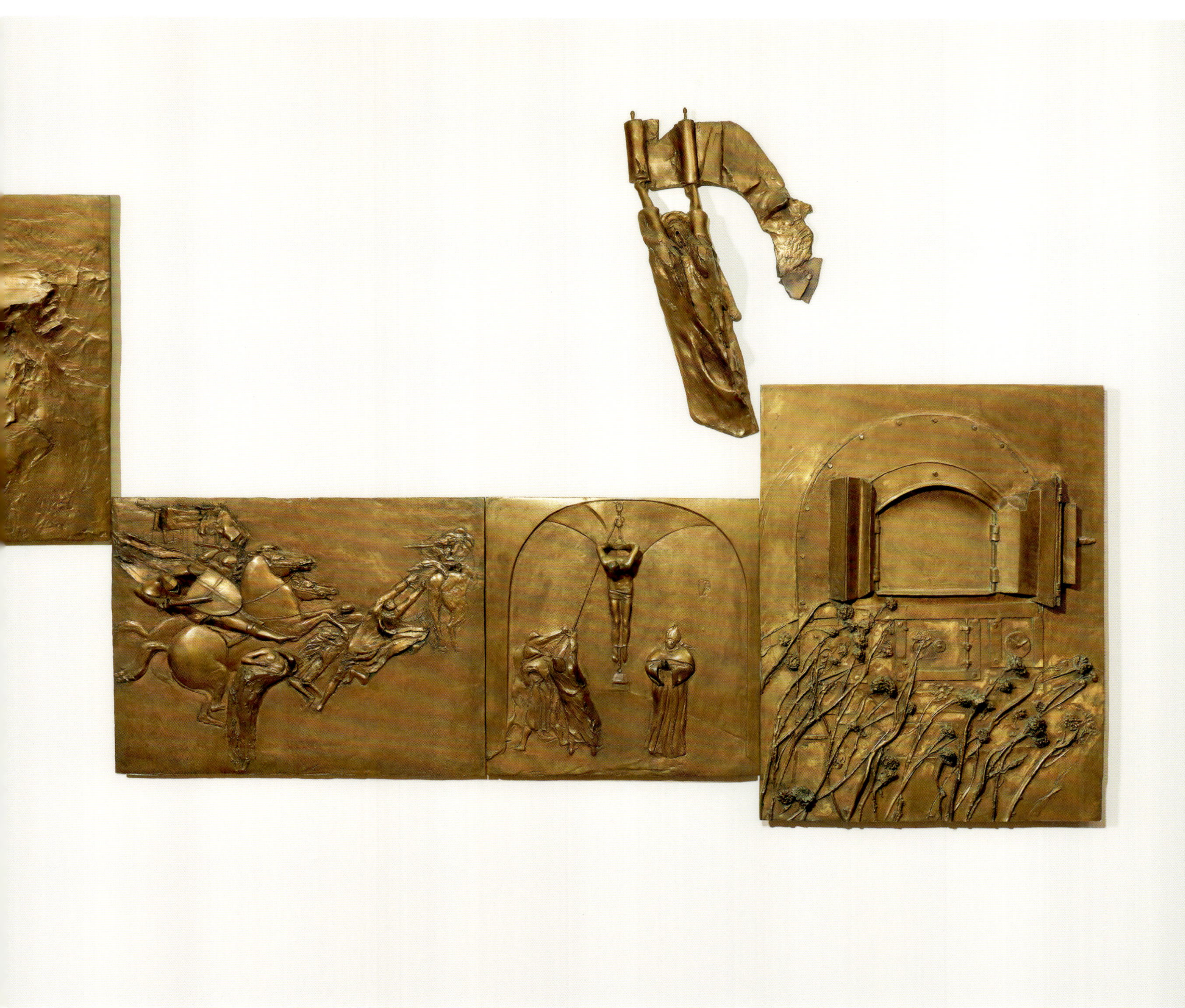

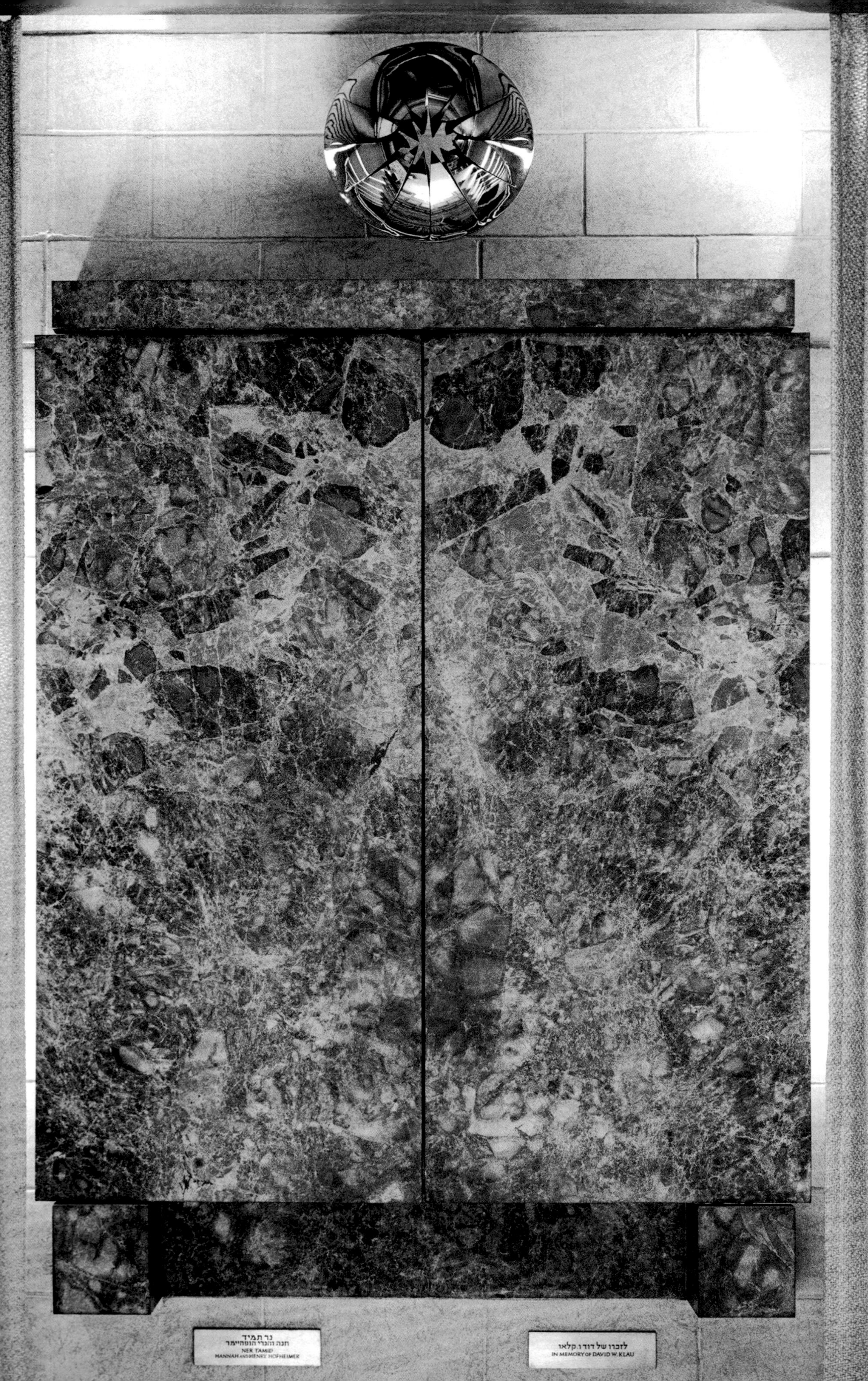

Plate 28
Luise Kaish. *Eternal Light*,
1974, bronze, 18 in. (45.7 cm).
Hebrew Union College,
Jerusalem, Israel

Plate 29
Luise Kaish. *Holocaust Memorial*, 1975, bronze,
79 ¼ × 60 ½ × 7 in.
(201.3 × 153.7 × 17.8 cm).
Collection, Jewish Museum,
New York, Gift of Mr. and
Mrs. Albert A. List

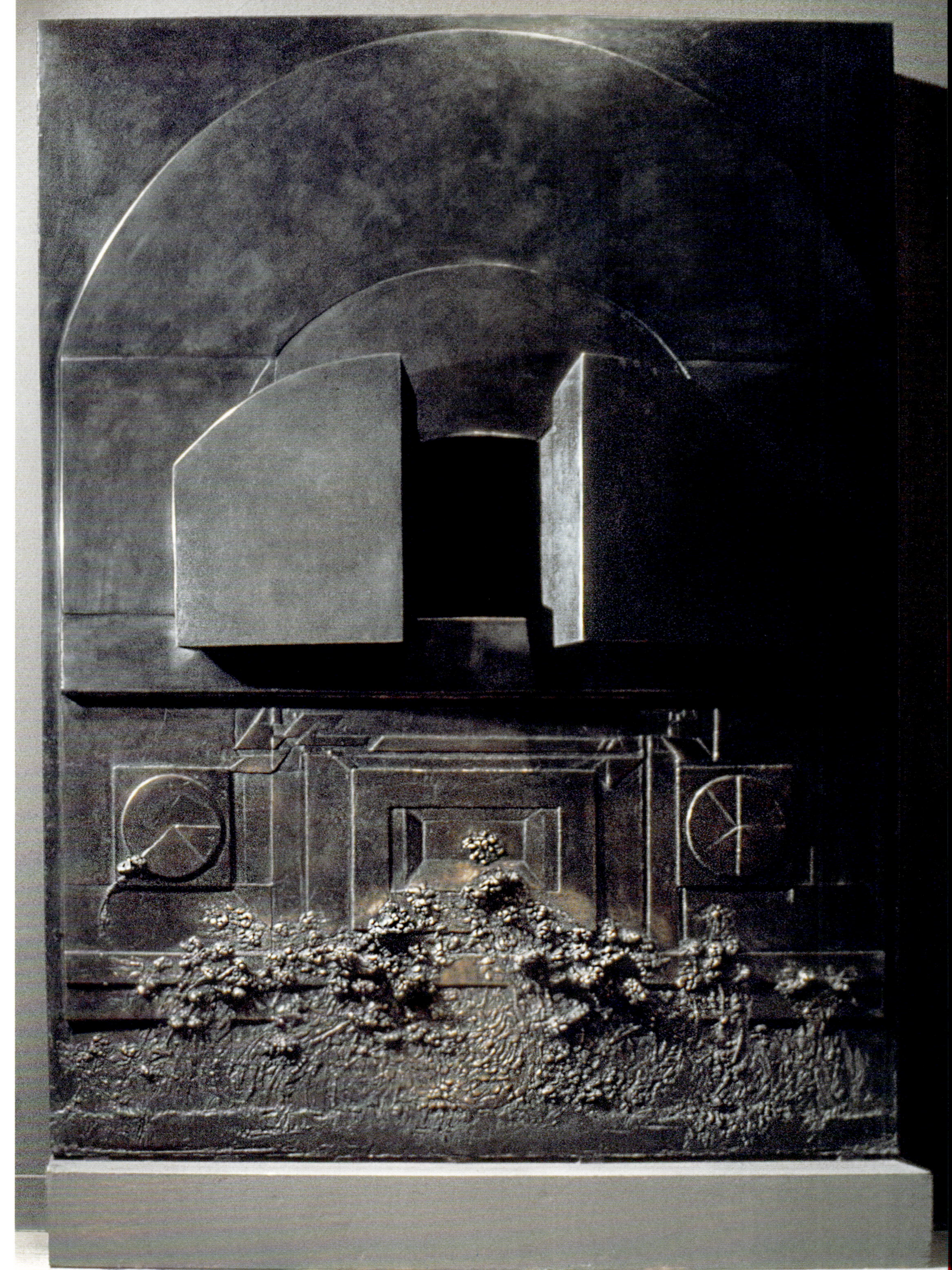

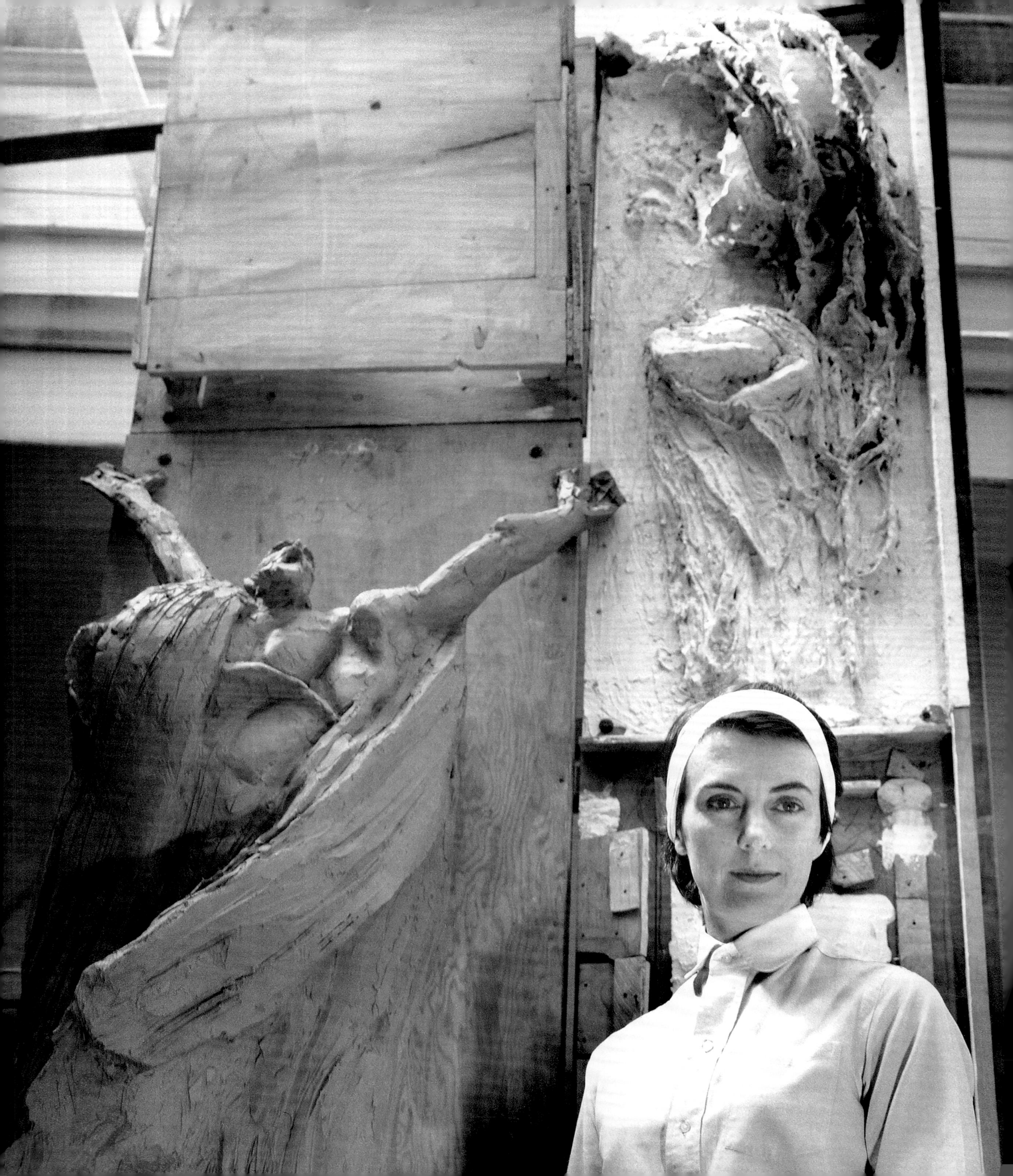

MANY ROUTES TO REVELATION

Samuel D. Gruber

Luise Kaish with *The Ark of Revelation*, MacDougal Street studio, New York, 1962

The most memorable picture of Luise Kaish shows the then-young five-foot-four artist atop a ladder at her MacDougal Street studio at work on her massive and masterful *The Ark of Revelation*, which when cast in bronze would weigh two tons (see frontispiece). In the 1950s she was one of a group of artists, many of them Jewish, who believed in figurative art as an expressive force even during the heyday of abstract expressionism and at the beginnings of pop art. Kaish was interested in form, but she also delved into matters of psyche and sprit. Her work is infused with uncommon emotional and spiritual energy that, when applied to synagogue and church commissions, includes overt religious content. In the introduction to the catalogue of Kaish's 1973 exhibition at the Jewish Museum, art historian Avram Kampf wrote: "There is a strong religious vein which runs through the work of Luise Kaish and which sets her apart from the sculptors of her generation. This religious element is a fundamental component of her work based on her own experience of the world and her own personal attitude to it."[1] Kaish read and studied widely in preparation for commissions. Even her more personal biblical bronzes developed from continued reading of the Bible and Louis Ginzberg's *Legends of the Jews*. Later, her *Ark Doors* for Temple Beth Shalom in Wilmington, Delaware, grew from the text of the Zohar and from what she'd learned from Gershom Scholem's book about Jewish mysticism (see Pls. 21, 22).[2]

Indeed, Kaish was an unashamedly Jewish artist and a maker of religious art. She brought intense intellectual scrutiny of religious belief and practice as well as genuine spirituality to all her work. Unlike many contemporaries whose synagogue art was a sideline, Kaish welcomed religious commissions, and gave them deep theological consideration along with painstaking artistic planning.[3] Her career and reputation grew from the positive reception of her biblical bronzes in the 1950s and from *The Ark of Revelation* for Temple B'rith Kodesh in Rochester, which was dedicated in 1964 (see Pls. 17, 18).

For Kaish, Judaism was not foreign baggage to be hidden or discarded. It gave her the opportunity to channel deep spiritual content and strong emotions into her art. She wrote frequently about her religious belief in relation to her expressive and contemplative art to prepare for her religious commissions, and to explain them both to her Jewish audiences and to a respectful but often uncomprehending art world. Kaish embraced Judaism in her work and life, but on modern terms. She was guided by her own family history and by several inspirational rabbis in her youth and early adulthood.

Kaish had grown up Reform in New York. Her father's family had settled in Louisville, Kentucky, in the 1820s, and had retained their Jewish identity and values. Kaish's mother, Elsa, grew up in a Polish Catholic family outside Detroit. She attended parochial schools, but after falling in love with her husband-to-be she converted to Judaism. Elsa joined the Free Synagogue in Flushing, New York, where the young family lived, and became a close friend of the rabbi Max Meyer and his family. [4] Elsa brought to Judaism a "depth of belief that was extraordinary. Sunday School at the synagogue and confirmation were all-important

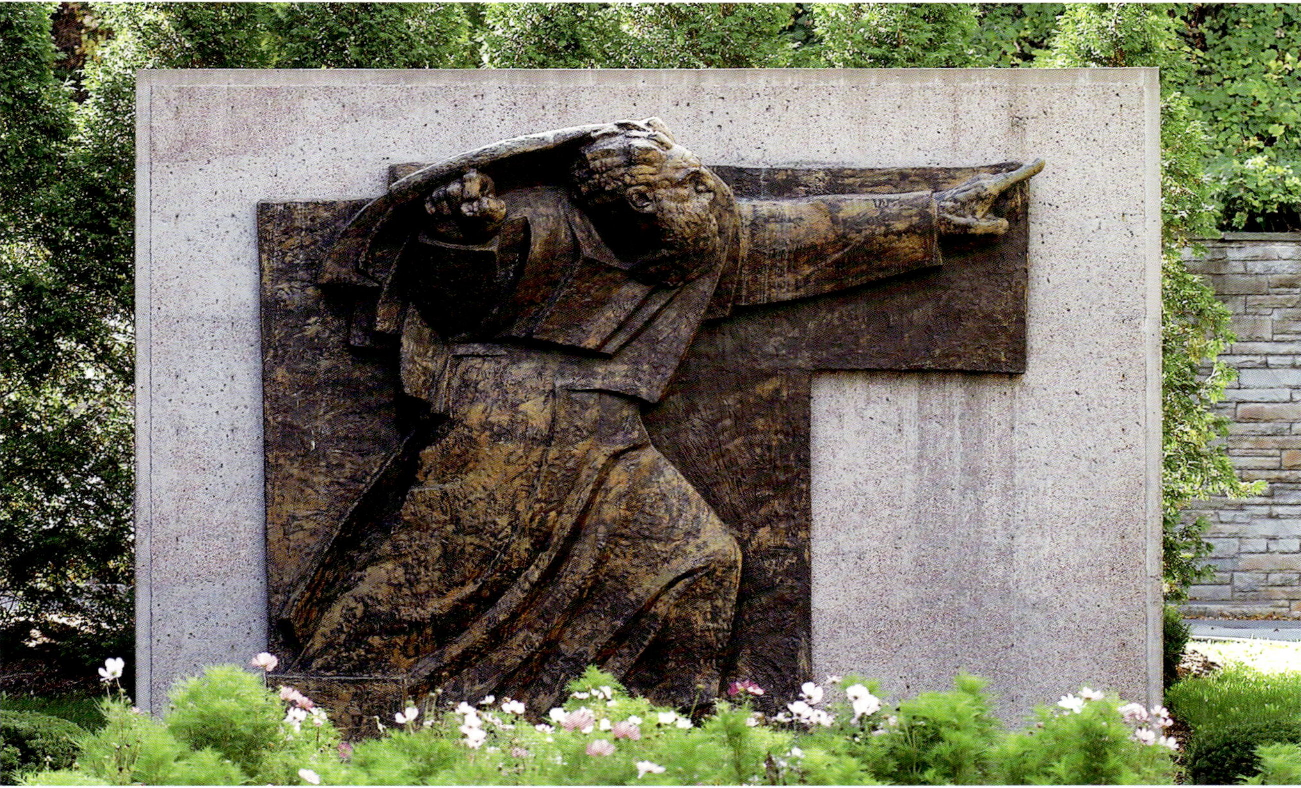

Fig. 29 Ivan Meštrović, *Moses*, 1952, bronze, 146 × 188 × 36 in.
(370.8 × 477.5 × 91.4 cm), Syracuse University, Syracuse, New York

for all the kids."[5] Kaish attended religious school with the broad-minded Rabbi Meyer, who took his young charges to visit churches of every denomination. He laid the foundation for Kaish's subsequent interest in religious art and architecture, and her willingness to accept religious commissions from Christians as well as Jews.

This was a very different environment from what many successful mid-twentieth-century American Jewish artists—often children of Eastern European Jewish immigrants or immigrants themselves—experienced. Unlike Kaish, they worked hard to move away from organized Judaism, synagogue association, and religious observance. Kaish, however, spent her youth moving closer to Judaism. Only a few contemporary sculptors, such as the Hartford-born Elbert Weinberg, strove to develop Jewish themes in a modern style as a major strain of their creative output.[6]

In 1947, after a year in Mexico, Kaish entered the new graduate program in sculpture at Syracuse University under the direction of Croatian sculptor Ivan Meštrović, whose teaching and work ethic heavily influenced Kaish in the early part of her career. Meštrović was Catholic; however, his first wife Ruža was Jewish, and she and her family were killed in the Holocaust, as were many of Meštrović's friends and colleagues. Photos of Meštrović's Syracuse studio, where Kaish spent time, include a Crucifixion, a Mother and Child, and various versions of Moses (Fig. 29), which Meštrović prepared for the never completed *American Memorial to Six Million Jews of Europe* on which he worked from 1949 until 1952, when Kaish was a graduate student.[7] Kaish knew much of Meštrović's work, including his

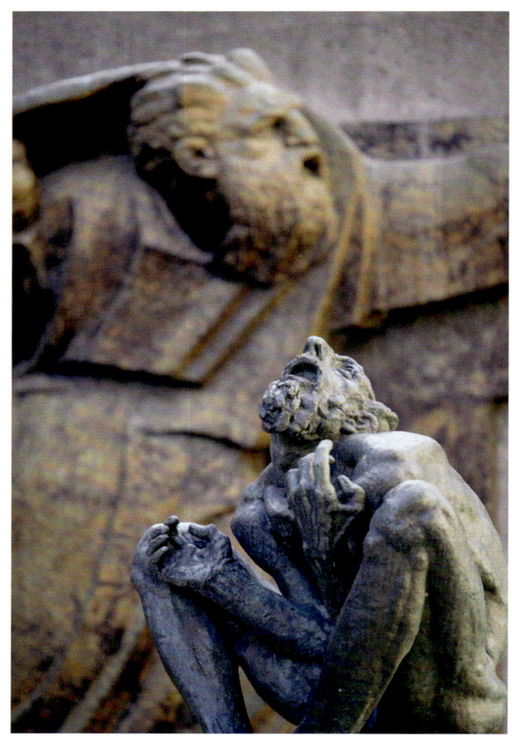

Fig. 30 Ivan Meštrović, *Job*, 1945, bronze, 49 × 40 in. (124.5 × 101.6 cm), Syracuse University, Syracuse, New York

supplicant figures of Job (Fig. 30) and Persephone, whose out-stretched arms would be echoed in the ecstatic poses of Kaish's Moses and other prophets. At Syracuse, Meštrović also created several sculptures of the Madonna, and Kaish's *Birth* (1948–50) and *Mother and Child* (1950) are influenced by her teacher's style (see Pls. 1, 2).[8]

Kaish did not carry the cultural experience of radical politics of so many Jewish artists of the pre–World War II era, such as William Gropper, who, in the aftermath of the Holocaust, began to produce artwork nostalgic for Europe's lost Jewish world—a world that he had previously rejected. Nor was she steeped in Orthodox Judaism or cultural Yiddishkeit, as were many pre-war artists such as Max Weber, the Soyer brothers, and Ben Shahn. Her American Jewish experience was fundamentally different from many Jewish artists in the emerging New York school with whom her own career overlapped, especially Mark Rothko, Adolph Gottlieb, Barnett Newman, Philip Guston, Ibram Lassaw, and Herbert Ferber, and a small number of women artists like Louise Nevelson, Helen Frankenthaler, and Lee Krasner. Kaish was aware of, but did not follow, the path of avant-garde European Jewish artists who arrived in America as refugees from Hitler's Europe, and who mostly championed the twentieth-century movements of cubism and surrealism. In recent European art, she was attentive to the work of Jacob Epstein, the American-born sculptor who had made a successful career in England; Jacques Lipchitz, the Lithuanian-born French sculptor who came to America as a refugee; and, of course, Meštrović, who was also a war refugee. Jews in Europe and America had embraced sculpture since the late nineteenth century, but the ranks of successful Jewish sculptors remained relatively small until after World War II. Kaish was one of many of her Jewish generation attracted to sculpture, though many followed the route of abstraction, and eventually minimalism.

Kaish, in her studies with Mestrovic and her absorption in the art history of Europe, began her early career more in the tradition of pre–World War II Jewish American sculptors such as William Zorach and the internationally known figural sculptor Nathan Rapoport, rather than more "modern" Jewish sculptors like Chaim Gross and Aaron Goodelman, who rarely, if ever, explicitly addressed Jewish themes in their work. Rapoport's heroic and monumental *Warsaw Ghetto Uprising Memorial* made headlines when it was unveiled in 1948,[9] just a year before Meštrović began work on his own Holocaust memorial for New York City, and before Kaish got to work on her heroic *Saltine Warrior*.

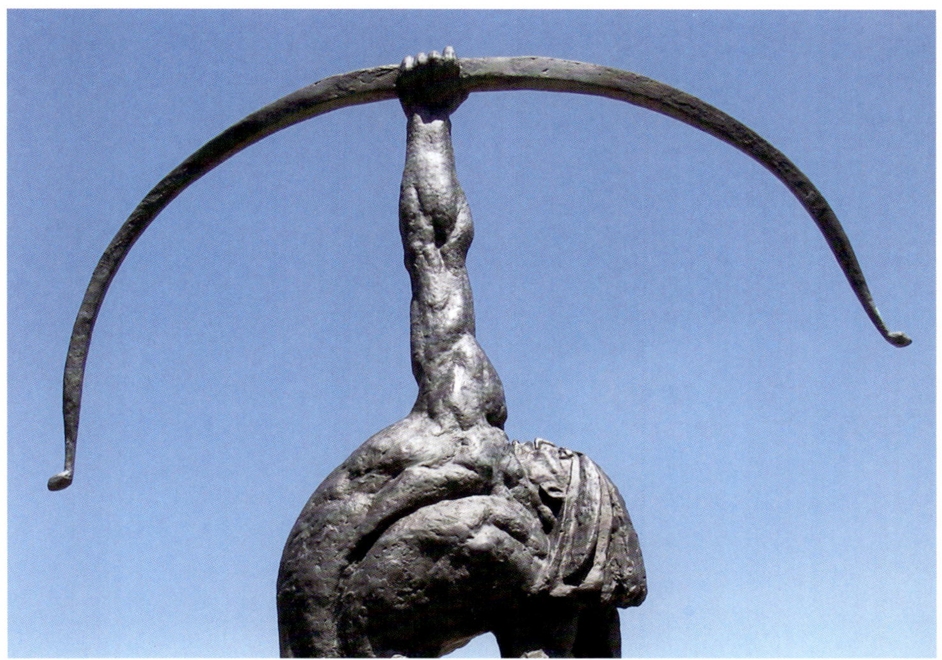

Fig. 31   Luise Kaish, *Saltine Warrior* (detail), 1951 (see Plate 16)

Fig. 32   Luise Kaish, Study of Oliver for the *Saltine Warrior*, 1950, Patinated plaster, lifesize

Saltine Warrior (1951)

Early in her career Kaish embraced the human figure as a tool for her ideas and emotions. She wrote: "I have always felt the human figure to be one of the most profound and dynamic of images to express the form and content of an idea."[10] As a student she "studied modeling, plaster casting, stone and wood carving in the round and in relief."[11] She "set out to master the figure . . . to be able to use it as an expressive force."[12] This aim came to powerful fruition in her early masterpiece *Saltine Warrior* (see Pl. 16). The sculpture was proposed in 1950 as a commission for Meštrović, who had already created the monumental *Spearman* and *Bowman* in 1928 for Congress Plaza in Chicago; Meštrović instead decided to have his students compete for the project, and each submitted a concept model.[13] Kaish won. Her bronze *Saltine Warrior* demonstrated virtuosity and originality that came close to equaling her mentor. The larger-than-life statue, unveiled on June 3, 1951, still stands on the Syracuse University Quad.[14] Kaish's sculpture of an Onondagan archer with bow aimed at the sky avoided caricature to create a portrait of explosive strength and nobility; the parallel arcs of the taut bow and the warrior's bent back are arranged architecturally and fraught with tension (Fig. 31). Kaish engaged the local Onondaga Nation to find a model for the work, leading to an artistically honest result that was also politically astute (Fig. 32).

Prophets (1956–57)

After the *Saltine Warrior*, Kaish stopped using models for her figures. She had already absorbed the contours and movements of the human body, which she then began to expressively adapt. She was an accomplished musician and, in her art, molded and sculpted the body like an instrument with which she could play a range of sensations and emotions. She grouped her figures using a visual language that hinted at larger concepts and ideals. In this she followed sculptors of the previous generation: Jacob Epstein,[15] Jacques Lipchitz, Alberto Giacometti, and Chaim Gross, for example—all of whom manipulated the human figure towards abstraction.

Kaish's artistic career quickly took off in Rochester, New York, where she and husband Morton moved in 1950. They joined Temple B'rith Kodesh and were befriended by Philip Bernstein, a leading American Reform rabbi cultured in art and music who would play a major role in Kaish's artistic and professional development. In 1951, Kaish received a grant from the Louis Comfort Tiffany Foundation allowing her to travel to Europe, where she was enthralled by medieval and Renaissance sculpture in stone and bronze. The Kaishes returned to Europe in 1956–57, settling in Rome, where she produced a group of forty-seven sculptures inspired by the Bible. Kaish was a thinker as well as a sculptor, and brought to her work an intellectual and creative interest in Jewish thought and tradition at the time. "I had the Talmud [and] *Legends of the Jews*, which I used as the sources for some of my work; we were very interested in the Kabbalah."[16] Her training allowed her seamlessly to marry the European (Christian) art tradition with Jewish themes.

These works, and others she completed upon her return, were spring points for larger commissions. *Trumpeters of Jericho* (1957; see Pl. 13) was followed by a menorah (1960) for Temple B'rith Kodesh, and *Jacob Wrestling with the Angel* (1957; Pl. 31), *Jonah Fleeing Nineveh* (1958–59; Pl. 30), and *The Great Blessing of Abraham* (1960; Pl. 32) led to the creation of *The Ark of Revelation* (1960–64; see Pls. 17, 18). These were "personal interpretations in some cases of a particular text, a visual distillation of a prophetic idea or revelation, or figures inspired by the emotional quality of prayer."[17]

Kaish worked in the lost-wax process at this time, explored sand casting, and produced welded sculptures in copper and bronze, which were exhibited in 1958 at the Memorial Art Gallery in Rochester and in Kaish's second show at the Sculpture Center, where they were well received. A large piece, *Abraham, Abraham* (1958), was donated to the Memorial Art Gallery.[18] In New York almost all the pieces were sold. The 1957 bronze *The Blessing (Two)* (see Pl. 14) was included in the Museum of Modern Art's 1959 exhibition of contemporary sculpture,[19] and was illustrated in both the local *Villager* newspaper and in the *New York Times*.[20]

About these works Kaish wrote: "These pieces are part of a group of works inspired by the Hebraic faith and tradition. Their source is the Bible and the living tradition as carried on in the synagogue. They are personal interpretations in some cases of a text of the Bible: as for instance, the figure of the angel of the Lord appearing to stay the hand of Abraham and substituting the symbolical ram for the beloved son, for me, one of the most powerful and important expressions of Jewish faith. In another instance, "I have striven to express the distillation of the prophetic impulse, as symbolized by the figure of the prophet on his camel in the desert, his arms raised in supplication to the lord God." [21]

Of her depictions of the visions of Jeremiah, Ezekiel, and Abraham, she said that "by juxtaposing two masses, one in the round, the other in suspended relief form, I sought to express that sense of presence, of the messenger envisioned within a great cloud, and the figure caught in the moment of greatest passion. This theme was to inform my figurative work in the years ahead."[22]

The Ark of Revelation (1960–64)

When Rabbi Bernstein visited the Kaishes in Rome in 1958, returning from Israel to Rochester, where his congregation was planning a new synagogue, he was extremely moved by the bronzes of the prophets. Bernstein had previously written in 1948 that Reform Judaism's role "was to recapture the spirit, the teachings, the way of life enunciated by the Hebrew prophets."[23] On seeing Kaish's works, he immediately knew he would like her to create art for the new temple. This visit would culminate in *The Ark of Revelation*, dedicated in 1964.[24]

In October 1959, Kaish had a good meeting with the synagogue architect Pietro Belluschi,[25] who liked her work and was suggesting window reliefs. Kaish, however, imagined her prophets adorning bronze doors, like those she had admired on churches in Italy. She confided to Bernstein that

> what is dearest to my heart, are the doors; the bronze doors with sculpture reliefs drawn from the great Hebraic figures and episodes of the Bible. I would liken my conception to the great doors in the world of art . . . Ghiberti in Florence, St. Zeno in Verona and Hildesheim in Germany. A work of art at the entrance to the Sanctuary where people would be able to see it, contemplate the reliefs, and touch them. I have found through the years that these sculptural doors and portals have been of the greatest sustained esthetic pleasure and interest.[26]

Kaish ended her letter on a strong note: "I know what I can do and believe in the doors. Nothing would please me more than to do them for your synagogue."[27] Bernstein forwarded her letter to Belluschi, who wrote back enthusiastically about Kaish's idea.[28] Very quickly, rabbi and architect came to see the doors not as a sanctuary entrance but as part of a great ark, the visual centerpiece of the synagogue. Ironically, in the final design, despite Kaish's initial inspiration, there would be no doors at all. The great bronze reliefs provide a frame within which is an open (curtained) space housing the Torah scrolls.

B'rith Kodesh's leadership offered Kaish the commission in August 1960.[29] This was a momentous event in synagogue art. First, this was the first commission granted to a woman for such an important piece of synagogue design. Second, there was full agreement that this *Ark* would be decorated with eighteen panels, almost all of which would include representation of a human figure. Arks in Europe, such as those at Druja and Boskovice,[30] as well as the late-nineteenth-century example in the Bialystoker Synagogue in New York,[31] were decorated with many animals, but few before *The Ark of Revelation* were adorned with human figures.[32]

One powerful aspect of Kaish's finished *Ark* is the pervasive agitation of its figures, and of the bronze surface. The touch of the artist's hand and the pull of her fingers are felt over every inch. This rough state echoes the doubts and uncertainties of patriarchs and prophets, and also speaks to the tempestuous time in which the *Ark* was made. Americans had recently lived through World War II and the Holocaust, and still lived in fear of nuclear attack. During the years of Kaish's contract for the *Ark*, Americans had witnessed the Cuban Missile Crisis, the March on Washington led by Martin Luther King Jr. (and many rabbis), and—just as the *Ark* was in the foundry—the assassination of President Kennedy.[33] Work proceeded smoothly except for small changes, such as the position of Moses's hands, to avoid appearance of Christological references. In October 1963, the *Ark* was at the foundry for casting.[34] It was installed in the spring and dedicated on April 3, 1964.

The *Ark* is a large work of eighteen bronze figural panels, sixteen of which illustrate scenes of God's presence, through direct revelation to prophets or through their actions. Panel ten is the functional *ner tamid* (eternal light), which projects above the *Ark* opening where the Torah scrolls are kept. The form of the *Ark* is based on Exodus 25: 18–23, which describes the cover of the Ark of the Covenant. (The final program for *The Ark of Revelation* can be found in Appendix A.)

Kaish wrote of the *Ark*, "I sought to give visual and symbolic form to the words of the patriarch and prophet in an unremitting dialogue with God . . . to have it reveal in the mysterious play of light over its forms the inner sense of being, of revelation, of covenant. An angel stays the hand of Abraham; Moses listens to words from the bush; seraphim burn the lips of Isaiah; Ezekiel is lifted over the valley of the dry bones."[35] The spirit of the work derives from intense engagement with the writing of the prophets and their emotional mix of exuberance, expectation, desperation, and loss. While attention has long focused on the figural representation, the real theme is about encountering God, and God's revelation to humanity (Fig. 33).

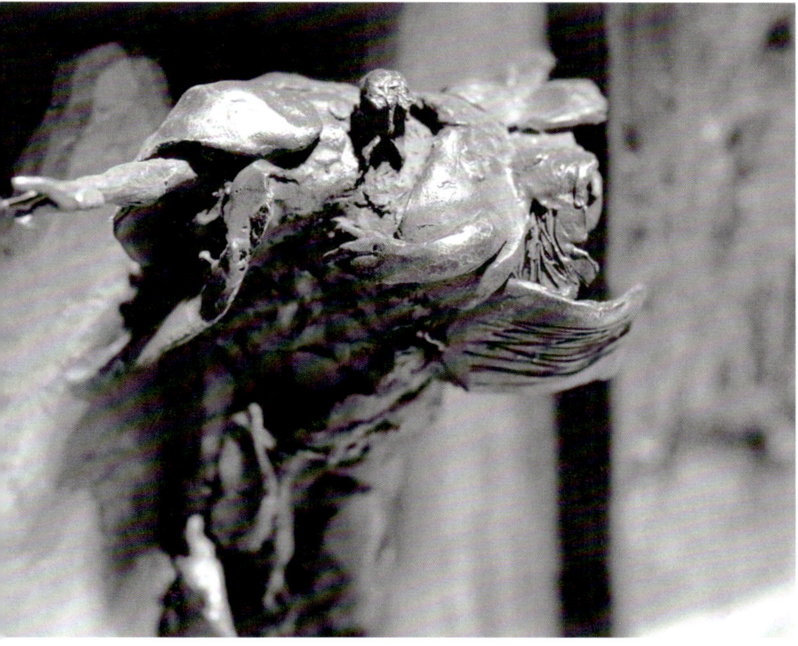

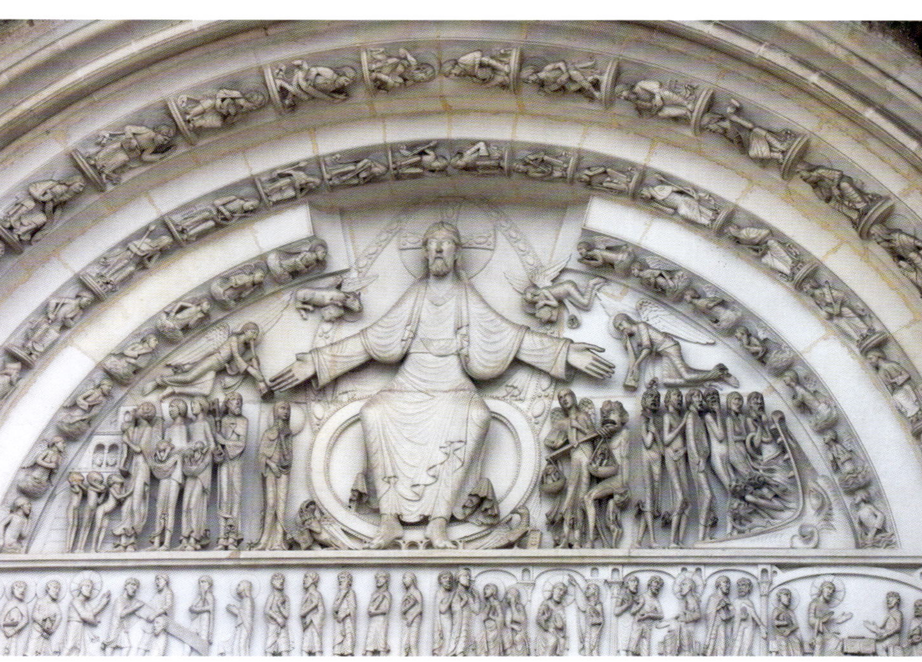

Fig. 33   Luise Kaish, *The Ark of Revelation* (detail), 1960–64 (see Plate 17)

Fig. 34   The tympanum of Vézelay Abbey, France

Stimulated by her work on the *Ark*, Kaish produced more bronze sculptures on biblical and prophetic themes. These include *The Great Blessing of Abraham* (1960–61; Pl. 32), *Boachim* (1964–65), *Expulsion from Eden: Relief* (1964; Pl. 36), the *Spice Container* (1965; Pl. 40), *Whither Thou Goest* (1965; Pl. 41), and *Chassid* (1966; Pl. 42).

Christ in Glory (1967)

The Ark of Revelation's success led to Kaish's next major commission, a monumental relief of the Christ in Glory created for the Holy Trinity Mission Seminary in Silver Spring, Maryland, which drew on her figural vocabulary and method from the *Ark*. Her experience with the *Saltine Warrior* (see Pl. 16) helped her create this monumental Christ figure, which weighs 3,300 pounds and is thirteen and a half feet tall and ten feet wide (see Pl.19).

Christ in Glory is a powerful work in high relief. Christ's outstretched arms are almost at right angles to the plane of his body; hanging high on the chapel wall, the figure levitates, as if about to fly into the space. He is set against an almost almond-shaped, gold-colored bronze background, suggesting medieval mandorlas like those at the Romanesque churches of Autun and Vézelay (Fig. 34), in which Christ is depicted with hands outstretched. Kaish's Christ brings his own celestial atmosphere into the chapel, imbuing the space with a bit of heaven.

Kaish said of the work that she "wanted to create a figure of Christ which would express the ecstasy the spiritual oneness of man with God,"[36] that same connection between human and God she strove to convey in *The Ark of Revelation*, though now embedded in monumental Christian form. For Kaish, there was no contradiction or competition. She told an

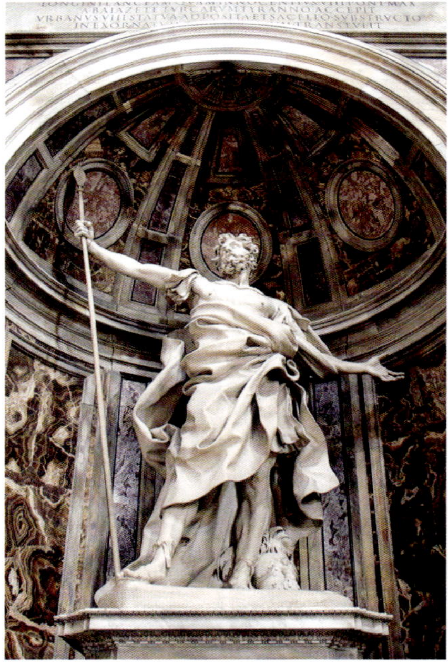

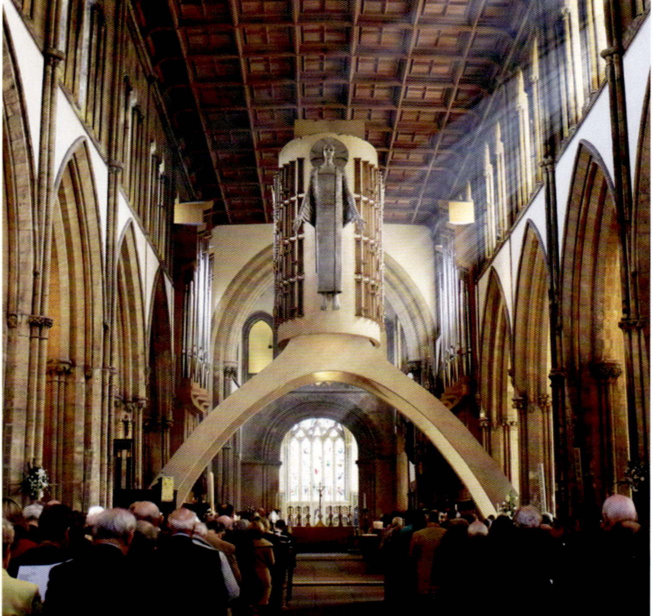

Fig. 35 Gian Lorenzo Bernini, *Longinus*, 1638, marble, 13 ft. (4 m) high, Basilica of St. Peter's, Vatican City, Italy

Fig. 36 Jacob Epstein, *Christ in Majesty*, 1954–55, aluminum, 16 ft. (4.9 m) high. Llandaff Cathedral, Wales

interviewer that "there was nothing in the morality that Jesus preached that cannot be found in the Hebrew Bible."[37]

The Christ figure recalls the ecstatic Moses of the Rochester *Ark*, but this Christ stretches his hands not to receive the (Old) Law, but to share it (the New Law of Christian faith). There are seeming yards of swirling baroque drapery around Christ's arms. As in the seventeenth-century sculpture of Bernini, the drapery is shaped by emotion, not exact anatomical features. This large figure recalls Bernini's crossing figures in the basilica of St. Peter's in Rome, especially St. Longinus, with his arms thrown wide in his moment of ecstatic realization and revelation (Fig. 35). Kaish was probably also aware of two monumental works by Jacob Epstein, whom she had met on her visit to England. One is a large exterior bronze relief of the Madonna and Child (1950) at Cavendish Square, London, in which the Christ Child has his arms extended; the other is a large figure of Christ in Majesty (1954–55) at Llandaff Cathedral in Wales, where Christ appears to float above the nave with arms lowered, but outstretched (Fig. 36).[38]

The Beth Shalom Ark Doors (1967–68)

Kaish could be abstract and cerebral, too. This served her well in her second large Jewish commission, the *Ark Doors* for Temple Beth Shalom, in Wilmington, Delaware, a Conservative congregation that rejected figural treatment (see Pls. 21, 22). The congregation's only specification was that the *Ark Doors* should include the Tablets of the Law, which were common in so many twentieth-century ark designs. But Kaish wanted more.

Rather than mimicking traditional representations of the tablets or simply giving them a new artistic framework, Kaish chose an entirely new interpretation. She turned to the Jewish mystical text of the Zohar, the thirteenth-century "Book of Splendor," for a deeper artistic vocabulary and spiritual context. Intensely studying the Zohar's rich imagery in the same way she'd previously delved into the prophetic writings, she discovered visual and plastic clues to shape her sculpture. She embedded the Commandments in a circle instead of the traditional tablet, making Torah a symbol of cosmic law. Avram Kampf wrote, "According to the Zohar, God emerges not out of chaos, but out of nothingness—out of the hidden hiddenness, and creates a world according to Torah, which preceded the creation of the world."[39]

Beth Shalom's Rabbi Jacob Kraft took it upon himself to interpret the doors in a written description, of which Kaish approved (see Appendix B). In his introduction Rabbi Kraft wrote that Kaish "has given an interpretation of the Ten Commandments based on the medieval, mystic conception of God as *Ein Soph*, the Infinite. The intention of the artist is to communicate to the viewer the larger meaning of the moment at Sinai; not only the revelation of the Ten Commandments, but the profound and enduring meaning seen through the eyes of the mystic."[40] Gone is the neat symmetry of the traditional tablets; instead, the letters are pushed and molded into the cosmic orb with a force of creating. The sculptor as maker recalls the physical act of Creation. As in Rochester, Kaish has molded the surface of the *Ark Doors*, but here she uses letters—the divine letters of the Torah that teach, inspire, and command, rather than the prophetic figures inspired by revelation.

The Wall of Martyrs (1972–74)

Temple Beth El in New Rochelle commissioned Kaish to create *The Wall of Martyrs*, a series of bronze reliefs that depicts Jewish martyrdom through history (see Pl. 27), while she was finishing a two-year Rome Prize Fellowship at the American Academy in Rome. Kaish extended her stay in Rome and threw herself into research and modeling for the project (see Appendix C).

The purpose of the memorial was to put the horrors of the Holocaust into a longer historical context, and encourage deeper understanding of three millennia of Jewish history. The proponents of *The Wall of Martyrs* subscribed to what historian Salo Baron termed the "lachrymose conception of Jewish history,"[41] promulgated by nineteenth-century historian Heinrich Graetz, which emphasizes periods of suffering and oppression in Jewish history much more than the many long periods of relative stability and cultural achievement. But in the wake of the Holocaust, and in the short period between the Middle Eastern wars of 1967 and 1973, this narrative was powerfully appealing. The massacre of Israeli athletes at the 1972 Summer Olympics in Munich further validated this understanding. Importantly,

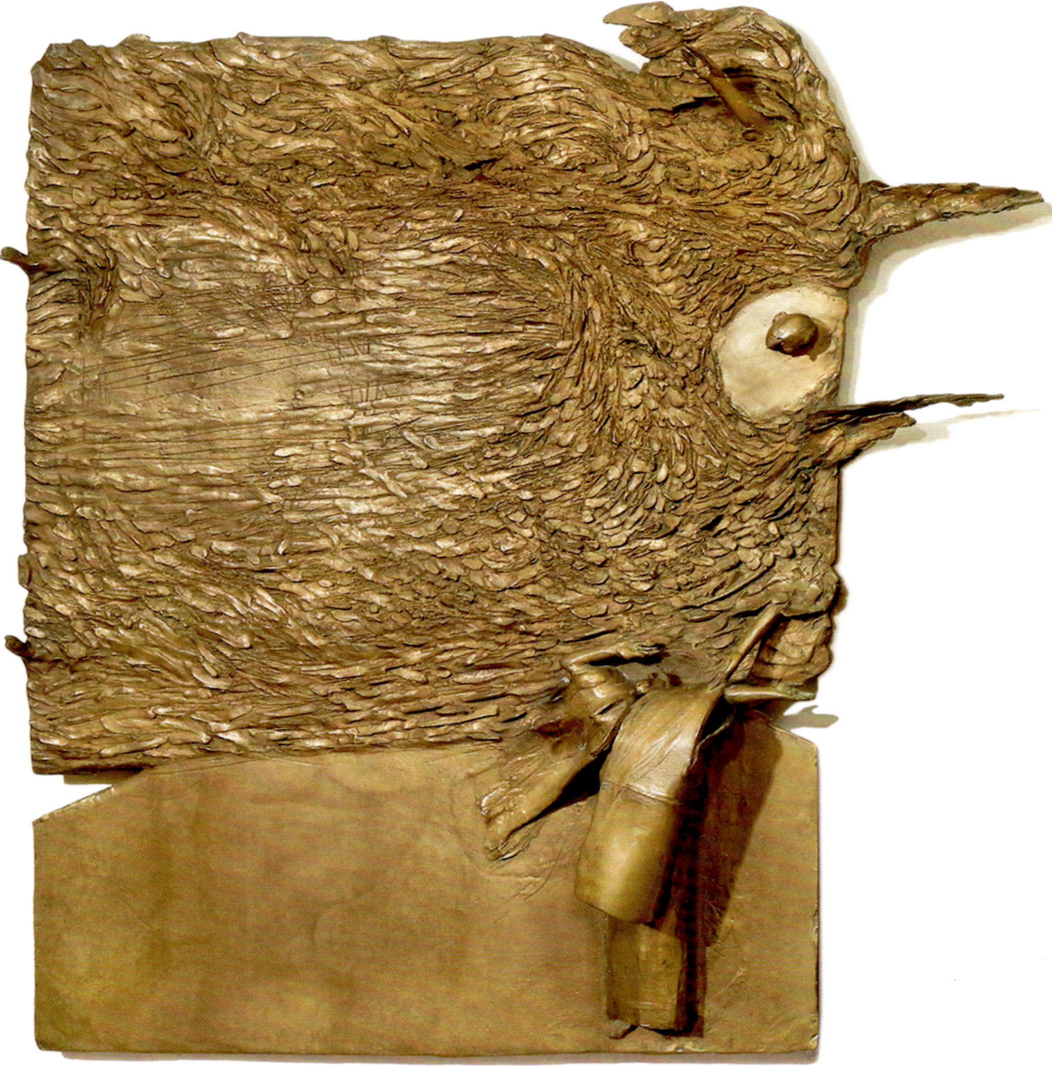

Fig. 37   Luise Kaish, *The Wall of Martyrs*, *The Eternal Martyr* (Panel 1), 1972–74, bronze, 37 ¼ × 40 ¼ in. (94.6 × 102.2 cm) (see Plate 27; Appendix C)

suffering gave Kaish the impetus to develop and depict the emotional language that combined symbol and narrative, and in many ways melded the literal and abstract qualities of the Rochester and Wilmington *Arks*.

Kaish began the martyr reliefs with a link to her earlier work, presenting a symbolic prophet figure speaking out against iniquity, with outstretched arms and open mouth to show ecstasy before an angel's hovering spirit (Fig. 37). The second panel depicts the flight from Jerusalem in 586 BCE, inspired by the words of Prophet Jeremiah in Lamentations 1:1: "How doth the city set solitary, that was full of people! How she has become as a widow." Jerusalem is engulfed in flames, while men and women flee to exile or worse (Fig. 38). This relief references Michelangelo's Sistine Chapel ceiling painting of the Flood, and also recalls more recent art of Jewish suffering and exile (Fig. 39).

The third panel shows the agony and strength of Rabbi Hananiah ben Teradyon, one of the Ten Martyrs recalled in the poem *Eleh Ezkerah*, recited on the Day of Atonement

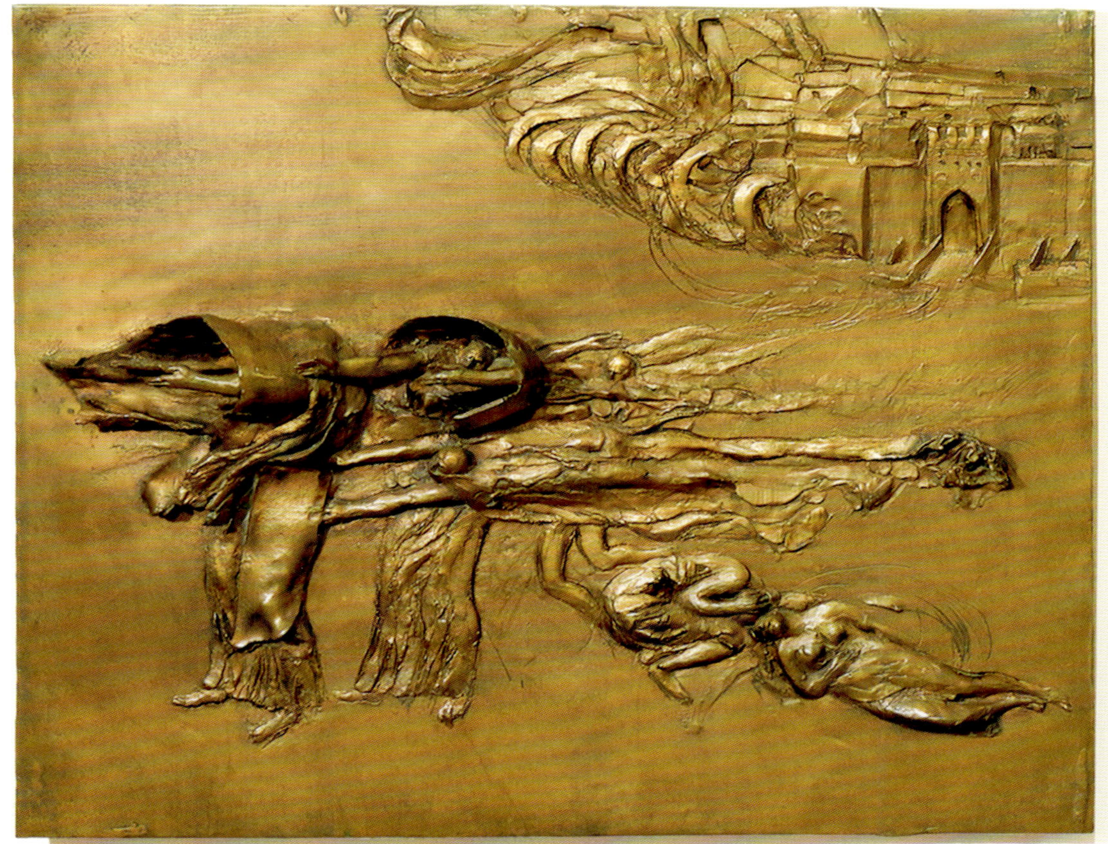

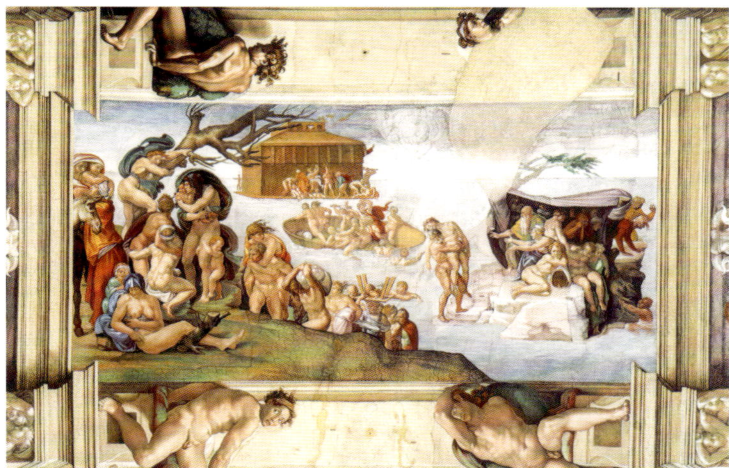

Fig. 38   Luise Kaish, *The Wall of Martyrs, The Flight from Jerusalem* (Panel 2), 1972–74, bronze, 28 ½ × 34 in. (72.4 × 86.4 cm) (see Plate 27; Appendix C)

Fig. 39   Michelangelo, *The Flood*, 1508–12, fresco, 10 × 18 ft. (3.05 × 5.49 m), Sistine Chapel, Vatican City, Italy

and the ninth of Ab. The rabbi was wrapped in the Torah and burned alive. Kaish shows him defiant, his arms outstretched at an angle to the edge of a circle—a suffering version of Leonardo's *Vitruvian Man*. When asked by his disciples "Master, what do you see?" he replied, "I see parchment burning, while the letters of the Torah soar upward."

In the fourth panel, as Kaish describes it, "the formidable face of rock, Masada is shown rising amidst the beautiful and desolate wasteland surrounding the natural mysteries of the Dead Sea."[42] In the fifth panel, a cavalcade of horses represents Crusader knights who,

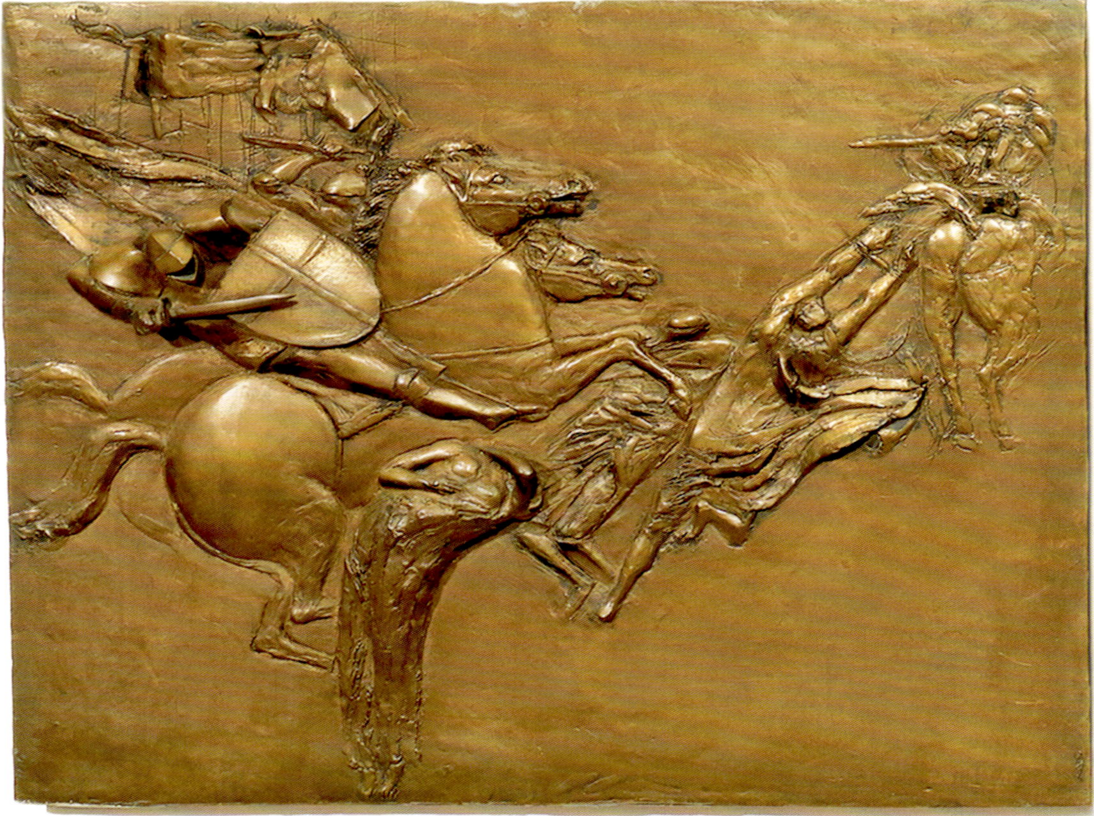

Fig. 40   Luise Kaish, *The Wall of Martyrs, The Crusades* (Panel 5), 1972–74, bronze, 25 × 33 ¼ in. (63.5 × 83.8 cm) (see Plate 27; Appendix C)

under the sign of the Cross, send Jewish victims fleeing. Again, Kaish refers to classics of European art. These could be Rhineland Jews, or Jews in Jerusalem, caught in the throes of a Paolo Uccello–inspired battle or hunt (Fig. 40).

The sixth panel, the simplest of the narrative designs, represents the Inquisition. A Jewish figure hangs from the center top of the relief, between two arches. Two figures at lower left pull at rope that tortures the victim, while a Christian bishop stands by on the right. The composition deliberately echoes a common arrangement in medieval and Renaissance scenes of Christ's Crucifixion. Here, however, the expected diagonal of Longinus's spear is a rope, and Jesus is a Jew, tormented by the Christian Church. The seventh panel, depicting the Chmielnitzki Massacre, is represented by a Chassid, shown holding aloft the sacred scrolls—torn, defiled, yet spiritually intact. The last panel moves to the Holocaust. There are no figures in the scene, only a crematorium oven, its open doors askew, surrounded by a field of flowers rising from the ashes (Fig. 41).

In this series of striking bronze reliefs, Kaish has given an abbreviated but powerful overview of millennia of Jewish suffering and martyrdom. For those knowledgeable about art, she also rewrites much of the Western art tradition to include Jewish history as part of the narrative.

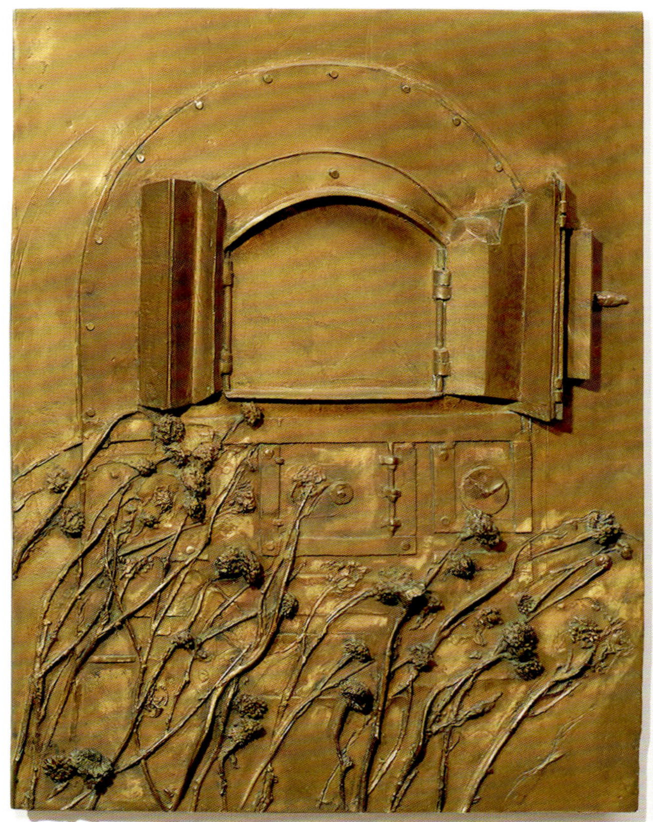

Fig. 41   Luise Kaish, *The Wall of Martyrs, The Holocaust* (Panel 7), 1972–74, bronze, 28 ¾ × 38 in. (73 × 96.5 cm) (see Plate 27; Appendix C)

Holocaust Memorial (1974–75)

Following the completion of *The Wall of Martyrs*, and Kaish's much-praised 1973 exhibit at New York's Jewish Museum, philanthropist Vera List commissioned the artist to create a Holocaust memorial for the entrance of the museum's new List Building, a modern addition to the Gothic-style Warburg Mansion (see Pl. 29). The memorial's imagery is closely linked to the final panel of *The Wall of Martyrs*. It is Kaish's most literal work, a bronze slab with a geometrized but explicit crematorium oven in high relief, based on her intensely emotional trip to Dachau in 1951. Though it had been more than a quarter-century since the horrors of the Holocaust became widely known, this was still an early memorial in the United States, and the first public memorial in New York City.[43]

Unfortunately, however, Kaish's memorial was removed during the museum's 1993 expansion of the Warburg Mansion and remains in storage.

Conclusion

Religious art, especially art that reflected and promoted Jewish religious history, ideals, and practice, was not Luise Kaish's only artistic output—far from it. Still, together these works are a remarkably coherent body of work that, by themselves, warrant Kaish's reputation as an innovative and influential artist of both vision and craft. Her willingness to inject these works with strong emotional content, and her insistence on rejecting dry tropes and stereotypes in the search for a new visual language, allow these works to remain fresh and exciting, as well as deeply rewarding on tactile, visual, and intellectual levels. Her religious work is not dogmatic or even didactic; it challenges viewers to consider the essence of religious traditions and observance, and to find that within themselves. Her works tell us there are many routes to revelation, but this begins as a personal quest.

Endnotes

1. Avram Kampf, "Introduction," in *Luise Kaish Sculpture*, exh. cat. (New York: Jewish Museum, 1973), 3.

2. Gershom Scholem's books in English continue to be widely read and very influential on contemporary Judaism. During Kaish's formative years it was his *Major Trends in Jewish Mysticism* (New York: Schocken Books, 1941) that held sway. The book was popular in America after 1946.

3. For the synagogue work through the mid-1960s by many of Kaish's contemporaries, see Avram Kampf, *Contemporary Synagogue Art: Developments in the United States, 1945–1965* (New York: Union of American Hebrew Congregation, 1966). Much of the best-known synagogue work of the 1950s and early 1960s was done to accent synagogues designed by Percival Goodman (1904–1989), the first architect to encourage the integration of modern synagogue architecture and modern art. Many pieces were entirely abstract but carried titles giving them biblical or Jewish associations: for example, *The Burning Bush* (1951) by Herbert Ferber (1906–1991) for the Congregation B'nai Israel in Milburn, New Jersey, and *Pillar of Fire* (1953) by Ibram Lassaw (1913–2003) at Temple Beth El, Springfield, Massachusetts. Other work tended to group Jewish symbols in a decorative arrangement, like Bernard Rosenthal's (1914–2009) large metal relief (1956) at Temple Emanuel in Beverly Hills, California.

4. Meyer was a graduate of the Jewish Institute of Religion, and then rabbi in Flushing from 1922 to 1963, when he was named rabbi emeritus. He was the prime mover in the development of the Free Synagogue of Flushing, a leader of the American Jewish Congress, and secretary of the New York Board of Rabbis. See "Dr. Max Meyer" (obituary), *New York Times*, December 31, 1981, https://www.nytimes.com/1981/12/31/obituaries/dr-max-meyer.html.

5. Morton Kaish, oral history with Liza Zapol, July 31, 2015, New York, transcript, 2, Luise Kaish archives.

6. On Weinberg (1928–1991), see Nancy Finley, *In the Grand Tradition: The Enduring Art of Elbert Weinberg* (Hartford, CT: Hartford Public Library, 2018), especially chapter 2, "No Graven Images: Weinberg's Judaic Sculptures."

7. On Meštrović (1883–1962) at Syracuse, see William P. Tolley, "Ivan Meštrović Comes to Syracuse University," *The Courier* 19, no. 2 (1984): 3–6; David Tatham, "Ivan Meštrović in Syracuse, 1947–1955," *Syracuse University Library Associates Courier* 32, (1997): 5–24. On the memorial, see Rochelle G. Saidel, *Never Too Late to Remember: The Politics Behind New York City's Holocaust Museum* (New York: Holmes & Meier, 1996).

8. *Mother and Child* was selected for inclusion in *American Sculpture 1951: A National Competitive Exhibition* at the Metropolitan Museum of Art.

9. On Rapoport (1911–1987) and the *Warsaw Ghetto Uprising Memorial*, see James Young, *The Texture of Memory: Holocaust Memorials and Meaning* (New Haven and London: Yale University Press, 1993). On his subsequent sculpture, see Richard Yaffe, *Nathan Rapoport Sculptures and Monuments* (New York: Shengold, 1980).

10. Luise Kaish, "Sculpture: A Poetic Force" (lecture, University of Washington School of Art, presented in conjunction with Battelle Research Center, Seattle, July 10, 1979), typescript, Luise Kaish archives, New York.

11. Luise Kaish, "Autobiographical Information Submitted in Application for a Guggenheim Fellowship," 1959, Luise Kaish archives.

12. Ibid.

13. Morton Kaish, oral history, 2016, Luise Kaish archives.

14. "Saltine Warrior Unveiled," *Syracuse Post-Standard*, June 4, 1951.

15. Kaish met Epstein on her first trip to England in 1951.

16. Luise Kaish, interview by the author, 2002.

17. Kaish, "Autobiographical Information."

18. "Statue Honors Forman's work in United Appeal," *Democrat and Chronicle* (Rochester), January 29, 1958.

19. *Recent Sculpture U.S.A.*, May 13–August 16, 1959, Museum of Modern Art, New York. Exhibition catalogue by Walter Bareiss and James Thrall Soby (New York: Museum of Modern Art, 1959), https://www.moma.org/documents/moma_catalogue_3359_300062192.pdf. *The Blessing (Two)* is illustrated in the catalogue.

20. "Recent Sculpture U.S.A.," *New York Times*, May 17, 1959 (with photo); "Village Sculptors in Museum Show," *Villager* (Greenwich Village, New York), July 16, 1959.

21. "Artist Statement on Biblical Bronzes," 1957–58, typescript page, Luise Kaish archives.

22. Luise Kaish, "Columbia Lifelong Talk," c. 1985, Luise Kaish archives.

23. Philip Bernstein, "What's Ahead for Reform Jews?" sermon, November 26, 1948, Philip S. Bernstein Papers, University of Rochester, New York.

24. The *Ark* at Temple B'rith Kodesh was prominently featured in Kampf's *Contemporary Synagogue Art*, with a stirring description and ten large photos; it was then included in Kaish's 1973 solo exhibition *Luise Kaish Sculpture* at the Jewish Museum, New York. Subsequently, the *Ark* was included in Samuel D. Gruber, *American Synagogues: A Century of Architecture and Jewish Community* (New York: Rizzoli, 2003), 122–27. Gruber wrote, "In its size and medium, and in its central location, this *Ark* is surely one of the major works of Judaica of the past half-century . . . even today. The presence of Kaish's figures on the *Ark* is an exciting shock."

25. Belluschi (1899–1994) was dean of Architecture at MIT and known for distinctive religious buildings, which in time included five synagogues. See Meredith Clausen, *Spiritual Space: The Religious*

Architecture of Pietro Belluschi (Seattle: University of Washington Press, 1992).

26. Luise Kaish to Philip S. Bernstein, October 23, 1959, Luise Kaish archives.

27. Ibid.

28. Pietro Belluschi to Philip S. Bernstein, November 17, 1959, Luise Kaish archives.

29. Garson Meyer, chairman, B'rith Kodesh Building Committee, to Luise Kaish, August 26, 1960, Luise Kaish archives.

30. On the Druja ark, see Bracha Yaniv, "Praising the Lord: Discovering a Song of Ascents on Carved Torah Arks in Eastern Europe," *Ars Judaica* (2006): 83–102. On Boskovice, see Olga Sixtová, Daniel Polakovič, and Arno Pařik, *Boskovice Synagogue: Guide* (Prague: Jewish Museum of Prague, 2002). Neither of these arks, however, would have been known to Kaish.

31. On the Bialystoker ark, see Gerald Wolfe and J. Fine, *The Synagogues of New York's Lower East Side* (New York: New York University Press, 1978).

32. The other example known to this author is *The Doors of the 36* (1956) at Temple Beth-El of Great Neck, New York, by Ilya Schor (1904–1961), consisting of highly stylized silver repoussé panels based on the Hasidic legend of the thirty-six wise and good humans who live in every generation. It is not known if Kaish knew of these recently completed doors. Schor's ark is fully illustrated in Kampf, *Contemporary Synagogue Art*, 204–7.

33. By December 1961, Kaish was working on a quarter-size model of the *Ark*, and final discussions were taking place about the *Ark's* interior, approach steps, and other details. Kaish's design was fully approved by the building committee in April 1962. At Rosh Hashanah that year Rabbi Bernstein added in a sermon, "we have not yet seen the masterpiece, the great focal point of our sanctuary, which a genius is fashioning for our *Ark*"; Philip S. Bernstein, "What Are We Doing," Rosh Hashanah evening sermon, September 28, 1962, typescript.

34. Philip S. Bernstein to Luise Kaish, March 27, 1963.

35. Luise Kaish, "Notes for B'rith Kodesh Talk and Wall of Martyrs," undated, Luise Kaish archives.

36. Quoted in caption for "Ecstasy," *Washington Post*, August 5, 1967.

37. Emery Grossman, "Interview with Kaish, Sculptor," *Temple Israel Light*, November–December 1966.

38. Leeds City Art Galleries, Henry Moore Centre for the Study of Sculpture, *Jacob Epstein Sculpture and Drawings* (Leeds: W. S. Maney & Son, 1989), 262–277.

39. Kampf, "Introduction," 4.

40. Ibid.

41. Salo W. Baron, "Newer Emphases in Jewish History," *Jewish Social Studies* 25 no. 4 (1963): 245–58. Reprinted in Salo W. Baron, *History and Jewish Historians: Essays and Addresses* (Philadelphia: Jewish Publication Society, 1964), 90–106.

42. As described by Morton Kaish.

43. On Holocaust memorials created at this time, see James Young, ed., *The Art of Memory: Holocaust Memorials in History* (New York: Jewish Museum, 1994).

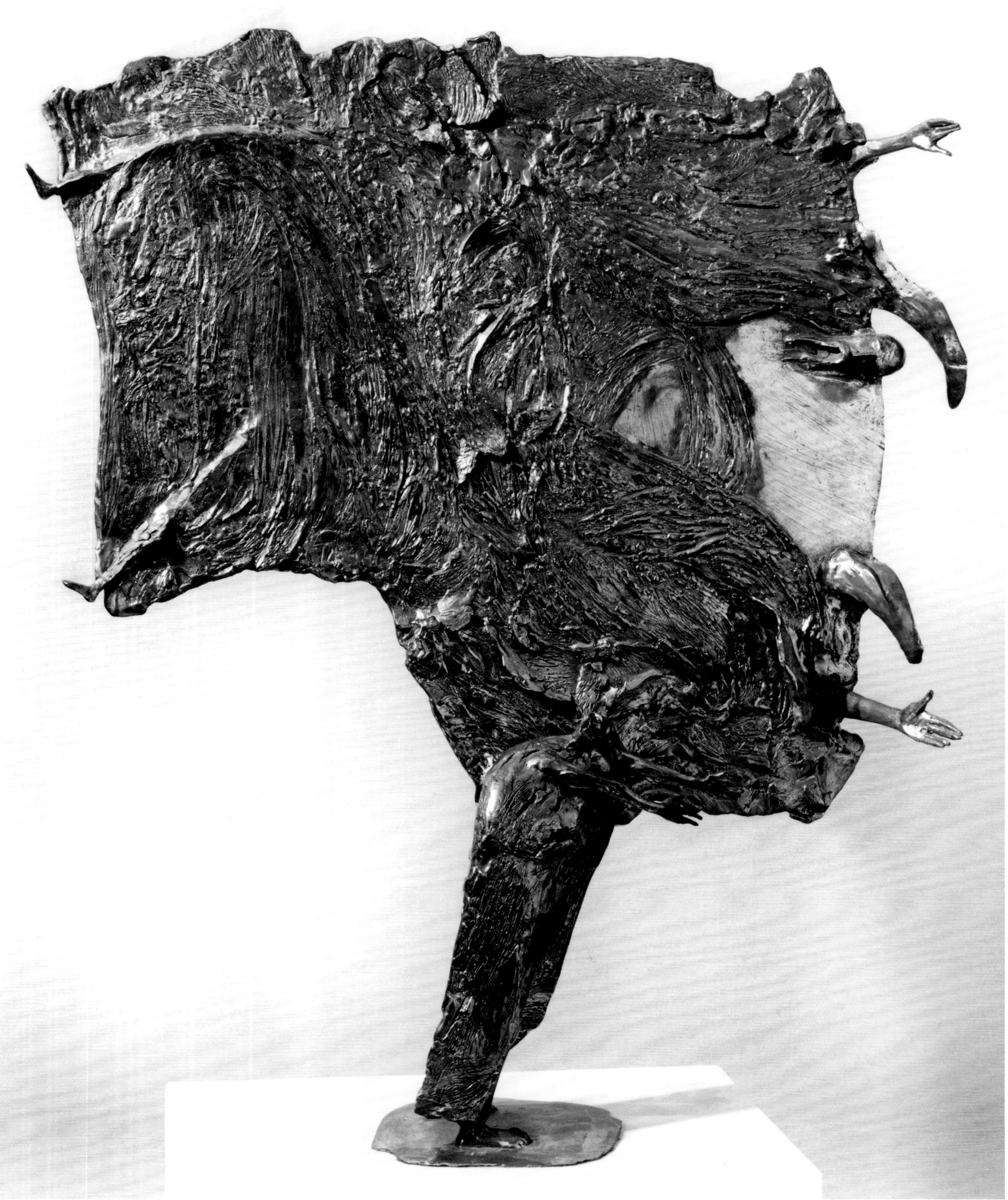

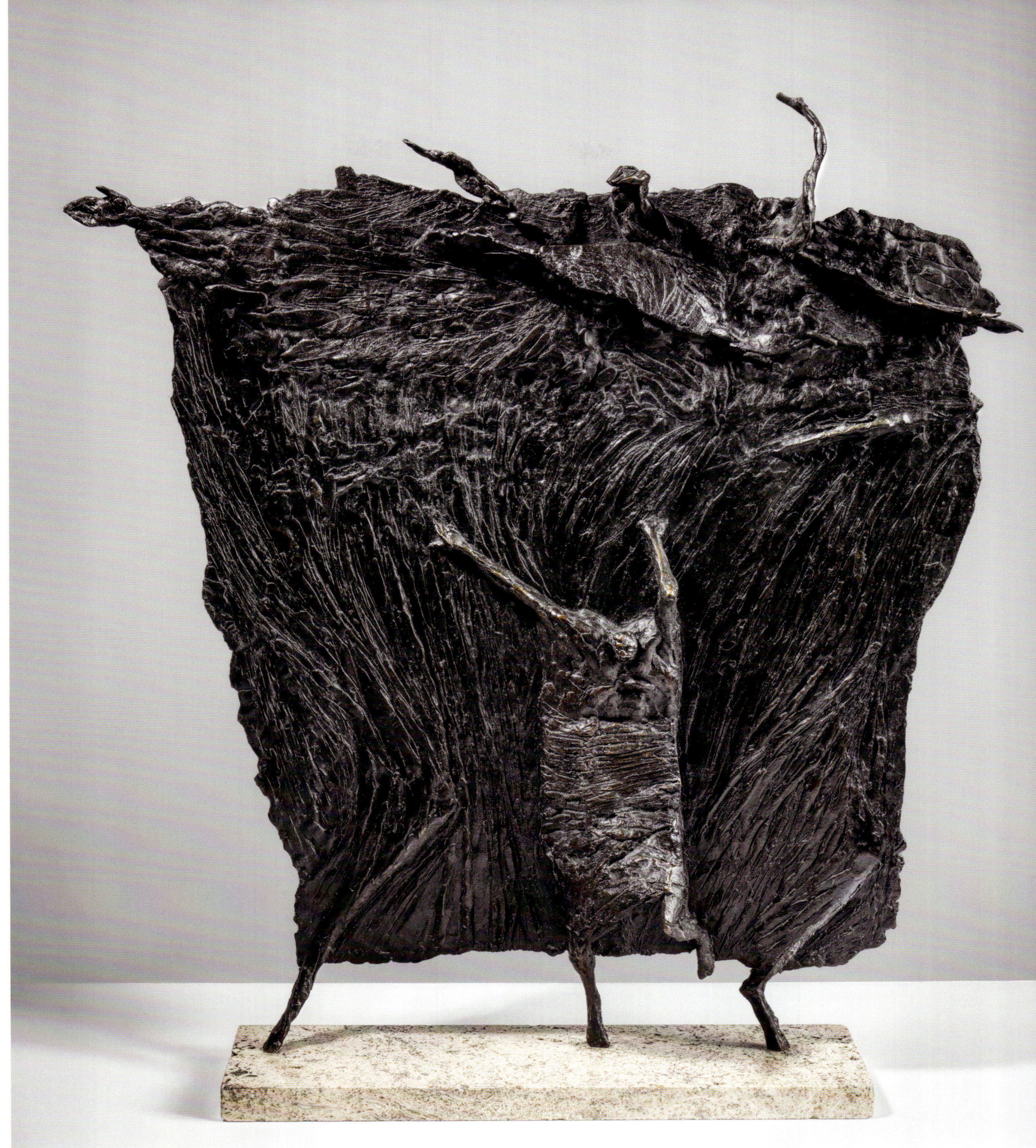

Plate 30
Luise Kaish. *Jonah Fleeing Nineveh*, 1958–59, bronze, 39 × 30 in. (99.1 × 76.2 cm). Collection, Jewish Museum, New York, Gift of Mr. and Mrs. Albert A. List Family

Plate 31
Luise Kaish. *Jacob Wrestling with the Angel*, 1957, bronze, 19 × 19 × 3 in. (48.3 × 48.3 × 7.6 cm)

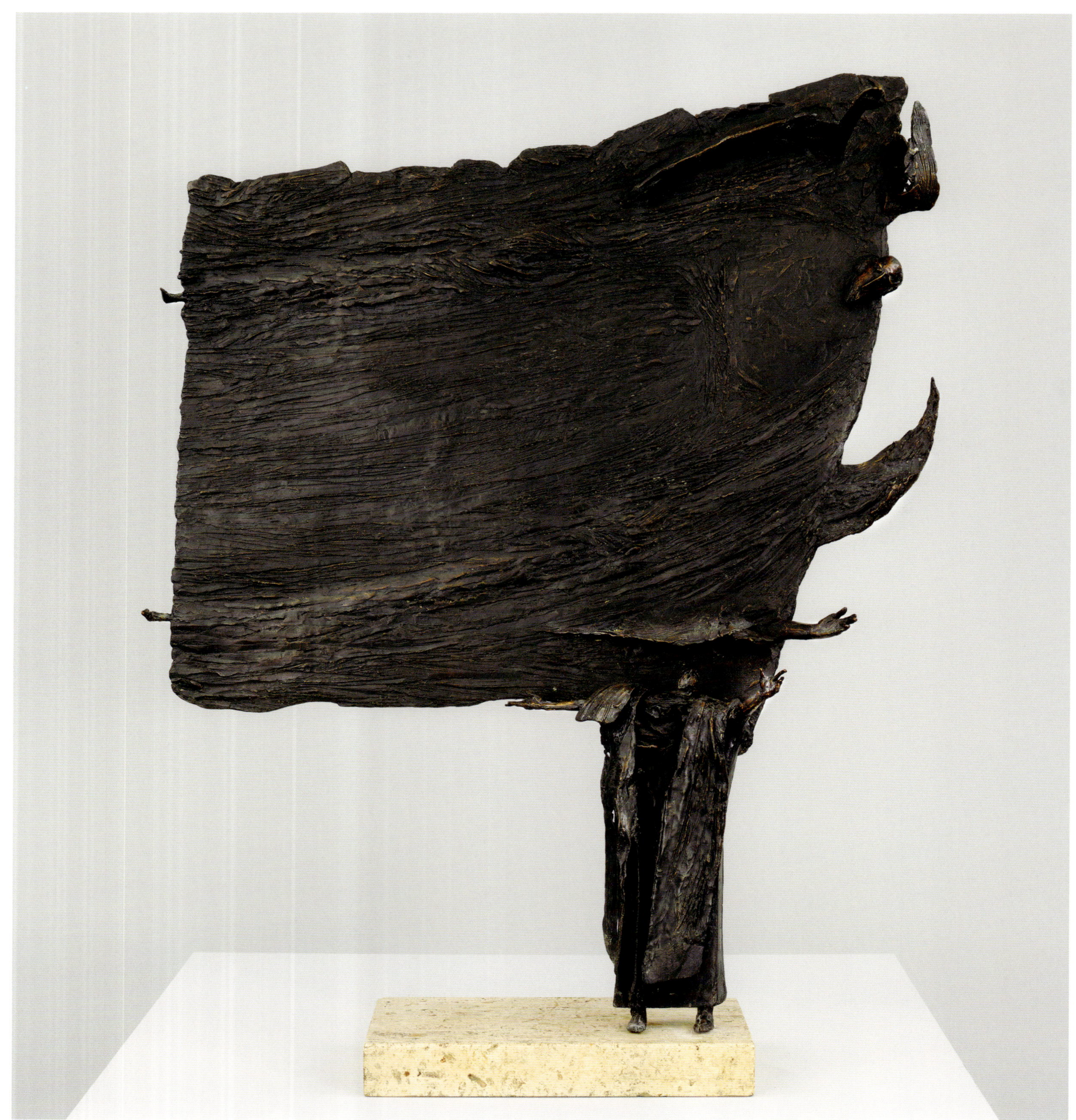

Plate 32
Luise Kaish. *The Great Blessing of Abraham*,
1960, bronze, 36 ¼ × 29 ¾ × 10 in.
(92.1 × 75.6 × 25.4 cm). Collection,
The Whitney Museum of American Art

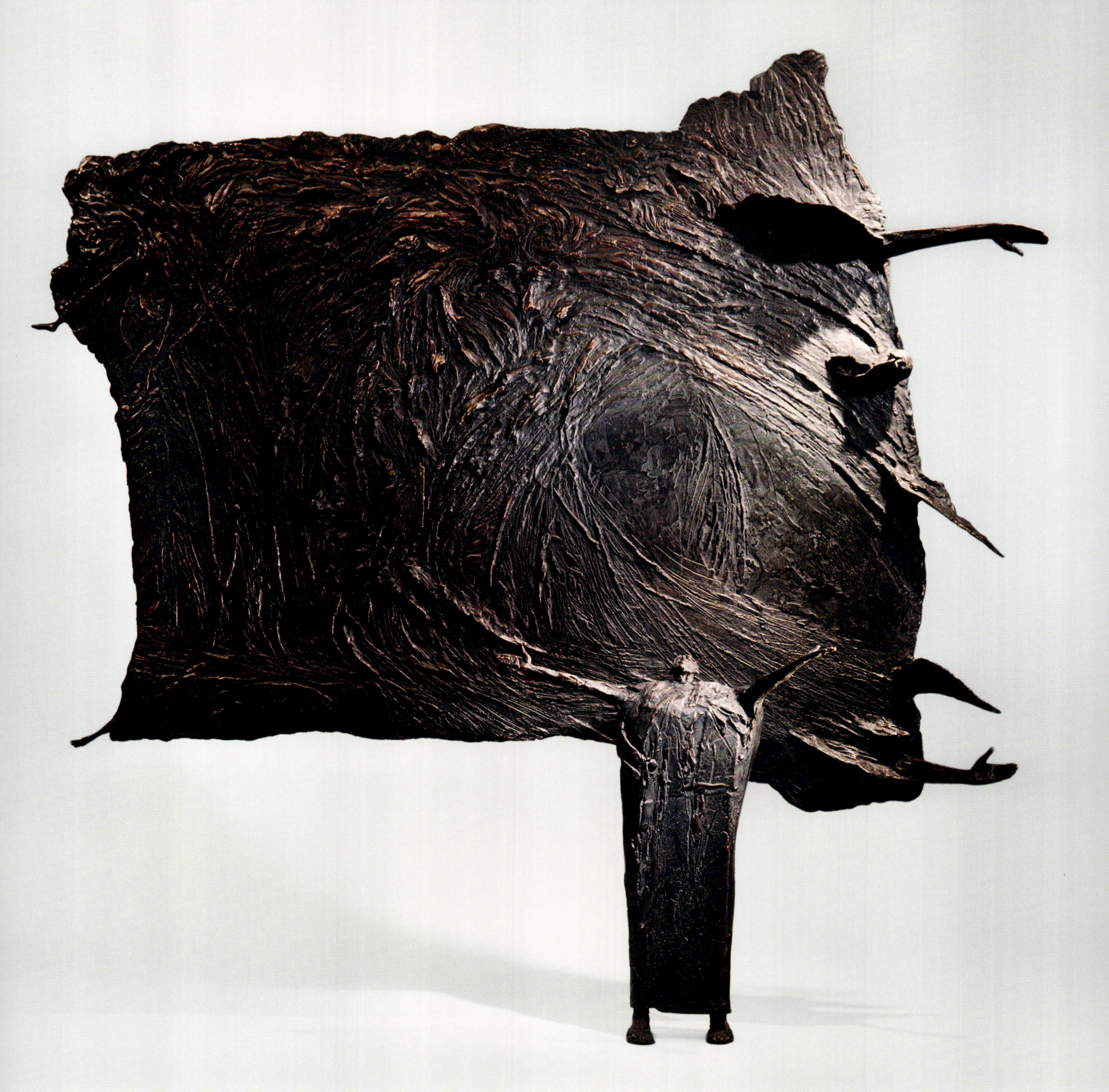

Plate 33
Luise Kaish. *Frederick the Great*, 1961, bronze,
39 ⅞ × 39 ⅞ × 7 ½ in. (101.3 × 101.3 × 19.1 cm).
Collection, Smithsonian American Art Museum, Gift of
Container Corporation of America

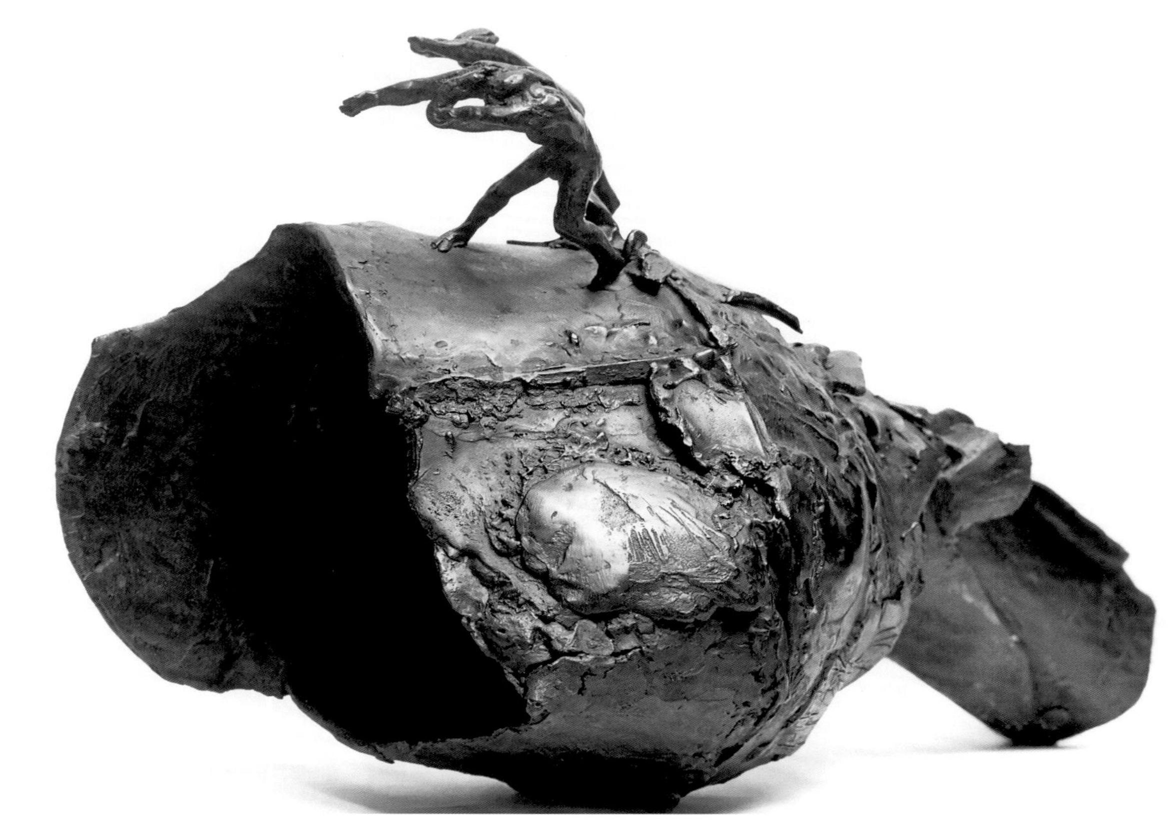
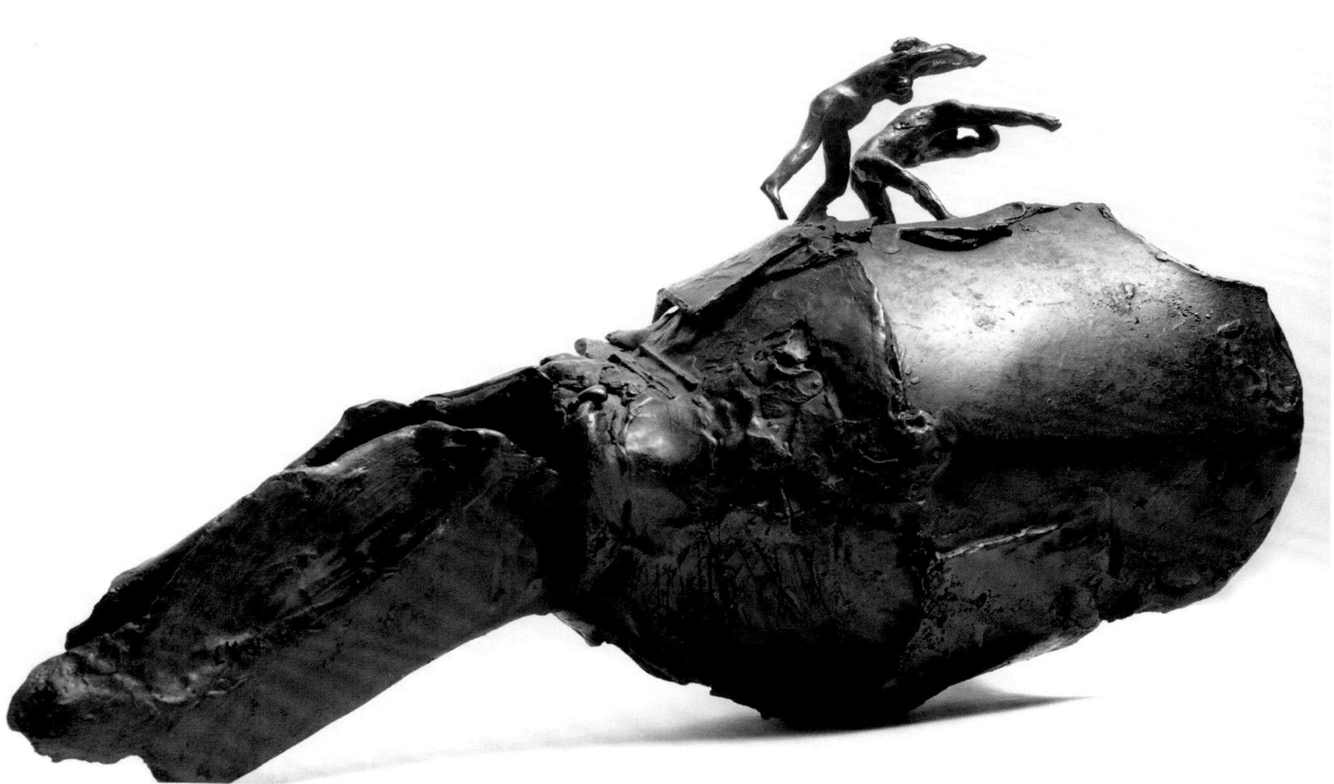

Plate 34
Luise Kaish. *Creation and Expulsion II*, 1965,
bronze, 12 × 21 in. (30.5 × 53.3 cm)

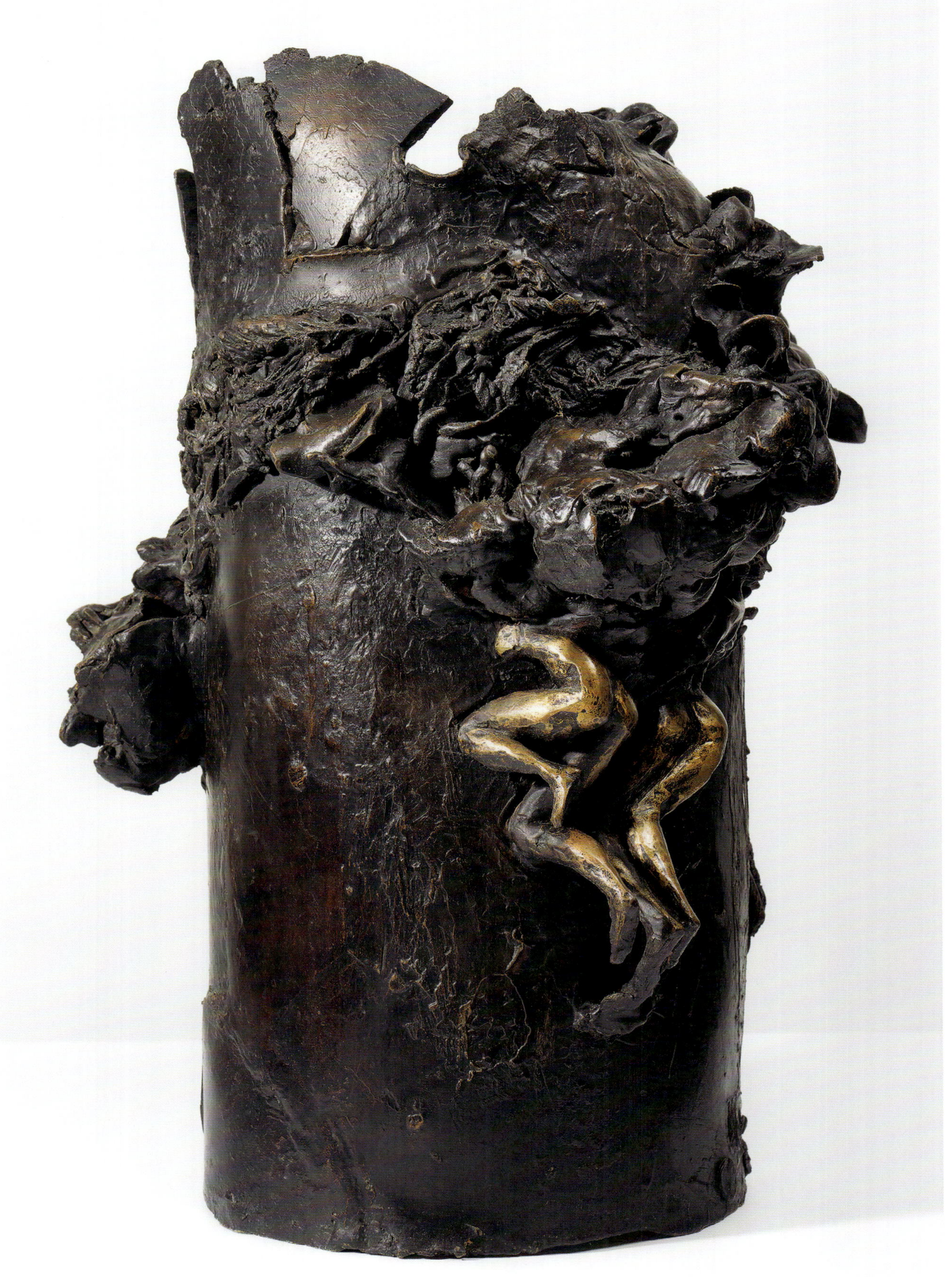

Plate 35
Luise Kaish. *Expulsion II*, 1964, bronze,
19 × 16 in. (48.3 × 40.6 cm)

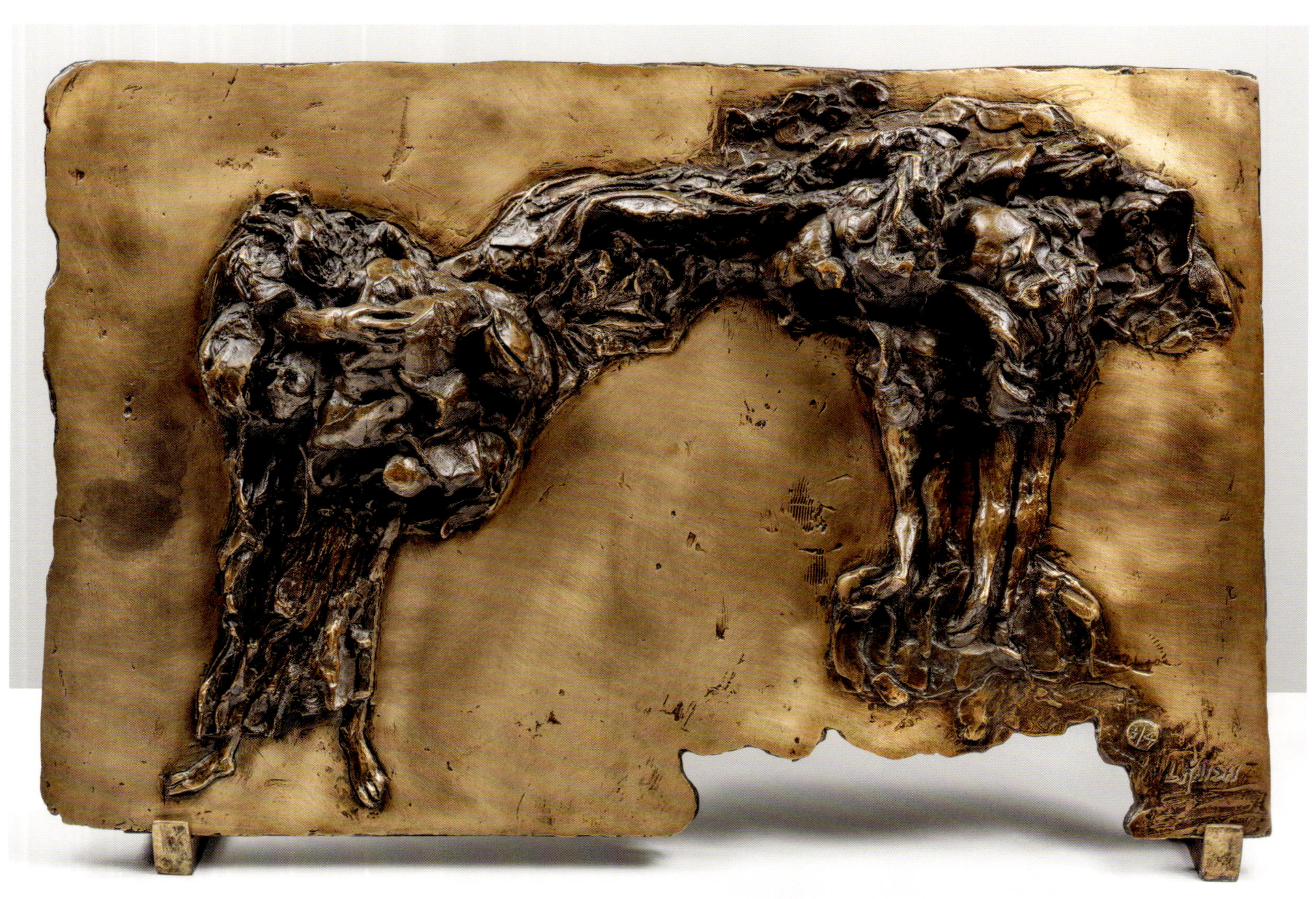

Plate 36
Luise Kaish. *Expulsion from Eden: Relief*,
1964, bronze, 15 × 24 in. (38.1 × 61 cm)

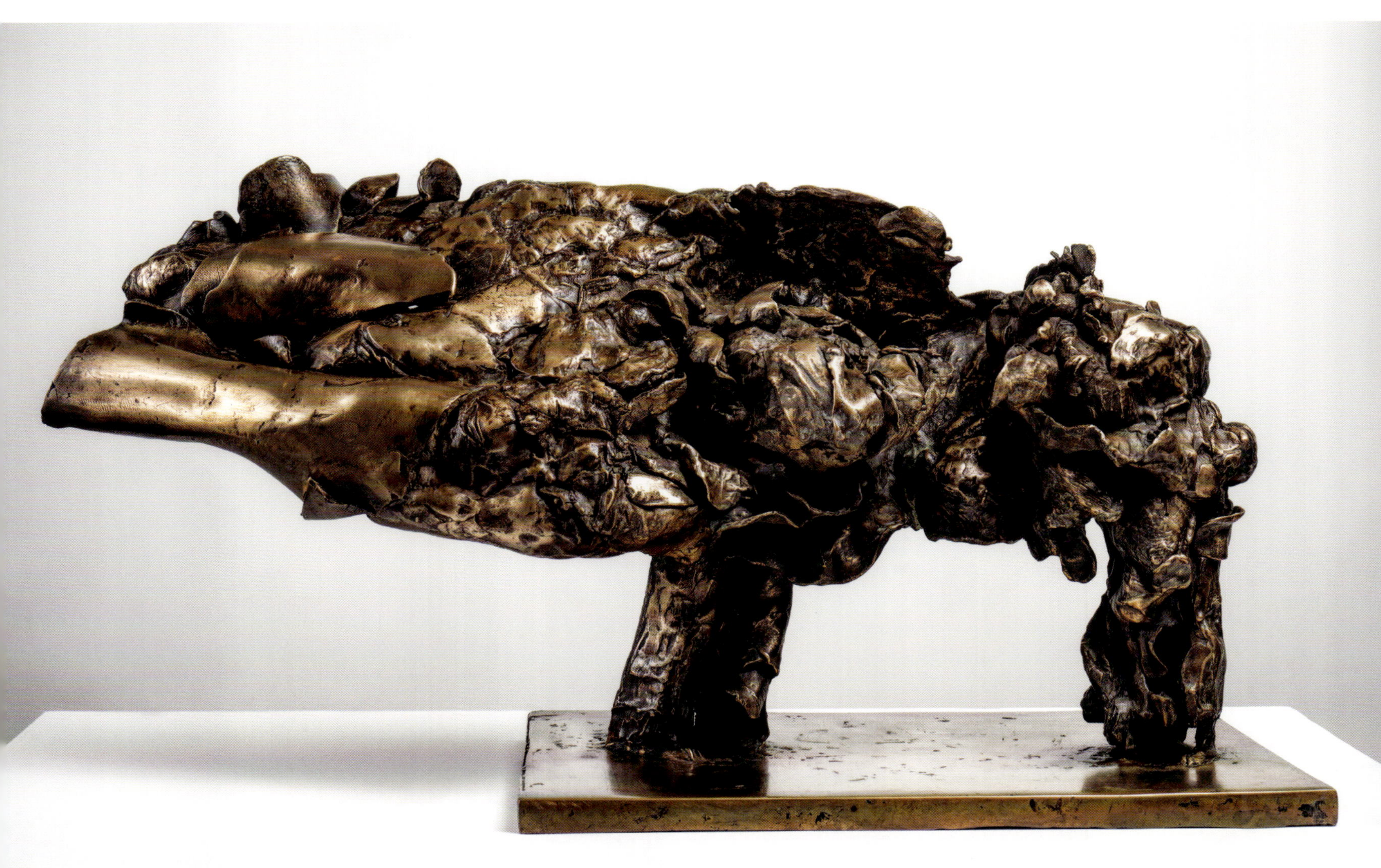

Plate 37
Luise Kaish. *Creation and Expulsion from Eden* (*Ulro*),
1964, bronze, 13 × 26 × 11 ½ in. (33 × 66 × 29.2 cm)

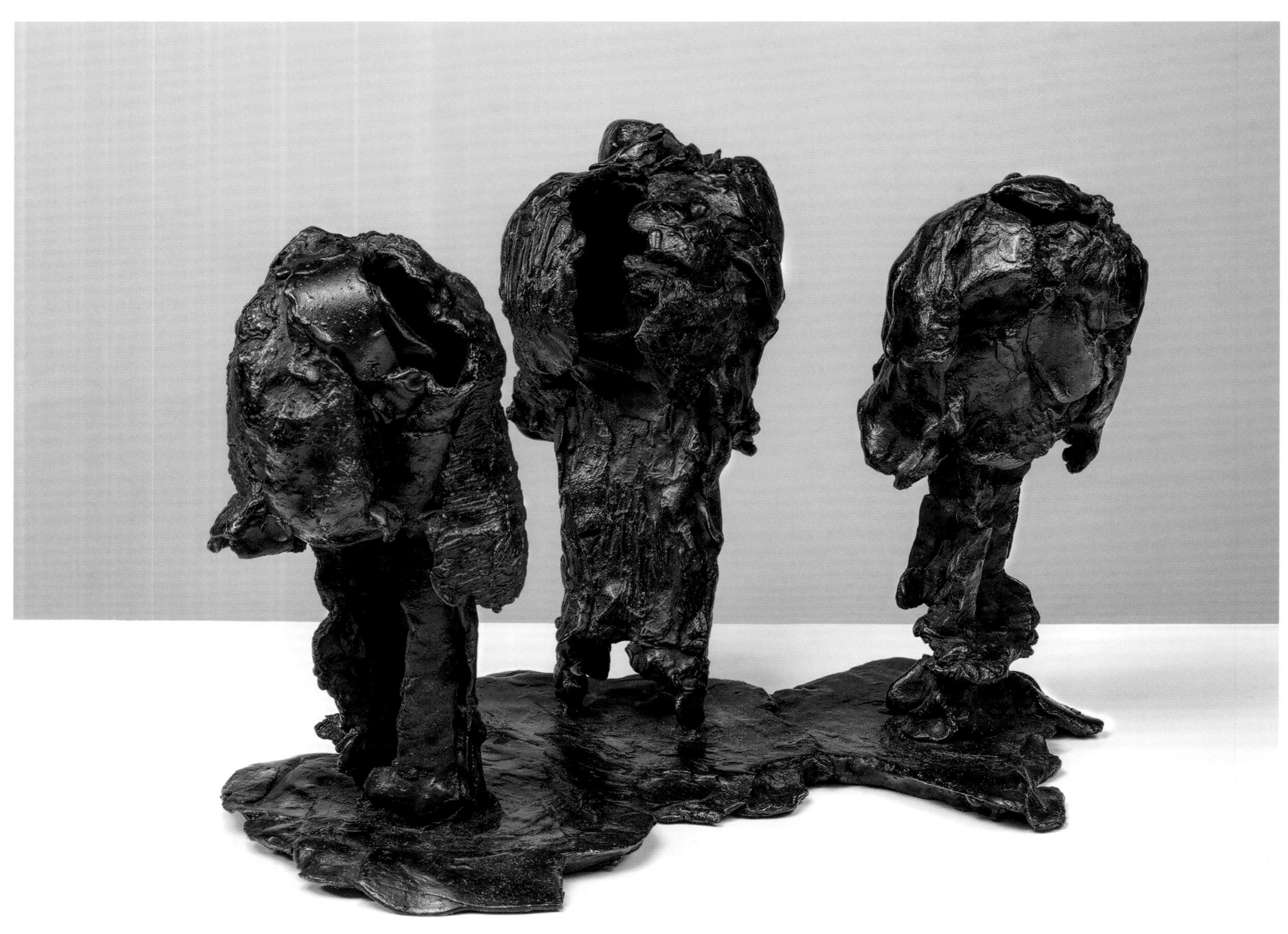

Plate 38
Luise Kaish. *Oracles III*, 1964, bronze, 9 × 14 in. (22.9 × 35.6 cm)

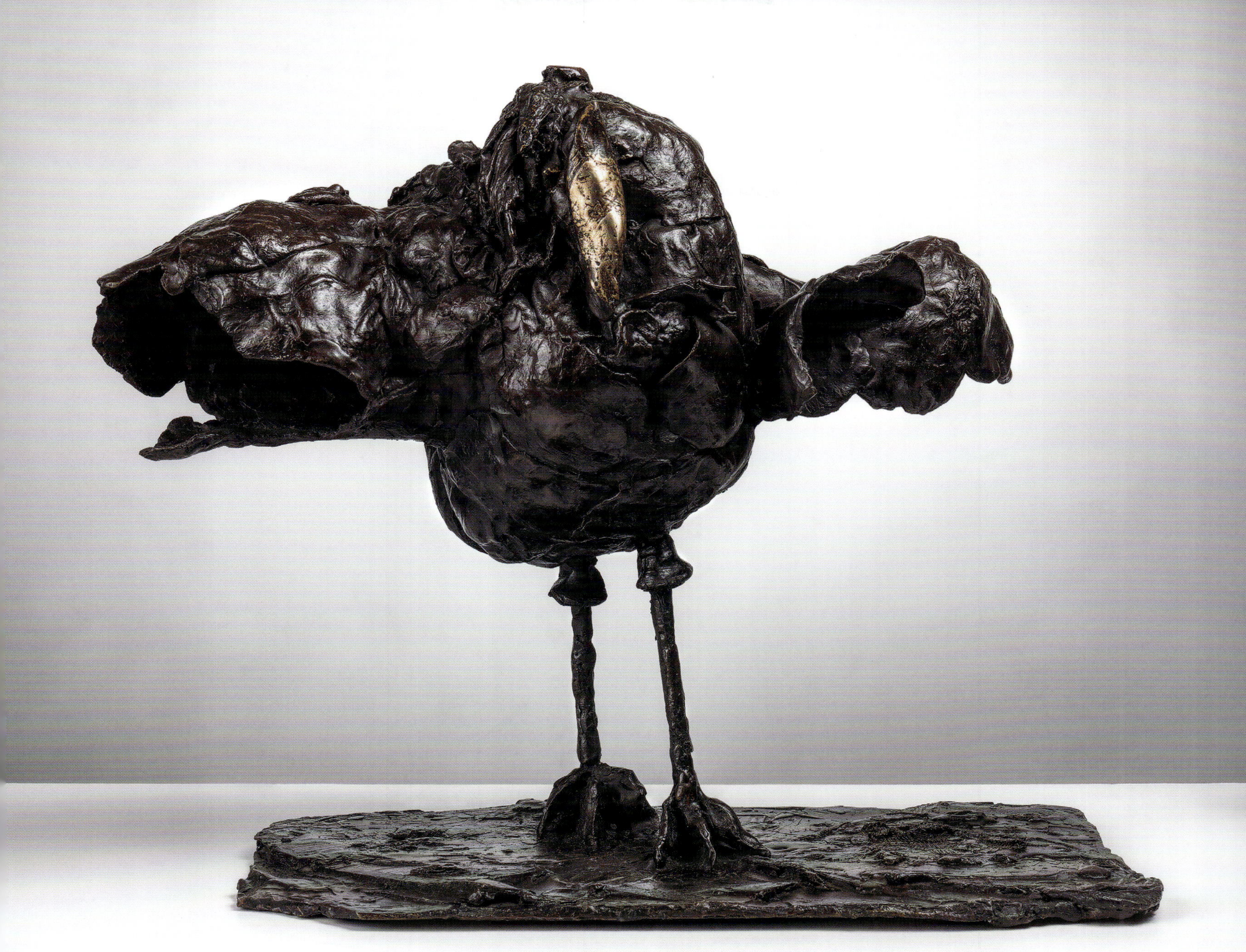

Plate 39
Luise Kaish. *Lucky Bird* (*Owl*), 1965, bronze, 15 × 18 in. (38.1 × 45.2 cm)

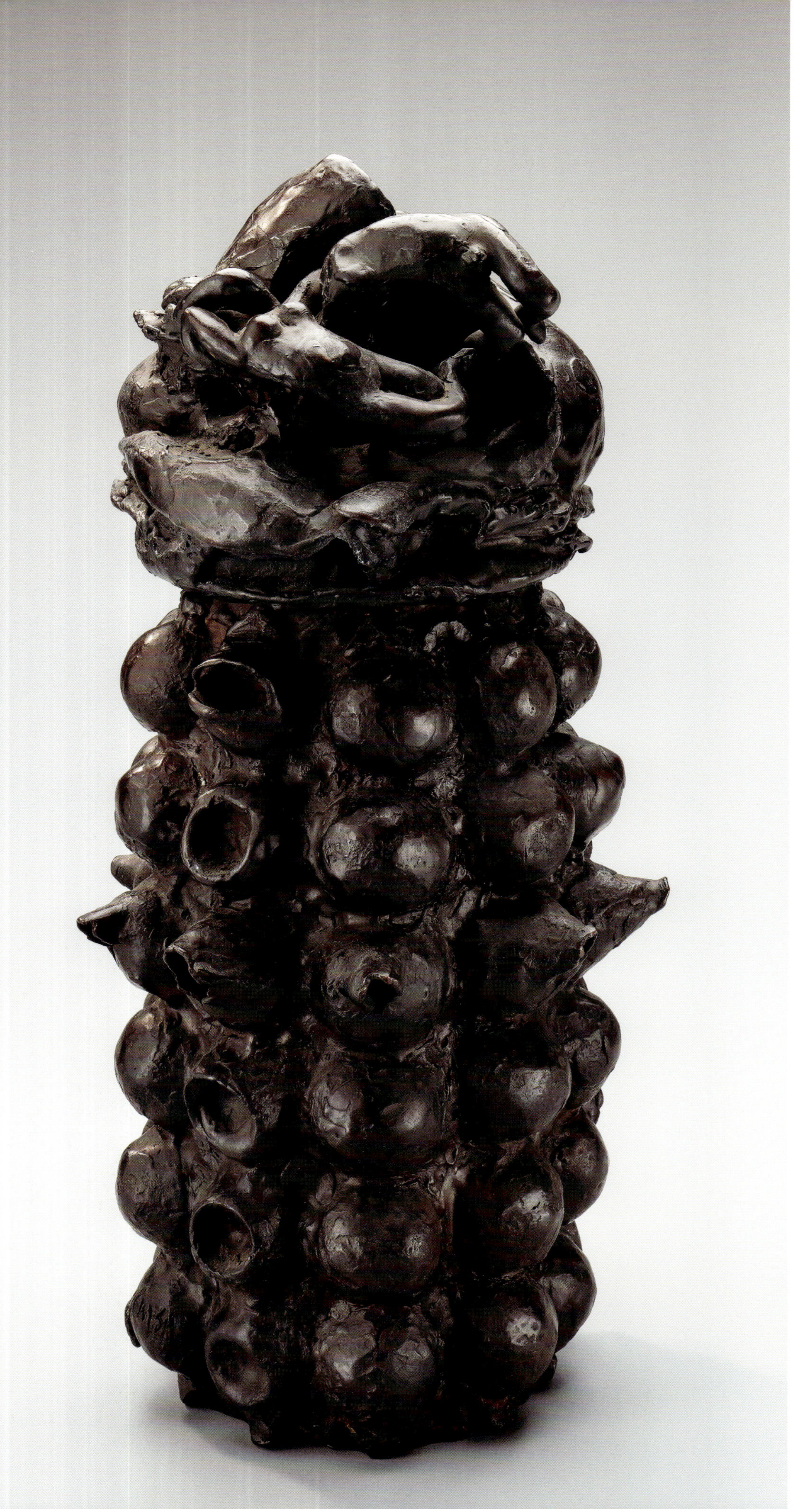

Plate 40
Luise Kaish. *Spice Container*, 1965, bronze, 16 ½ × 6 ¾ in. (41.9 × 17.1 cm). Collection, Jewish Museum, New York. Commission: Dr. and Mrs. Leo J. Koven Fund, in honor of the 50th wedding anniversary of Mr. and Mrs. Max N. Koven

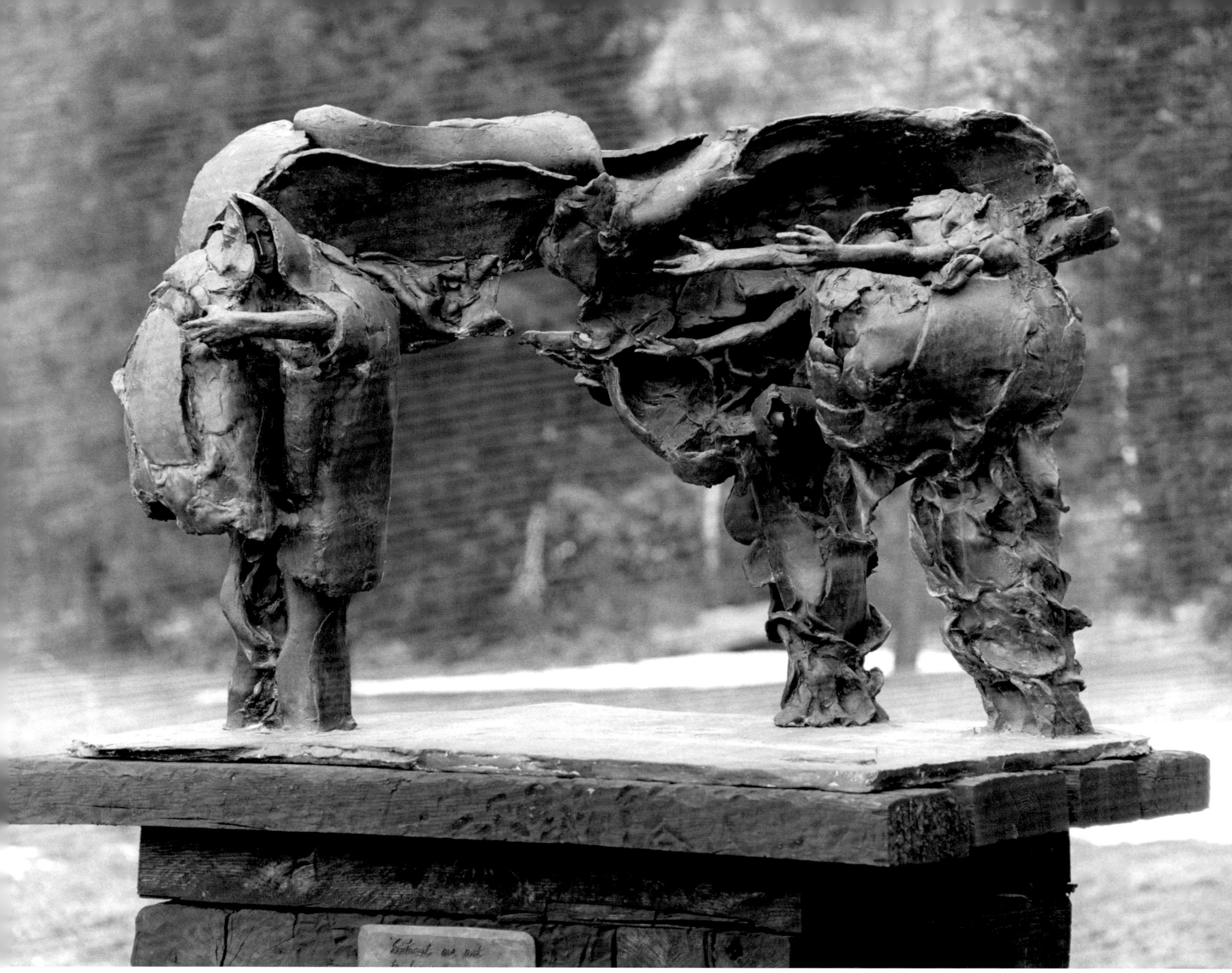

Plate 41
Luise Kaish. *Whither Thou Goest* (Ruth Rodgers Memorial),
1965, bronze, 32 × 34 × 45 in. (81.3 × 86.3 × 114.3 cm).
Temple Israel, Westport, Connecticut

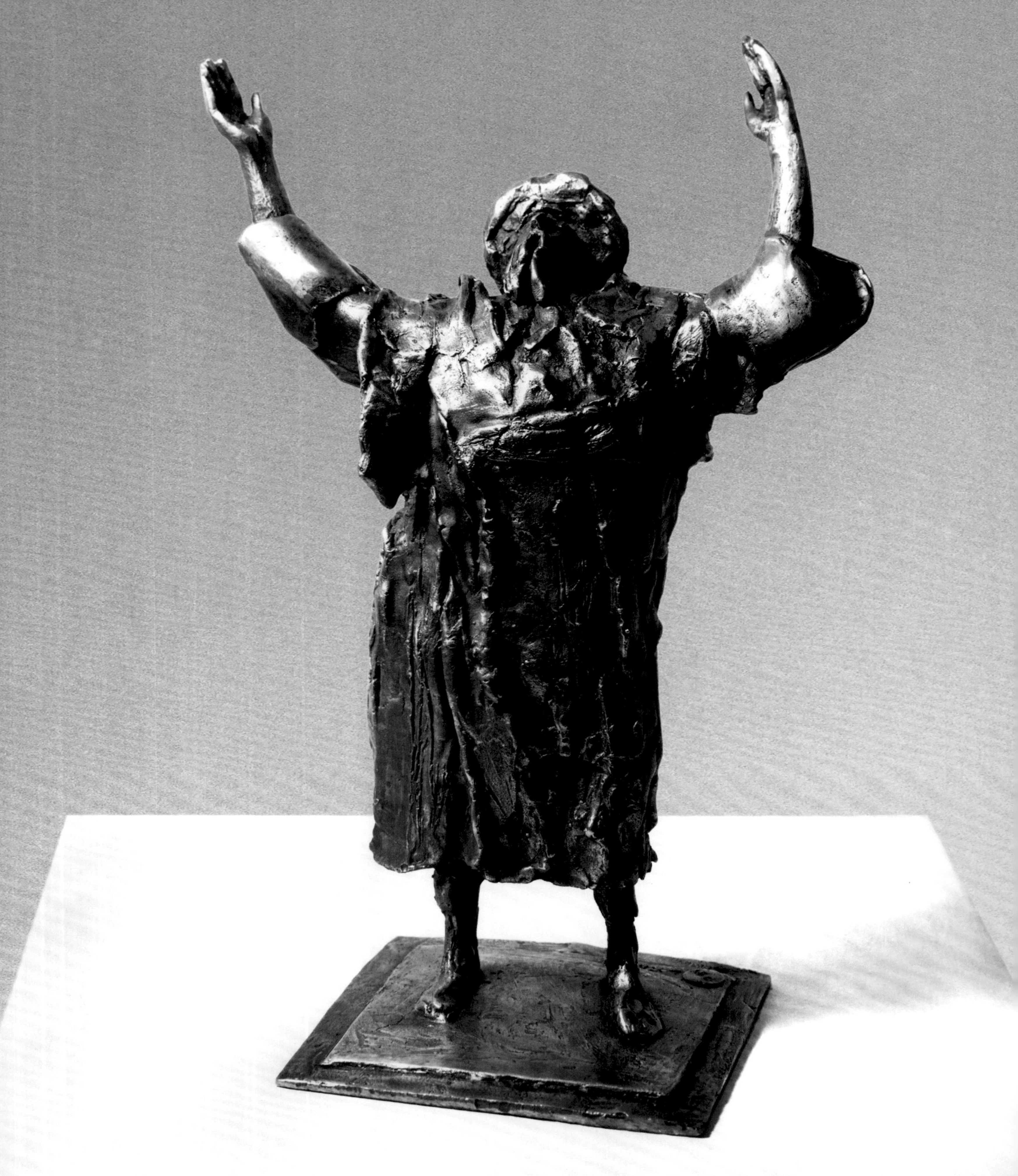

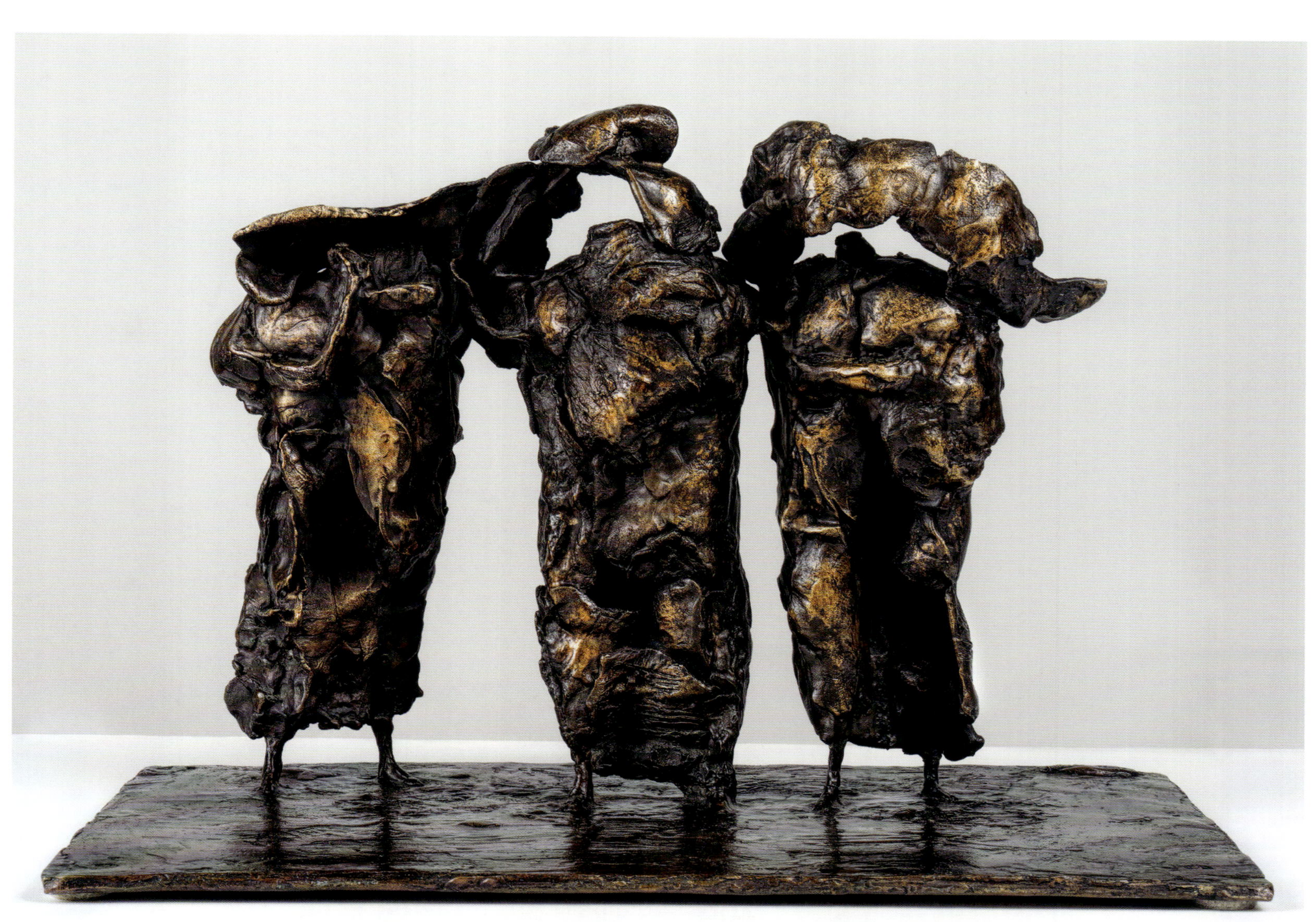

Plate 42
Luise Kaish. *Chassid*, 1966, bronze,
11 ¼ in. (28.6 cm) high. Collection,
Jewish Museum, New York, Gift of
Mr. and Mrs. Jacob Shulman

Plate 43
Luise Kaish. *Oracles I*, 1965, bronze,
10 × 14 ¼ in. (25.4 × 36.3 cm)

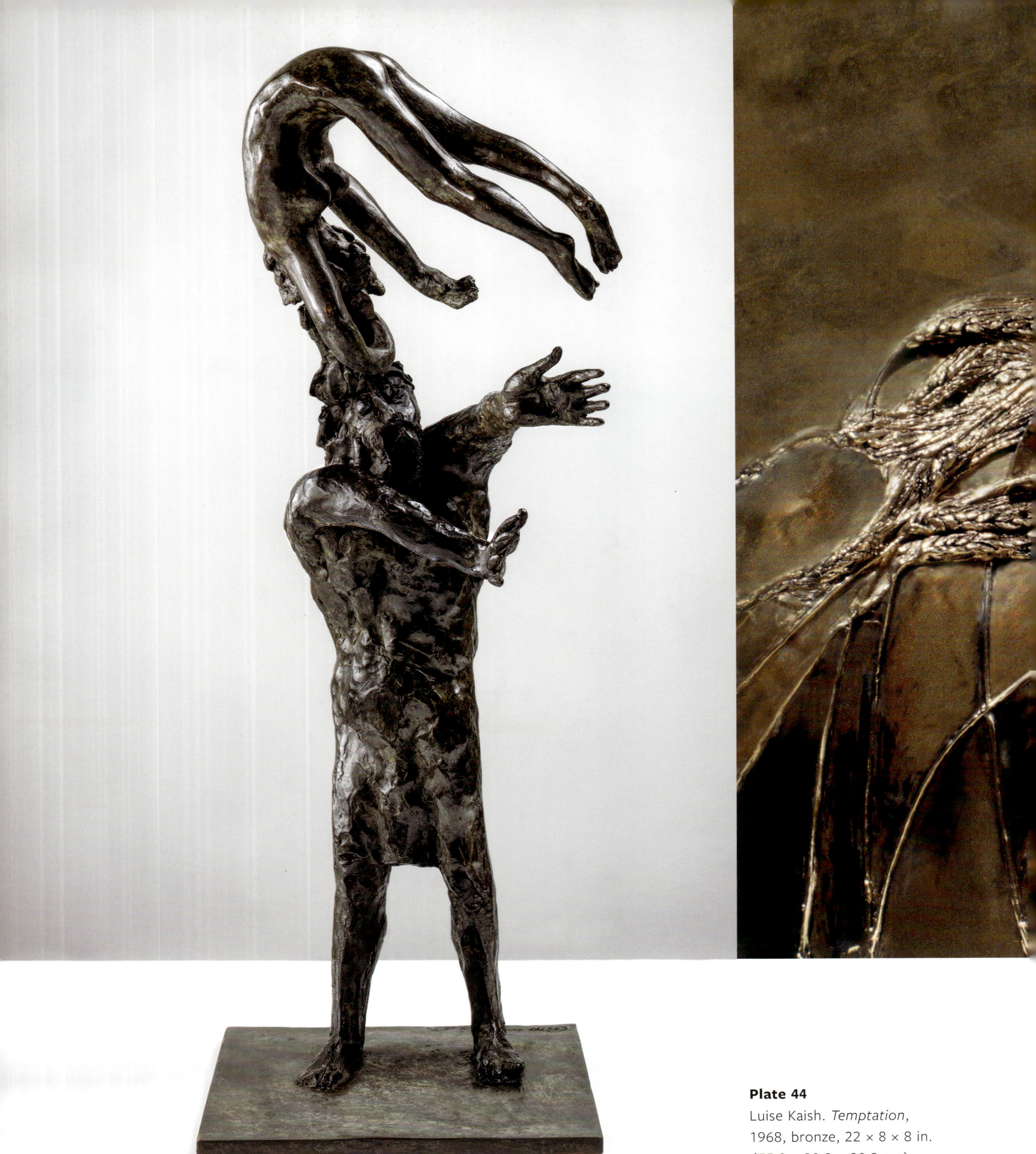

Plate 44
Luise Kaish. *Temptation*,
1968, bronze, 22 × 8 × 8 in.
(55.9 × 20.3 × 20.3 cm)

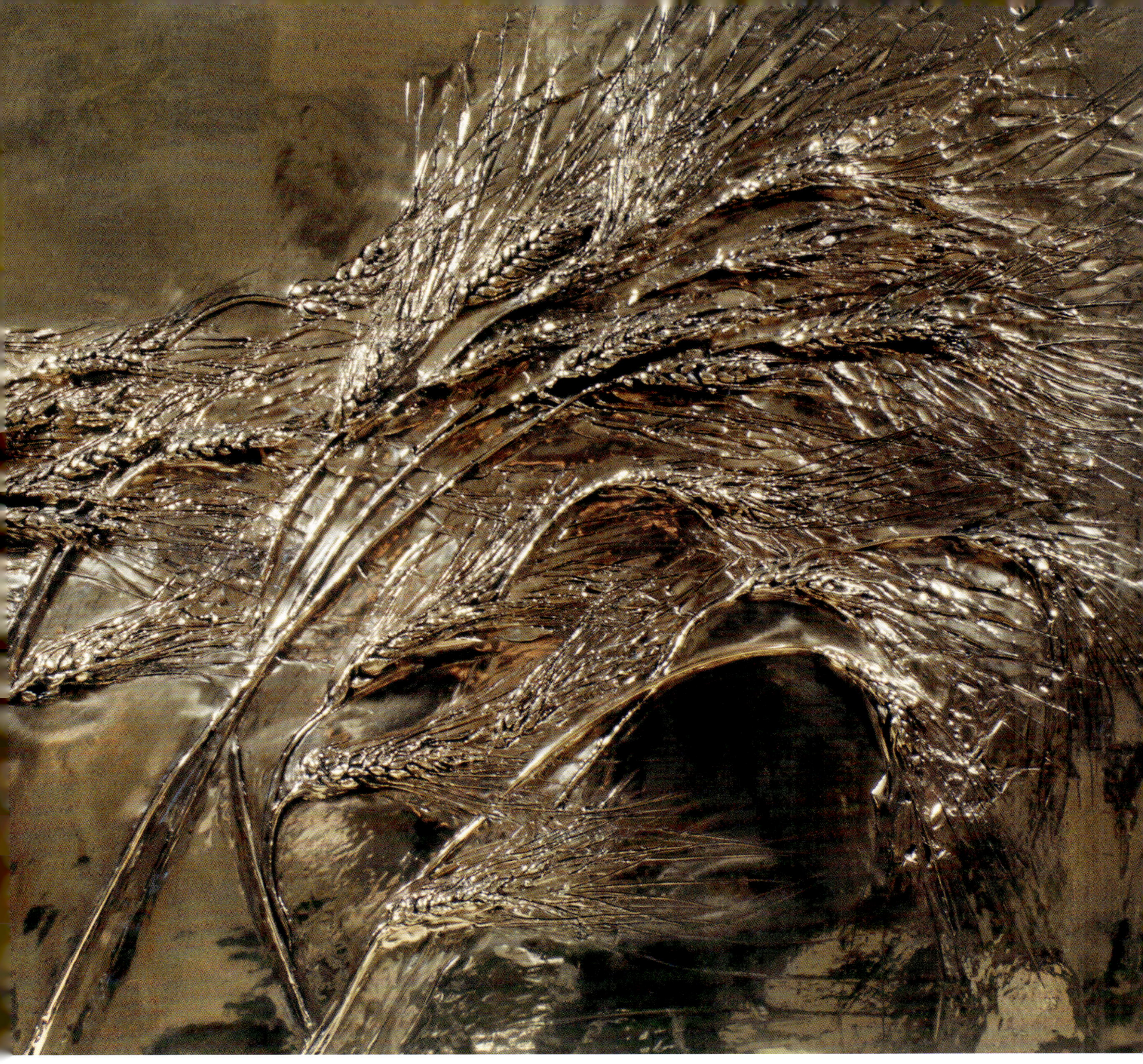

Plate 45
Luise Kaish. *Wheat*, 1968,
bronze, 18 × 25 ½ in. (45.7 × 64.8 cm)

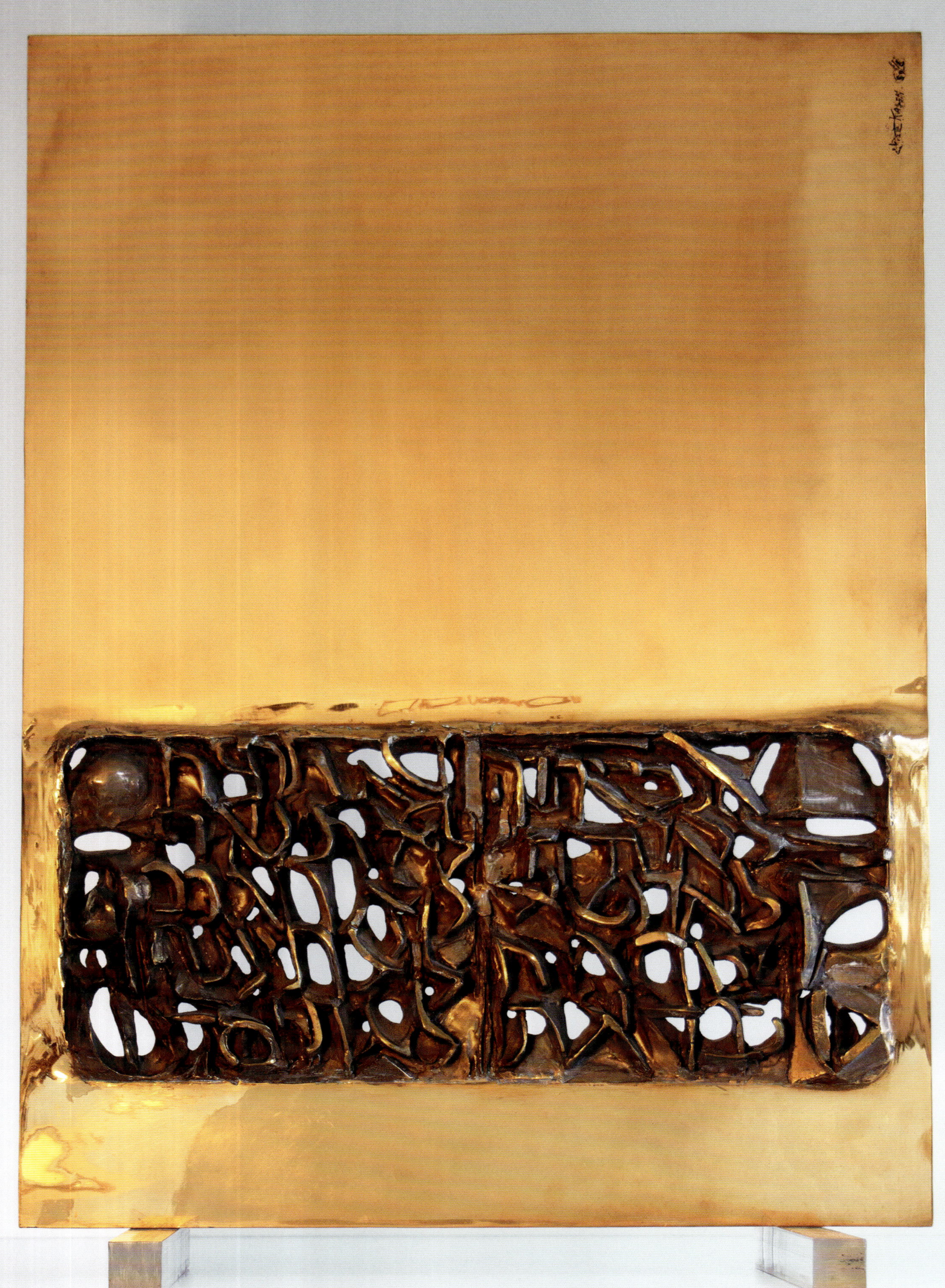

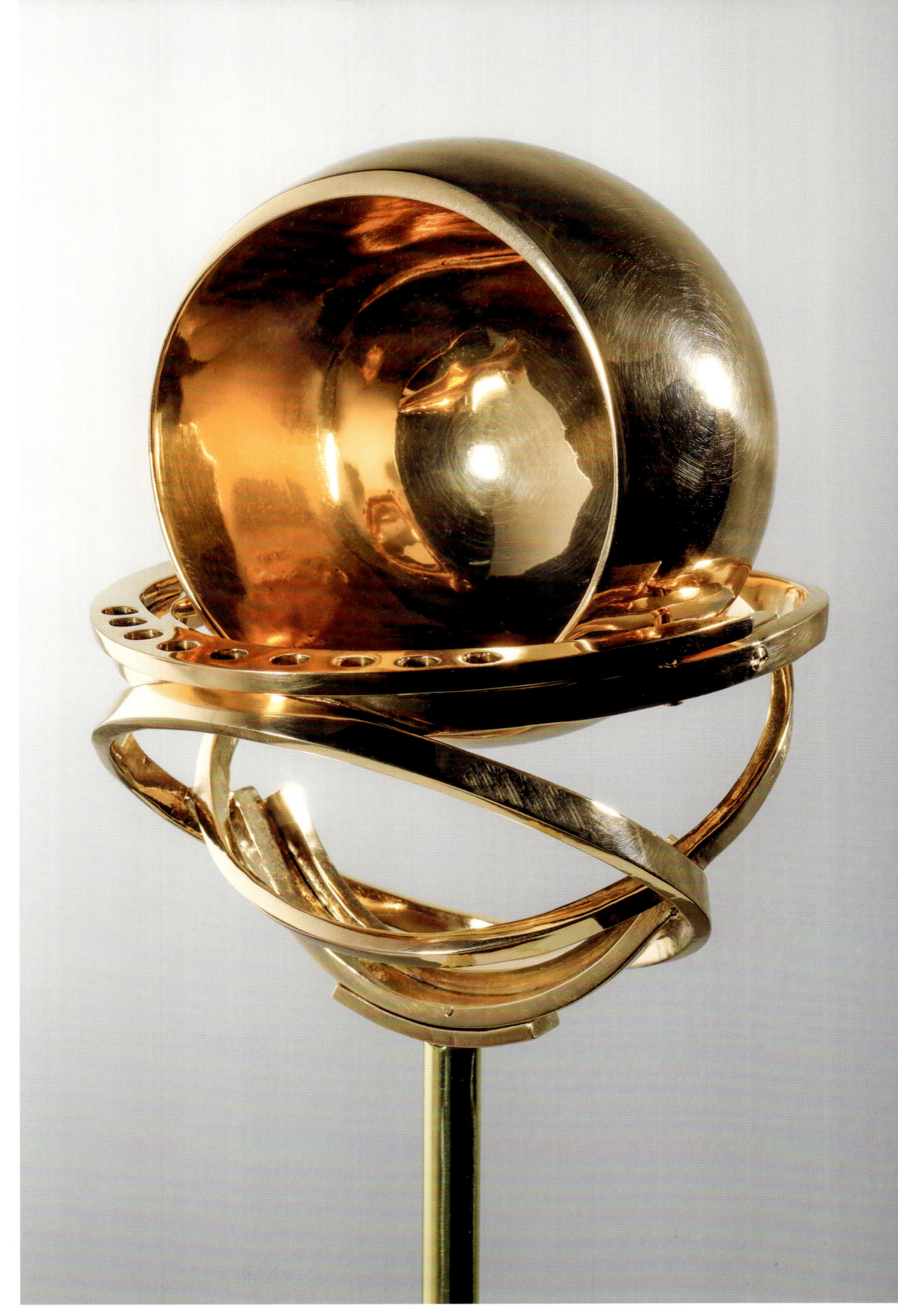

Plate 46
Luise Kaish. *Architectural Relief Study,*
Screen and Doors (*Ten Commandments*),
1968, polished bronze, 24.5 × 18 in.
(62.2 × 45.7 cm)

Plate 47
Luise Kaish. *Menorah*, 1970, Everdur bronze,
8 × 8 in. (20.3 × 20.3 cm)

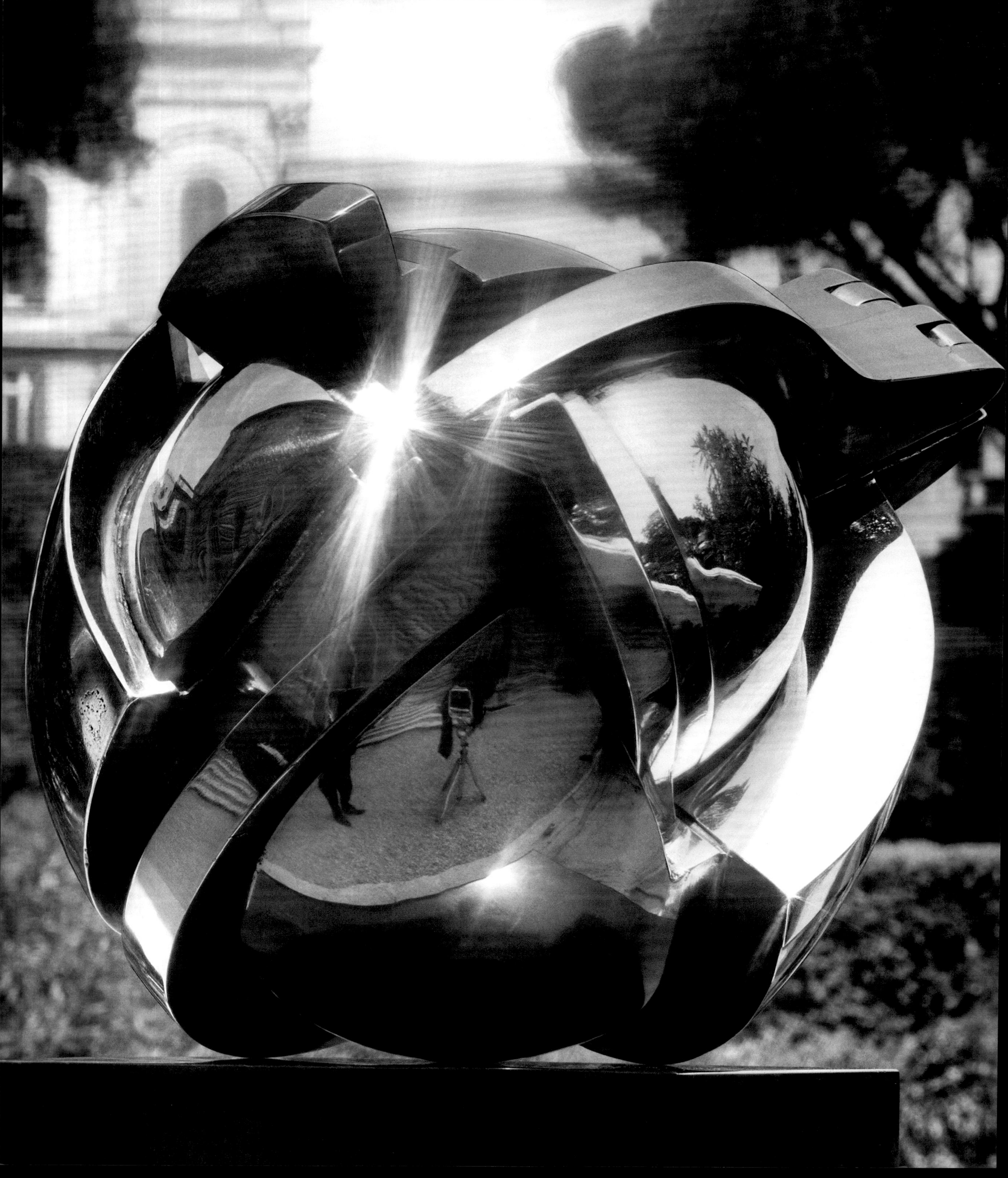

AN ART OF THE SPIRIT

Eleanor Heartney

These works raise the question of what one wants from art. They are not "controversial" and thrilling in that sense—not a kilometer's worth of sticks laid end to end on a gallery floor, not a Super Realist plastic lady or gentleman that makes the banal briefly weird. Speaking a language of our time, they deal with the timeless themes of art: nature and our relation to it, feeling and sensation as kinds of knowledge, the beauty of physical being.[1]

–Roger Lipsey

These words, written by art historian Roger Lipsey in a 1981 review of the work of Luise Kaish, pose an important question. What, indeed, do we want from art? After a century of modernism, postmodernism, and now, perhaps, post-postmodernism, the answer to this question remains remarkably unclear. Art has been construed in so many ways. It has been seen as a reflection of the world, an instrument for probing the psyche, and a thing in itself, grandly disconnected from life as we otherwise know it. Art has also been considered at various times a tool for social change, an expression of individual or group identity, and a summons to visual pleasure. But, curiously, one of the most obvious answers to the question above is also one that is rarely proposed by contemporary commentators: art has, throughout history and across cultures, offered a bridge between the worlds of matter and spirit.

Today this aspect of art tends to make people uncomfortable. The history of modern art has often been written as a flight away from the spiritual, cast here as the lair of superstition, prejudice, and unreason. Progress in art has meant progress away from anything that smacks of religious belief. Alfred Barr's famous 1936 chart of the family tree of modern art explained its evolution in terms of a mechanical schema of reaction and counterreaction.[2] Clement Greenberg's influential formalism argued for an art purged of external reference, a state epitomized for him by the drip paintings of Jackson Pollock. Harold Rosenberg, in a review of an exhibition at the Jewish Museum in New York that included Kaish's work, denied any role in avant-garde art for "ethical and religious beliefs inherited from ancient creeds." In fact, he sniffed, "In the perspective of art since the Second World War, Jewish references in a painting increase the odds against its being a good painting."[3] Even today, these attitudes linger. Despite widespread repudiation of other aspects of mid-century iconoclasm, the eviction of spirituality from serious art remains gospel for the majority of critics and curators.

But if critics, curators, and historians have been leery of the spiritual in art, artists are not. The result has been a strangely distorted account of modern and contemporary art in which artists whose own words affirm their spiritual quests are recast to fit a secular narrative. Piet Mondrian becomes a precursor to formalism and minimalism, despite his own deep interest in Theosophy. Jackson Pollock is a pioneer of "pure painting" despite his longstanding immersion in Jungian archetypes and psychology. Andy Warhol is the slick salesman of secular consumer culture despite his daily attendance at Catholic Mass.

So, it should not be surprising that Luise Kaish, whose work cannot be disentangled from her spiritual journey, should seem to fit uncomfortably into the received narrative of contemporary art. She recognized as much, remarking in a 1985 interview: "I haven't been so art-smart. At the time I was doing the work called religious, it was very 'out'. That was in the fifties and sixties. The figure was out. My feeling is that in future times when you look back you will see a world of abstraction and minimalism and Luise Kaish sticking out like a sore thumb."[4] And yet, as Roger Lipsey says, in the quotation that opens this essay, the very thing that makes Kaish's work less than trendy is the thing that makes it compelling. Her art attempts to look beneath the surface and to explore universal themes of belief, hope, existence, and our connection to the infinite. In the same interview, she noted that her work "expresses the striving of man after God, his desire to form a continuous pattern of identification with the source of all being."[5]

What is an art of the spirit? To follow this thread through Kaish's long and productive career is to realize that spiritual art is not defined by any particular style, material, form, or iconography. Nor is it necessarily art that is overtly religious (though that can be one manifestation of the spiritual in art). In her life, Kaish worked with bronze, stainless steel, stone, oil paint, ink, collage, and acrylic and created everything from monumental bronze sculptures, whimsical welded animals, and reflective stainless-steel spheres to abstract collages, luminous landscape paintings, and representations of the cosmos. The thread that unites these works is something less obvious. We might characterize it as an idea of connection that comes from the sense of the universe as a living thing. Or as Kaish put it in an article published in 1988: "My work is based on a sense of continuity. Life and death are unimportant. Despite the different conditions of our lives we meet at the end. One discovers the true impulse as one goes along."[6]

Luise Kaish came of age as an artist in mid-twentieth-century New York, a time when rupture was in the air. Avant-garde art was dominated by what Harold Rosenberg termed "The Tradition of the New" and nothing was more *retardataire* than a preoccupation with history. But while Kaish lived for a time in Greenwich Village, that hotbed of postwar bohemianism, and was acquainted with the burbling cauldron of what would be dubbed the New York school, she was not interested in making a clean break from the past. Rather, Kaish, especially during the early decades of her career, was preoccupied with affirming contemporary art's link to art history. Her studies and extensive travels affirmed for her the continuing power of tradition, and in particular art's role in articulating eternal truths and its capacity to express spiritual values. In considering her work during the 1950s and 60s, Roger Lipsey maintains that she "belonged to the centuries-old Italian figurative tradition as much as to the American avant-garde."[7] In fact, during her three-year stay at the American Academy in Rome, her husband Morton recalls that she tended to interact as much with historians, architects, musicians, and classicists as with other artists.[8]

Kaish's interest in the figurative tradition may have begun with her early studies with Ivan Meštrović, a Croation émigré and follower of Rodin who gained renown for stylized heroic sculptures dealing with mystical and religious subjects. Meštrović's arrival in Syracuse followed a series of dramatic and life-threatening experiences. An adamant anti-fascist, he was a well-established sculptor with an international reputation when he was forced, in 1943, to flee his native country to avoid execution. He sought refuge in Rome, and at the war's end refused an invitation to return, believing that Tito's communism was as antithetical to human liberty as Hitler's fascism. A chance encounter with William Pearson Tolley, Syracuse University's chancellor and president, yielded an invitation to serve as a sculpture professor at the university. It was there that Kaish studied with Meštrović as part of a small coterie of specially selected students. Along with skills in clay modeling, wood carving, and stone cutting, she became acquainted with the power of monumental sculpture.

Following graduation, Kaish embarked on her life-long travels. In Paris, she was entranced by Auguste Rodin's *Gates of Hell* (1880–1917). In Florence, she discovered the *Gates of Paradise*, a pair of gilded bronze doors created by Lorenzo Ghiberti for the Baptistery of San Giovanni. Her self-education continued with a study of Romanesque architecture and statuary, and included pilgrimages to the eleventh-century Bernward doors of the Hildesheim Cathedral in Germany, and the twelfth-century doors of the basilica of San Zeno in Verona, Italy. Such works presented complex realizations of biblical stories.

These experiences proved invaluable when Kaish embarked on her own series of ecclesiastical commissions. Works she created for Temple B'rith Kodesh in Rochester, New York; the Holy Trinity Mission Seminary in Silver Spring, Maryland; and the Beth El Synagogue Center in New Rochelle, New York, reveal her mastery of figurative storytelling in bronze. But while Kaish found herself increasingly in demand as the creator of powerful religious sculptural tableaux, she was also immersing herself in a study of the Jewish mystical tradition of the Kabbalah.[9] This pointed her in a new direction.

Based on the Zohar, a collection of written, mystical commentaries on the Torah, Kabbalah takes a variety of forms. The underlying thread is a vision of the essence of God that posits a continuum between Creator and Creation. God as the first cause is identified with light—the Zohar refers to *Ein Sof*, or "limitless light"—whose emanations create the

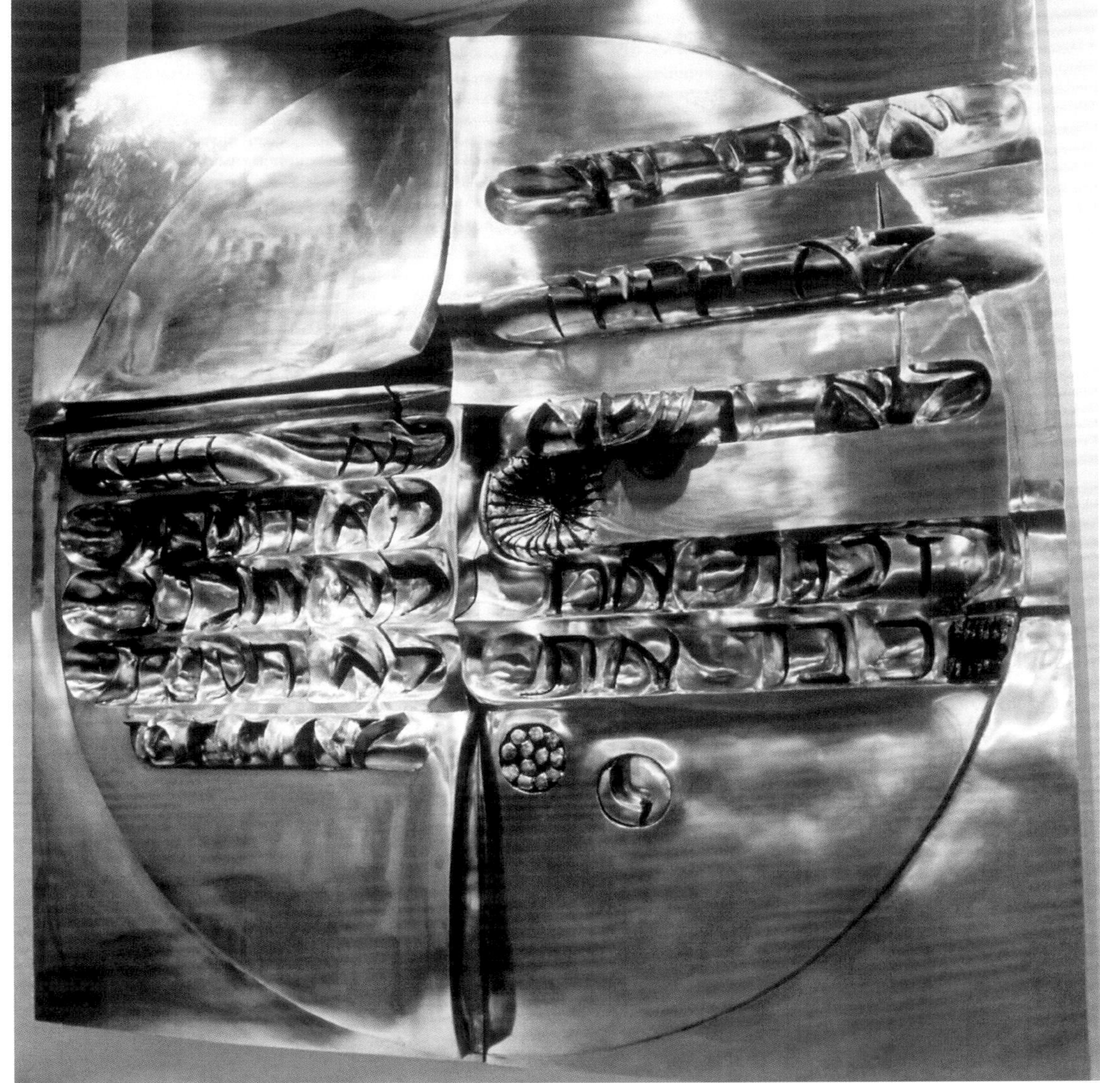

Fig. 42   Luise Kaish, *The Beth Shalom Ark Doors*, 1967–68 (see Plate 21)

multiple levels of reality. These emanations are the ten lights of the *Sefiroth,* the channel between God and Creation, each of which represents Divine Revelation in the world. *Kav* is the ray of direct light emerging from the *Ein Sof* that brings the world into existence. Kaish's study of the Kabbalah was to have a profound influence on her artistic practice.

In 1967 Kaish received a commission from Temple Beth Shalom in Wilmington, Delaware, to create a set of ark doors. As this was a Conservative congregation for whom figuration would not be appropriate, Kaish sought an abstract visual language to express the mystical truths she was exploring in the Zohar. The result was *The Beth Shalom Ark Doors* (1967–68), a breakthrough work in which she integrated the Ten Commandments with the kabbalistic concepts of *Ein Sof, Sefiroth* and *Kav* (Fig. 42). In this commission, she represented the *Ein Sof* as a large polished bronze circle that slides apart to reveal the curtain sheltering the Torah. Inscribed on the circle are the letters of the Ten Commandments based on a script found in the Dead Sea Scrolls. Linear grooves symbolize the *Sefiroth,* and small circular mounds symbolize the Twelve Tribes of Israel. Two large abstract menorahs flank the doors while a bronze form representing Eternal Light hangs above (see Pls. 21, 22).

Here a complex set of ideas is held together in an elegantly simple composition. The glowing surface of the polished bronze becomes the embodiment of the idea of light that underlies the Kabbalah. In its use of abstracted metaphors, the commission reveals Kaish's evolving sense of art's relationship to spirit. As she remarked in an interview for *Columbia Magazine* in 1985, "I think imagination, intuition, creativity come from places other than the pragmatic." She added that texts like the Kabbalah "are at the root of all imagination—that capacity to sense something beyond the obvious and to search for that something."[10]

Her husband Morton describes her spirituality in similar terms: "She somehow felt a one-ness with the Universe beyond anyone I've ever known."[11] Following the Beth Shalom commission, this sensibility became even more intense. One detects in Kaish's work a move away from literal and doctrinal expressions of religion toward a more mystical embrace of the immanence of the Divine in all things. This search subsequently took her beyond Kabbalah into an exploration of a wide range of other spiritual ideas and traditions. Her intellectual curiosity allowed her to skip across conventional boundaries between traditions and disciplines as she wove together her own vision of the spiritual.

An avid researcher and collector of ideas, Kaish left behind scores of files documenting her explorations. These provide invaluable insight into her thinking. Materials gathered in a folder labeled "Philosophy" suggest the range of the sources she sought out as she formulated her own personal belief system. There are notes about Henri Bergson's concept of the *élan vital*, the creative force responsible for growth and evolution, as well as his rejection of linear time for the experience of duration. Other reference points include the writings of Henry James, Samuel Taylor Coleridge, Heinrich Heine, and Allan Bloom; explorations of the concepts underlying Japanese aesthetics and Chinese painting; and, perhaps most significantly, definitions of the concept of animism. One handwritten text cites "animism . . . the belief that natural objects, nature phenomena and the universe itself possess souls." Another refers to "The doctrine that God is the transcendent reality of which the material universe and man are only manifestations. It involves a denial of God's personality and expresses a tendency to identify God and nature."[12] A quotation copied from the book *When the Tree Flowered: The Fictional Biography of Eagle Voice, a Sioux Indian* underscores her departure from an anthropomorphic perception of God. The passage in the book comprises a prayer to a deity who is one with nature: "Grandfather, Great Mysterious One! You have been always, and before you nothing has been. There is no one to pray to but you, you are older than all need, older than all pain and prayer. The star nations all over the heavens are yours, and yours are the grasses of the earth."[13]

Kaish's animistic turn emerged from her immersion in Kabbalah. It also seems to have fed an obsession with NASA. Her archives include folders full of articles on the 1969 moon

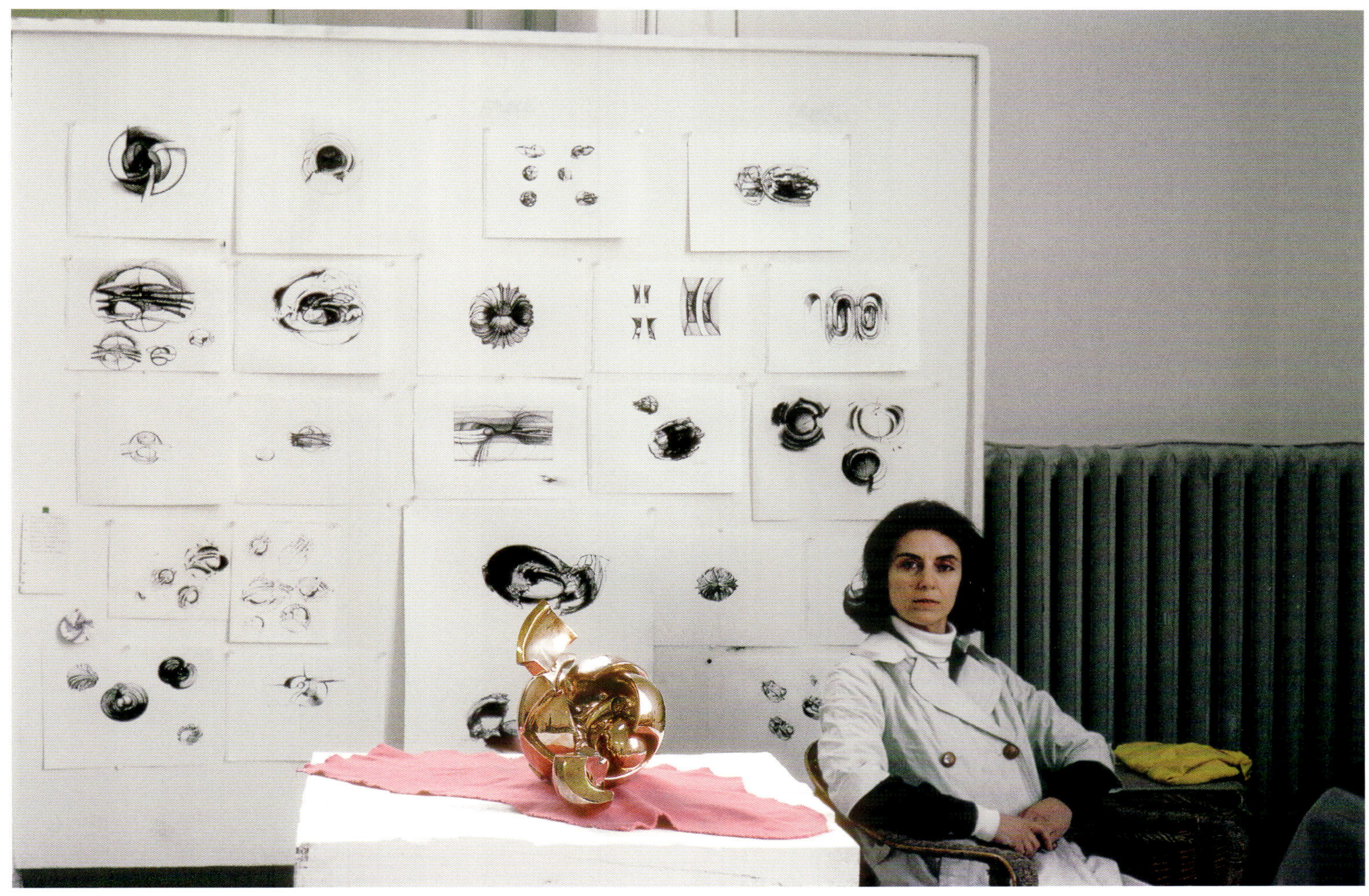

Fig. 43   Luise in her studio at the American Academy in Rome, 1970–72

landing and the space program. Morton Kaish notes that she avidly followed coverage of the space launches and expressed the desire to be buried in deep space. As she explained in a statement that appears on her memorial program, "for me the Universe holds an endless fascination. Beautiful as is this earth, I do not wish to be buried in it at death. The thought that my dust, our dust, could be mingled with the matter of star building, released in space to become part of the creative act, perhaps joined with the Almighty . . . What a fantastic journey that would be, and where I would wish to journey." On June 25, 2019, her ashes were launched, along with those of other luminaries including Skylab's Bill Pogue, *Star Trek*'s James Doohan, and planetary scientists Eugene Shoemaker and Eric De Jong, from Cape Canaveral, Florida, aboard the SpaceX Falcon Heavy rocket.[14] For Kaish, who clearly saw an "analogy between space travel and spiritual revelation," it was the ultimate expression of her belief in the oneness of the universe.[15]

Kaish's spiritual search drew her away from the literalism of figuration. She continued in her post–Beth Shalom period to create figurative works on commission, including her 1972–74 *Wall of Martyrs* for Beth El Synagogue Center in New Rochelle. However, in her personal work, she was increasingly drawn to abstraction. One indication of this is the

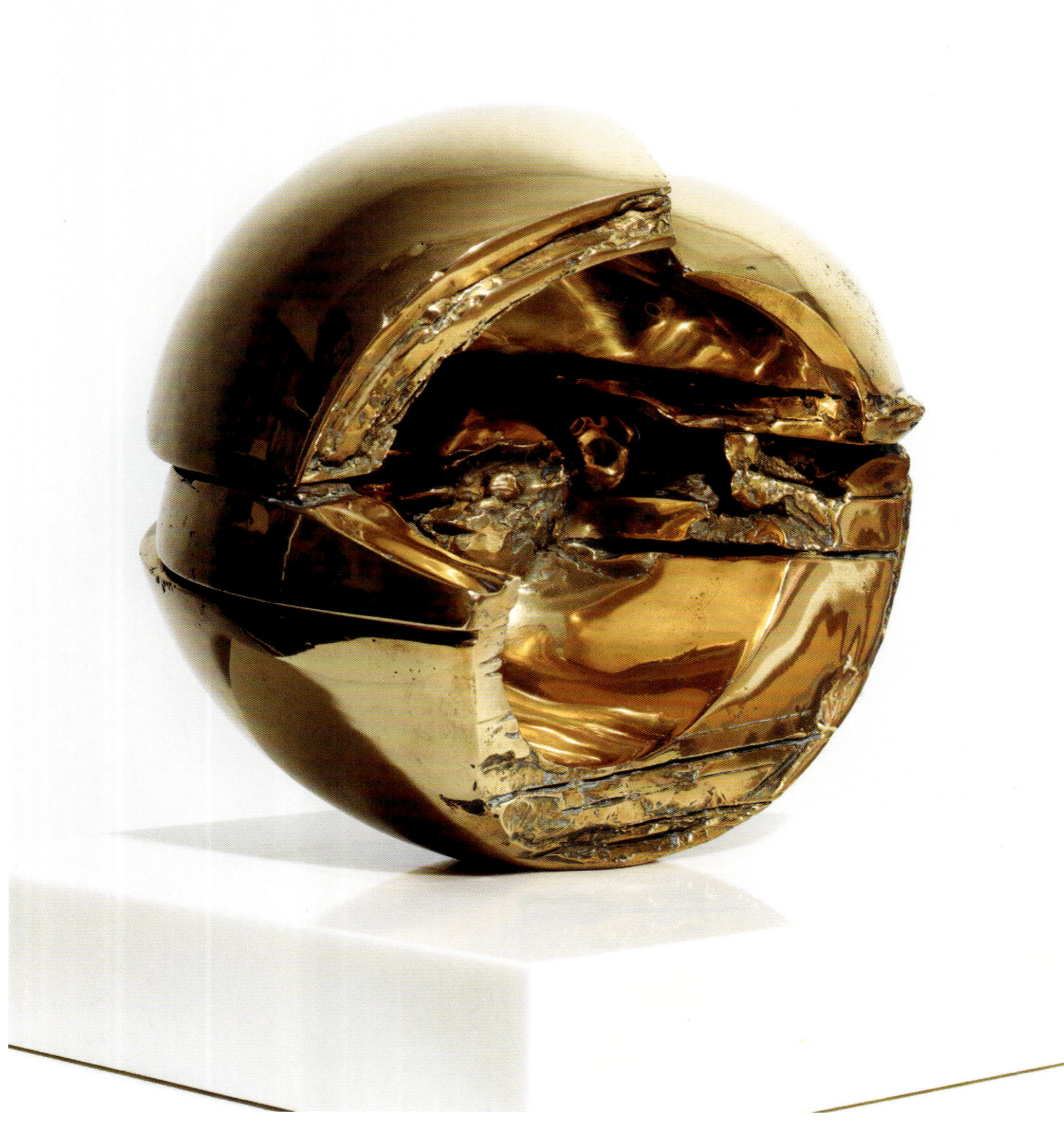

Fig. 44　Luise Kaish, *Cosmos with Unborn Planet*, 1971–72, polished bronze, 8 in. (20.3 cm) diameter

series of spherical works that she began in 1970 (Fig. 43). These abstract sculptures are created in polished aluminum, stainless steel, and bronze, and have broken reflective surfaces, which she described as seeking to "express in plastic terms a conception of form and light interacting upon each other by a series of intersecting planes . . . capable of transforming both themselves and the environment."[16] Titles such as *In the Beginning, Cosmos with Unborn Planet* (Fig. 44), *Star Void*, and *Sphere* (Fig. 45) indicate Kaish's efforts to dissolve the boundaries between nature, religion, and science. She also created a series of stainless steel works she titled *Voyages*, whose curving planar surfaces capture and distort the visible world around them. As with the spheres, light glances off the polished surfaces, replacing the sense of mass with a shimmering play of reflections (Pls. 49, 50).

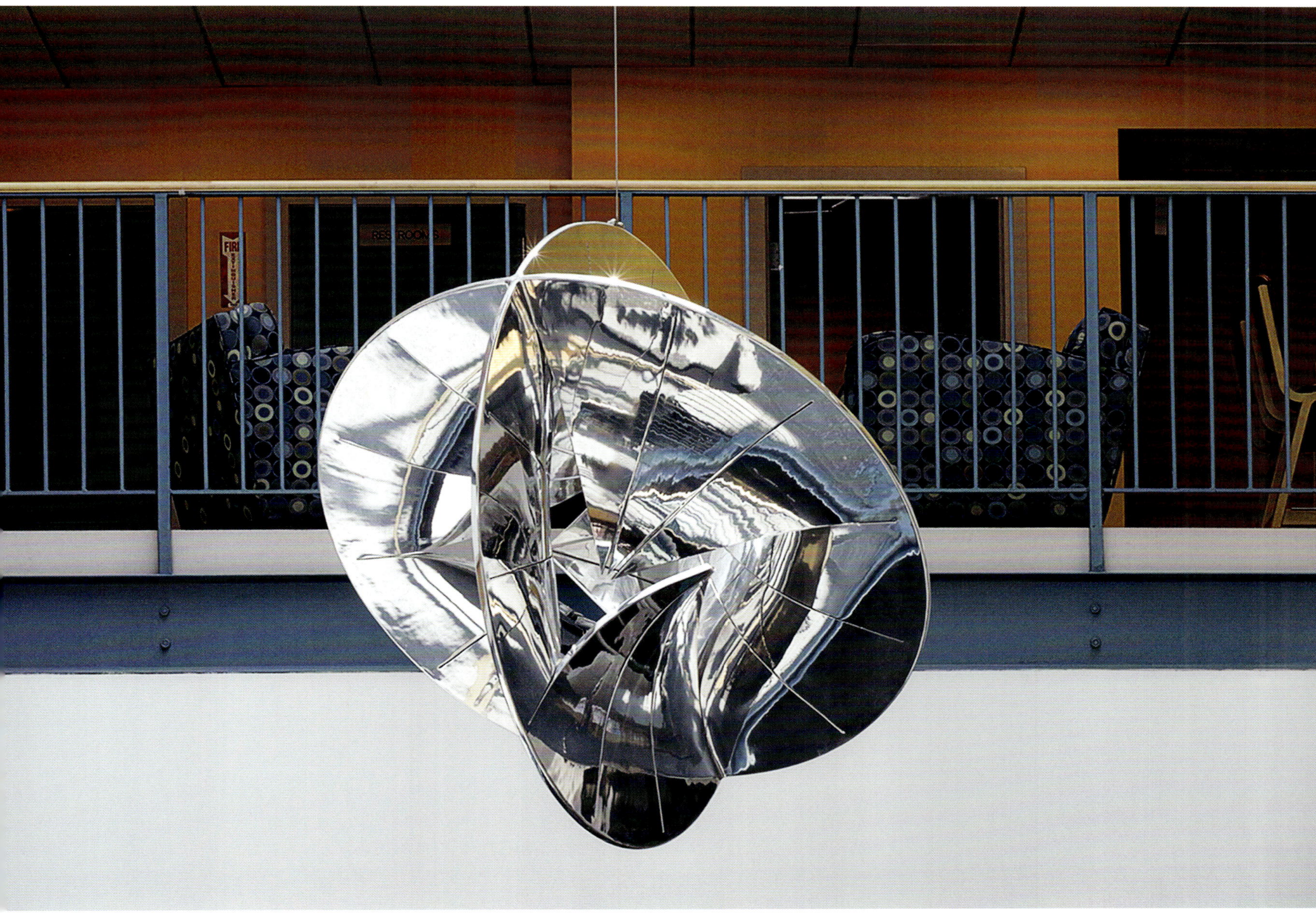

Fig. 45　Luise Kaish, *Sphere*, 1976 (see Plate 53). Collection, Hood Museum, Dartmouth College

In her notes on these works, Kaish mused, "light is symbolically identified with animism, the belief in the soul as spirit, the breath of life. It is also one of the most affecting and real plastic forces a sculptor must comprehend for what we really see form by is light."[17]

In using the language of abstraction to express her spiritual explorations, Kaish was very much in sync with what author Charlene Spretnak has termed "the spiritual dynamic in modern art."[18] Reading against the grain of conventional histories that emphasize the formalist underpinnings of the emergence of abstraction in twentieth-century art, Spretnak maintains instead that spirituality was the driving force behind modernism. Her examination of key figures like Gauguin, Van Gogh, Kandinsky, Malevich and Klee reveals the depth of their spiritual concerns. Spretnak offers an alternative history of modern art that is in keeping with the ideas explored in a groundbreaking 1986 exhibition titled *The Spiritual in Art: Abstract Painting 1890–1985*. Organized by Maurice Tuchman for the Los Angeles County Museum of Art, that show argued that "the genesis and development of abstract art were inextricably tied to spiritual ideas current in Europe in the late nineteenth and early twentieth centuries."[19]

Spretnak and Tuchman maintain that modernist abstraction was born of a desire to transcend the material, visible world at a time when mechanistic theories of science and labor were threatening to reduce human life to what Kandinsky referred to as "the nightmare of materialism."[20] This is a history that was largely suppressed by mid-century critics like Clement Greenberg and Harold Rosenberg and is only recently gaining widespread recognition. As Roger Lipsey has noted, "Abstract art was born a religious and metaphysical art, and only later came to seem a bodily thing when its spiritual aspiration was ignored or misunderstood."[21]

Evidence of the spiritual dynamic has long been hiding in plain sight. There are obvious examples, including a plethora of commissions by major artists for sacred spaces: Matisse's Rosary Chapel (1949–51, Vence, France); Barnett Newman's *Stations of the Cross* (1958–66, National Gallery of Art, Washington, D.C.); the Rothko Chapel (1964–67, Houston, Texas); and Adolph Gottlieb's Torah ark curtain for the Congregation B'nai Israel synagogue, Millburn, New Jersey (1950–51, now in the Jewish Museum, New York). Such works could once have been (and often were) dismissed as one-offs—works created by artists whose work more generally aspires to a secularized sublime; it is much clearer today that the spiritual concerns of these artists were central to their work. As Rothko once remarked, "The people who weep before my pictures are having the same religious experience I had when I painted them."[22] But moving beyond the literal is the question of how spiritual concerns shape work that is not overtly symbolic. Here, again, the mainstream tendency has been to dismiss or even ridicule spiritual readings of abstract work. Harold Rosenberg's remark in the aforementioned review of the Jewish Museum show is exemplary. He says, "Luise Kaish's circular construction in polished aluminum is no more Judaized by being 'The Cabalistic Sphere' than it would be Germanized by being entitled 'Nietzsche: The Eternal Return.'"[23]

Such remarks date from an era when the theories of the critic trumped the words of the artist. Today commentators are more prone to acknowledge artists' own descriptions of their intentions. The growing acceptance of art's spiritual dimension is also aided by the current fracturing of art-world consensus in the wake of globalism, multiculturalism, and feminism. Artists who were once considered outliers are finally getting their due. The explicitly spiritual concerns in the work of artists like Hilma af Klint and Hyman Bloom may have once made critics squeamish; now they and other artists are being awarded full-scale retrospectives, and their writings and concerns are seen as integral to their work.

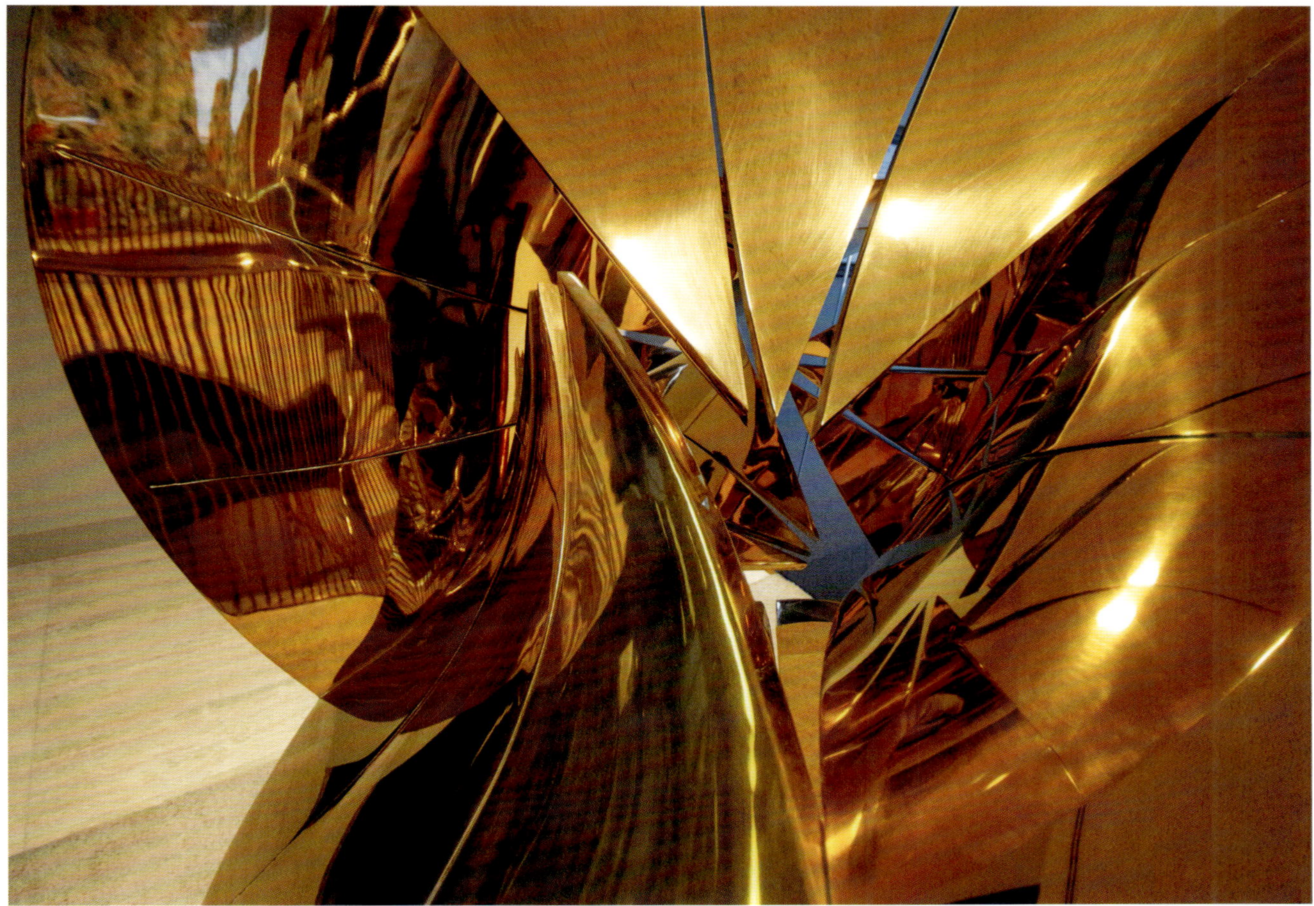

Fig. 46   Luise Kaish, *La Lumière* (detail), 1975–76 (see Plate 57)

Meanwhile, discussions of the work of artists long in the spotlight—such as Anselm Kiefer, Agnes Martin, and Bill Viola—now routinely examine their spiritual interests.

Kaish further articulated the ideas emerging from the Beth Shalom *Ark Doors* and the spheres and *Voyages* in subsequent commissions like *Eternal Light* (1974; see Pl. 28), created for Hebrew Union College in Jerusalem, and *La Lumière* (1975–76; Pl. 57), commissioned by the Continental Grain company in New York. Both expanded on the spherical form to explore the spiritual significance of light. *Eternal Light* is a polished bronze circular form that expresses the Twelve Tribes of Israel as sections of the circle pulling up from the center. As Morton Kaish notes, "each [is] subtly different, each reflecting its own burst of light, and it becomes a work literally blazing with energy."[24] *La Lumière* presents a pair of intersecting circular forms that, like *Eternal Light*, pull out from the center. Again, the movement of light is crucial. As Kaish herself described, "The polished segments reflect back on each other, and as the sculpture moves, they create a series of square and triangular images (Fig. 46). The key is that it reflects itself as well as what is around it. Life and art are always revealing themselves. . . . The concept is an ancient one. Light has held mysterious qualities in all cultures and for all ages. One finds references to sun and light in literature and the arts. This sculpture is a crystallization of that idea. . . . Light is the source of all living things."[25]

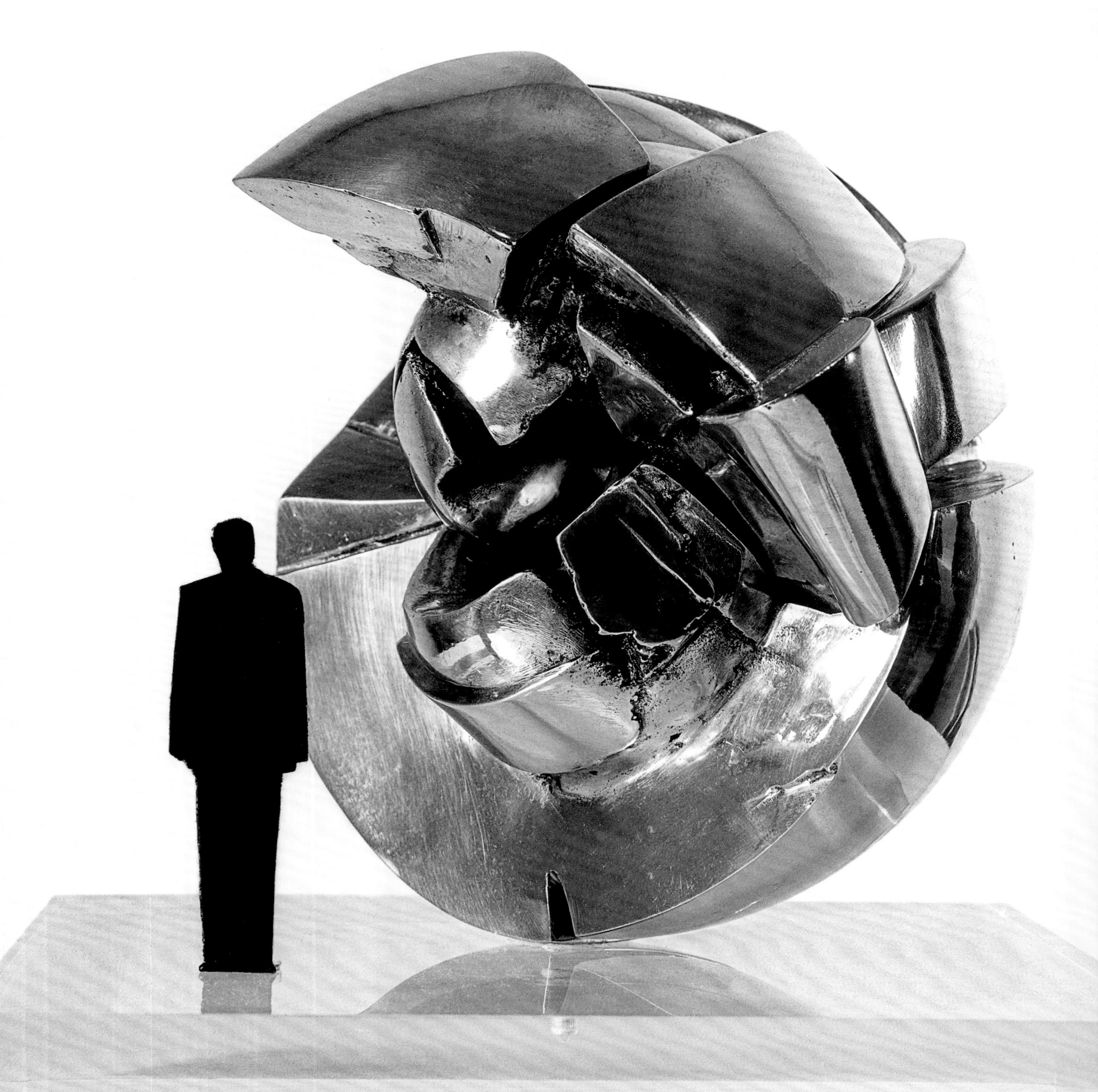

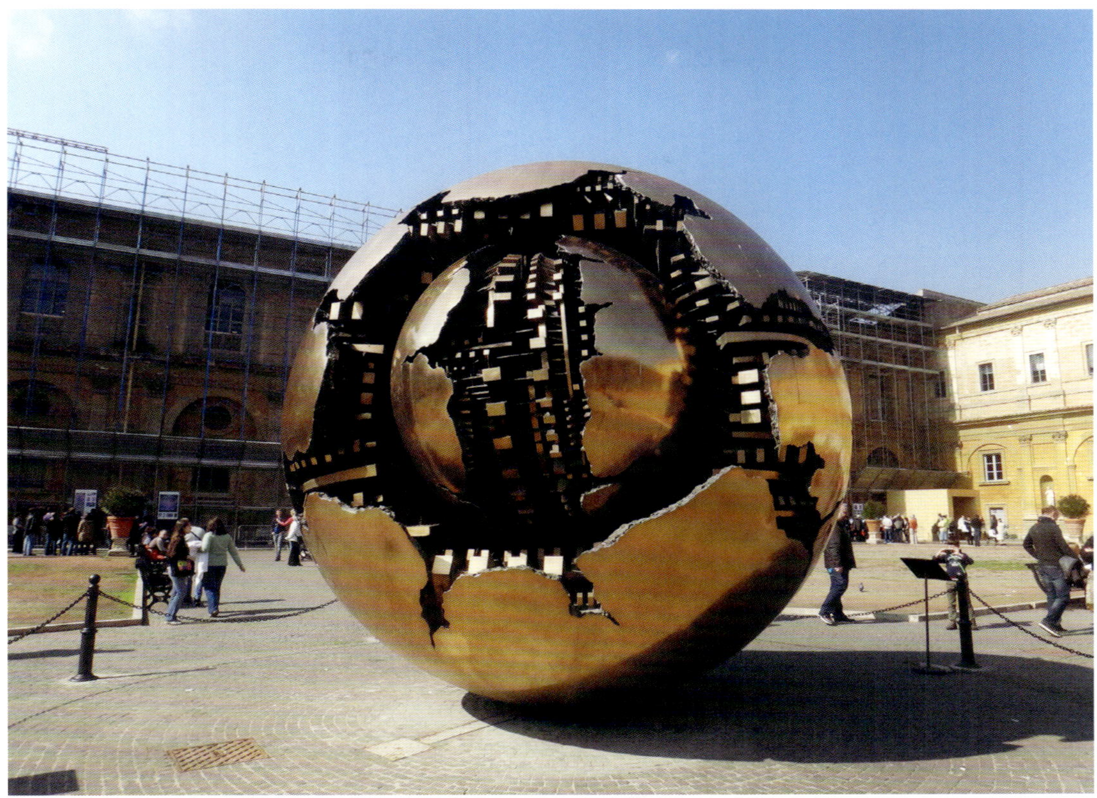

Fig. 48   Arnaldo Pomodoro, *Sphere within Sphere*, circa 1963, bronze, 13 ft. (4 m) diameter, Cortile della Pigna, Vatican City, Italy

Works like these reveal Kaish's connections to kindred spirits working out of other belief systems. She belongs to a group of contemporary artists who explore a kind of sacred geometry and share a sense of the mystical continuity between nature, humanity, and the cosmos. Most obvious, perhaps, are links between her spherical sculptures and the works of Italian sculptor Arnaldo Pomodoro, with whom she shared a foundry during her stay in Rome (Fig. 47). Morton Kaish was told by long-time resident sculptor Herzl Emanuel that the two of them met at the foundry and shared a great mutual respect and admiration. Pomodoro's *Sfera con sfera* (*Sphere within Sphere*) series, like Kaish's spheres, involves the breakdown of the spherical shape and the play of light across the spheres' polished bronze surfaces (Fig. 48). Pomodoro's spheres, one of which is installed on the grounds of the Vatican, are characterized by a tension between the idealized spherical form and jagged crevices that seem to be eating it away from within. He has described his concept in terms that suggest a darker version of Kaish's reflective eternal light and her *In the Beginning* series: "The sphere is a marvelous object, from the world of magic, wizards, whether it is of crystal or bronze, or full of water . . . It reflects everything around it, creating such contrasts that it sometimes is transformed, becoming invisible, leaving only its interior, tormented and corroded, full of teeth."[26]

A more celebratory version of the sphere appears in the work of James Lee Byars, a flamboyant performance and installation artist who returned frequently to the sphere as a symbol of cosmic perfection (Fig. 49). Balls of various materials and sizes, many of

Fig. 47   Luise Kaish, *Untitled, New Planet*, circa 1971, bronze, 10 in. (25.4 cm) diameter

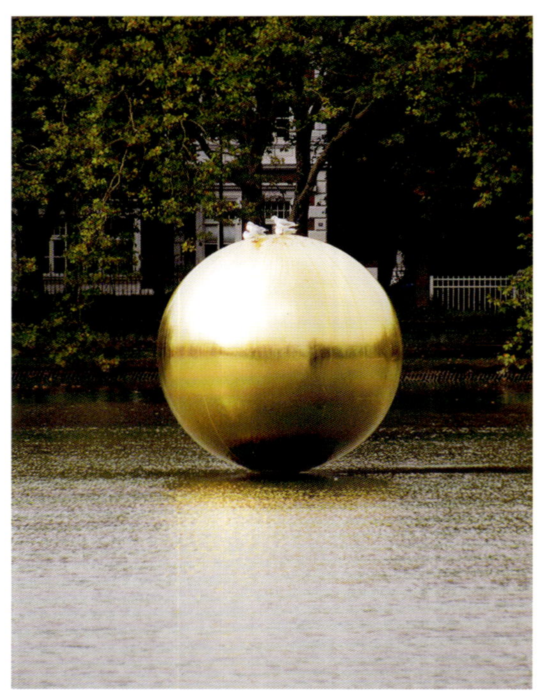

Fig. 49 James Lee Byars, *Golden Sphere*,
1992, plaster with gold leaf, 10 ft. (3 m) diameter.
Schloss Benrath, Düsseldorf, Germany, 2010

them gilded, appear frequently in his work, often presented in shrine-like settings, which reflect a personal philosophy informed by his interest in such diverse spiritual traditions as Japanese Noh theater, platonic forms, medieval alchemy, and the writings of figures such as T. S. Eliot and Ludwig Wittgenstein. In one of his most famous performances he staged his own "departure from the world" within a gold-leafed room with a glass sarcophagus and five crystals. Seen in this context, Byars' spheres suggest an unreachable and untouchable state beyond human experience, and perhaps reachable only by death.

A third version of sacred geometry appears in the works of Anish Kapoor, an Indian-born British artist whose lexicon includes spheres, domes, pyramids, and columns. In his sculptures and installations these forms are transformed and dematerialized through materials including powder pigment, red wax, and polished stainless steel. Much of Kapoor's work revolves around the dichotomy between presence and absence and form and void. This is made manifest in his Chicago *Cloud Gate* (2006), a huge elliptical archway of highly polished stainless steel that becomes an undulating reflection of its surroundings, as well as in quieter works involving pigment-filled circular cuts in walls or stone that seem to sink back into infinity (Fig. 50). Musing on the slippage between interior and exterior in his work, Kapoor has remarked, "What is inside it is as profoundly mysterious as what is in the cosmos and in many ways identical to it. Body, spirit and cosmos are both poetically potent and interdependent."[27]

Throughout the 1970s Kaish continued to create sculptures and sculptural commissions, but she also, increasingly, turned her attention to two-dimensional works. These tend to have less obvious religious content, using other means to express her vision of a world filled with spirit and centered on the mystical significance of light. There are, for instance, her burntworks, in which she was, in a sense, painting with fire, piecing together singed fragments of canvas in compositions that talk about elements consumed and transformed. Throughout the 1970s and into the early 1990s she worked on a number of collage series, including the abstract multimedia *Portals* (see Figs. 63, 65; Pls. 72, 73, 76). These hark back thematically to the ecclesiastical doors of her figurative commissions, while also referencing the notion of a threshold between the worlds of matter and spirit. Kaish characterized a series of collages titled *Lovers Houses* as fantasy houses with wings as if to fly away (see Figs. 61, 62, 64; Pls. 75, 78–81). Many contain vertical or horizontal stripes that she

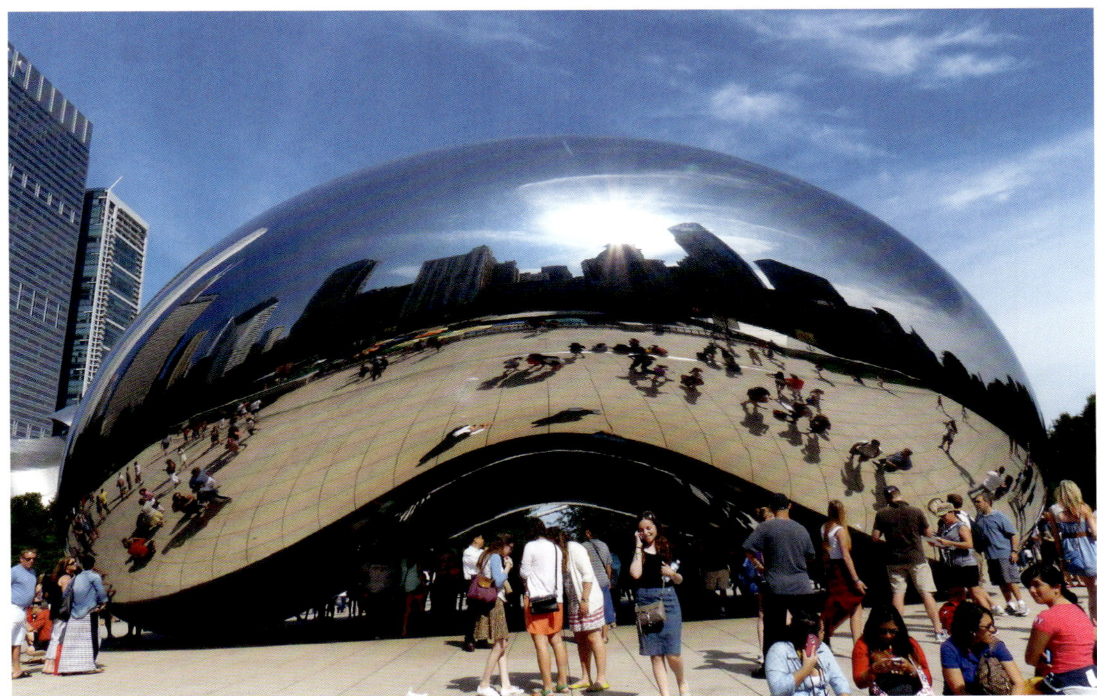

Fig. 50 Anish Kapoor, *Cloud Gate*, 2006, stainless steel, 33 × 42 ft × 66 ft. (10 × 13 × 20 m),
Chicago Millennium Park, Chicago, Illinois

related to the breaks in her spheres. Both the collages and the spheres, she points out,
present geometric shapes designed so light passes through their centers.[28] There is also
Broadway Babies, a series of colorful compositions inspired by the flamboyant characters
she saw walking down the streets of upper Manhattan (see Pl. 77). In 1981 she had an exhibition of collages at the Staempfli Gallery. In the exhibition brochure she described the
works in terms that tie them to her longtime concern with nature, space, and spirit, noting,
"I like to think of these landscape collages as brief poems, as worlds in themselves, where
through the very smallness of the window, we can glimpse the stars of the universe."[29]

In the 1990s and early 2000s, with her health failing, Kaish stayed close to home, creating a series of luminous landscapes based on her secret spot in Riverside Park. In 2012,
she also began creating maquettes for a series of axonometric bronze reliefs (Fig. 51; see
Pls. 101–3). These, Morton Kaish reports, were intended as culminations of her ideas about
light, spirit, and geometry.[30] Sadly, they were never realized as the pierced three-dimensional
relief sculptures she intended.

We return to Roger Lipsey's question: What do we want from art? For Kaish there
was never any doubt. In a *Columbia Magazine* interview from 1985 she maintained that art

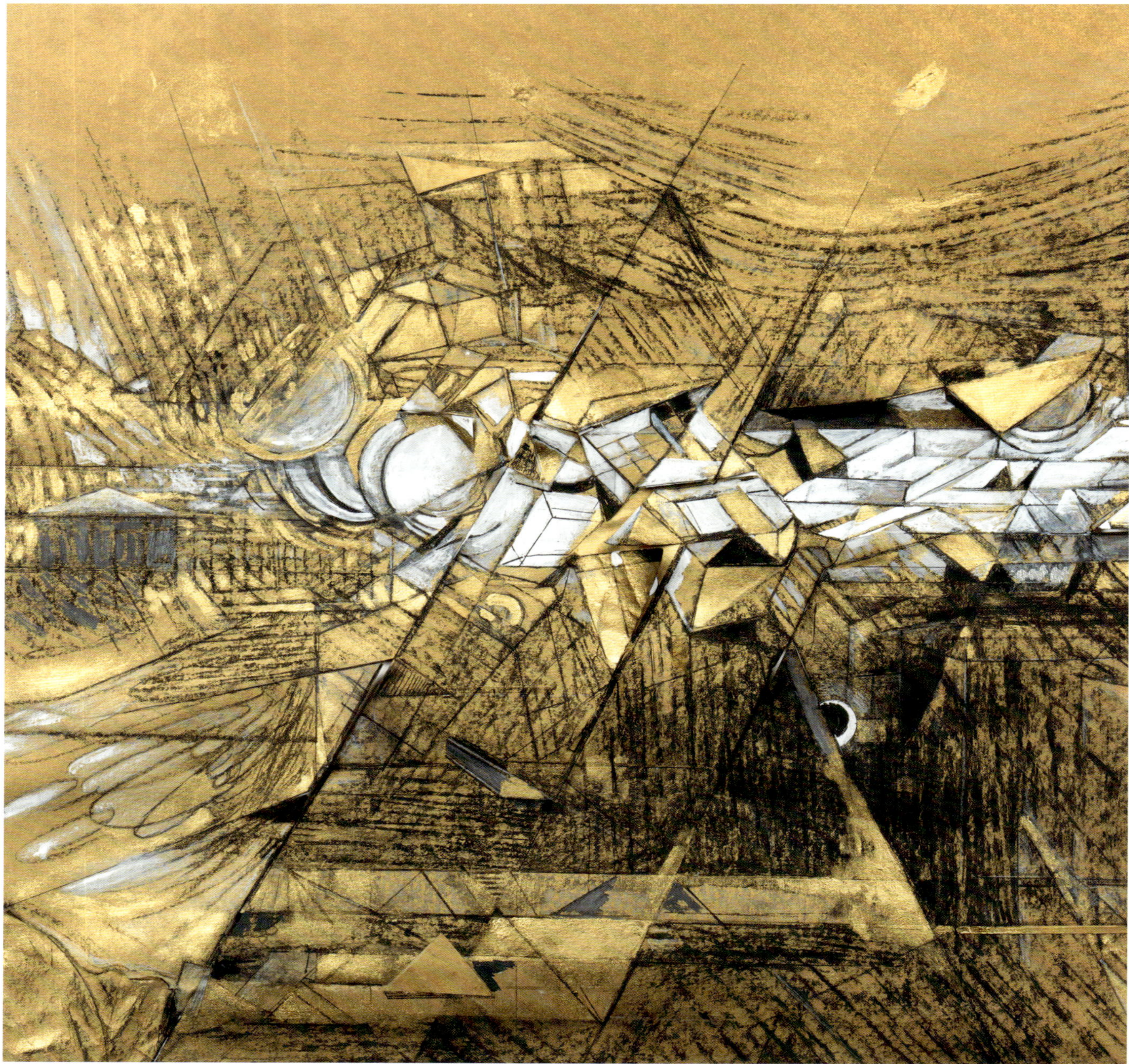

Fig. 51   Luise Kaish, *The Wind Is Blowing* (detail), maquette for axonometric bronze relief (detail), 2012 (see Plate 103)

"influences the way we think, the way we regard our culture . . . art can be used to elevate and coalesce or fragment and disintegrate."[31] Her profound and varied body of work offers an alternative to the more materialistic, commercially driven orientation of so much contemporary art. In the process it provides a compelling reminder of how much we lose when we neglect art's spiritual dimension.

Endnotes

1. Roger Lipsey, "Luise Kaish's Small Worlds," *Arts Magazine* 56, no. 3 (November 1981): 160.
2. Barr's chart was reproduced on the dust jacket of *Cubism and Modern Art*, exh. cat. (New York: Museum of Modern Art, 1936).
3. Harold Rosenberg, "Jews in Art," *New Yorker*, December 22, 1985, 66.
4. Quoted in Linda Mandeville, "A View of Her Own: Artist Luise Kaish," *Columbia Magazine*, February 1985, 22.
5. Ibid., 20.
6. Quoted in Sherry Chayat, "Art: Kaishes Take Different Paths Beyond Reality," *Rochester Herald Journal*, Summer 1988, 22.
7. Roger Lipsey, memorial essay, 2013, Luise Kaish archives, New York.
8. Morton Kaish, interview by the author, May 16, 2019.
9. *Kabbalah* is also spelled *Kabalah*, *Cabala*, and *Qabala*.
10. Mandeville, "A View of Her Own," 22.
11. Morton Kaish, oral history with Liza Zapol, July 31, 2015, New York, transcript, 56, Luise Kaish archives.
12. Luise Kaish archives.
13. John Gneisenau Neihardt, *When the Tree Flowered: The Fictional Biography of Eagle Voice, a Sioux Indian* (New York: Pocket Books, 1973), 52.
14. Marcia Dunn, "SpaceX Launches Falcon Heavy with Satellites, Experiments," *SFGate*, June 25, 2019.
15. Charlotte Streiter Rubinstein, *American Women Sculptors* (Boston: C. K. Hall & Co., 1990), 360.
16. Luise Kaish, unidentified typescript, n.d., Luise Kaish archives.
17. Ibid.
18. Charlene Spretnak, *The Spiritual Dynamic in Modern Art: Art History Reconsidered, 1800 to the Present* (Basingstoke, UK: Palgrave Macmillan, 2014).
19. Maurice Tuchman, "Hidden Meanings in Abstract Art," *The Spiritual in Art: Abstract Painting 1890–1985*, exh. cat. (Los Angeles: Los Angeles County Museum of Art, 1986), 17.
20. Wassily Kandinsky, *Concerning the Spiritual in Art*, trans. Michael T. H. Sadler (New York: Dover, 1977), 2.
21. Roger Lipsey, *An Art of Our Own: The Spiritual in Twentieth Century Art* (Boston: Shambhala, 1974), 21.
22. Selden Rodman, *Conversations with Artists* (New York: Devin-Adair, 1957), 93, reprinted as "Notes from a Conversation with Selden Rodman, 1956," in Mark Rothko, *Writings on Art: Mark Rothko*, ed. Miguel López-Remiro (New Haven: Yale University Press, 2006), 119.
23. Rosenberg, "Jews in Art," 6.
24. Morton Kaish, oral history with Liza Zapol, 43.
25. Quoted in "Discover 'La Lumière,'" *Continews*, Spring 1978.
26. Greater Des Moines Public Art Foundation, "Sphere Within a Sphere," 2019, https:// dsmpublicartfoundation.org/public-artwork/ sphere-within-a-sphere/.
27. Anish Kapoor, "Blood and Light: In Conversation with Julia Kristeva," in *Anish Kapoor Versailles*, ed. Alfred Pacquement, exh. cat. (Paris: RMN–Grand Palais, 2015), https://anishkapoor.com/4330/blood-and-light-in-conversation-with-julia-kristeva.
28. Mandeville, "A View of Her Own," 23.
29. *Luise Kaish: Recent Collages*, exh. cat. (New York: Staempfli Gallery, 1981).
30. Morton Kaish, interview with the author, May 16, 2019.
31. Mandeville, "A View of Her Own," 20.

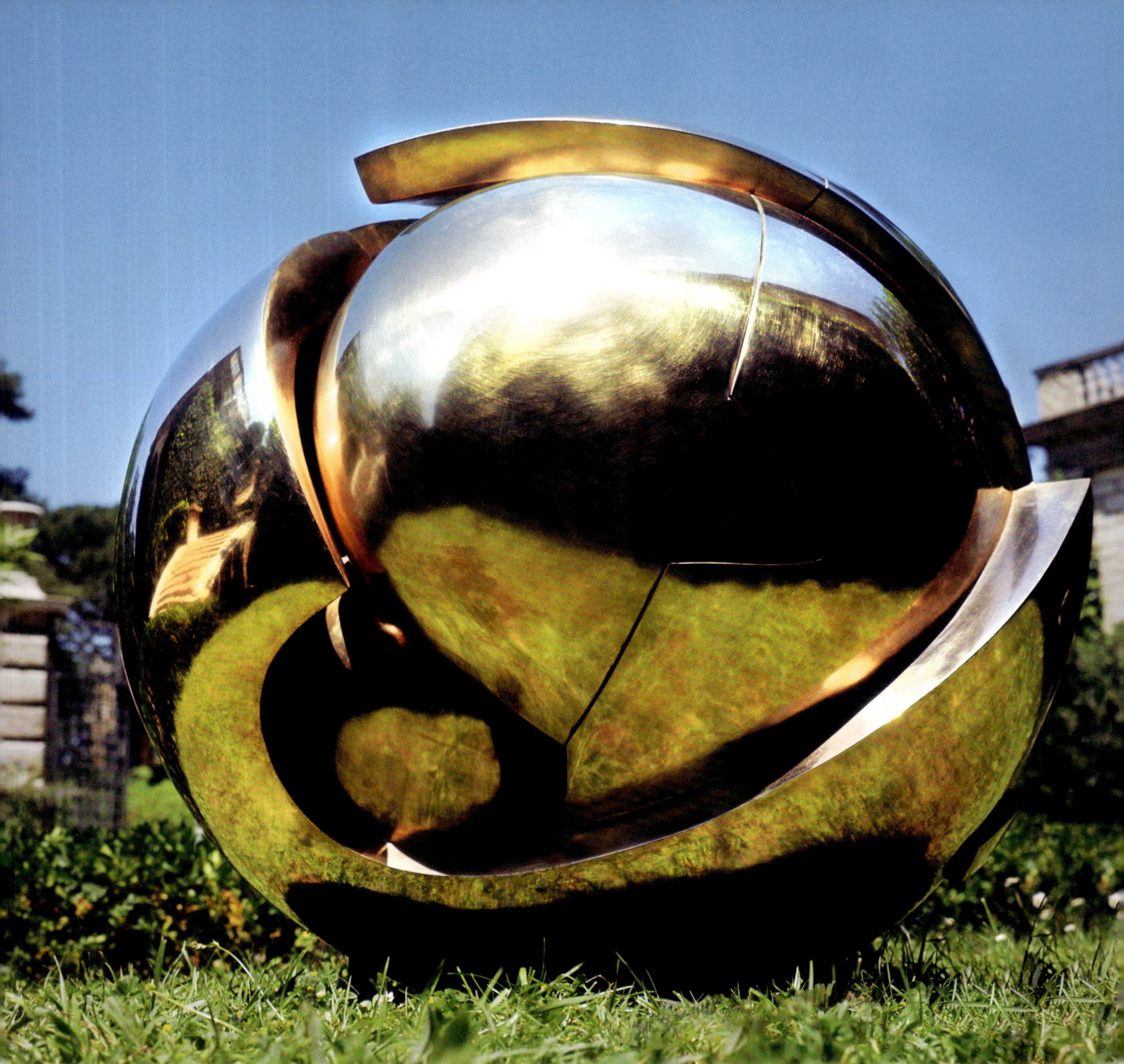

Plate 48

Luise Kaish. *In the Beginning*, 1970, polished bronze,
29 in. (73.7 cm) diameter

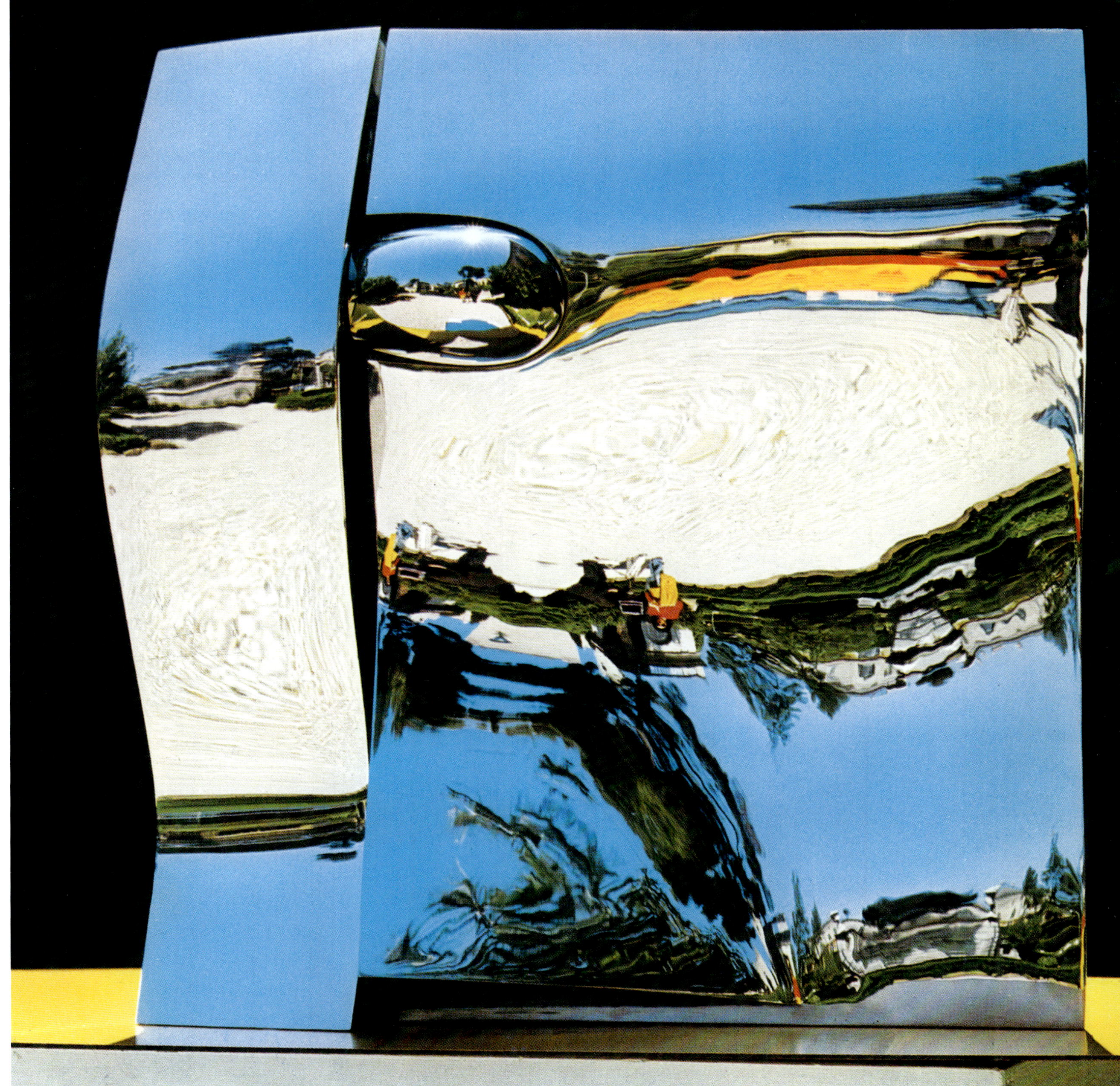

Plate 49
Luise Kaish. *Voyage II*, 1971, stainless steel, 22 × 21 × 8 in.
(55.9 × 53.5 × 20.3 cm)

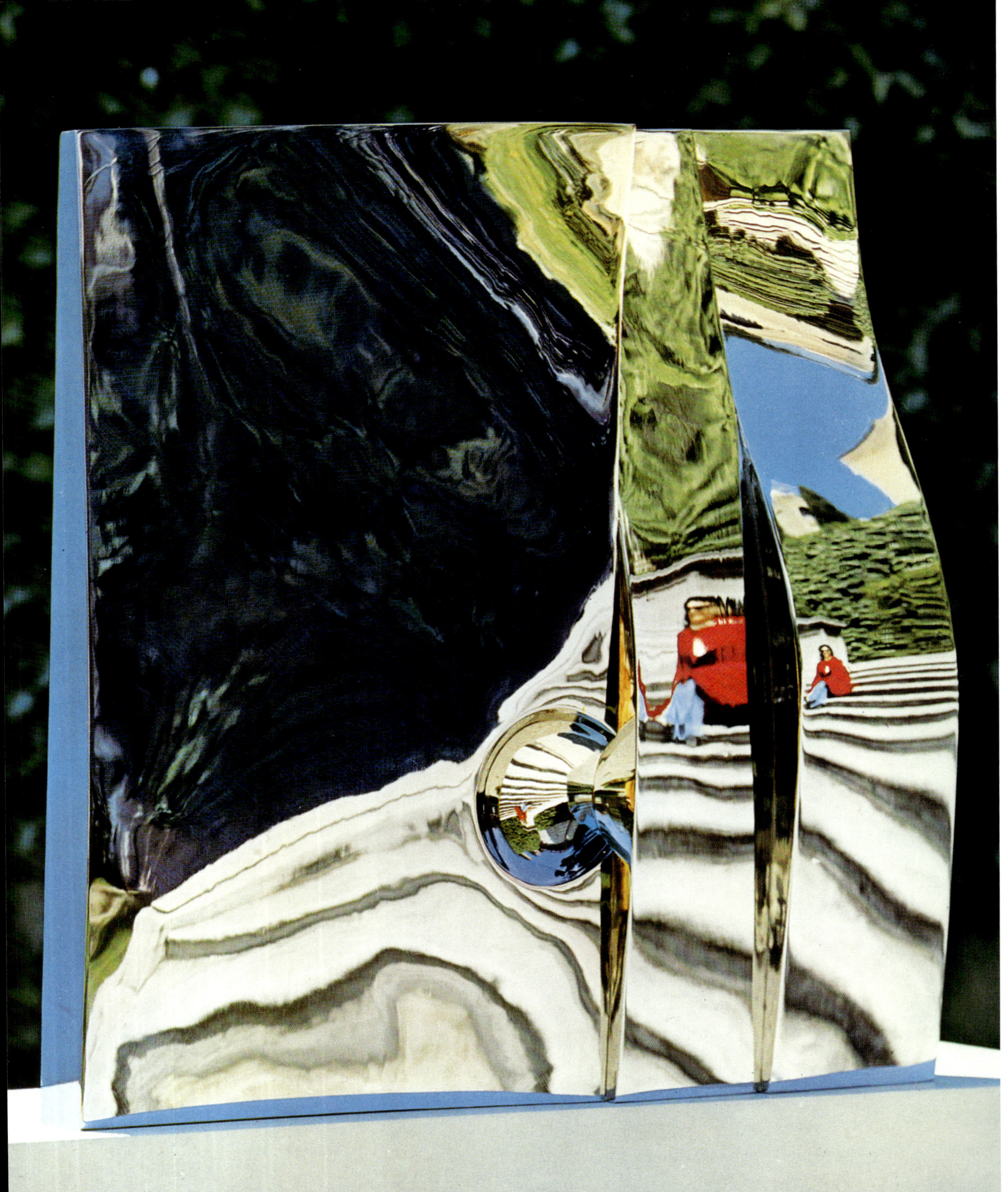

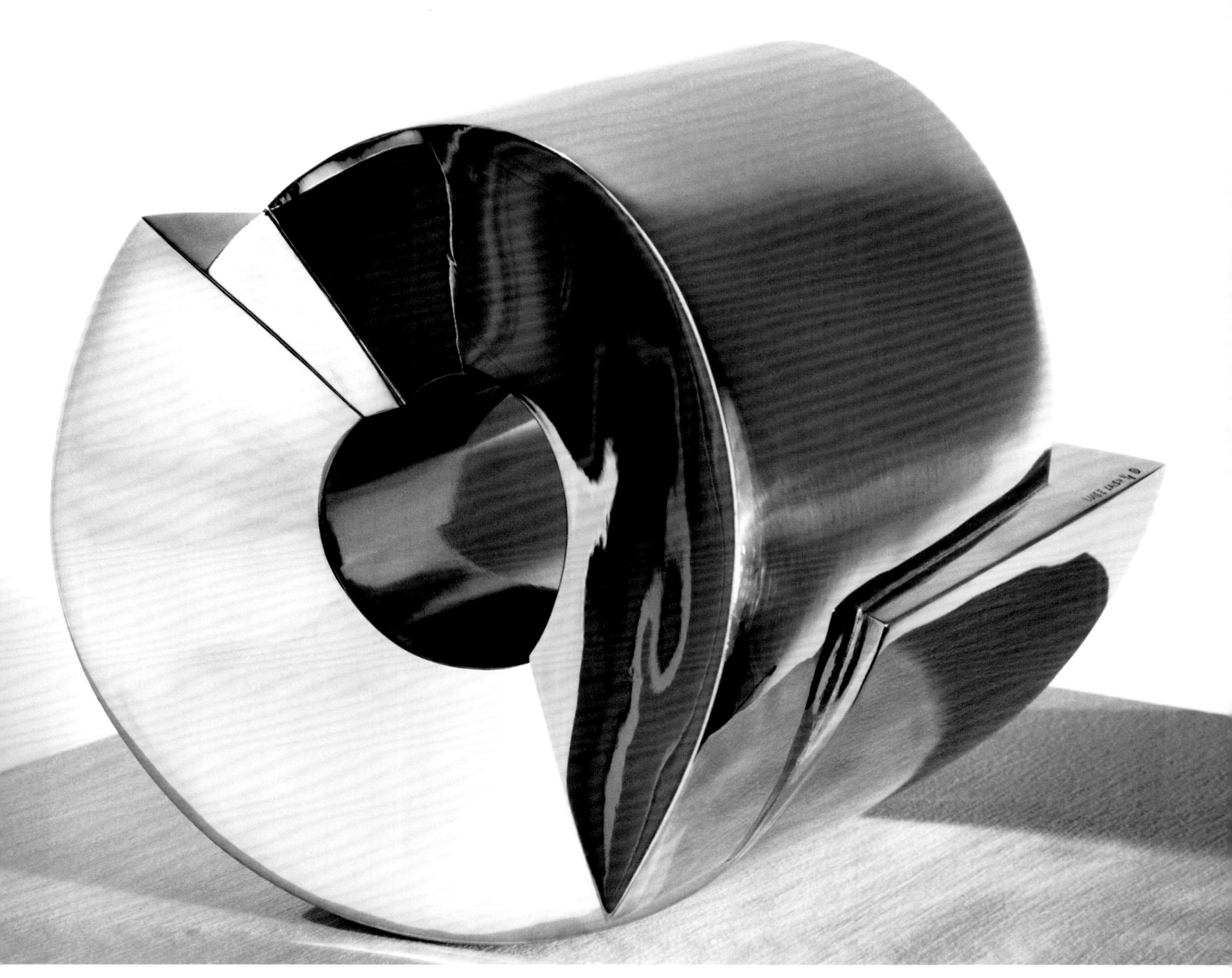

Plate 50
Luise Kaish. *Voyage I*, 1971, stainless steel,
29 × 29 × 6 in. (73.7 × 73.7 × 15.2 cm)

Plate 51
Luise Kaish. *Star Void*, 1971, stainless steel,
8 × 8 × 8 in. (20.3 × 20.3 × 20.3 cm)

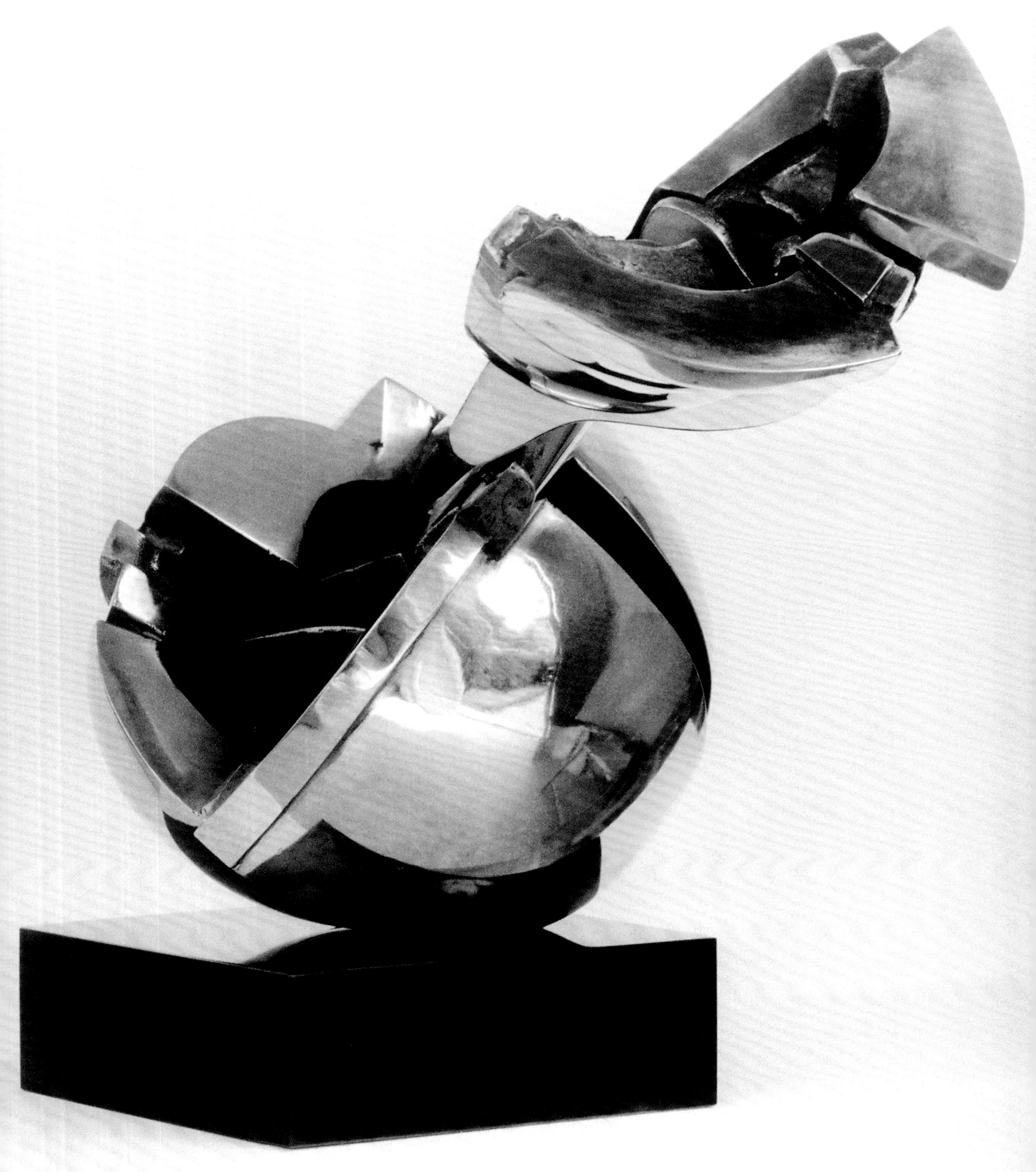

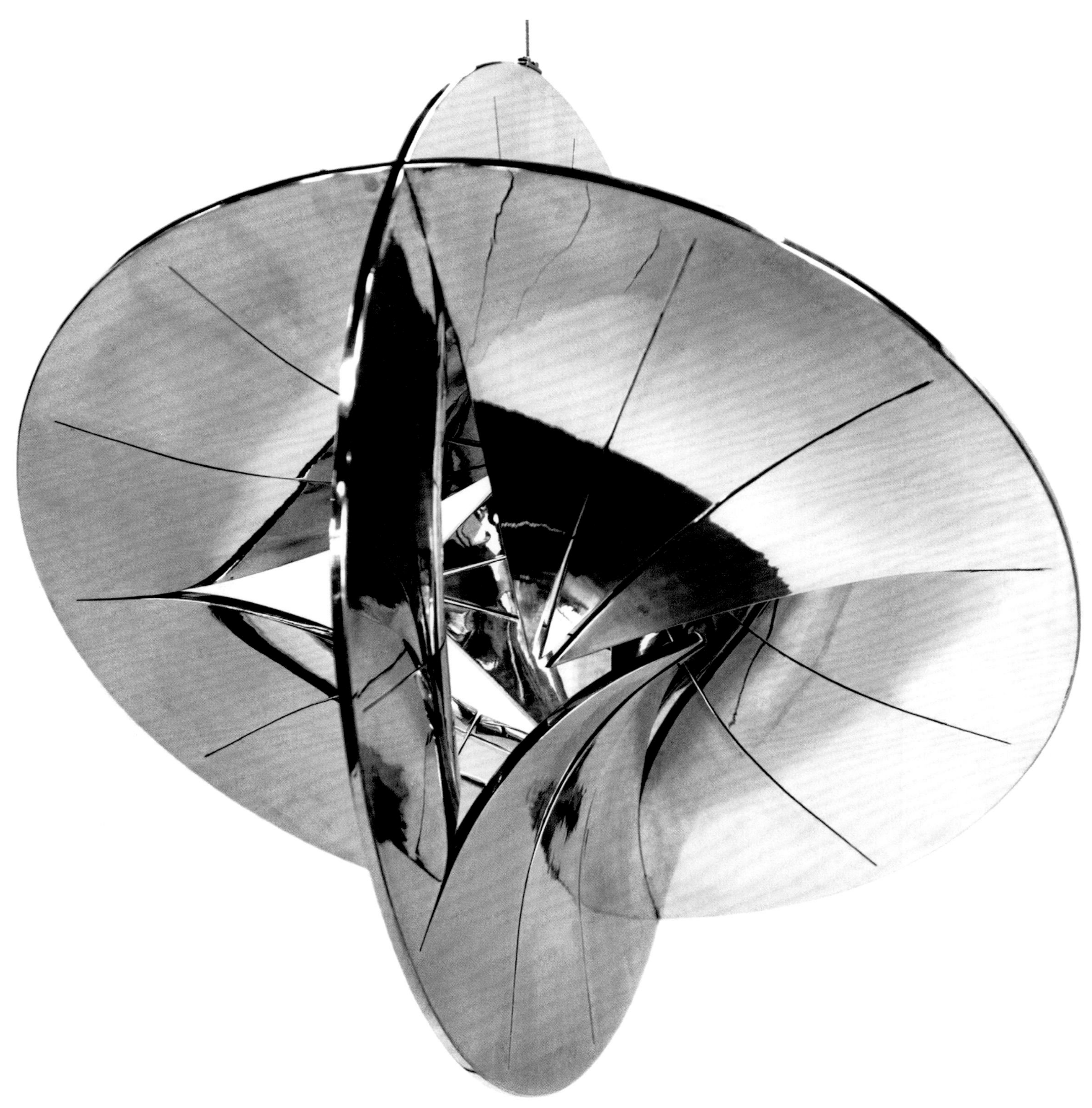

Plate 52
Luise Kaish. *In the Beginning IV*, 1972,
bronze, 10 × 11 in. (25.4 × 27.9 cm)

Plate 53
Luise Kaish. *Sphere*, 1976, polished
aluminum, 39 in. (99.06 cm). Collection,
Hood Museum, Dartmouth College 1976

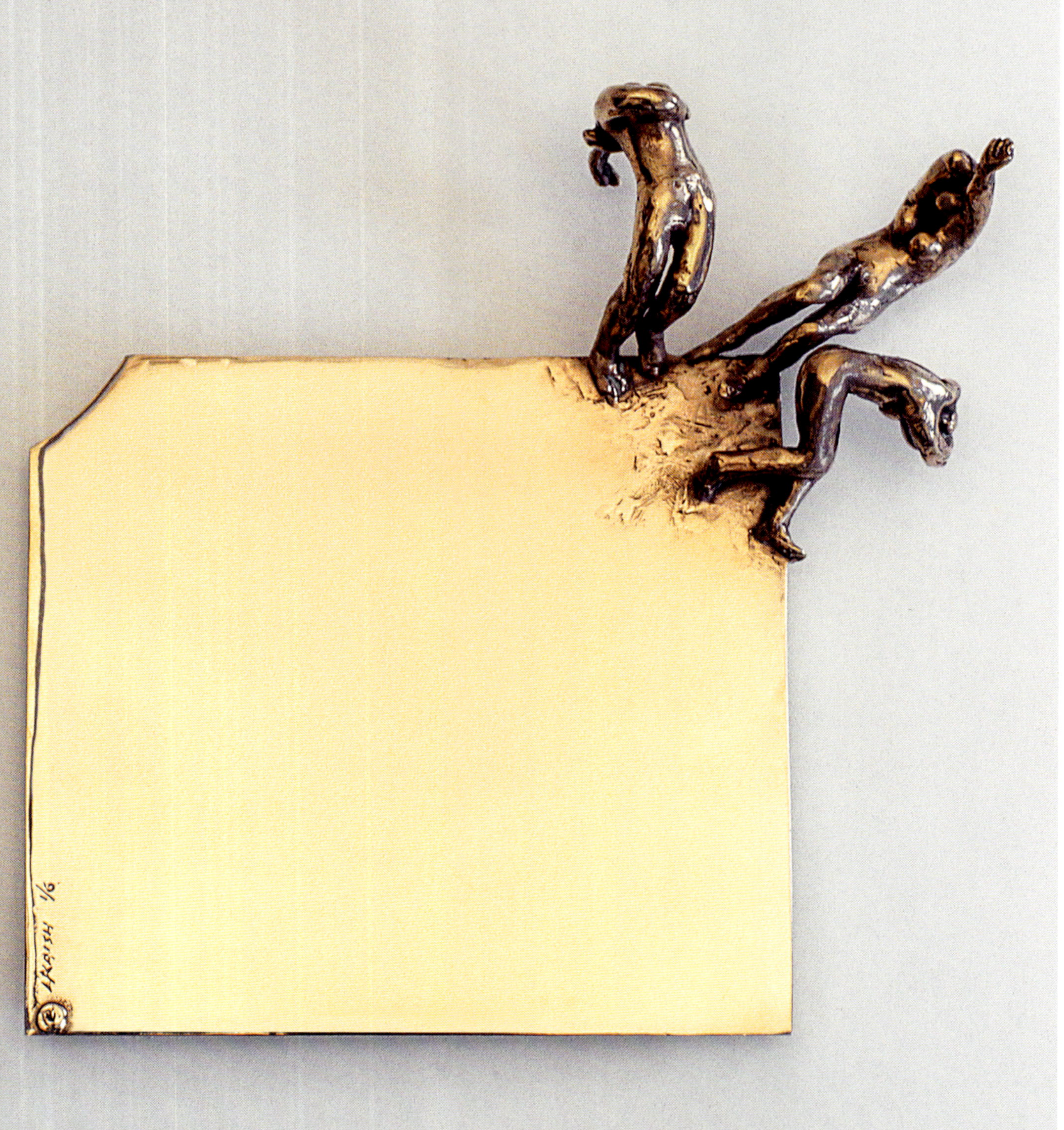

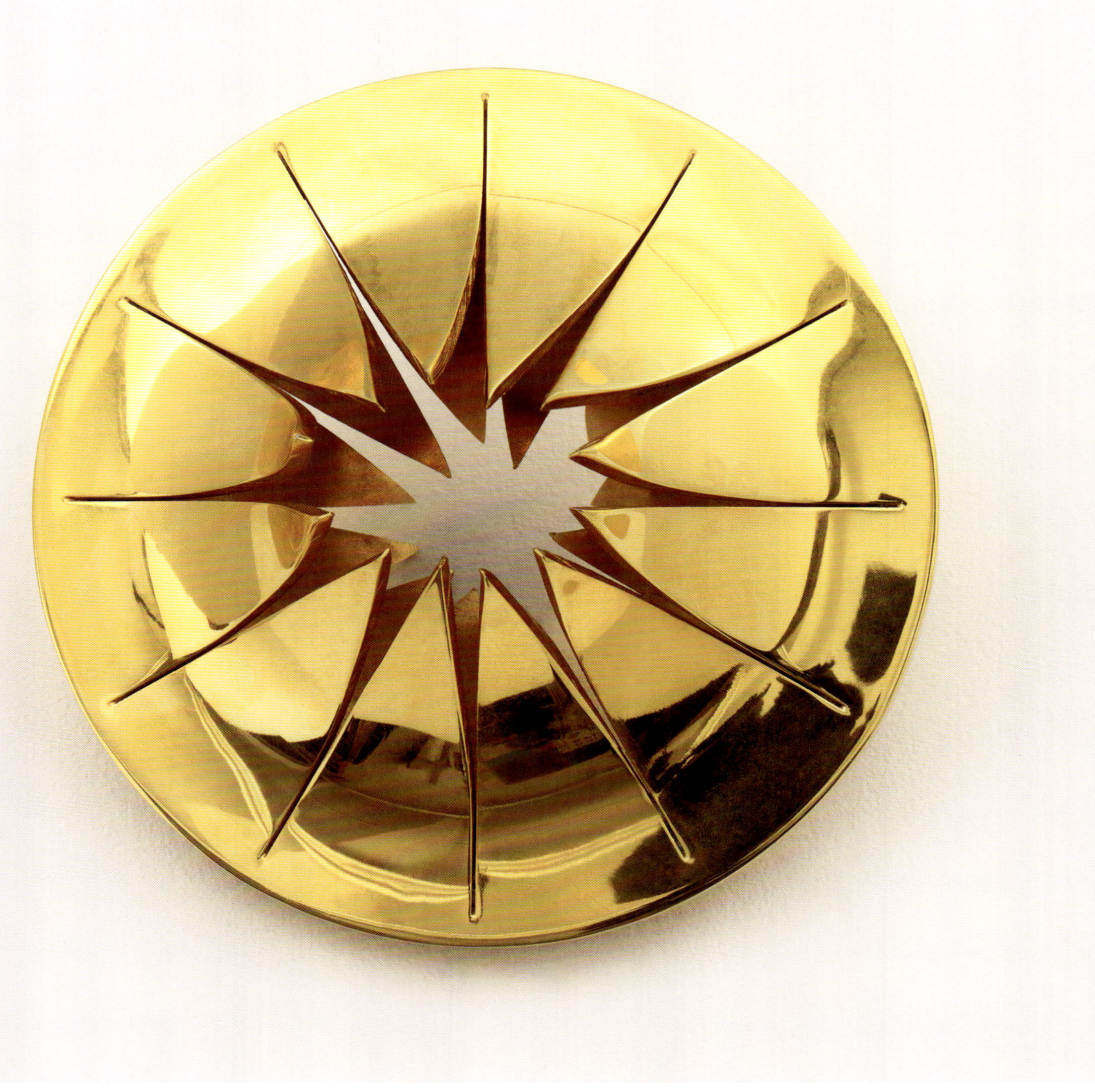

Plate 54
Luise Kaish. *Flight from Jerusalem II*, 1973,
bronze, 11 × 11 in. (27.9 × 27.9 cm)

Plate 55
Luise Kaish. *Twelve Tribes A*, 1973, bronze,
gold plated, 5 ½ in. (14 cm) diameter

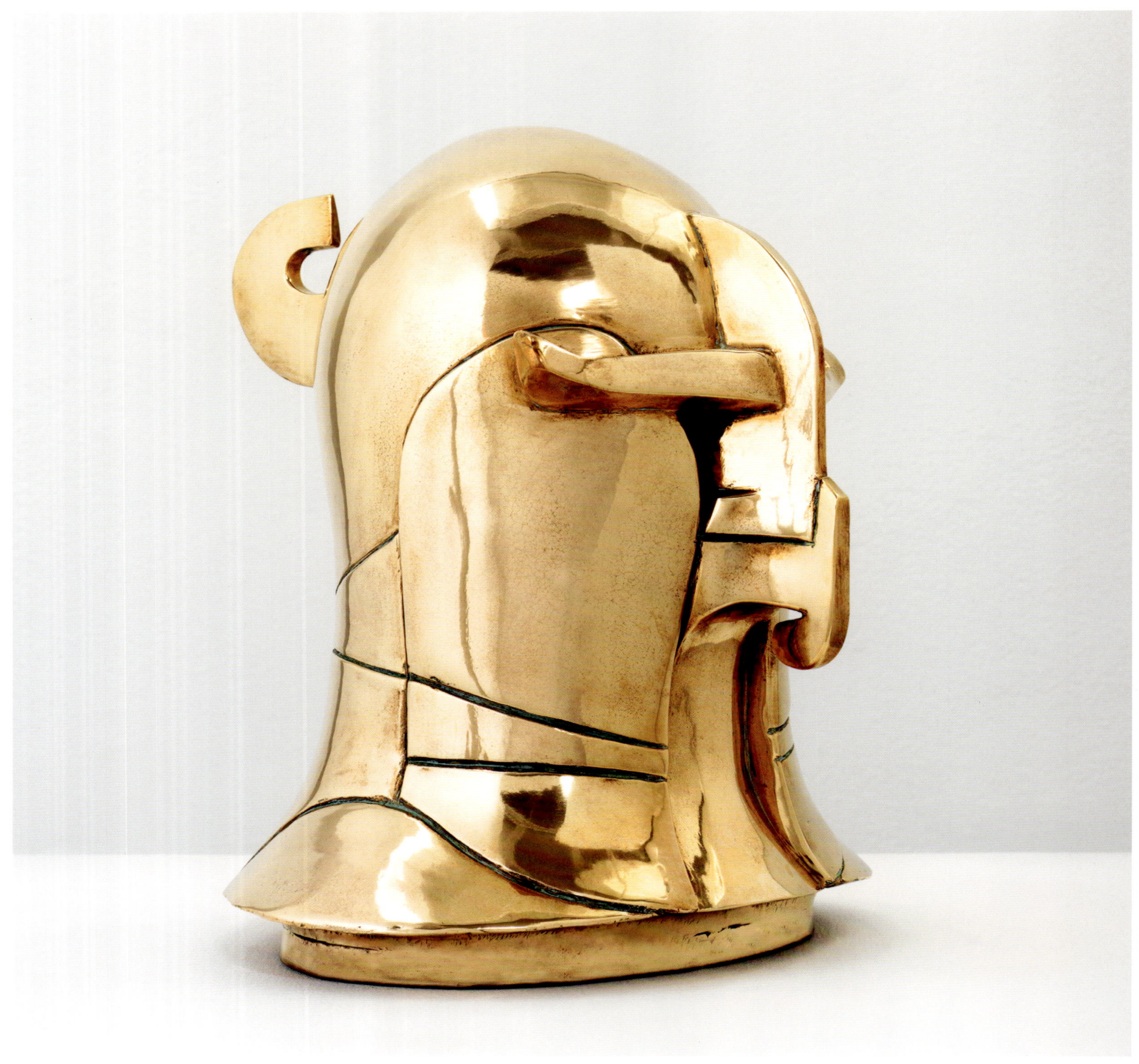

Plate 56
Luise Kaish. *Barbarosa* (*Crusader Head*), 1973, bronze,
10 ½ × 9 × 10 in. (26.7 × 22.9 × 25.4 cm)

Plate 57
Luise Kaish. *La Lumière*, 1975–76, polished bronze,
48 × 48 × 48 in. (121.9 × 121.9 × 121.9 cm). Collection
of Continental Grain Company, New York

146

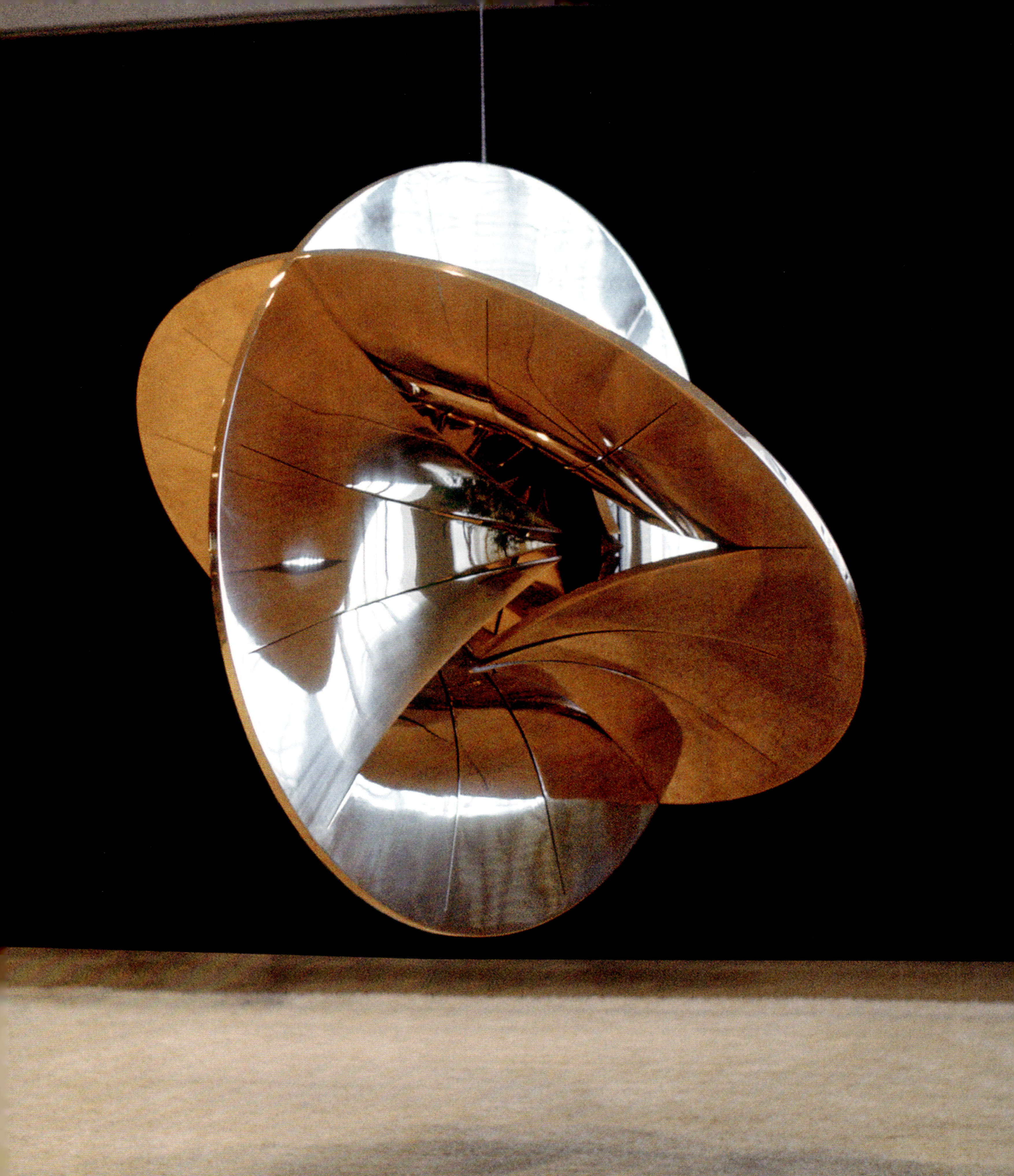

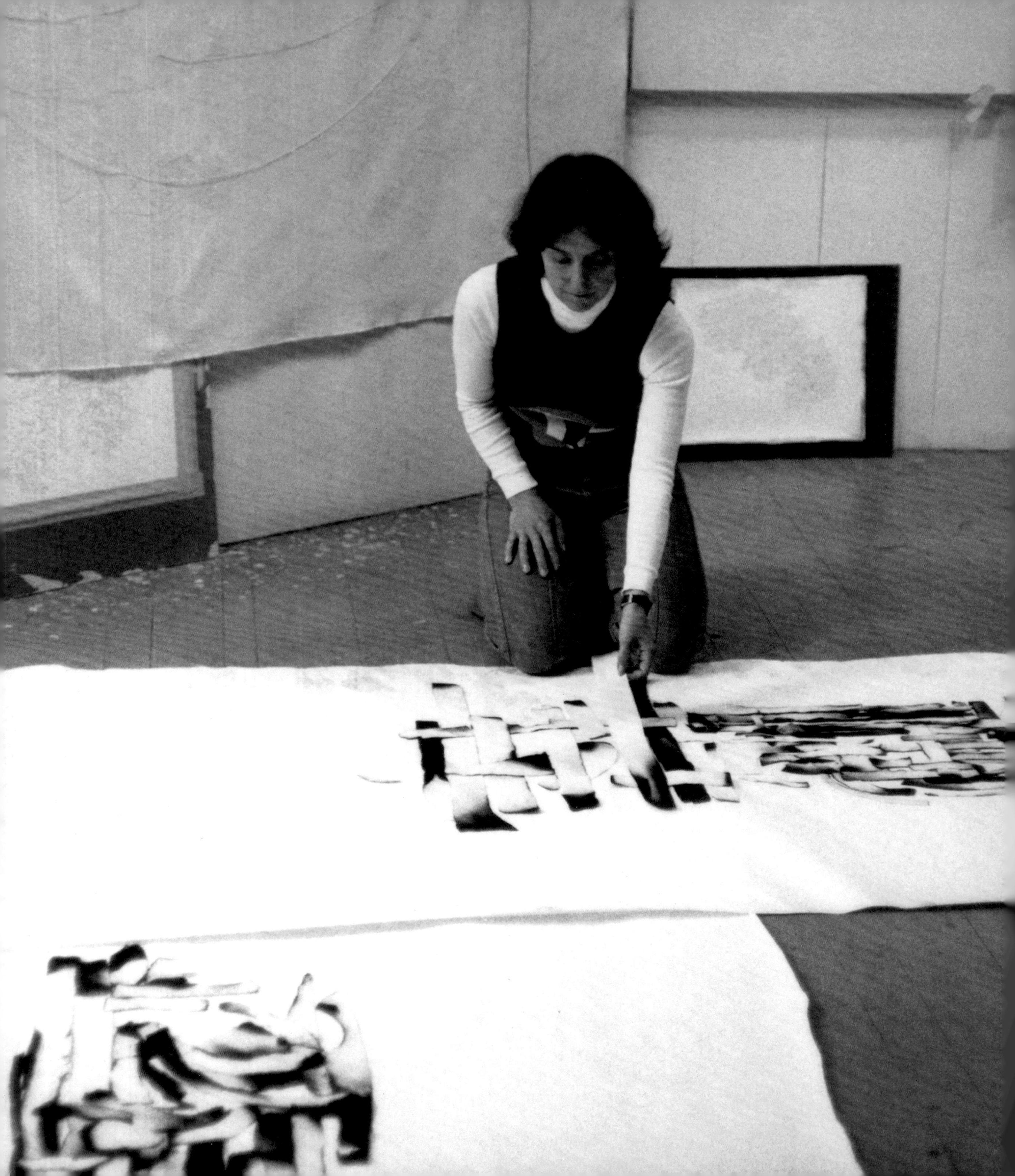

ABSTRACTION/ FRUSTRATION/ TRANSFORMATION

LUISE KAISH'S BURNTWORKS

Norman L. Kleeblatt

Luise Kaish with a burntwork, MacDowell, 1976

Artists refer to the reality within oneself, to art as yoking together the subjective and objective.[1]

–Luise Kaish

The term *multifaceted* aptly describes the career of Luise Kaish. As with many artists, her professional life was filled with dualities and contradictions. She worked as a painter and sculptor, creating art in scales from modest to monumental. Like many of her generation, her practice included periods focused either on figuration or abstraction, sometimes using these principles in tandem or even fusing them in single works.[2] Trained in the United States by both European and American teachers, she looked to artists on both sides of the Atlantic for collegiality and camaraderie. Kaish's inspirations and sources included both the contemporary and the historical.[3] She was both wife and colleague to her fellow-artist husband, Morton Kaish; given the numerous reports and anecdotes about their personal and professional relationship, one might even call them partners in crime. Unlike many women artists of her time, but closer to the narratives of women artists today, she planned her family carefully and found time and great joy in both motherhood and family.

Tragic aspects of twentieth-century world history played a major role in Kaish's expression, as did spirituality and philosophy, nature and nurture. Kaish learned about the Holocaust as its scope and reality were first revealed in the mid-1940s. Like many artists of her generation, as well as the previous, this tragic presence in her art was natural for individuals coming of age during World War II. Large-scale commissions were a large part of her career, especially during the period from 1951 to 1976. Such monumental projects provided numerous physical and conceptual challenges, and also demanded serious technical, management, and negotiating skills. Kaish also enjoyed the isolated, intimate encounters of art making in her studio. There she confronted the myriad formal problems of her time, as well as the technical potentials and constraints of material and construction.

On a personal level, she also expressed her subjectivity as a spiritual being, a woman, a teacher, an administrator, a practicing Jew, the wife of an artist, and a mother.[4] These subjective aspects were closely related to the emotive range of her work, which ran the gamut from celebratory to tragic—the latter inevitable to artists of her generation and stated succinctly in historic comments about the necessary role of contemporary art in fusing the "tragic and timeless."[5] Though highly personal, Kaish's artworks—especially her commissions—were meant to be experienced by others, engaging not only particular communities but also individuals.

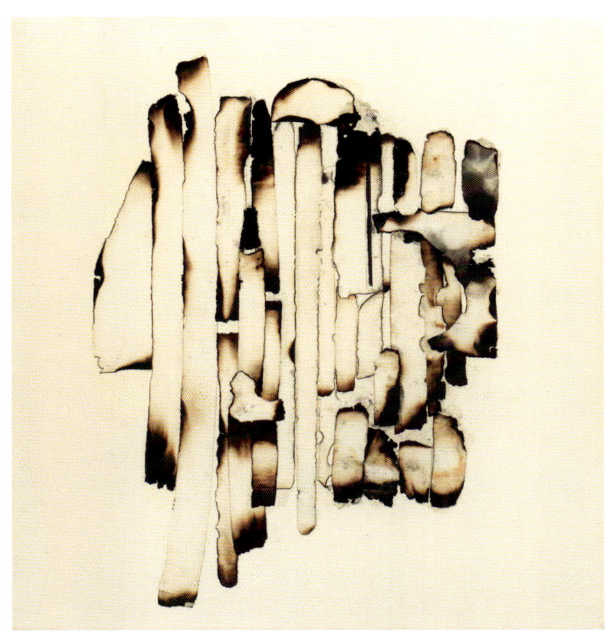

Fig. 52 Luise Kaish, *Firepond I*, 1976 (see Plate 60)

Within Kaish's long career, I focus here on a decidedly specific group of works from the 1970s. She dubbed this group "burntworks," a moniker that reflects both the physical reality of their invention as well as the formal issues Kaish was working to resolve at the time. *Firepond I* of 1976 is one example of the collages she created from strips of burnt canvas (Fig. 52, Pl. 60). In this instance, she keeps the individual elements clearly separated and neatly aligned in vertical strips. With *Untitled* of 1976–79, later on in the evolution of the series, Kaish tightly aligns the burnt, variegated shapes in a way that segregates the different intensities of char to create an effect of color tonalities that one might consider sfumato (Pl. 61). As unique as they were transformative in her oeuvre, the intangible ideas embedded in these works and the physical processes she deployed to make them were crucial to her subsequent practices. This is especially true of her later two-dimensional pieces.[6] Toward the end of her life, Kaish noted that the burntworks had never before been exhibited.[7] Yet these works offer key insights into Kaish's experimental nature, and into her manner of thinking and creation. Given her preoccupation with the fusion of objectivity and subjectivity, Kaish's burntworks are inevitably laden with symbolic and metaphorical references as well as emotional charge.

The burntworks had their origin in a moment of chance that occurred during the couple's residency during the summer of 1975 at the MacDowell in New Hampshire. Kaish's practice was evolving from sculpture, and she was experimenting with the dimensionalities of collaged canvas, working in a studio with a huge stone fireplace. Her husband, Morton, described the scene:

> She was having a tough day. Nothing is working as she wants it to. Frustration. Maybe this canvas relief wasn't such a good idea, after all?
>
> Midday, in total frustration, Luise lights a fire and she tosses her morning's work into the flames and sits back exhausted. And then, a wow moment. Revelation!
>
> As the canvas burns and curls, she sees rich black and brown tones that are being created by the fire. They're bold, they're subtle, and she knows they could never be made or matched by paint or pigment . . . She snatches it all out of the fire, dragging the burning strips onto the stone floor, and begins to recompose, to layer and to cut and to arrange.[8]

Kaish quickly realized that in the detritus of the works she had attempted to destroy she had found a medium that, in her words, was both "basic" and "raw." She detected that these scraps of singed canvas offered a "wide chromatic scale . . . quality of tone [and] value that could never be achieved with pigment."[9] The scorched remnants led Kaish to further exploration and ultimately to a new material and synthetic means of fabrication. Ever dialogic—even disputatious—in her thinking, she recognized the oppositions and juxtapositions of her discovery, and the need within her art for "resolving contradictions." In her notes on the burntworks, Kaish observed the fragments as "burnt images," which she collaged or layered onto canvas. She used "burning to create both depth and frontality—illusionistic space which could move both as recessive & aggressive."[10] In seeing these formless burned scraps as images, Kaish confirms their existence in a space that is at once abstract and representational, formal and emotional.

In her mind, the results were works of subtle energy and physical sensuousness in which—as with both her two- and three-dimensional works—she sought to make light the animating force of her art.[11] This was, of course, somewhat contradictory, given that Kaish was attempting to create light from extinguished fire. Individually and as a group, the burntworks series operates on multiple levels. By situating them within a historical, spiritual, philosophical, and religious matrix, I hope to demonstrate how they were at once unique within Kaish's oeuvre, essential to her subsequent practice, as well as an expression of artistic sensibilities and strategies of her time. Contexts for these works are manifold, and include historical and contemporary deployments of collage, and also a specific female reading of that artistic form. The works must also be read in terms of strategies of destruction among postwar artists, not only as a means of editing what artists saw as chaff from their careers, but also as a metaphor and means of creation. This later mode of operation has its conceptual basis in Lurianic Kabbalism, with which Kaish, given her literary interests and its popularity during the 1970s, would have been familiar.

On a purely formal or tactile level, the burntworks were closely connected to the practices of collage, that transformative artistic invention of the early twentieth century, and its more recent sculptural evolution: assemblage. This practice had been explained, exhibited, and codified in William Seitz's historic exhibition *The Art of Assemblage* presented at the Museum of Modern Art in 1961.[12] As a sculptor, Kaish recognized that the three-dimensional aspects of her collages made the concept of assemblage entirely relevant to her burntworks. In the delicacy of her construction and the care she took in their production, Kaish's burntworks might be related to the subtle mid-century collages of Anne Ryan, an artist Kaish admired,[13] and also to the well-known assembled sculpture of Louise Nevelson, alongside whom she exhibited in the prescient exhibition *American Women: Twentieth Century* of 1972.[14]

Kaish's burntworks, begun in 1975, must also be considered as *femmage*, a newly expressed rubric from the idea of women artists' impulse toward collaging from the scraps and waste of daily life, already a women's vernacular process in the eighteenth and nineteenth centuries. This idea was first discussed among a group of feminist artists in 1977 not long after Kaish began the series; the term was officially coined by the *New York Times* art critic Grace Glueck around 1978. Kaish's burntworks exhibit various characteristics of femmage enumerated by artists Melissa Meyer and Miriam Schapiro in their important essay on this practice published in 1978 in the pioneering feminist art publication *Heresies*: the works were made by a woman, incorporate the activity of saving and collecting, contain elements of covert images (Kaish had seen "burnt images" in the charred remnants from which she created her first burntworks), celebrate private or public events, and use abstract forms to create a pattern.[15]

The burntworks, neither entirely flat nor entirely sculptural, must be considered a hybrid phenomenon. Comprised of the salvaged detritus from Kaish's attempt to destroy work she considered a failure, this new and unlikely medium provided structural challenges as well as opportunities for invention. Not least, it necessitated that Kaish use different processes, which impacted her subsequent practice. The burntworks fit strategically with Kaish's abstract painting/collage technique, astutely described by Richard Martin as "inflected by painting, tearing away, building up, burning, scarring, scraping, bandaging, painting, salving, and painting again."[16] Martin compares Kaish's use of such processes on canvas to the intimacy of human skin itself. It is evident that many aspects of the technique that Martin observes in Kaish's art evolved from the challenges she encountered and partially resolved in the burntworks. In some sense, they forced her to play with different, less compliant materials, which required new forms of manipulation.

There is still much to say about the formal aspects of Kaish's burntworks. Yet it is the initial act of destruction that links them closely with the often personally destructive deeds of a number of artists of her time. Such acts of artists' annihilation of their own work recur frequently in the annals of postwar art, observed by the noted critic Harold Rosenberg in his iconic article "The American Action Painters" in 1952.[17] Both Barnett Newman and Robert Motherwell also destroyed—or supposedly destroyed—their early works, but for somewhat different reasons. Newman claims to have destroyed most of his work from before 1944 as he set out to transform the nature of his art, using increasingly abstract means and minimal compositions. The goal for his new work was to forge an art that was spiritually inflected and highly personal.[18] While Newman wanted to start in this new direction with a clean slate, it appears that Motherwell may have destroyed or hidden his earlier works to support the claim that he, one of the youngest of the abstract expressionists, was also the only first-generation member of the movement who had never painted representationally.[19] If Newman's reason for destroying his works was internal, having traversed a major artistic hurdle and found a new path, one might consider Motherwell's motive for concealing his past work strategically promotional: seeking to create a unique position for himself within

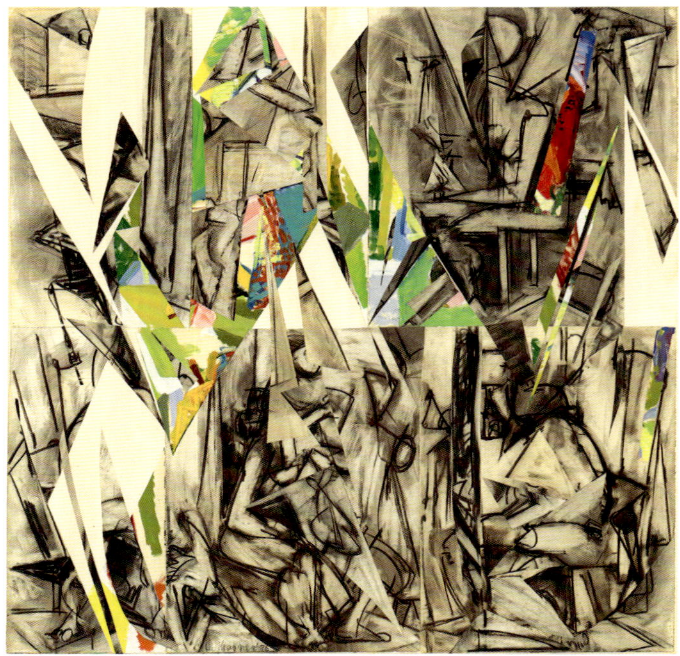

Fig. 53 Lee Krasner, *Imperative*, 1976, oil, charcoal, and paper on canvas, 50 × 50 in. (127 × 127 cm). National Gallery of Art

the abstract expressionist pantheon. Kaish, in comparison, intensely watched the destruction of the works she attempted to obliterate and saw in their process of decomposing a potential raw material for experimentation. This experiment became for Kaish a new artistic direction.

Kaish's colleague Louise Nevelson was another artist known to destroy works. Essentially, Nevelson burned works from her shows in which nothing sold.[20] She was likely as furious with the financial and reputational disappointments of her exhibitions as Kaish was with the aesthetic frustrations of the act of painting. Yet Nevelson gives her reason for the works' destruction as purely practical: she simply had no place to store them.[21] The artist and noted teacher Hans Hofmann had taught his students that it was perfectly sensible to destroy unsuccessful paintings, partially or totally. In fact, he often partially destroyed or altered his students' works as part of his pedagogical process.[22] One of Hofmann's most important students and disseminators of his teachings was Lee Krasner, another woman artist whom Kaish knew and who showed alongside Kaish in the early 1970s. Krasner destroyed many of her early cubist works from the 1940s, when she was working with Hofmann, only to rediscover and reuse the fragments to create massive series of collages, from 1953 to 1955 and then again from 1975 right up to her death in 1984 (Fig. 53).[23] Krasner's and Kaish's technique of saving and repurposing defaced, unsuccessful fragments certainly echoes the attributes of femmage expressed in Meyer and Schapiro's treatise.

It was John Baldessari who made the ultimate gesture of artistic annihilation. In 1970 he burnt all the works he had painted between 1953 and 1966 to create a new, entirely conceptual piece in his *Cremation Project*, the deliberate climax of the artist's desire to create work from the ashes of earlier work (Fig. 54). Though such an aggressive, premeditated tactic stands in sharp contrast to Kaish's act of frustration and her more reverent attitude toward art making, Baldessari's destructive impulse nevertheless offers resonances with Kaish's formal and emotive concerns. In relation to the notion of destruction and completely applicable to Kaish's work, Kerry Brougher incisively observes, "destruction became embedded not only in the imagery of many artists, but more deeply in their work, in their actions and ways of thinking about art itself, and even how they experienced the world

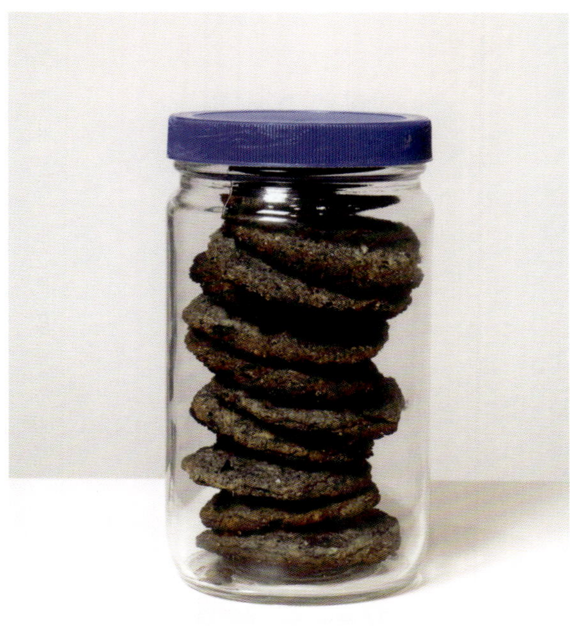

Fig. 54   John Baldessari, *Cremation Project with Corpus Wafers* (*Version 2*) (detail), 1970, glass jar with plastic lid, cookies (with ashes), recipe card, original affidavit of publication, newspaper page, and six color photographs, mixed media, dimensions variable

and their place in it."[24] This type of practice is closely linked to the notion of the tragic as a subject for art, so common in the wake of World War II, the Korean War, and the Vietnam War, to name but a few examples. Artists' vision about the place of such practice seems to have particular significance within Kaish's philosophical and ideological sensibilities.[25] Both Baldessari and Kaish knowingly burned their paintings, Baldessari's act being wholly planned, Kaish's totally spontaneous. Baldessari's destruction proceeded from calculation; Kaish's grew out of frustration. However, Kaish's ultimate saving of the canvas fragments from complete destruction by fire was an act of rescue that provided her with the materials for creation. One might call it creation by salvation.

Although Kaish did not use the term "destructive," she considered her burntworks creations made by "subtraction, not addition," in which her art fused intimately with her process of working.[26] Repurposing the scorched fragments required impeccable attention to detail: How would she use the scraps? Did she help them along? Did she cut them into more useful, repeating shapes to create coherent compositional elements? Would she re-singe parts of them to balance the formal weight of each compositional element? Such procedures were likely the case, as is evident in the repeated and similarly shaped vertical strips more or less evenly edged with dark smoky char that she used in *Firepond I*.[27] The meticulous cohesion of the individually chosen and worked scraps contrasts flagrantly with the spontaneous destructive act that formed the new materials she would use. A film of the artist at work—in action, so to speak—would be useful here in observing and decoding Kaish's process.

Recently encountering the *Untitled* (*MacDowell*) work of 1976 (Fig. 55) for the first time, I was struck by the collision of chance and calculation that came together in this and related burntworks. Many of the scorched scraps must have fallen apart along the edges where the burning was extinguished. Kaish must have carefully saved and sorted each piece, tidying them to create cohesively shaped collage elements. In the face of the

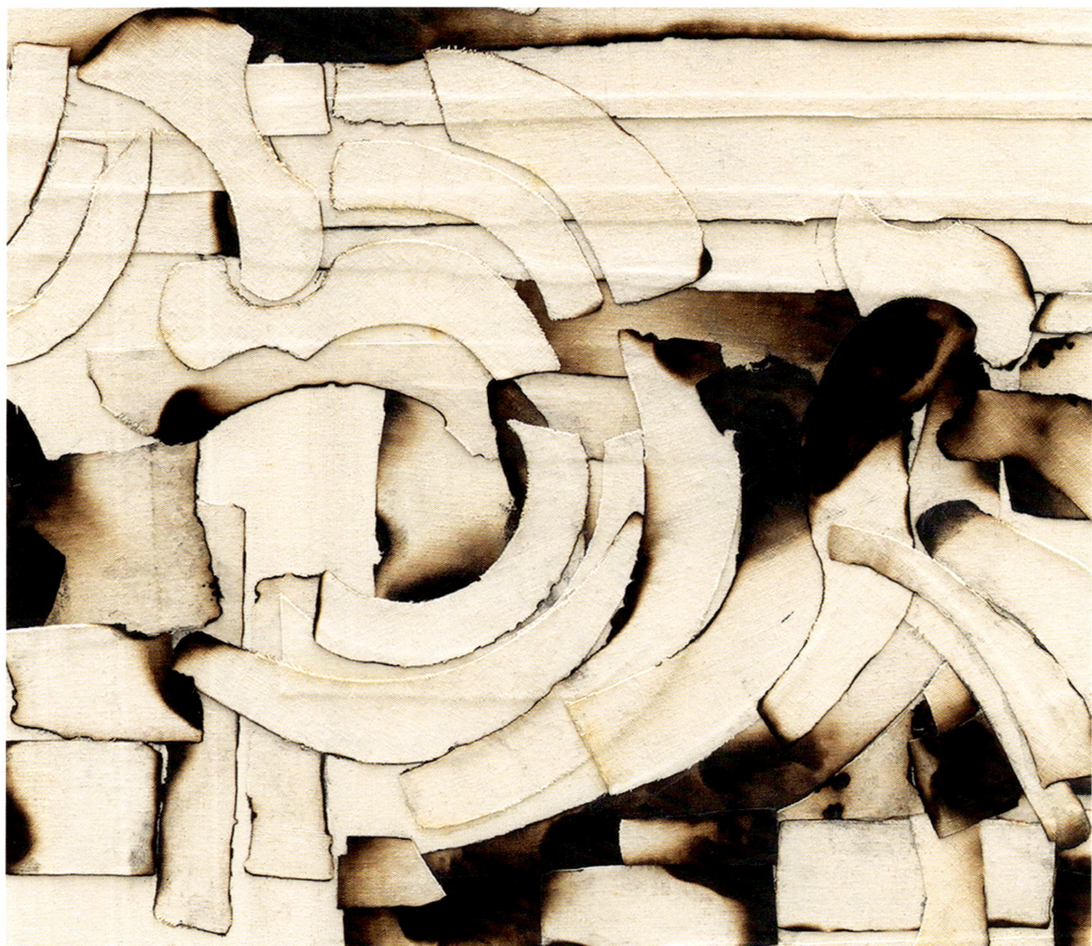

Fig. 55 Luise Kaish, *Untitled* (*MacDowell*) (detail), 1976 (see Plate 58)

chaos of this initial act of destruction, her careful arranging, composing, and adhering of the burnt fragments onto new unprimed linen canvases feels somewhat paradoxical. Her process contrasts greatly with the destructive gestures and assembled deteriorated materials of some artists based in Southern Europe whose work she must have known from her time in Rome, such as Alberto Burri, Lucio Fontana, Manolo Millares, and Antoni Tàpies, to name but a few (Fig. 56).[28] My first impression was that Kaish's burnt canvas elements were precisely applied like poultices or bandages to a wound, an observation confirmed by my subsequent reading of Richard Martin's remarks about Kaish's working technique. There is a restorative aspect to Kaish's fabrication, as if by capturing the elements and tenderly gluing them onto a new support, she could heal the destructive forces that had enveloped her raw material. Something like this is what she must have meant in her rather elliptical remarks on the burntworks: "art and a way of working fuse . . . poetic, visionary . . . capacity to identify . . ."[29] Here Kaish assembles her words in a fragmented, stream-of-consciousness manner consistent with process by which she assembles her burnt elements on canvas.

Kaish has strong spiritual connections with classic Jewish mystical texts, particularly the Kabbalah and the Zohar. In the Jewish rabbinic and literary tradition, such texts have been continually reinterpreted in the context of contemporary situations, and Kaish emphatically

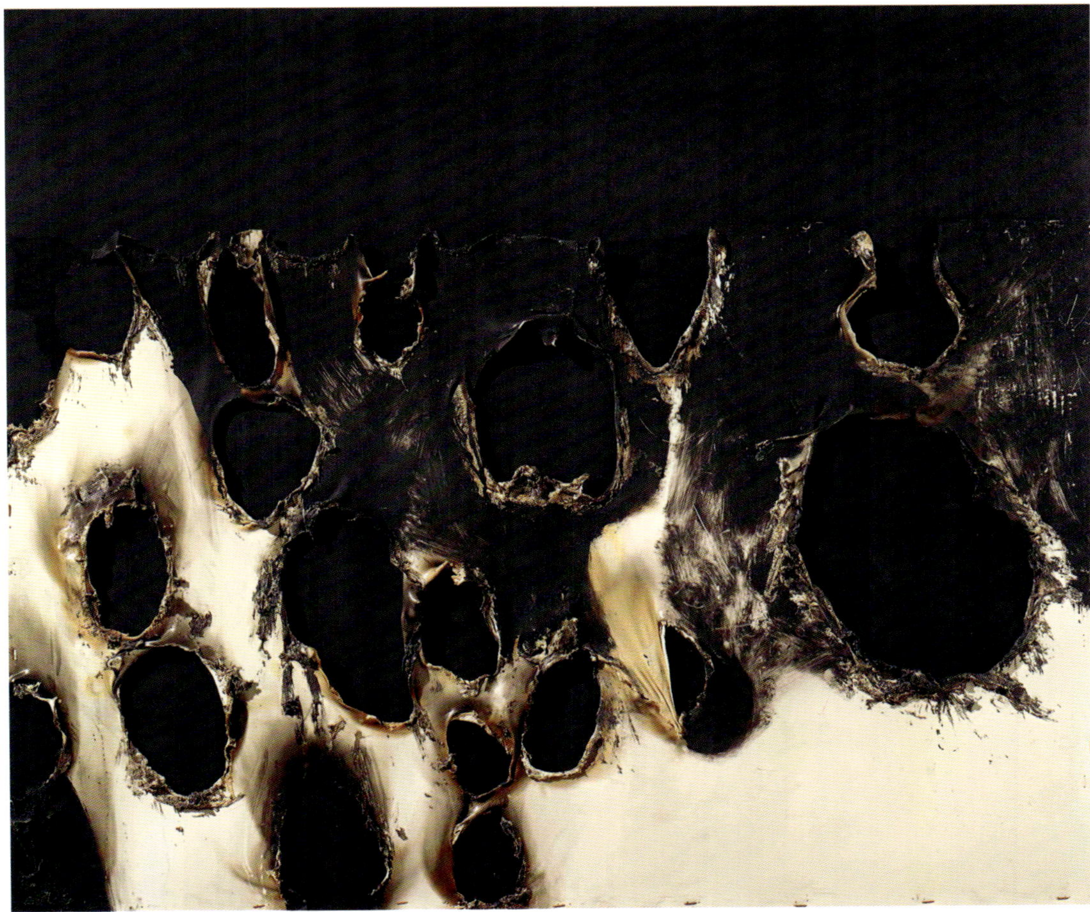

Fig. 56   Alberto Burri, *Combustione Plastica*, 1956, mixed media plastic and acrylic on canvas, 37 ½ × 39 ½ in. (85.7 × 100 cm)

states that, for her, "The Bible . . . the Zohar . . . the Cabbala [sic] have been sources of poetic & symbolic imagery."[30] Highly relevant to the physical fabrication and psychological foundations of Kaish's burntworks is the kabbalistic notion of the "breaking of the vessels" and the related concept of *tikkun*, or healing the world. Emerging from earlier mystical texts, the idea, evolved from the Zohar, was brilliantly articulated and reformulated by the sixteenth-century Jewish scholar Isaac Luria.[31] Luria sought to clarify earlier mystical texts, not about only God and the creation of the world and human beings, but also the forces of good and evil and the separation of the sacred and profane, as well as the individual's responsibility to the deity, the world, and fellow beings. The concept of the "breaking of the vessels" is one early basis for the notion of creation through destruction. In kabbalistic explanations of the origins of the world and human beings, divine light was contained in shells, with outer layers of "thicker" light holding inner reserves of "purer" light. These two forces ultimately fought each other and imploded, releasing the purer light mostly to its divine source and the "thicker," less pure light to lower levels considered tainted or evil. These compromised shells, holding less pure light, are ultimately the basis of the material world. Within these shells or husks (*Quelipot*) remained divine sparks of purer illumination, which allowed not only for their continued existence but also the restorative forces possible through human intervention known as *tikkun*.[32] As the twentieth-century scholar of Jewish mysticism Gerhsom Scholem explains:

> This primal space is full of formless, hylic forces, the Kelipoth [*Quelipot*]. The process of the world consists of giving shape to these formless forces, making something out of them. As long as this has not been done, the primal space, and in particular its lower part, is the stronghold of darkness and evil.[33]

Kaish must have been familiar with the scholarly work of the renowned Isaac Luria, and certainly with Gershom Scholem, whose iconic book *Major Trends in Jewish Mysticism*, first published in 1941, had by the 1960s become a virtual bible for American intellectuals.[34] Despite Scholem's depth of scholarship, the volume was often critiqued as being inadequate in itself for true understanding of the Kabbalah.[35] In any event, this was a foundational, somewhat revolutionary, text for postwar Jewish thinking, which required less-rationalist options in the wake of World War II, the Holocaust, and Hiroshima. Scholem's interpretation of *tikkun* had by the 1970s become a concept well acknowledged as essential within various religious, intellectual, and secular Jewish societies in the United States. And *tikkun*, the commitment to healing and improving the world, became as natural as it seemed necessary in the catastrophic wake of the Holocaust. Cynthia Ozick was one among a considerable group of scholars and writers who were admirers of Scholem's thought and scholarship. In an article in the *New Yorker*, Ozick observes:

> The concept of tikkun, the reintegration of what has been fragmented, the correction of confusion, the return to harmony. In this way, the Kabbalists of Galilee (e.g. Luria and company) through a cosmological myth of exile and redemption, were able to map a people's shattered experience and adumbrate a vision of restoration.[36]

Kaish's "bandaging and salving" of the saved fragments in her burntworks seem an apt analogy to the "breaking of the vessels" and the restoration of the world, both physically and metaphorically (Fig. 57). The burntworks were not collages of pure destructive force, as with artists such as Burri and Millares. Rather, Kaish took the remnants of destruction and transformed them into salvaged wholes, works that not only are highly organized and transcendent in nature, but that use, imply, and perhaps even emanate light. During the time Kaish was working on this project, she commented that she sought "to express the idea at its moment of greatest passion . . . gathering light, restructuring it, filtering it through forms subtle and complex." She spoke, referencing C. G. Jung, of her desire for a "visionary mode of creation . . . a state of participation mystique . . . a reality beyond the personal psychological experience, as beyond science, mathematics, and the armour of reason."[37] Her

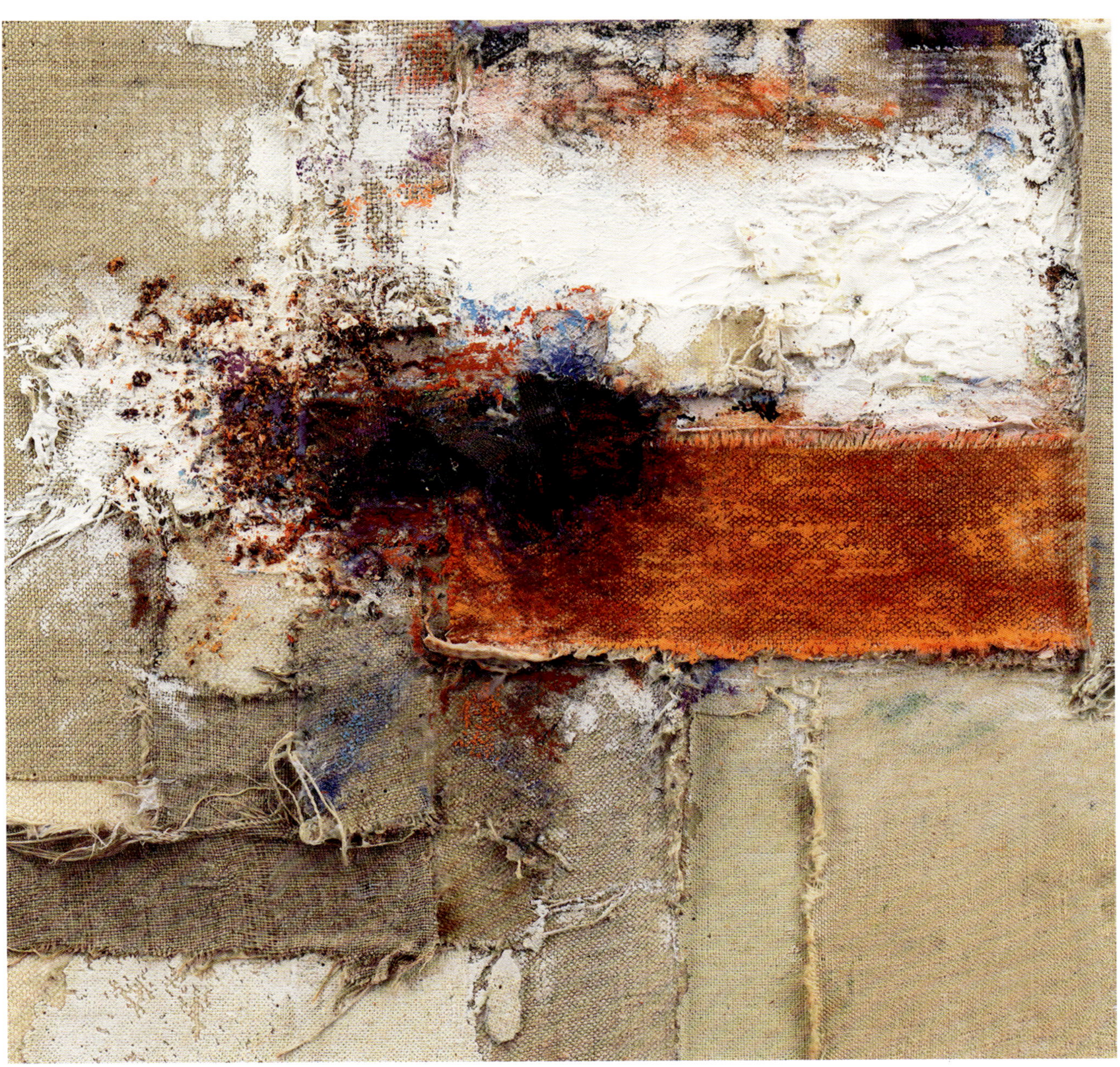

Fig. 57 Luise Kaish, *Mistaya* (detail), 1979–81 (see Plate 66)

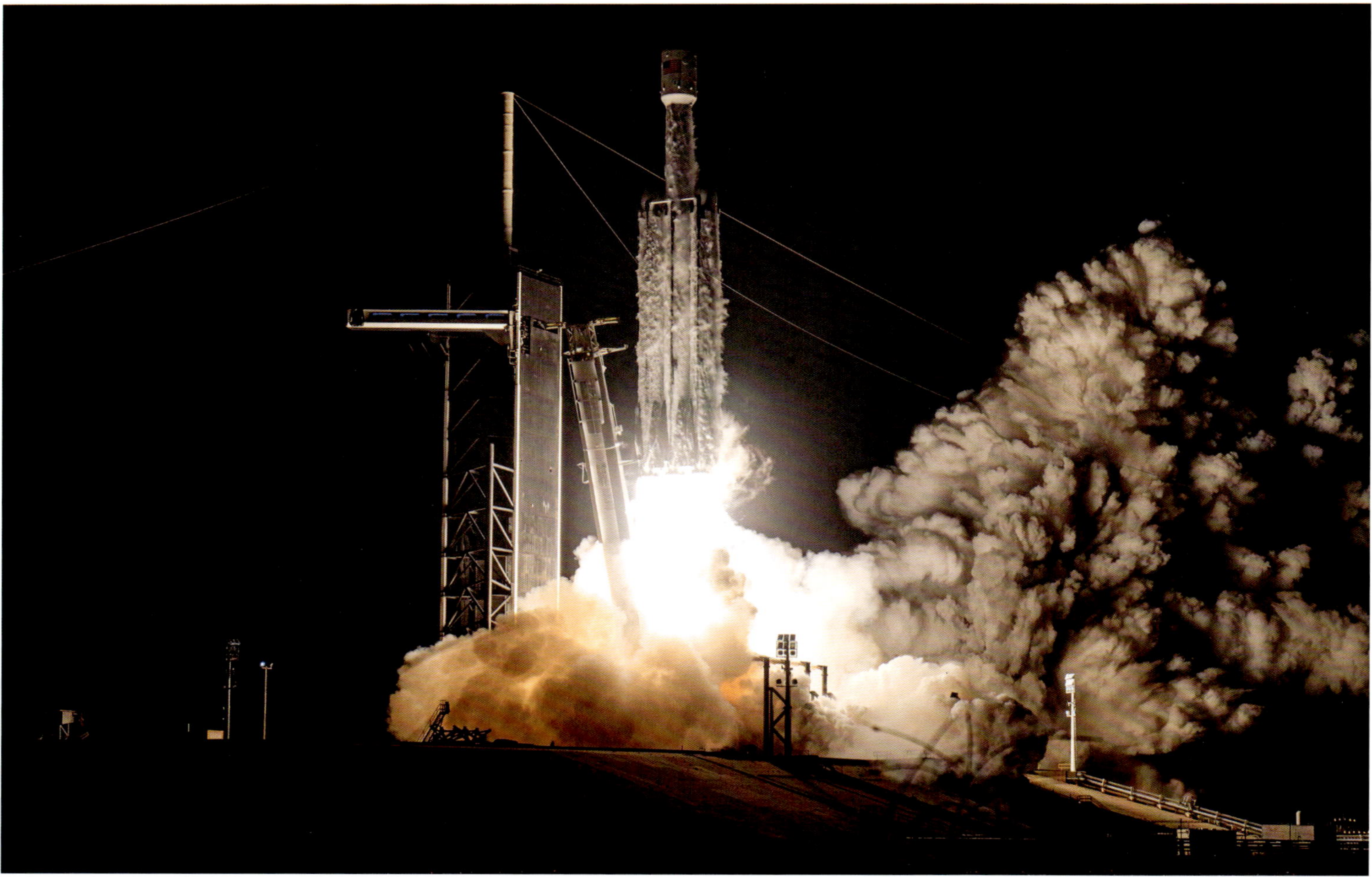

Fig. 58   Luise's spirit joins the cosmos aboard SpaceX Falcon Heavy rocket, Cape Canaveral, Florida, June 25, 2019

thoughts in this text continue with the concept that art and religion offer bridges between the soul of man and God. Kaish's thinking at the time of creating her burntworks, and the processes endemic to them, certainly demonstrate that she fused her intellectual interest in the spiritual, mystical, historical, and religious with the formal, structural, and material processes of their design: destruction, creation, salvation, reincarnation.

Afterlife / After Life

In a 2014 interview about his late wife, Morton Kaish observed that, with her burntworks and later pieces, Kaish had become absorbed increasingly with kabbalistic ideas, especially the notion of *Beth Shalom* (House of Peace). He acknowledged that Kaish had always been "fascinated, literally, with the earth and the heavens," one curious consequence of which was that she became a passionate follower of NASA since its early years when the United States launched humans into space. This fascination with "the spirit of the physical cosmos," Morton noted, might be considered a near preoccupation. During her time at the American Academy in Rome, Kaish began to sculpt more abstractly, using essential forms related to the planets, the sun, the universe, and the unknown—and, by extension, to creation itself.

This spatial, cosmological obsession reached such a point for Kaish that she decided that, upon her death, she wished her ashes to be dispersed in space.[38] In her words: "As you may know, for me, the Universe holds endless fascination. Beautiful as is this earth I do not wish to be buried in it at death. The thought that my dust, our dust, could be mingled with the matter of star building, released in space to become part of the creative act, perhaps joined with the Almighty . . . what a fantastic journey that would be."[39] On June 25, 2019, Kaish's ashes were sent into space on the third voyage of the SpaceX Falcon Heavy rocket, along with those of approximately 150 other posthumous passengers.[40] Kaish did not wish her ashes to travel "simply into orbit, or to the moon, but [into] deep space, the realm of infinity" (Fig. 58).[41]

In her final act, Kaish had conceived something far larger, more complex, and infinitely more intimate than John Baldessari's *Cremation Project*. Albeit brilliant, Baldessari's burning of thirteen years of his painting was meant as a conceptual act, and one that, all irony aside, remained a tangible object, a work of art at its most reductive. It is evident that Kaish was less interested in the conceptual than in the fission of the palpably material and the ethereal sublime, the objective and subjective, the corporeal and the spiritual. Her ashes so distributed, Kaish's final creative idea emerged from her stated longing, both personally and professionally, "to push beyond whatever may be beyond."[42]

Endnotes

1. Luise Kaish, "Lecture for an Unknown Occasion," c. 1983–89, Luise Kaish archives, New York.

2. Frequently mentioned among postwar artists who shuttled between representation and abstraction are Willem de Kooning (1904–1997) and Philip Guston (1913–1980); Grace Hartigan (1922–2008), though less often cited as an example, might well be added to the list.

3. Luise Kaish, conversation with Samuel Gruber, 2002, typescript, 1. Here Kaish talks about her travels during the early 1950s to France, Italy, and Switzerland looking at Romanesque, baroque, and Renaissance art and architecture.

4. Louise Nevelson (1899–1988), Lee Krasner (1908–1984), Grace Hartigan (1922–2008), and Eva Hesse (1936–1970) are but a few examples of artists juggling multiple personal and professional priorities.

5. Adolph Gottlieb (1903–1974) and Mark Rothko (1903–1970) famously made their edifying observations public in 1943 in an open letter to *New York Times* art editor Edwin Alden Jewell: Adolph Gottlieb and Mark Rothko to Edwin Alden Jewell, June 7, 1943, Mark Rothko papers, undated and 1943, Archives of American Art, Smithsonian Institution, Washington, D.C. The letter was quoted in its entirety in Jewell's response: "The Realm of Art: A New Platform and 'Globalism' Pops into View," *New York Times*, June 13, 1943, sec. 2, p. 9. See also John P. O'Neill, ed., *Barnett Newman, Selected Writings and Interviews* (New York: Alfred A. Knopf, 1990), 151, 153–44.

6. Though basically two-dimensional, according to Kaish's comments, all her art was impacted by her background as a thinker in three dimensions. In the introduction to the catalogue for a solo exhibition at Staempfli Gallery in 1981, Kaish remarks, "For me, working on canvas, as a sculptor, has always been like encountering a 'stop here' sign.

It's vertical, impenetrable, a wall. I want to punch a hole in it—to see the light fall, sense the space. I want to create a window, a space for one's visual imagination to move, through and into. By using the burnt canvas, I was able to join my imagination with the physical needs of a sculptor: to deal at first hand with a tactile material. I build, layer, tear and rebuild my canvas reliefs, at times contemplatively, at times in a frenzy of energy"; *Luise Kaish: Recent Collages*, exh. cat. (New York: Staempfli Gallery, 1981).

7. Luise Kaish, "Thoughts and Comments on Century Exhibition: Luise Kaish 2012," Luise Kaish archives.

8. Morton Kaish, oral history with Liza Zapol, May 26, 2016, New York, transcript, 45, Luise Kaish archives.

9. Luise Kaish, "Notes on Artistic Philosophy," 1976–80, Luise Kaish archives.

10. Luise Kaish, "Notes on Burntworks," c. 1976–80, Luise Kaish archives.

11. Ibid., back of previous page.

12. William Chapin Seitz, *The Art of Assemblage*, exh. cat. (New York: Museum of Modern Art, 1961). Seitz's show may well have been influenced by Alan Solomon's 1958 exhibition *Collages and Constructions* held at the Andrew Dickson White Gallery then at Cornell University.

13. Morton Kaish and Sarah McCollum Williams, conversation with the author, June 18, 2019.

14. Ida Kohlmeyer and Lowell Adams, *American Women: Twentieth Century*, exh. cat. (Peoria, IL: Lakeview Center for the Arts and Sciences, 1972).

15. Miriam Schapiro and Melissa Meyer, "Waste Not, Want Not: An Inquiry into What Women Saved and Assembled— Femmage," *Artcritical*, June 24, 2015, https://www.artcritical.com/2015/06/24/femmage-by-miriam-schapiro-and-melissa-meyer/; originally published in the feminist journal *Heresies* (Winter 1978): 66–69.

16. Richard Martin, "Luise Kaish," *Arts Magazine* 59, no. 2 (October 1984).

17. Noted in Russell Ferguson, "The Show Is Over," in *Damage Control: Art and Destruction Since 1950*, by Kerry Brougher, Russell Ferguson, and Dario Gamboni, exh. cat. (Washington, DC: Hirshhorn Museum and Sculpture Garden; Munich: DelMonico; New York: Prestel, 2013).

18. Newman (1905–1970) destroyed all of his works completed prior to 1944, and, as he explained in a letter to critic Clement Greenberg in 1955, "I first created my concept and developed my present style in 1944–45" (quoted in O'Neill, *Barnett Newman*, 204).

19. Some of Motherwell's (1915–1991) earlier figurative works did survive. See, for example, his painting *La Belle Mexicaine (Maria)*, 1941, oil on canvas, 29 ½ x 23 ¾ in. (74.9 x 60.3 cm), Dedalus Foundation, New York, exhibited recently in *Robert Motherwell: Early Painting*, September 7– October 28, 2017, Paul Kasmin Gallery, New York. See also Catherine Craft, *An Audience of Artists: Dada, Neo-Dada, and the Emergence of Abstract Expressionism* (Chicago: University of Chicago Press, 2012), 79. Craft mentions the role of destruction for artists including Krasner and Motherwell.

20. Nevelson (1899–1988) destroyed works from two early shows that were poorly received: one at Nierendorf Gallery in 1940 (see Burt A. Folkart's obituary for Louise Nevelson in the *Los Angeles Times*, April 19, 1988); the other a 1943 exhibition on the theme of the circus at the Norlyst Gallery that she participated in (see Roni Feinstein, *Louise Nevelson: A Concentration of Works from the Permanent Collection of the Whitney Museum of American Art*, exh. cat. (New York: Whitney Museum of American Art, 1987), 4.

21. Laurie Wilson, *Louise Nevelson: Light and Shadow* (London: Thames & Hudson, 2016), 41.

22. Tina Dickey, *Color Creates Light: Studies with Hans Hofmann* (British Columbia: Trillistar Books, 2011).

23. Ellen G. Landau, *Lee Krasner: A Catalogue Raisonné* (New York: Harry N. Abrams, 1995), 126–52; esp. "Remark," p. 596.

24. Kerry Brougher, "Radiation Made Visible," in Brougher, Ferguson, and Gamboni, *Damage Control*, 33. The destructive impulse in post-war art was codified by Brougher, Ferguson, and Gamboni in the 2013 Hirshhorn exhibition and catalogue, *Damage Control: Art and Destruction Since 1950*.

25. Kaish, "Notes on Artistic Philosophy," 1976–80. Gustave Metzger (1926–2017), the founder of auto-destructive art in Great Britain, is a relevant example of the more general destruction practice for art in the United States. This is all the more true with reference to Kaish, as Metzger's art evolved from his personal history and Jewish identity. He was on the children's transport from Nazi Germany to Britain, and most of his family was murdered in the Holocaust.

26. Kaish, "Notes on Artistic Philosophy," 1976–80.

27. Morton Kaish and Sarah McCollum Williams, conversation with the author, June 18, 2019.

28. Many of these Italian and Spanish painters did show in the United States during the 1960s and 1970s.

29. Kaish, "Notes on Artistic Philosophy," 1976–80.

30. Ibid.

31. Gershom Scholem, *Major Trends in Jewish Mysticism* (New York: Schocken Books, 1995), esp. 265–68.

32. Lawrence Fine, "Tikkun: A Lurianic Motif in Contemporary Jewish Thought," in *From Ancient Israel to Modern Judaism: Intellect in Quest of Understanding; Essays in Honor of Marvin Fox*, vol. 4, *The Modern Age: Theology, Literature, History*, ed. Jacob Neusner et al. (Atlanta, GA: Scholars Press, 1989), 35–53.

33. Scholem is noted for his "scientific" attention to mystical theories. Yaakov Dwek recounts a frequently told story of Professor Saul Lieberman's introduction to Scholem at the Jewish Theological Seminary of America lecture. Lieberman is quoted as saying, "Non-sense is nonsense, but the history of nonsense is very important science." This comment is indicative of the scientific positivism that prevailed in Jewish studies at the time. See Yaakov Dwek, "Gershom Scholem and America," *New German Critique* 44, no. 3 (132) (November 2017): 69.

34. Ibid., 63.

35. Ibid. Such was the basis for the debate around art critic Tom Hess's mystical, Jewish interpretation of the work of artist Barnett Newman. See Dwek, "Gershom Scholem and America," 73–74; Thomas Hess, *Barnett Newman*, exh. cat. (New York: Museum of Modern Art, 1971).

36. Cynthia Ozick, "The Heretic: The Mythic Passions of Gershom Scholem," *New Yorker*, August 25, 2002, https://www.newyorker.com/magazine/2002/09/02/the-heretic.

37. Kaish, "Notes on Artistic Philosophy," 1976–80.

38. Morton Kaish, oral history with Liza Zapol, 47.

39. Memorial Program for Luise Kaish, Central Synagogue, New York City, March 11, 2013.

40. The SpaceX Falcon Heavy rocket launched on June 25, 2019, was designed to orbit the earth for twenty-five years, and carried only half of Luise's ashes. The remainder awaits a forthcoming flight into deep space.

41. Marcia Dunn, "SpaceX Launches Falcon Heavy with Satellites, Experiments," *SFGate*, June 25, 2019, https://www.sfgate.com/business/article/SpaceX-launches-Falcon-Heavy-with-satellites-14048483.php.

42. Morton Kaish, oral history with Liza Zapol, 47.

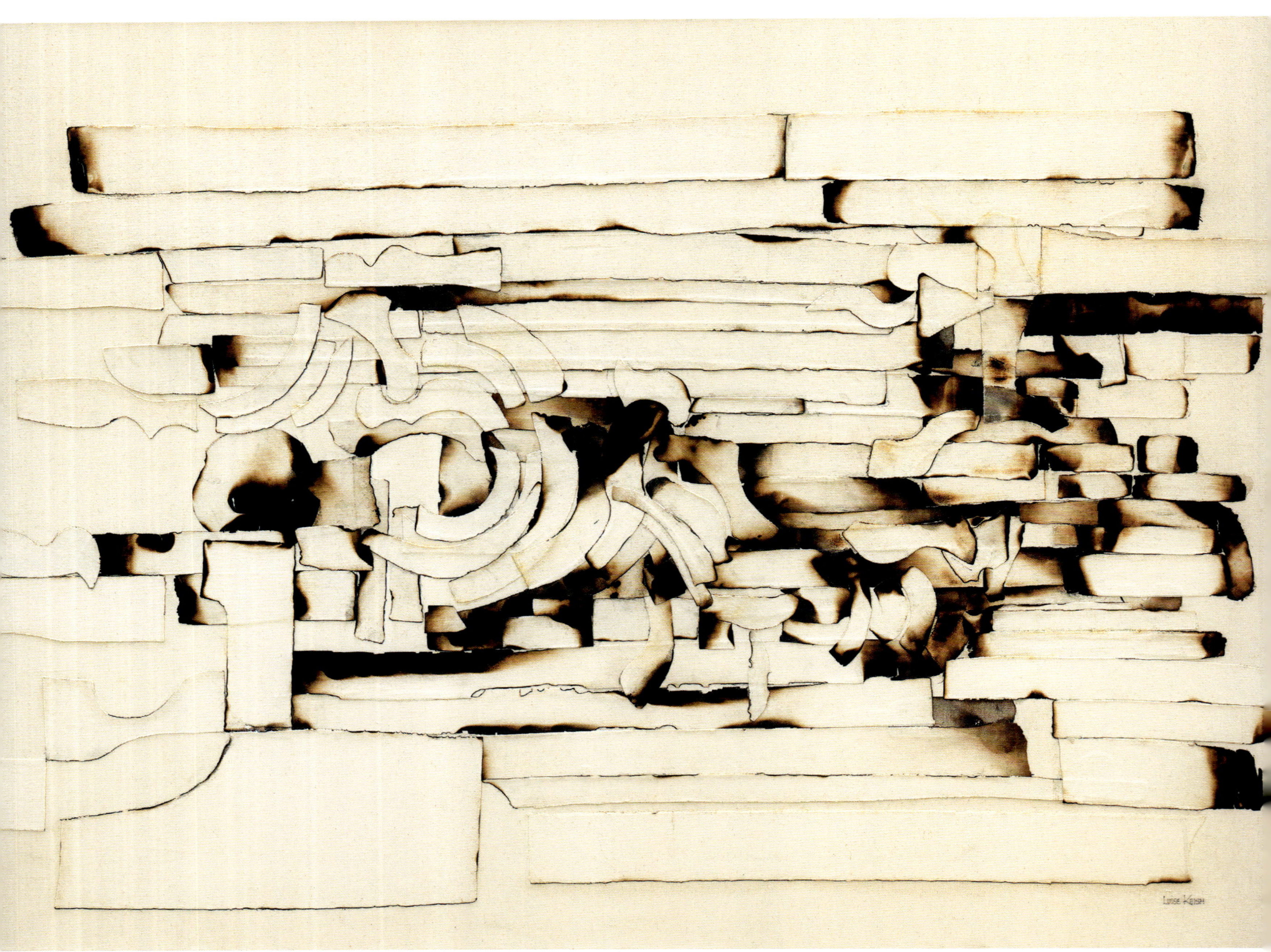

Plate 58

Luise Kaish. *Untitled* (*MacDowell*), 1976, burnt canvas collage,
42 × 58 in. (106.7 × 147.3 cm)

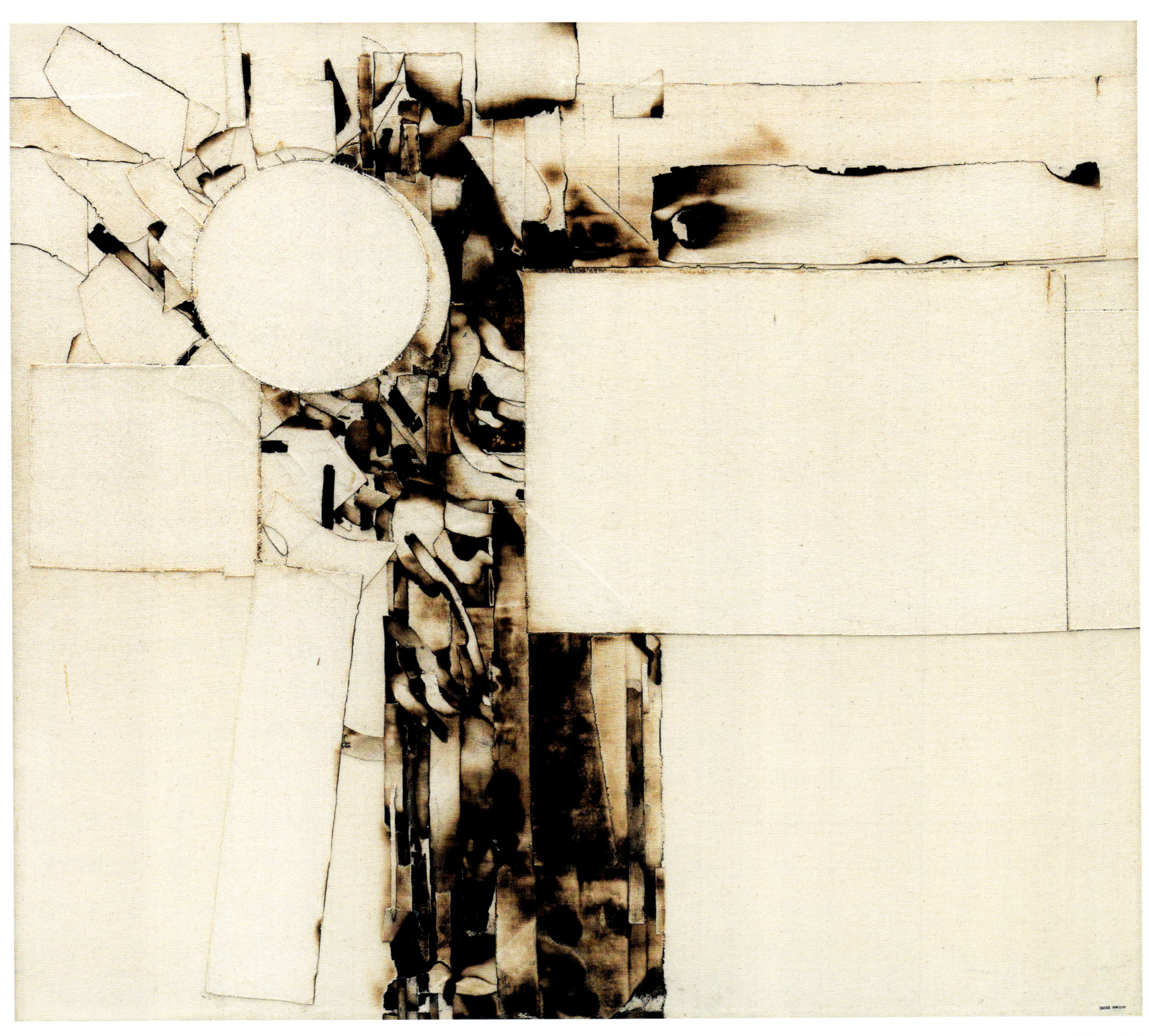

Plate 59
Luise Kaish. *Monadnock I*, 1976, burnt canvas collage,
48 × 48 in. (121.9 × 121.9 cm)

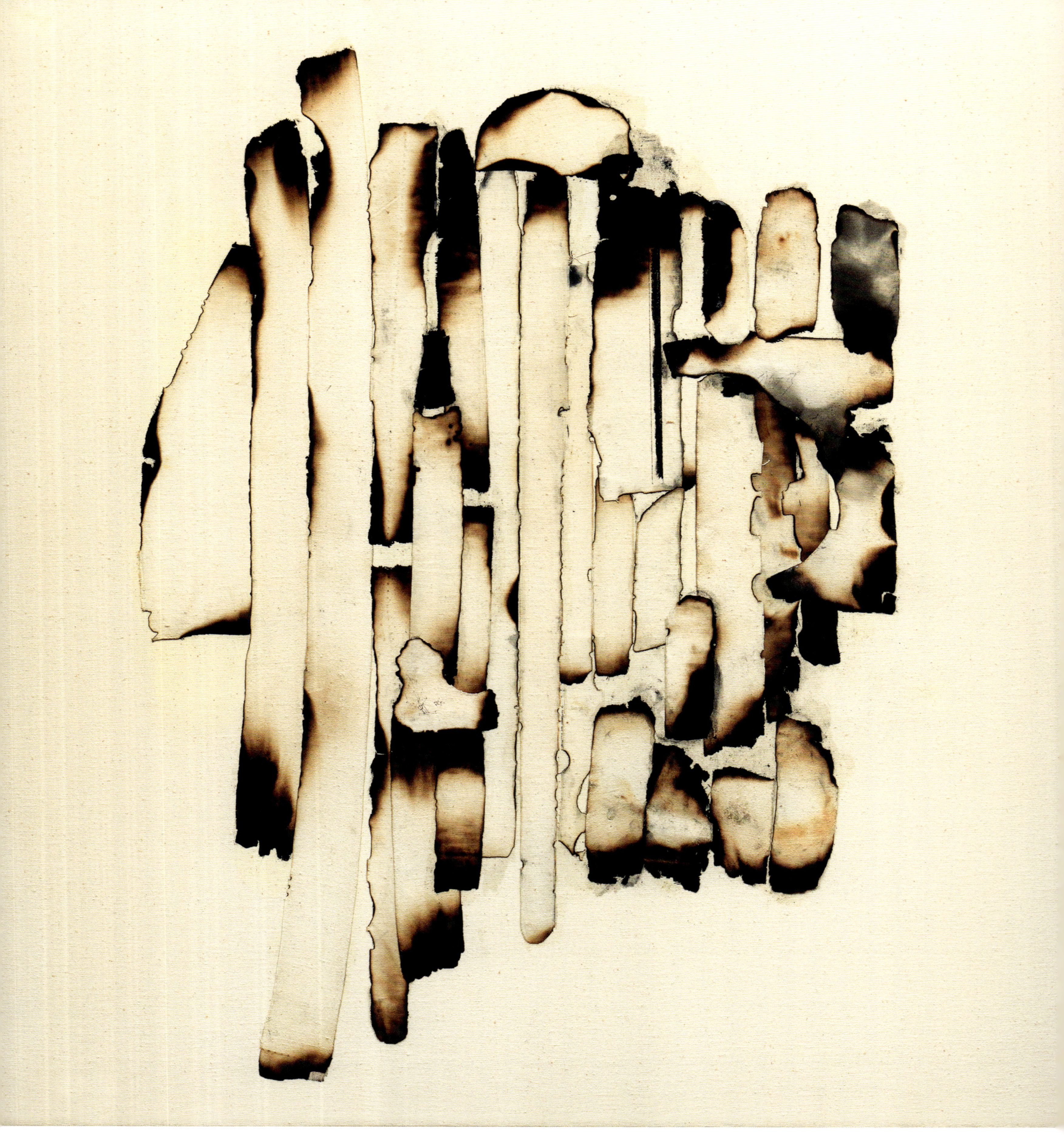

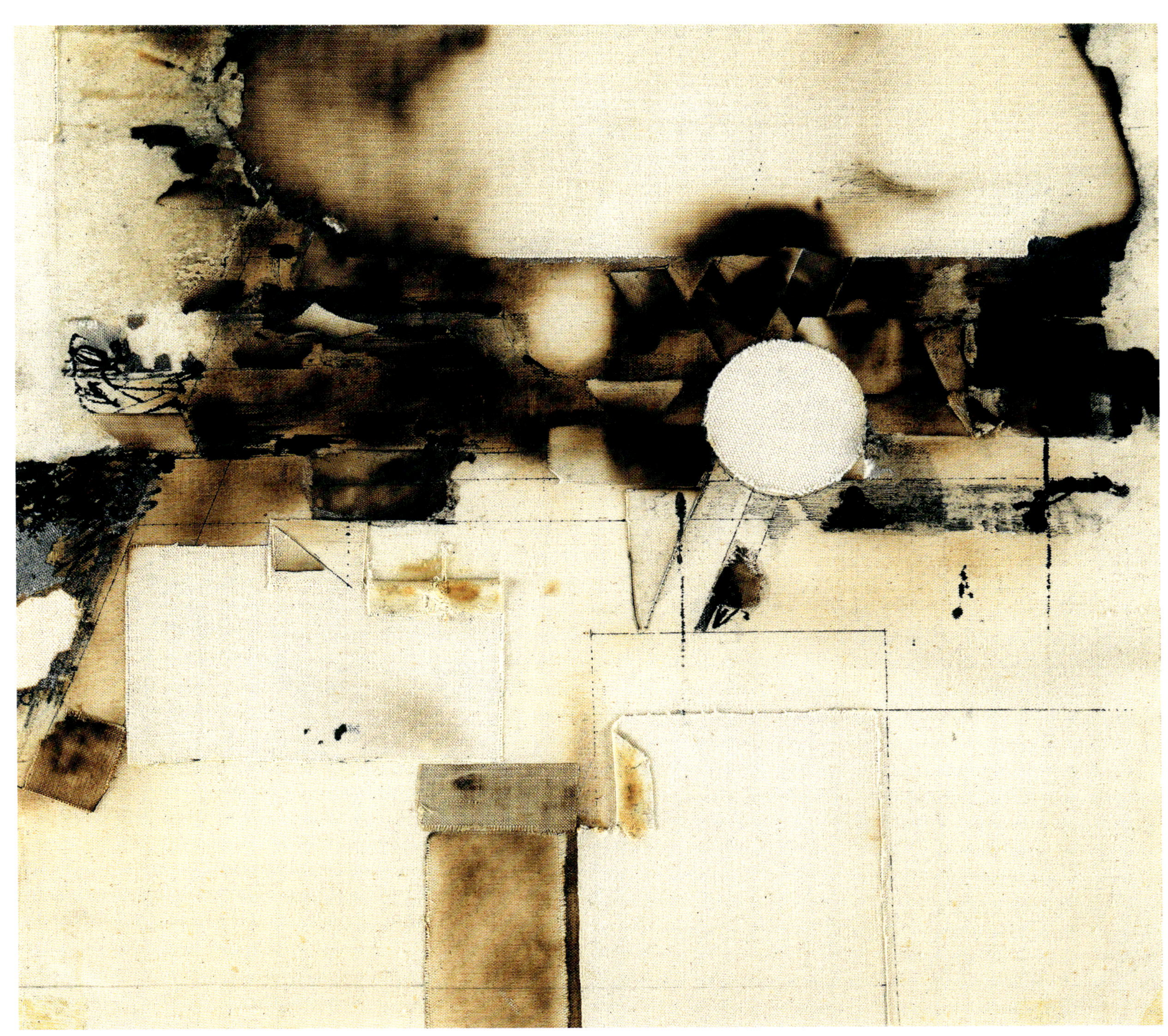

Plate 60
Luise Kaish. *Firepond I*, 1976, burnt canvas collage,
36 × 34 in. (91.4 × 86.4 cm)

Plate 61
Luise Kaish. *Untitled*, 1976–79, burnt canvas collage,
16 × 16 in. (40.6 × 40.6 cm)

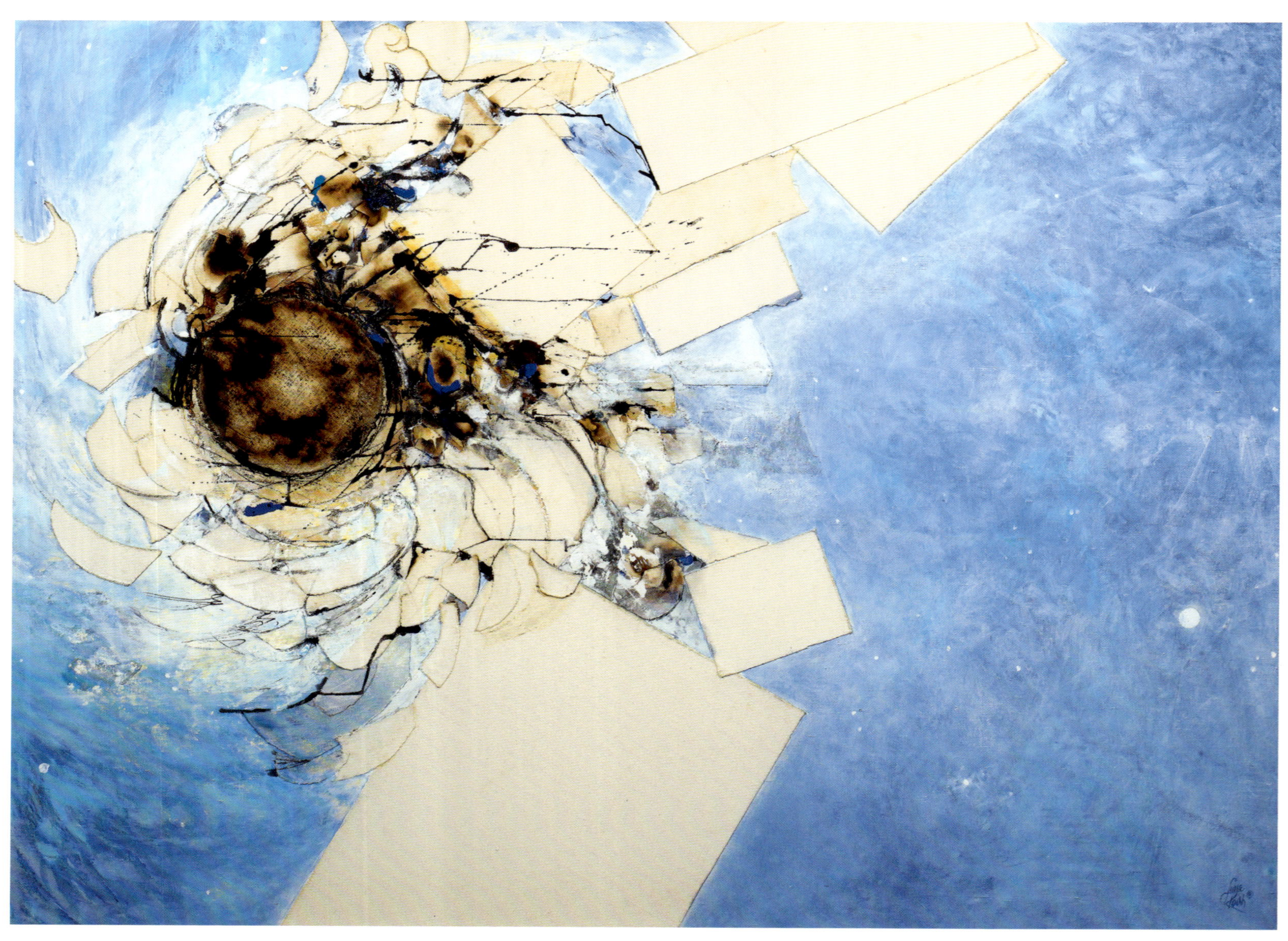

Plate 62
Luise Kaish. *Poet in Two Worlds* (*Deep Space*), 1975–78,
burnt canvas and acrylic collage, 50 × 68 in. (127 × 172.7 cm)

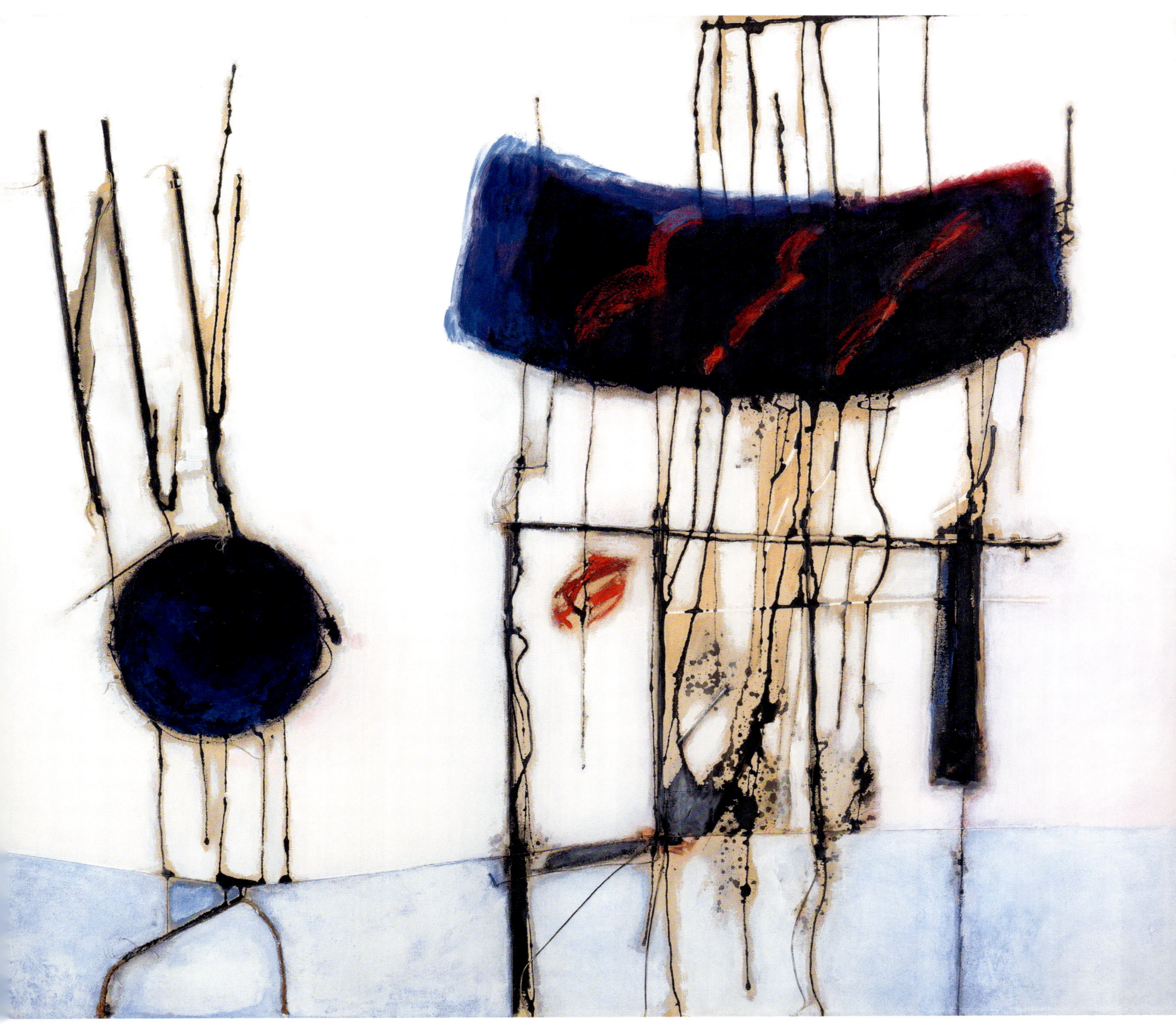

Plate 63
Luise Kaish. *Hanging Orb* (*After Japan Trip*), 1976,
acrylic, india ink, and string on canvas, 60 × 72 in. (152.4 × 182.9 cm)

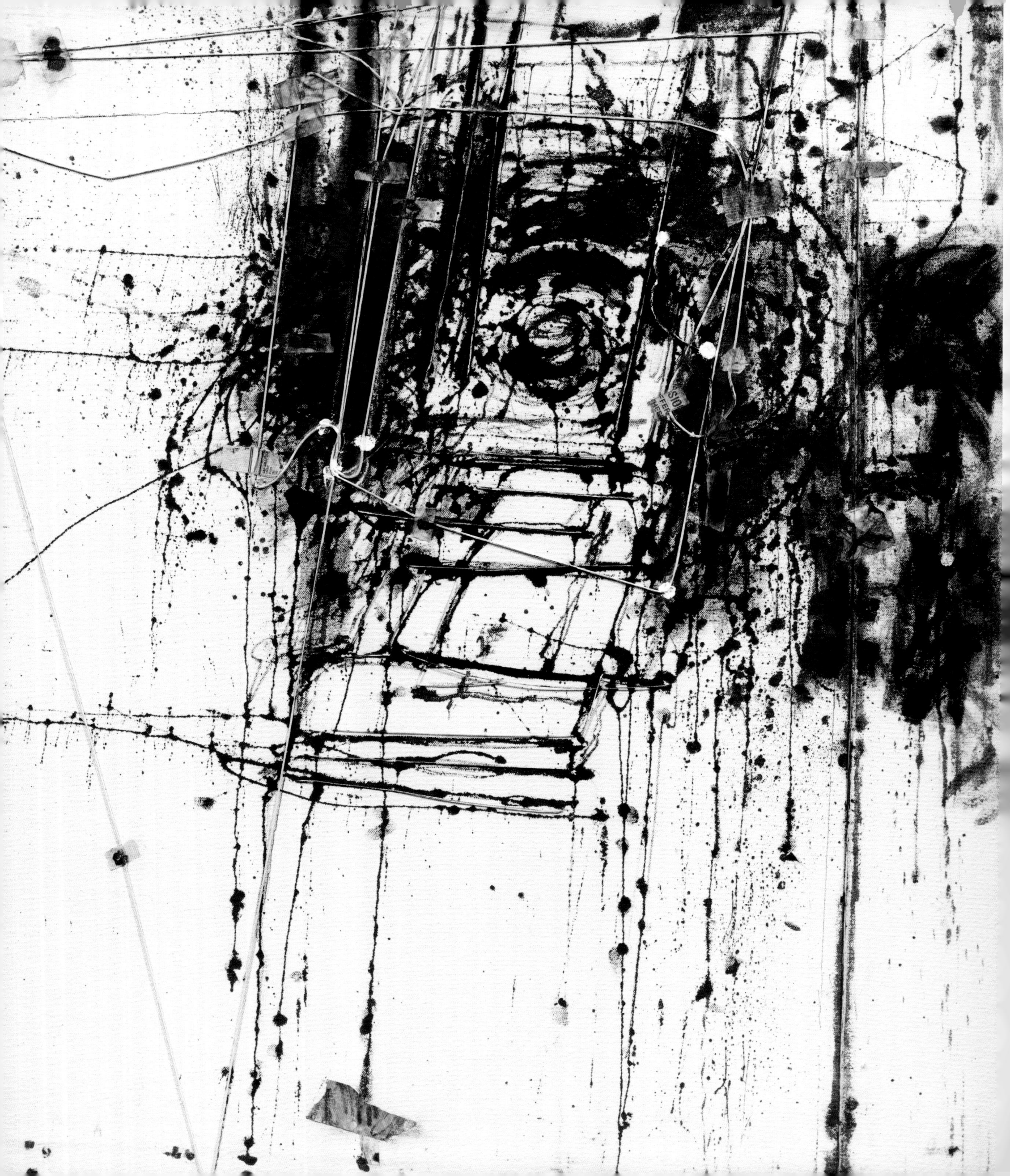

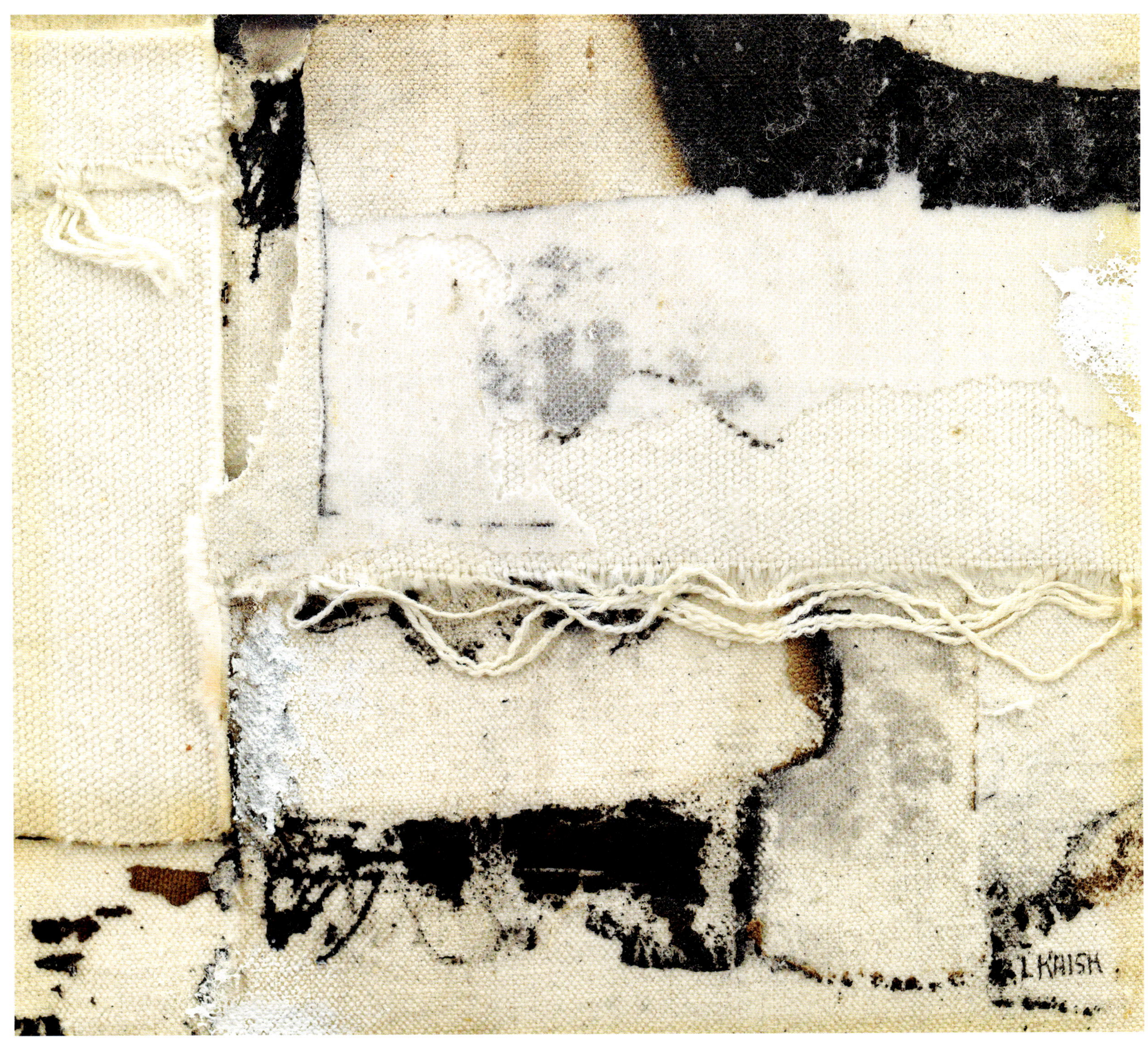

Plate 64
Luise Kaish. *Ink and String on Canvas*,
1976–85, ink and string on canvas, 36 × 32 in.
(91.4 × 81.3 cm)

Plate 65
Luise Kaish. *Burntworks 14*, circa 1979–81, collage,
mixed media on canvas, 5 ½ × 5 ½ in. (14 × 14 cm)

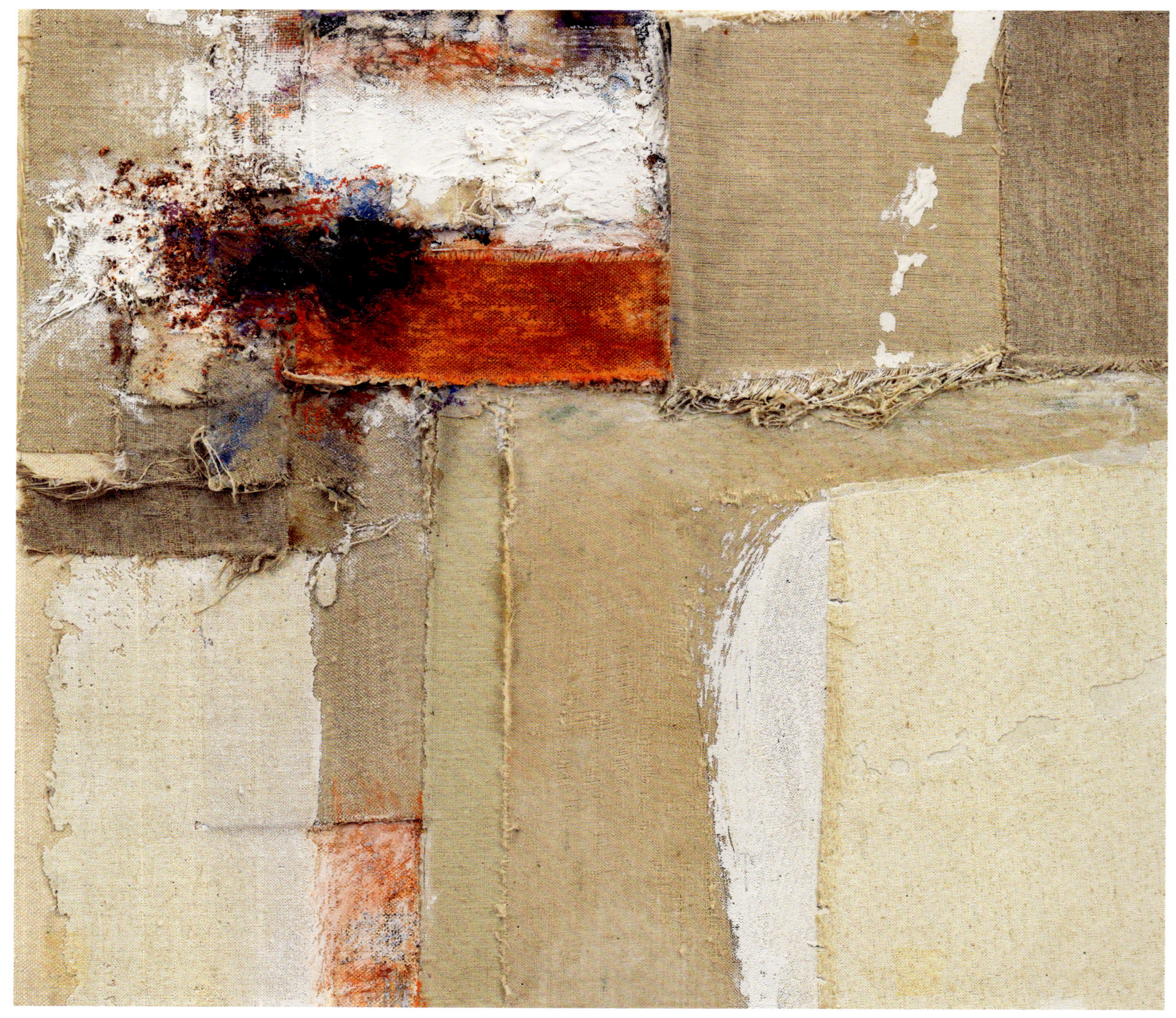

Plate 66
Luise Kaish. *Mistaya*, 1979–81, mixed media,
12 × 13 ½ in. (30.5 × 34.3 cm)

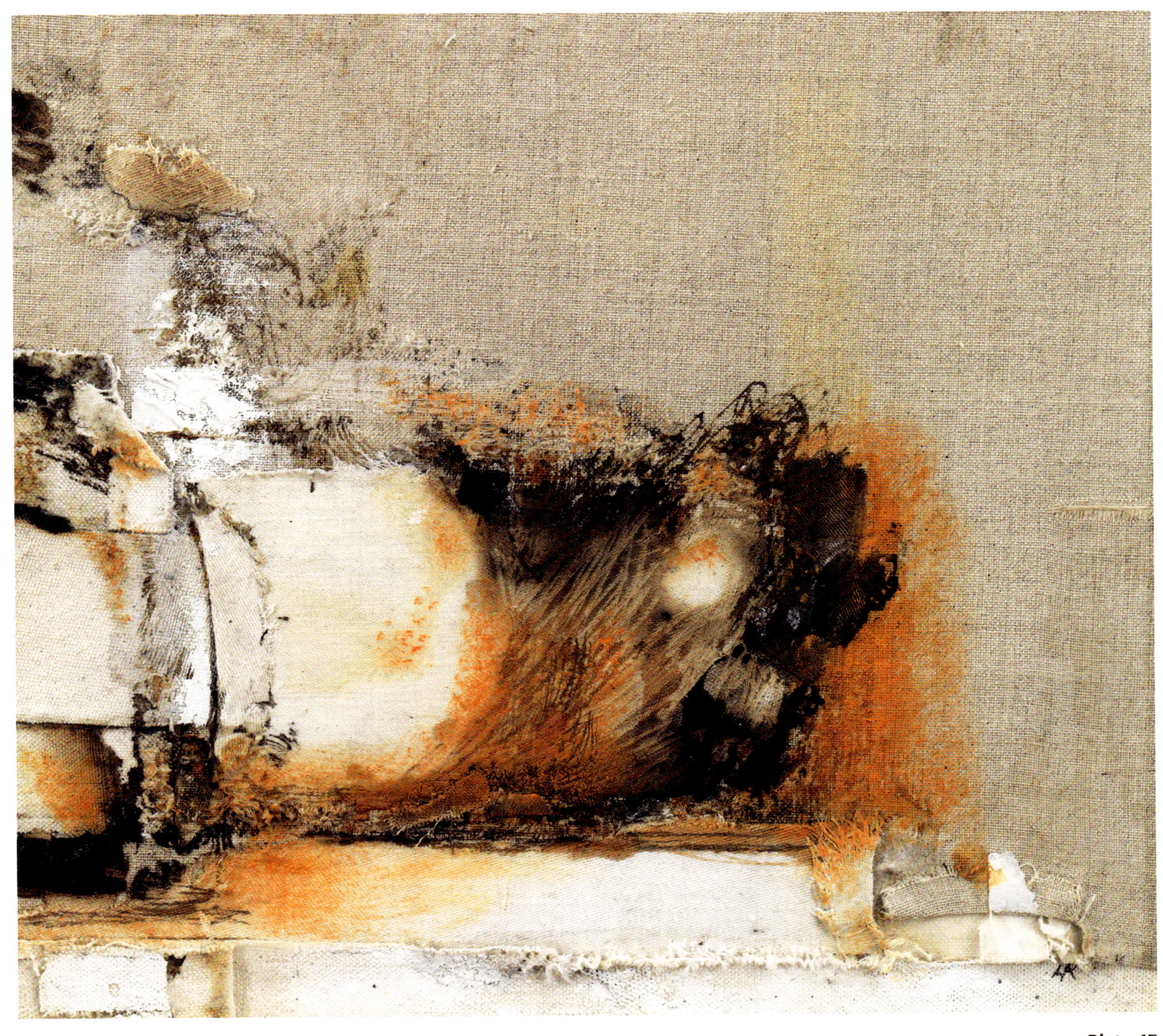

Plate 67
Luise Kaish. *Storm I*, 1980, collage, mixed media,
8 ½ × 9 ½ in. (21.6 × 24.1 cm)

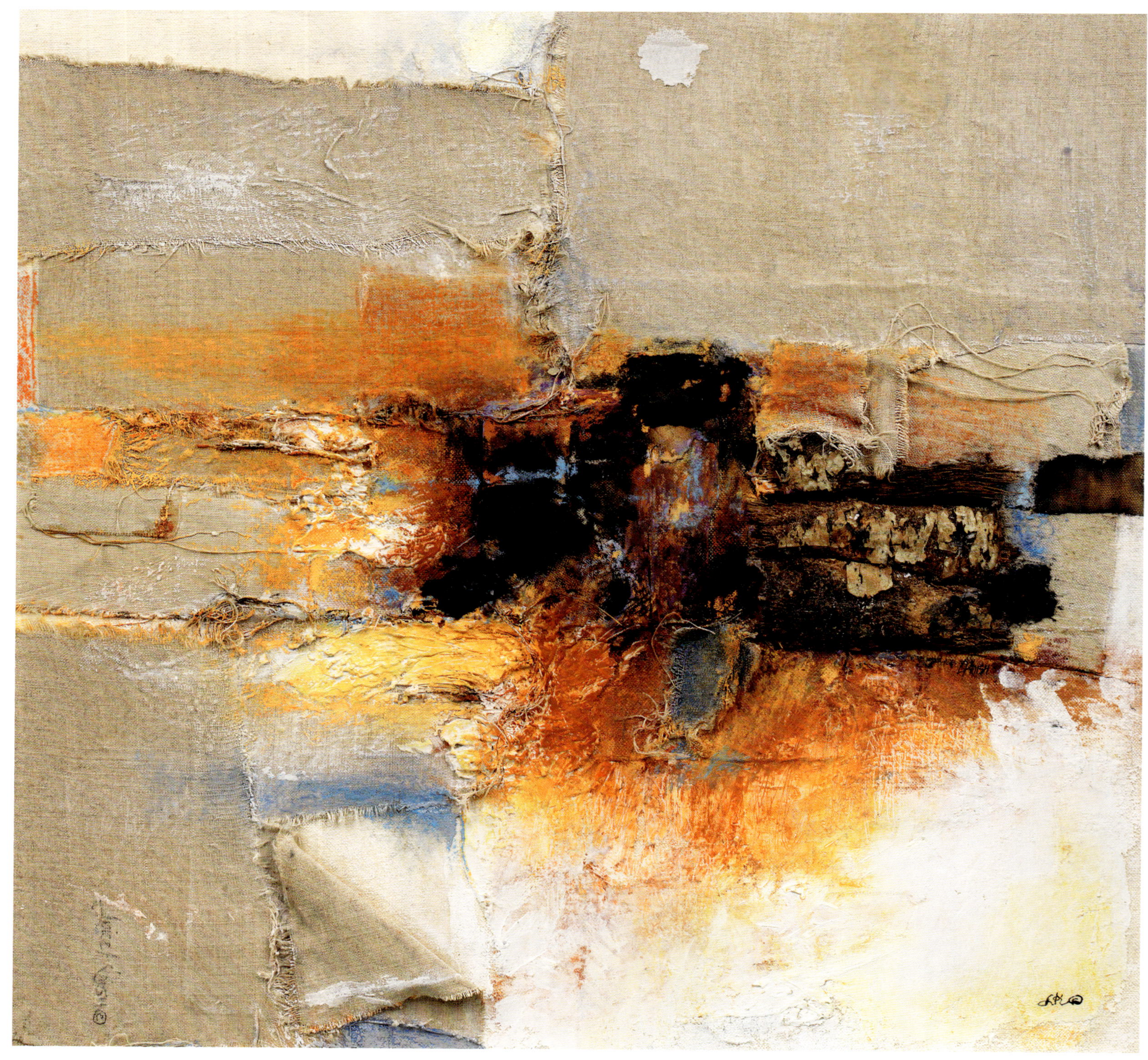

Plate 68
Luise Kaish. *Aspen*, 1981, mixed media,
20 × 24 in. (50.8 × 60.96 cm)

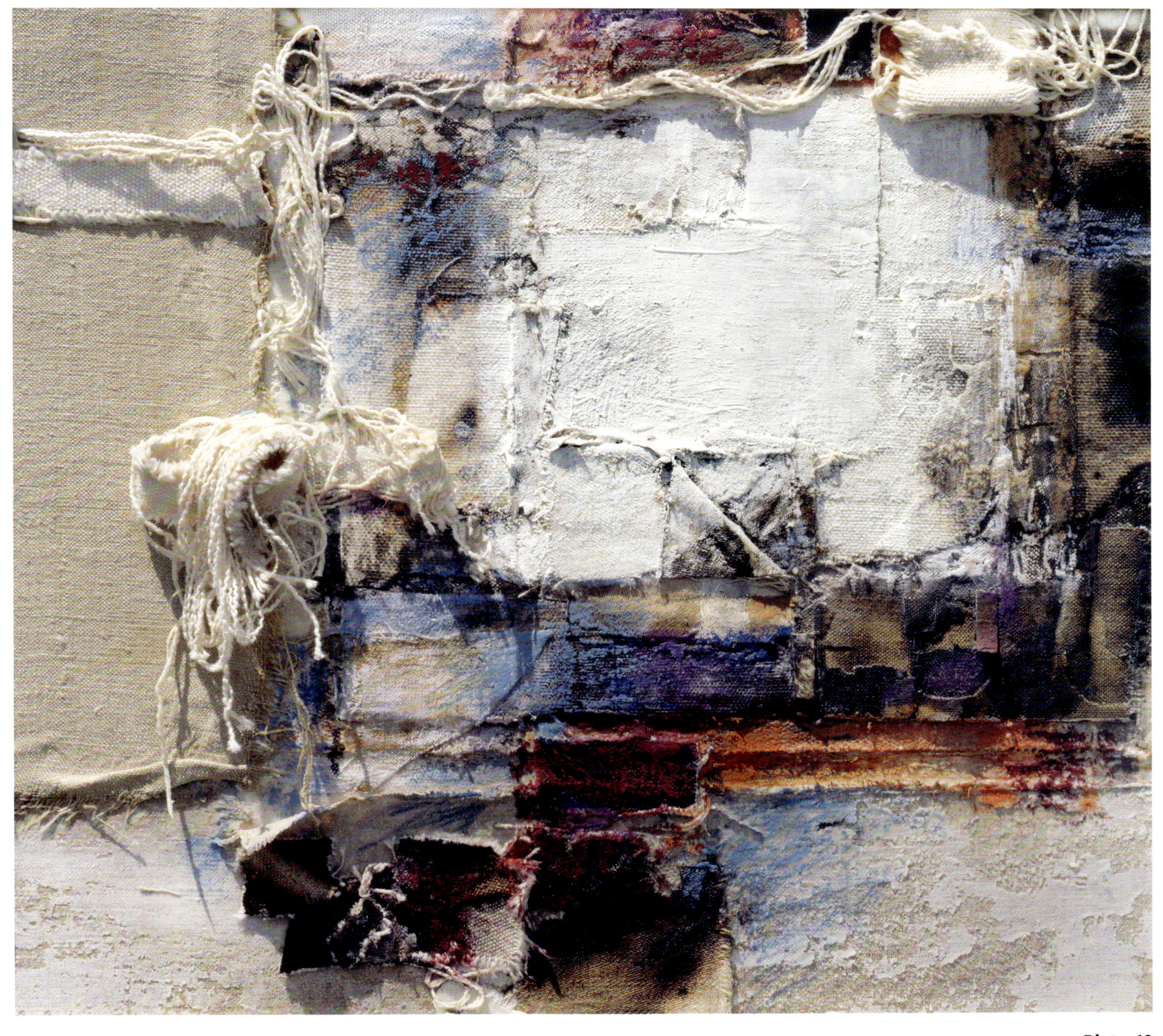

Plate 69
Luise Kaish. *Layers and Levels*, 1980, collage,
mixed media on canvas, 10 ⅝ × 11 ⅝ in. (27 × 29.5 cm)

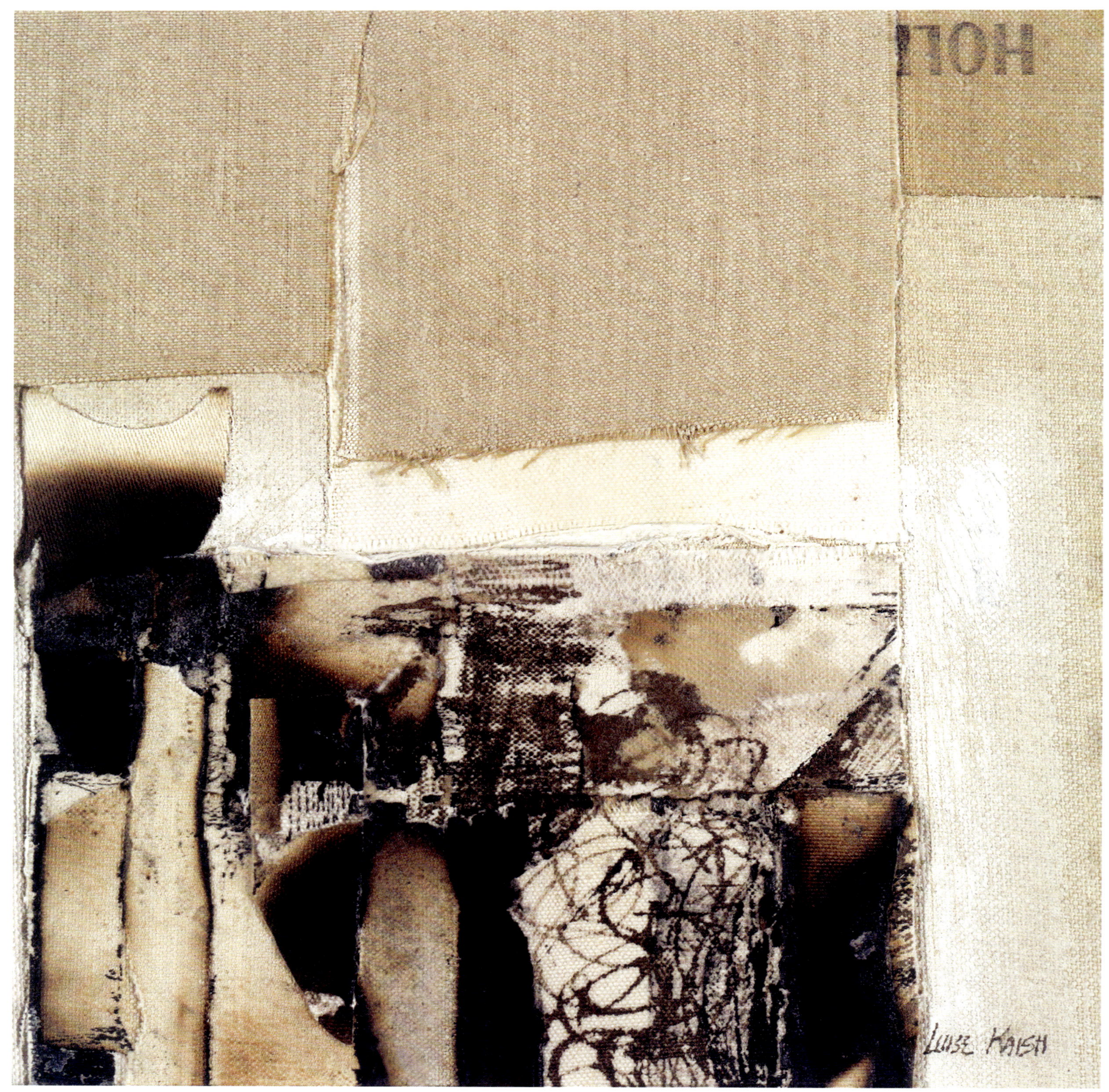

Plate 70
Luise Kaish. *Glacier Bay II*, 1983–84, collage,
mixed media on canvas, 18 ½ × 16 ⅜ in. (47 × 41.6 cm)

Plate 71
Luise Kaish. *H.H.H.*, 1981, oil, cut and pasted canvas, thread on canvas,
37 ¾ × 29 ¾ in. (95.9 × 75.6 cm). Collection, The Metropolitan Museum of
Art, Gift of Charles Z. Offin Art Fund, Inc.

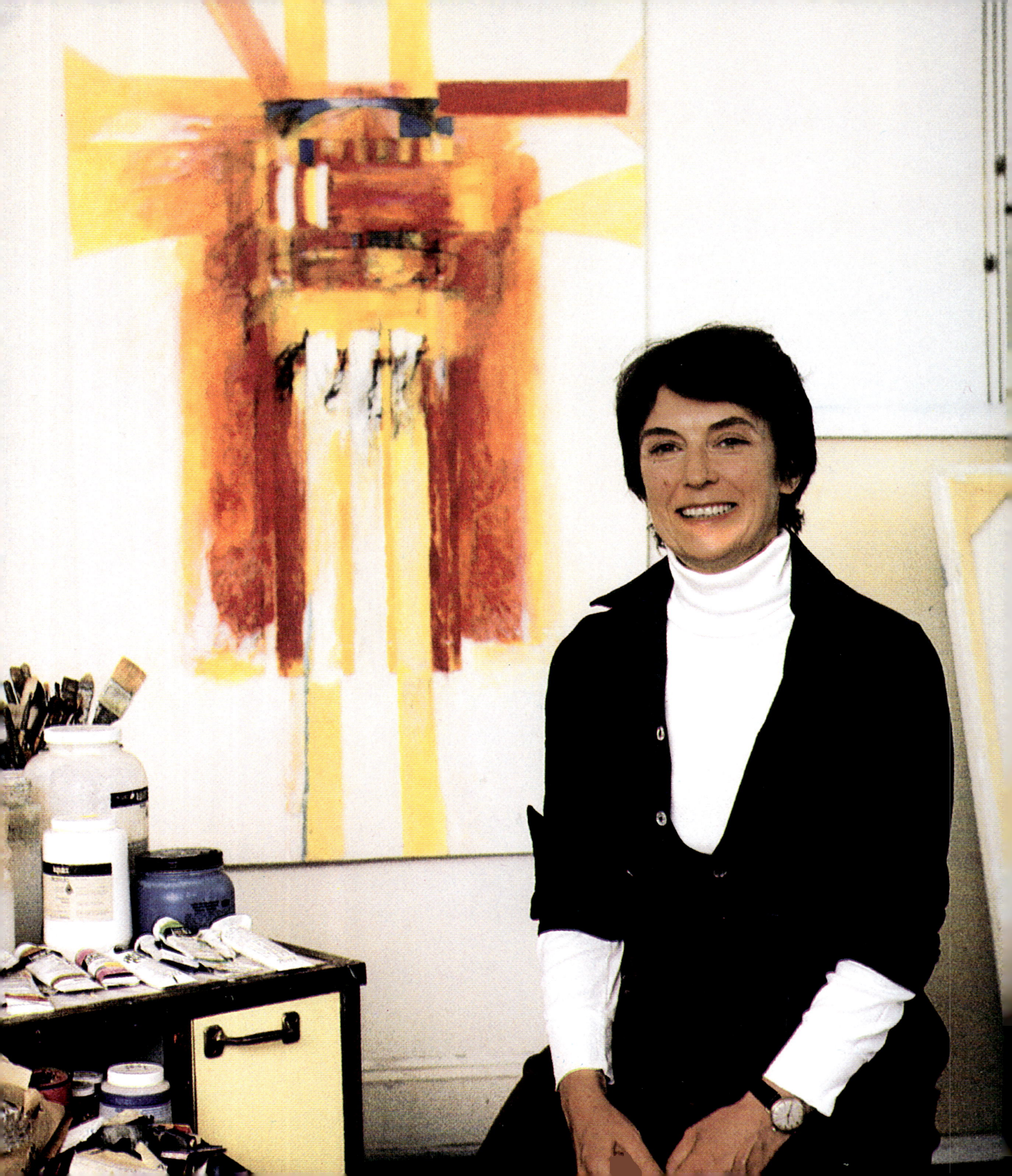

PLACE AND JOURNEY

THE LATER ART OF LUISE KAISH

Roger Lipsey

Luise Kaish in her studio, *Columbia Magazine*, New York, 1985

I am looking at a collage of modest dimensions: *From the City*, dating to 1980 (Fig. 59). If we are to understand the art of Luise Kaish from that time forward, we might first engage with this work. I'm told that over the years she kept it on a wall in her study; there must be a reason for that. I grasp that she may have thought of it as, among other things, a transcription of high-rise buildings, but that is hardly all it is. Were that so, it would have more to do with Augustine's City of God than with Kaish's neighborhood. One feels addressed by a symbol of her making that somehow—but how?—reaches past subjective symbol making. She valued a passage in the writings of C. G. Jung, which she quoted as follows: "A great work of art is like a dream: for all its apparent obviousness, it does not explain itself and is never unequivocal . . . A reality beyond personal psychological experience . . . beyond science and mathematics, and the armor of reason."[1] We are in a realm of that kind. Let's find our way.

We are odd creatures: we accept at once, without thinking about it, a torn, layered canvas with ragged edges. In any art tradition or era other than our own, those features would instantly condemn a work—but for us, familiar for more than a century with cubist collage and influenced through and through by our ragged global history of disasters and threats, torn-ness is part of our intimate knowledge. What Kaish firmly shows us exists upon a seemingly improvised canvas. That is an ambiguity, but as she once said in an artist's talk, "I like ambiguity. I like clarity."[2]

Kaish was a speculative thinker, a caring explorer of the cosmos revealed by science and of the cosmos revealed by religious traditions. With equal ardor, her mind could trace up to both the stars of the night sky and to God in his still more secret realm. Kaish's decades of work as a sculptor fulfilling monumental commissions for sacred art in Jewish and also Christian sanctuaries invisibly nourish the art of her later years: works on canvas, diminutive in comparison to much of her work as a sculptor. The force of that work is still evident. "I want, I seek . . . ," she once wrote.[3] A powerful impulse moved in her, early and late. We can expect the abstract imagery of her later years to cohere, in new ways, with what came before.

What, then, of this canvas? We see a progression from right to left of three rectangles suggesting vessels, linked but characterized in wholly different ways. The first, at right, is empty, marked with tears, possibly burns, incompletenesses. In context it reads as an incipience or undisclosed potential. The marks and burns call our attention to the vessel without revealing what it is: yes, ambiguous. The middle vessel is vastly more energized in an orderly way, with horizontal brushstrokes suggesting the circulation of contained energy. At the top of this middle vessel, a suggestion of energy rising, still largely contained. And, at left, a perfectly wonderful figuration of energy released, a joyous burst of vitality.

We would do well now to let go of most of these words. Kaish was a maker of icons, and icons exist silently in the world they create or the world in which they participate. In the great traditions of iconography—for example, Orthodox Greek and Russian—participation

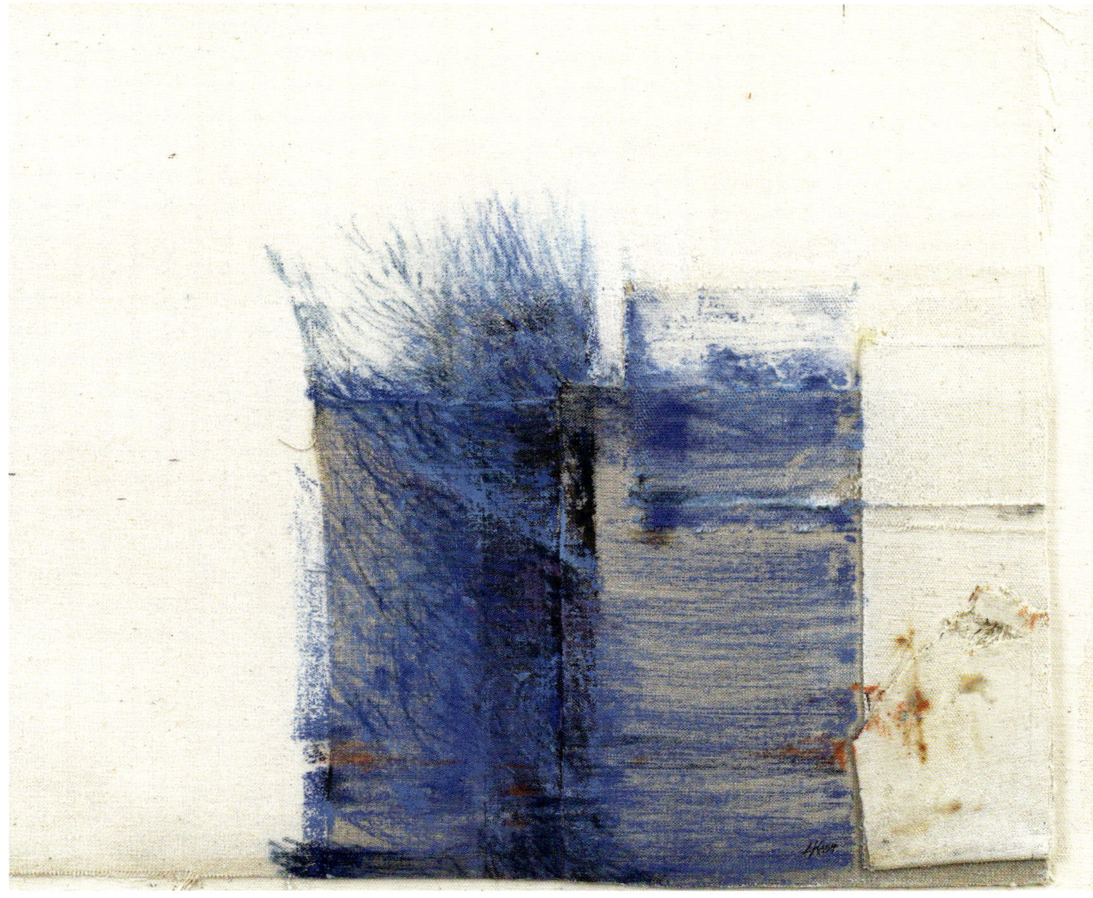

Fig. 59 Luise Kaish, *From the City*, 1980, mixed media, 11 × 13 ½ in. (27.9 × 34.3 cm)

in the stream of tradition is crucial: St. George slaying the dragon must look precisely like St. George slaying the dragon, the composition and its details settled and clear. Only when the icon is faithfully bound into its tradition is it "active," endowed with a spark of the saint's presence. In the art of our time, when artists of spiritual temperament have no shared iconographic tradition near at hand, those with the instincts of an icon maker per-force find their own visual language. Their imagery is unlikely to enshrine a saint's presence or state a traditional religious theme; nonetheless there is *something*—something we feel as viewers—that invites a hushed, contemplative approach. Kaish's art is of this kind. Her later collages and paintings are filled with energy, inventiveness, vitality, and celebration, yet they invite us to linger, to become perceivers, to question the image and ourselves. There is a match: the image encodes some aspect of human nature and experience, yet it exists also in its own silent world.

The mystery explored in this particular work is *development*: from virtually nothing, sheer incipience or potential, through a stage of cradling or containment, to full expression. From nothing to something: an aspect of the artist's creative journey, and of our own. If this work commands and rewards attention, that is owing to the novel, subtly austere icon of development that Kaish discovered in her mind and sets before us.

This notion of discovery in the mind is central for Kaish. In the notes for one of her talks in the later years, she puts it this way:

> For myself as an artist I could best describe what happens as the following. I SEE the works in my head. They are visual. Much as a composer hears a musical theme, or the writer puts together words, or the individual sees images in his dreams. How this happens or why I do not know. I only know that it is. Then comes the task of transferring that inner vision into concrete terms. Sometimes I will begin to work and the reality does not fit the vision. What is in my head does not emerge in either the form or the manner of its conception. This is the point at which all artists work and often rework their ideas. Do the forms express what one feels? . . . Some works spring through this transitional stage fully realized. This is the moment of pure ecstatic joy.[4]

"How this happens or why I do not know. I only know that it is": these are poignant words, recognizing the artist's vision as a mystery to be received with gratitude—and surprise— and elaborated in a spirit of obedience; inspiration is also a command. Kaish is not alone here. Franz Schubert was once asked by a musical family to compose a celebratory chorale on a poem already chosen. As he read through the poem—unfamiliar, lovely—the music began singing in his mind. He delivered the score a few days later, a magnificent thing.[5]

Kaish was a learned artist. She had seen, studied, and absorbed everything, so to speak—visited innumerable monuments and museums; traveled and lived at length, both physically in Europe and imaginatively in virtually all periods of Western art. It was this, in part, that made her an ideal teacher and department chair at Columbia University. But she wore her learning lightly; that was important, too. A truly beautiful canvas, *The Butterfly Net, The Priory,* dating to 1998 (Fig. 60; Pl. 92), reveals intimate familiarity with the late-nineteenth-century art of the Nabis in Paris; it is as if she is one of them—a peer of the young Pierre Bonnard, Édouard Vuillard, Maurice Denis, and others in their circle. She dons their sensibility, with a gesture also toward Matisse's landscapes and interiors. The striking thing is that this work isn't derivative; it is altogether her own, masterful rather than imitative, yet it breathes nostalgic homage to brilliance a century earlier in Paris. This is visual poetry, the remaking of things seen into a new, affectionate vision. "My angels were always telling stories," Kaish wrote.[6] This must be one of those tales.

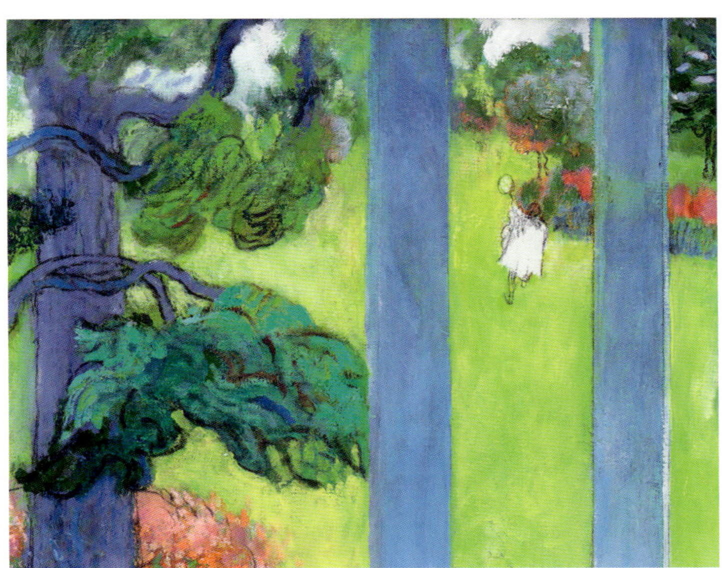

Fig. 60 Luise Kaish, *The Butterfly Net, The Priory* (detail), 1998
(see Plate 92)

When artists return again and again to a theme—remember Monet's gardens and his patient attention to Rouen Cathedral in all weather—we can be sure that they are in pursuit. Kaish's extended series of *Lovers Houses*, as she called them, is such a pursuit. "We are lovers," she has written about these works. "We . . . existing in the common search, separate and sharing . . . this house of between-ness and the keening to return. . . . We cognize structure, imaging in sequential progressions of color, tactile and light-refracting. Time implied and space implied, my *Lovers Houses*, love. And wait."[7] Her words are not analytic, not clad in what Jung called "the armor of reason"; they are a poetic parallel to the images.

She made enclosures where intimates can meet, often with a bilateral design acknowledging the lovers' distinctiveness within their shared house. Kaish's preference for brilliant color and contrast is evident in many of these works. "I want pulsating rhythms and vibrations of color," she once wrote, "at maximum saturation to pervade the works. The use of the repetition of color and shape is to intensify those aspects."[8] Her visual vocabulary belongs to modernist tradition—to the fabulously engaging color grids of Paul Klee, to the splashes and seeming insouciance of more recent masters such as Robert Rauschenberg—but once again the vision is all her own. The icon tradition is not far off: the sun's rays illuminating the left side of the magical enclosure in *Lovers House I* (Fig. 61) recall the centuries-old imagery of Pentecost, when the apostles are touched by rays of light from above. Kaish provides a house for lovers that is open to higher energy: the "keening to return" isn't theoretical, it is a response to that light, which ensures that return is real not imaginary, possible not impossible. The lovers, whoever they are, have a joyous shelter now for their passion for one another, but it is a stage not a stopping place.

The *Lovers Houses* series is a meditation on the nature of love. Kaish offers more than one mood, more than one style or moment of relationship. In a work from a few years later, 1987 (Fig. 62), we encounter a house for contemplative lovers: cool colors, strict geometry, a space for meditators looking together toward the austere cosmos intuited by ancient and Renaissance thinkers. "I use certain basic geometric figures such as point, straight line, circle, triangle, and square, as symbolic values. The basic energies of the universe," Kaish wrote in the years when she was elaborating the series.[9]

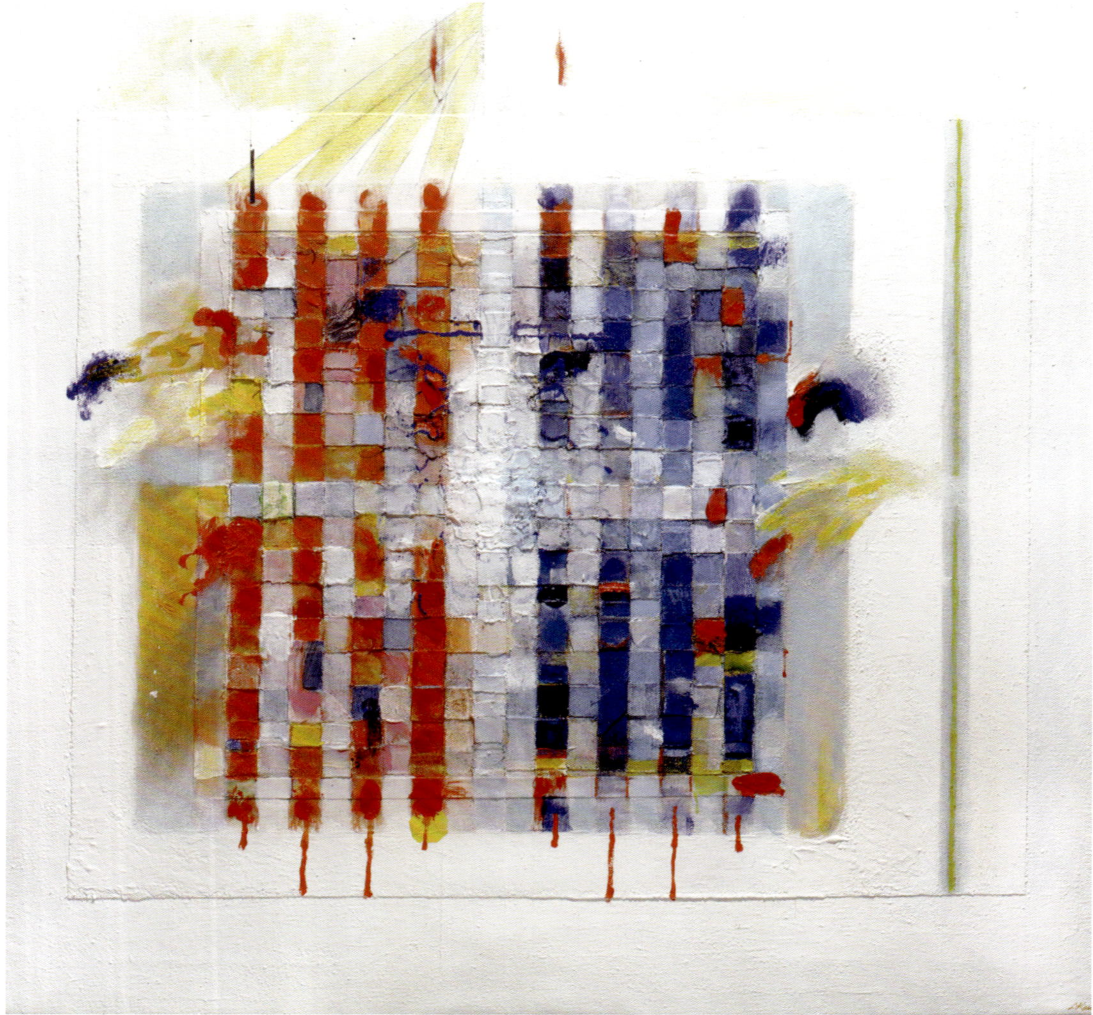

Fig. 61 Luise Kaish, *Lovers House I,* 1983–84, mixed media, 28 × 30 in. (71.1 × 76.2 cm)

One further canvas from this series, *Lovers House E* (Fig. 64), dating to 1983–84, occupies a mid-point between the lovers' houses and a second theme we might explore, portals. Who are the lovers here? Perhaps more Shiva and Parvati, a divine marital pair in Hindu tradition, than earthly lovers. Their house brings to mind an altar, aflame with color, endowed with intricate compartments for images or carvings, and—again, quite in the Indian tradition—with worshipful birds and other creatures. The work is small, just ten inches square, a jewel or all-but-secret offering to the gods and goddesses who teach us by their example how to love.

A lovers' house, but also a portal: an opening toward something more than we commonly know. The complex structure of *Lovers House E* recalls the monumental bronze *Ark*s from Kaish's earlier decades as a sculptor. The ark in Jewish houses of worship is an enclosure for the scroll of the Torah, the five books of Moses, but also a portal toward the history and meaning and language of relations with the divine. Kaish's *Portals* will be difficult to trap in words—and I have no wish to do that. But we nonetheless need a few words. Chosen from among many examples, perhaps just two canvases can show us what we need to see.

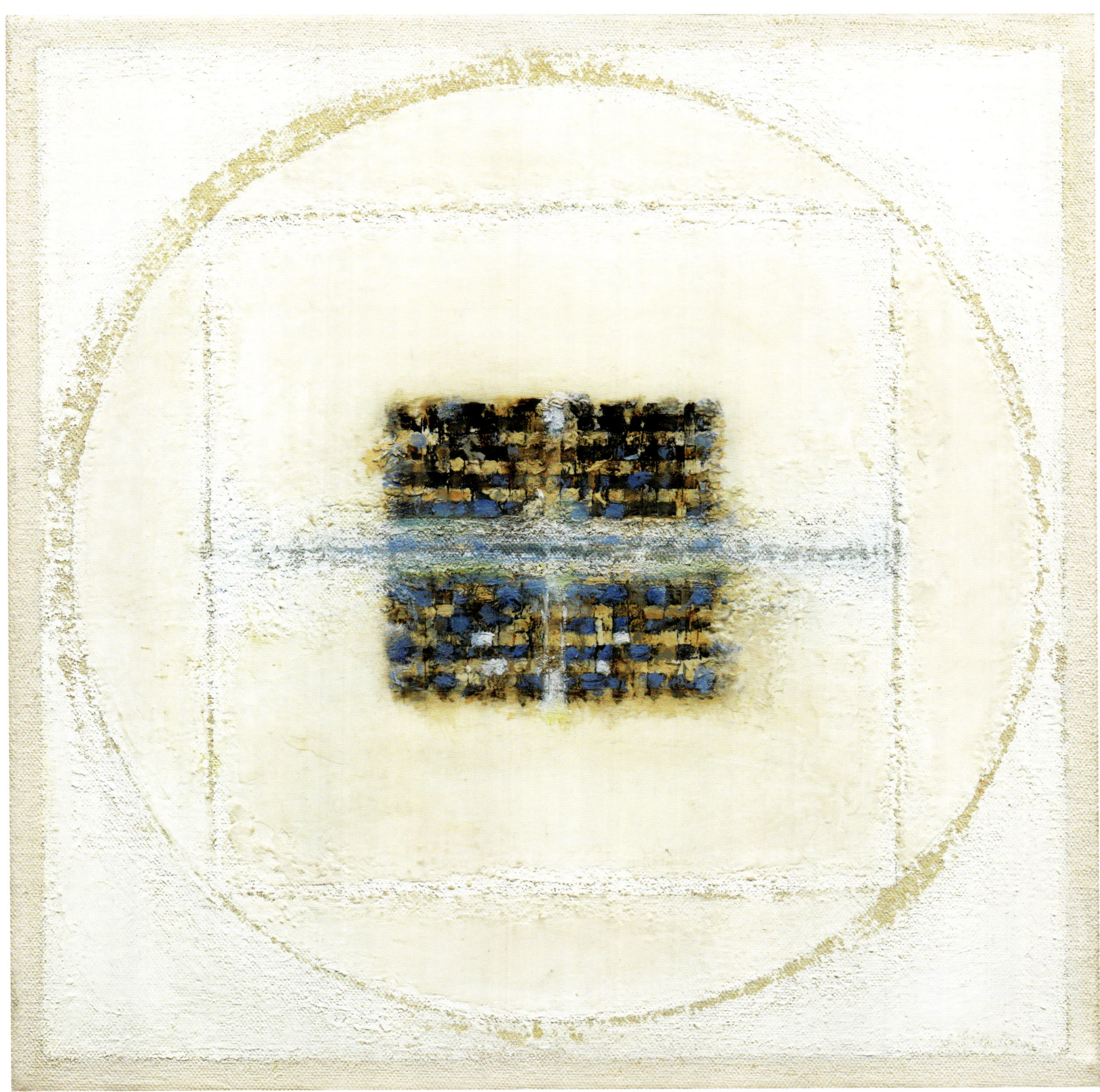

Fig. 62 Luise Kaish, *Lovers House*, 1987, mixed media on canvas, 13 × 13 in. (33 × 33 cm)

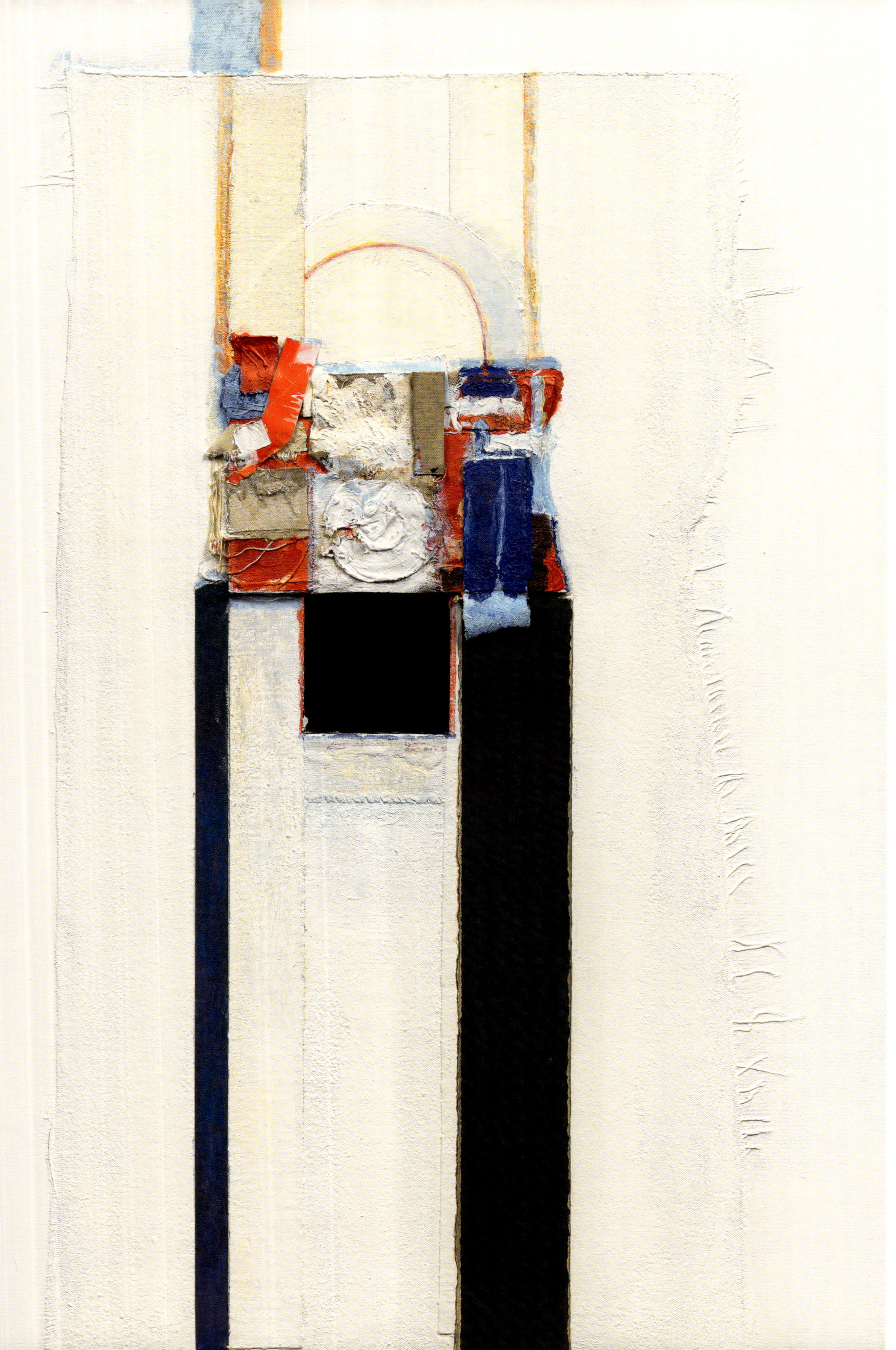

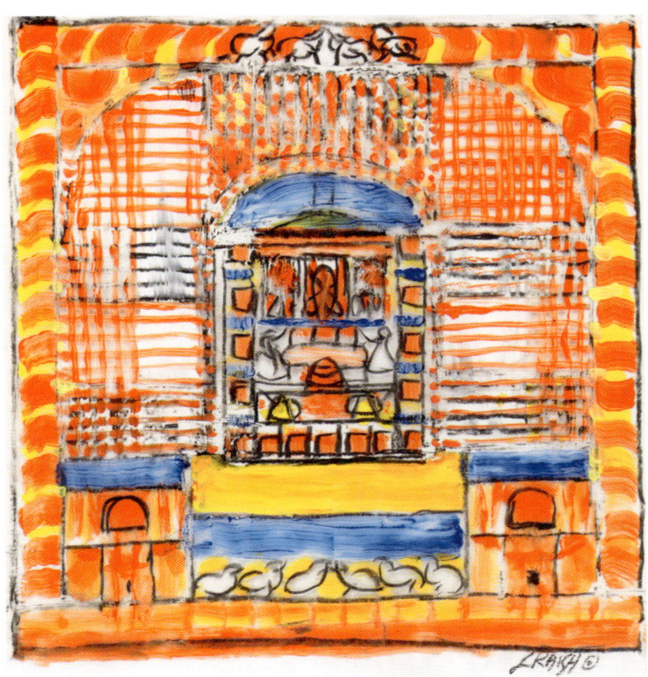

Fig. 64   Luise Kaish, *Lovers House E*, 1983–84, mixed media on canvas, 10 × 10 in. (25.4 × 25.4 cm)

Somewhere in her notes, Kaish speaks of working sometimes most deliberately and at other times in a "frenzy," as she put it, as if the creative impulse couldn't wait for deliberation to run its course.[10] Both deliberation and a fearless willingness to follow impulse are evident in her series *Portals*. *Portal V* (Fig. 63), dating to 1983–84, has both qualities: an architectonic order of clearly stated vertical pillars provides a calm setting for a mighty "lintel" of contrasting colors, patches, and asymmetries. A central curl in thick impasto—reading as an icon of unstoppable energy—surmounts a recollection of the early Russian avant-garde, Malevich's *Black Square* of 1915, an icon of kenosis, of the place where energy retreats and stops without losing its power. I doubt that Kaish went through an additive thought process as she brought this overall image to life; it is more like the outcome of a process partly foreseen, partly midwifed without foreknowledge. This striking canvas is an invitation to fullness of life if we care to pass through the portal.

The tendency evident in the lintel of *Portal V* led to numerous other works in the series, such as *Portal VII* (Fig. 65), from the same period. Here the architectonic elements, assuring us that there is after all a portal, are overwhelmed by tempestuous imagination: enter here if you dare! Again our learned artist takes her place in modernist tradition—there are recollections of Kandinsky's bold abstractions and the meticulous linear structures and spatial planning of cubism—but the work is all Kaish's own.

Some passionate souls are demure as you meet them; they keep their passion private, to be shared only on certain occasions in certain ways. Luise Kaish was of that kind: teacher, wife, mother, and more than willing to play those roles fully and sincerely. Yet she once spoke of the "visual ecstasy of the expression of ideas."[11] She burned inside with an unyielding, self-renewing flame. Her art burns still.

Fig. 63   Luise Kaish, *Portal V*,
1983–84, mixed media on canvas,
33 ¾ × 22 in. (85.7 × 55.9)

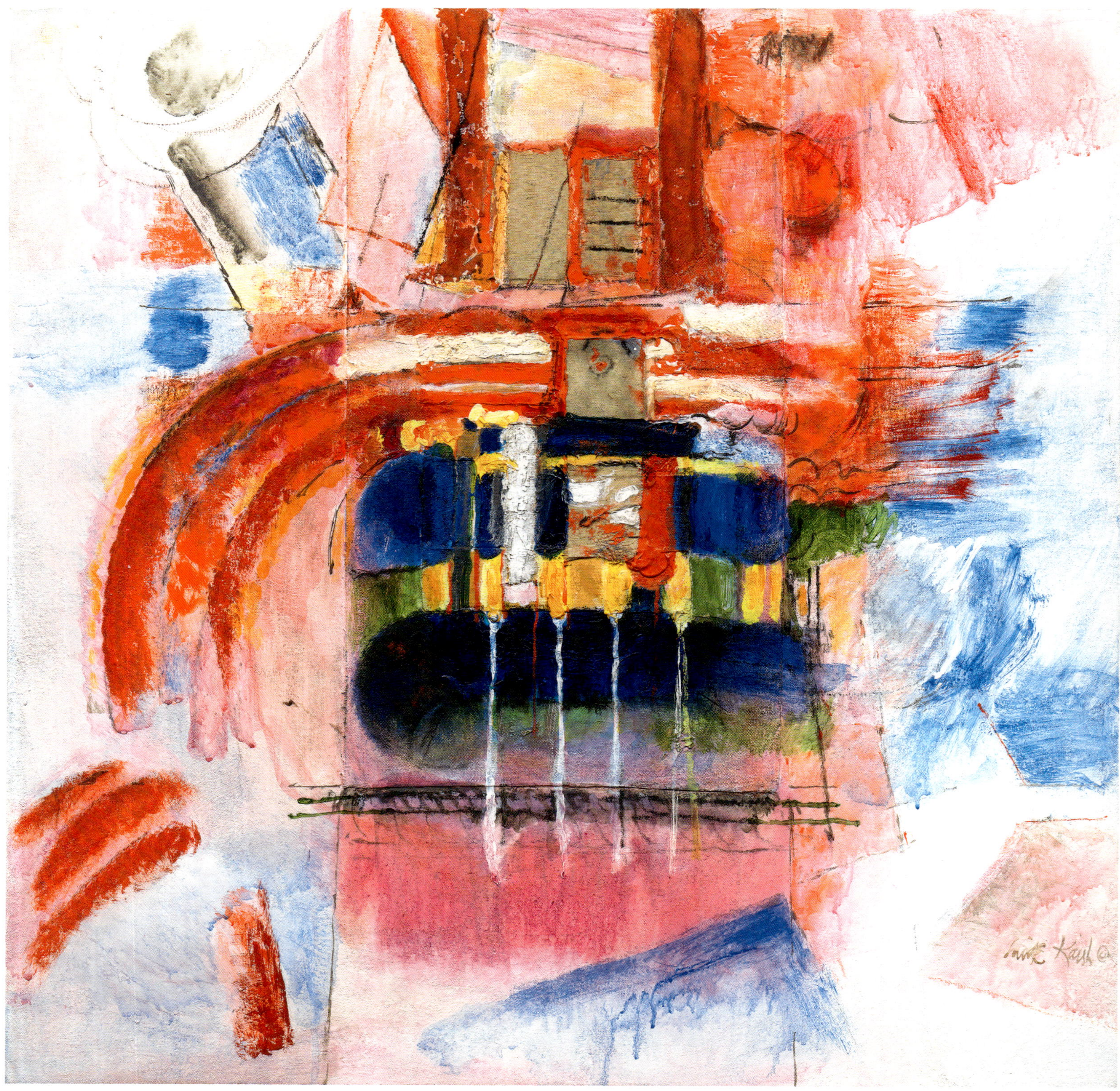

Fig. 65 Luise Kaish, *Portal VII*, 1983–84, mixed media on canvas,
30 × 30 in. (76.2 × 76.2 cm)

Endnotes

1. Luise Kaish, "Sculpture: A Poetic Force," (lecture, University of Washington School of Art, presented in conjunction with Battelle Research Center, Seattle, July 10, 1979), typescript, Luise Kaish archives, New York.
2. *Luise Kaish: Recent Collages*, exh. cat. (New York: Staempfli Gallery, 1981).
3. Luise Kaish, lecture notes for an unknown occasion, c. 1983–89, Luise Kaish archives.
4. Luise Kaish, unidentified typescript, n.d., Luise Kaish archives.
5. *Ständchen* (*"Zögernd leise"*), op. posth. 135, D920. See Christopher H. Gibbs, ed., *The Cambridge Companion to Schubert* (Cambridge: Cambridge University Press, 1997), 153–54.
6. Luise Kaish, handwritten notes, n.d., Luise Kaish archives.
7. Luise Kaish, unidentified typescript, c. 1981–88, Luise Kaish archives.
8. Luise Kaish, lecture notes for an unknown occasion, c. 1983–89.
9. Ibid.
10. *Luise Kaish: Recent Collages*.
11. Luise Kaish, handwritten notes, n.d.

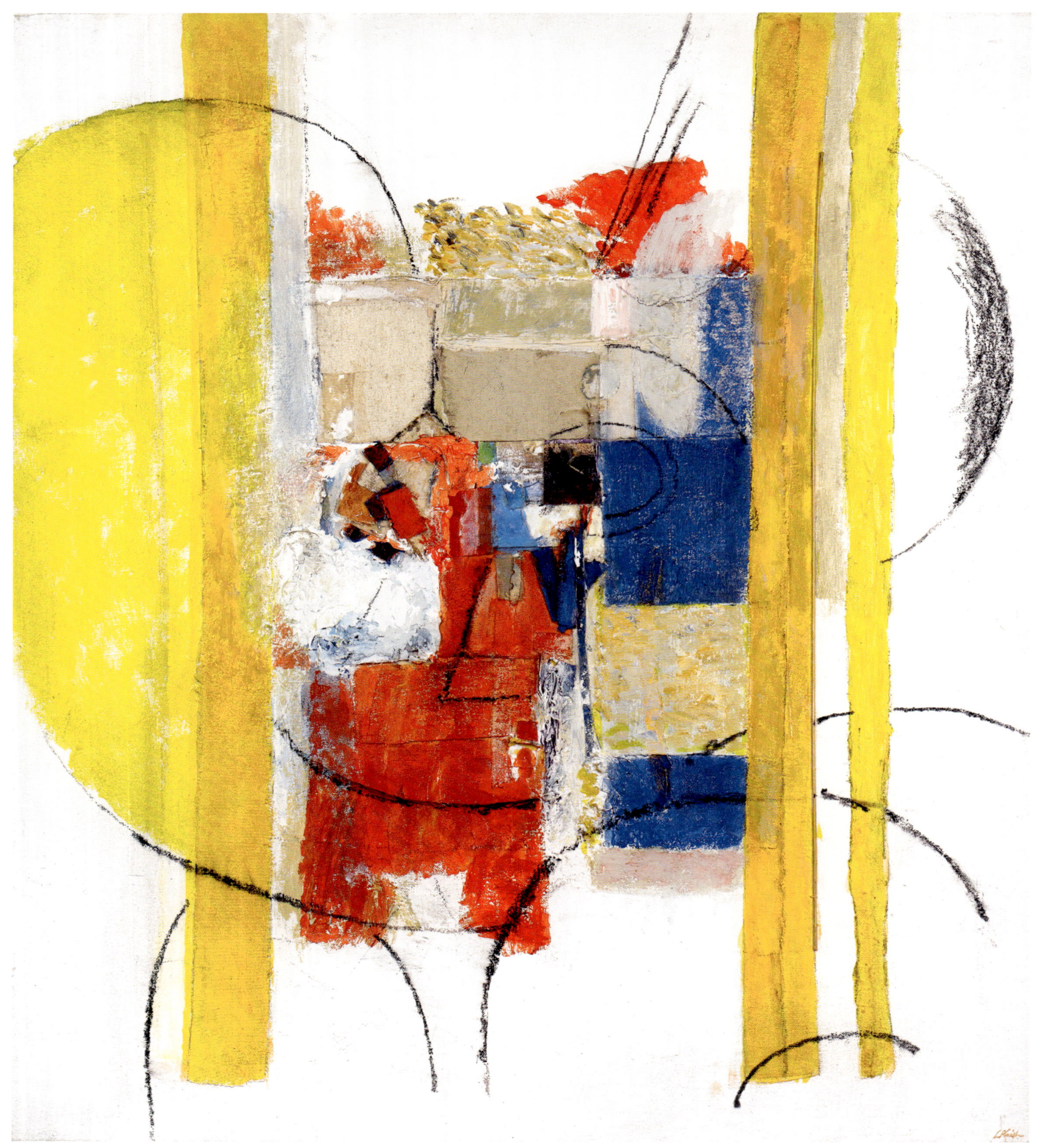

Plate 72
Luise Kaish. *Portal IV*, 1983–84, collage, mixed medium on canvas,
32 × 28 in. (81.3 × 71.1 cm)

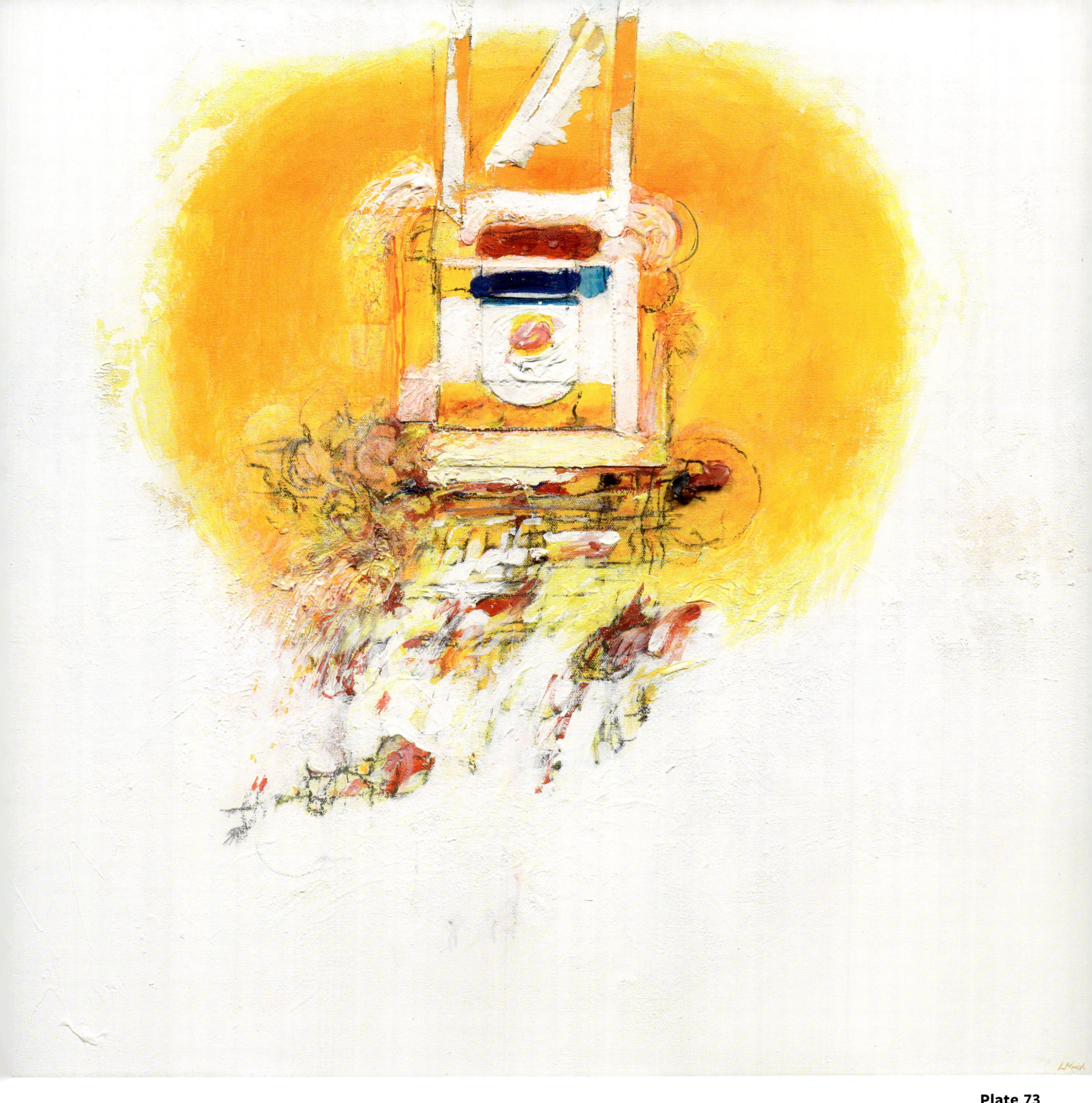

Plate 73
Luise Kaish. *Portal II*, 1983–84, collage, mixed media on canvas,
26 ¾ × 26 in. (67.9 × 66 cm)

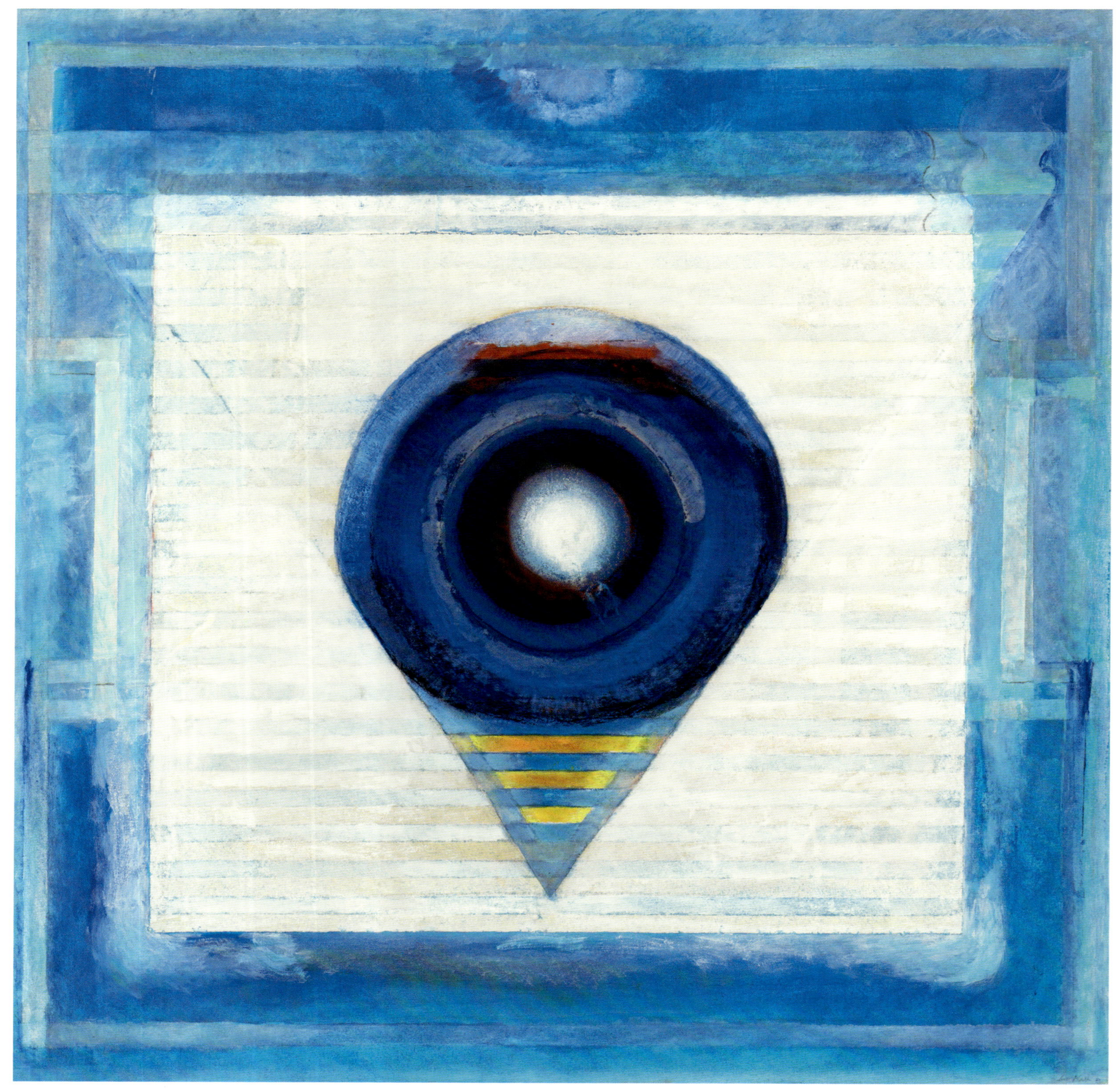

Plate 74

Luise Kaish. *New York Blue*, 1985–87, collage, acrylic on canvas,
48 × 48 in. (121.9 × 121.9 cm)

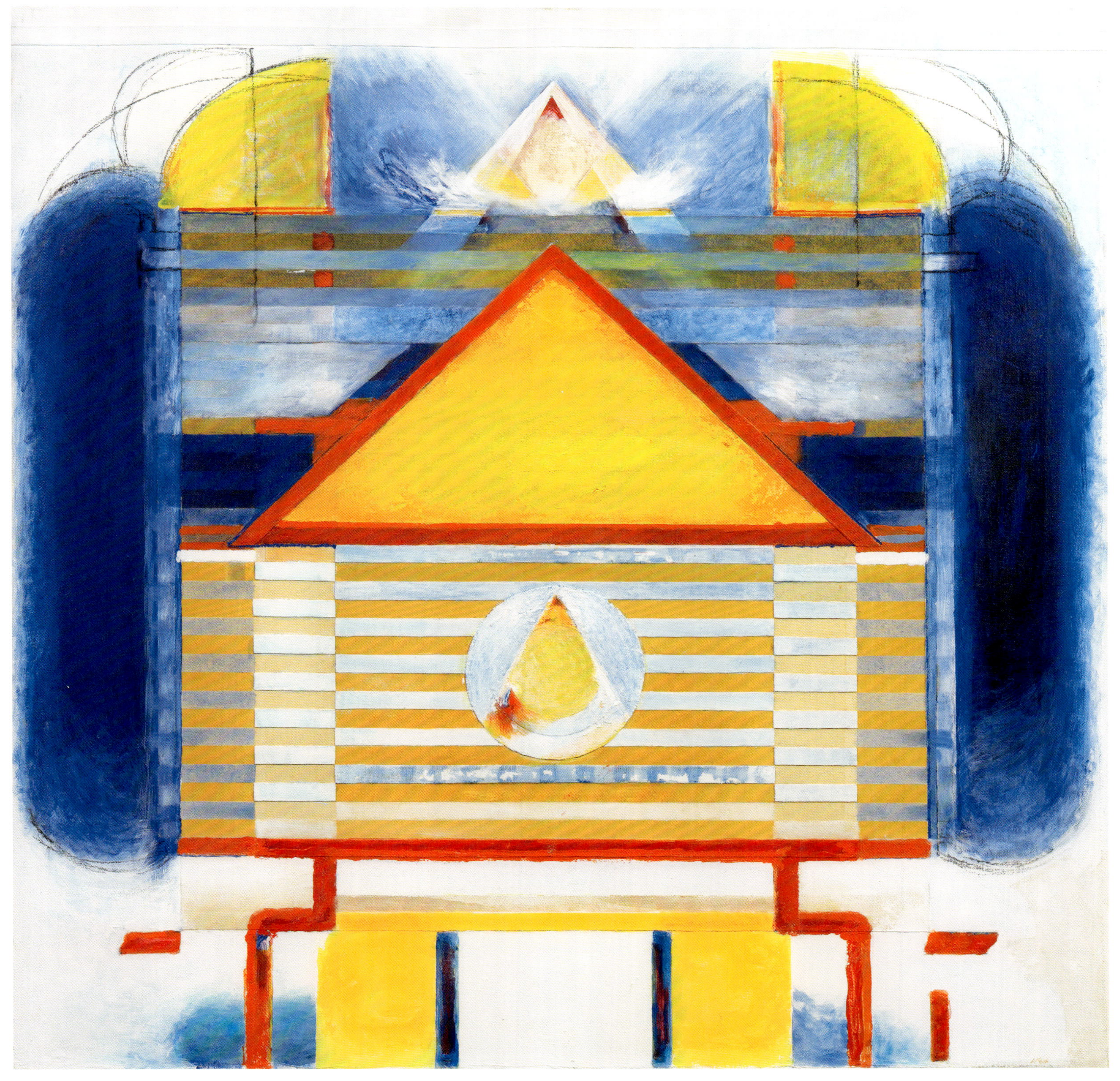

Plate 75
Luise Kaish. *Lovers House III*, 1983–84, collage, mixed media on canvas,
47 ½ × 47 ½ in. (120.7 × 120.7 cm)

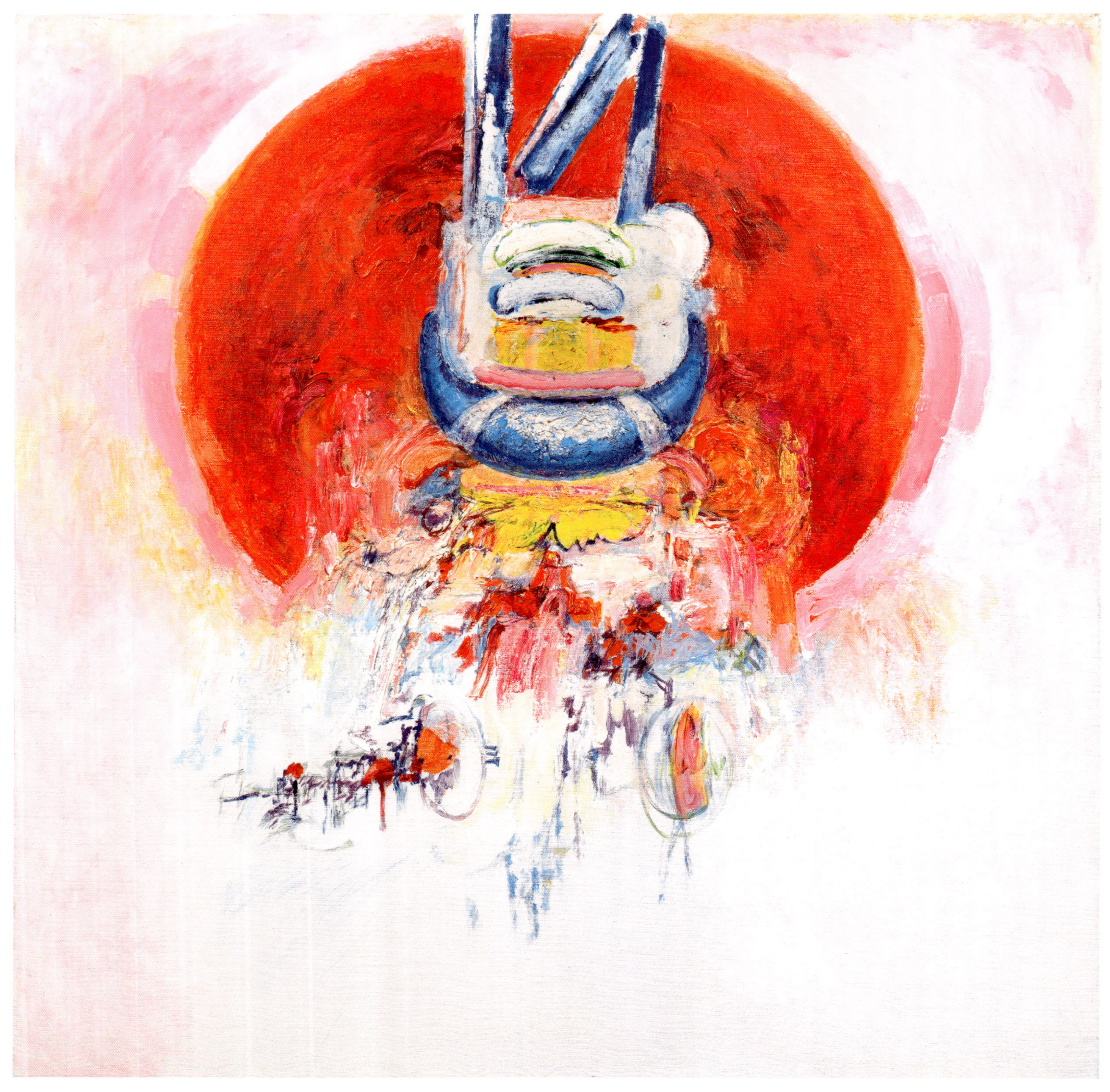

Plate 76
Luise Kaish. *Portal VIII*, 1985, acrylic on linen, 48 × 48 in. (121.9 × 121.9 cm)

Plate 77
Luise Kaish. *Broadway Baby and All That Jazz*, 1984–2006, mixed media, 55 × 33 ¾ in. (139.7 × 85.7 cm)

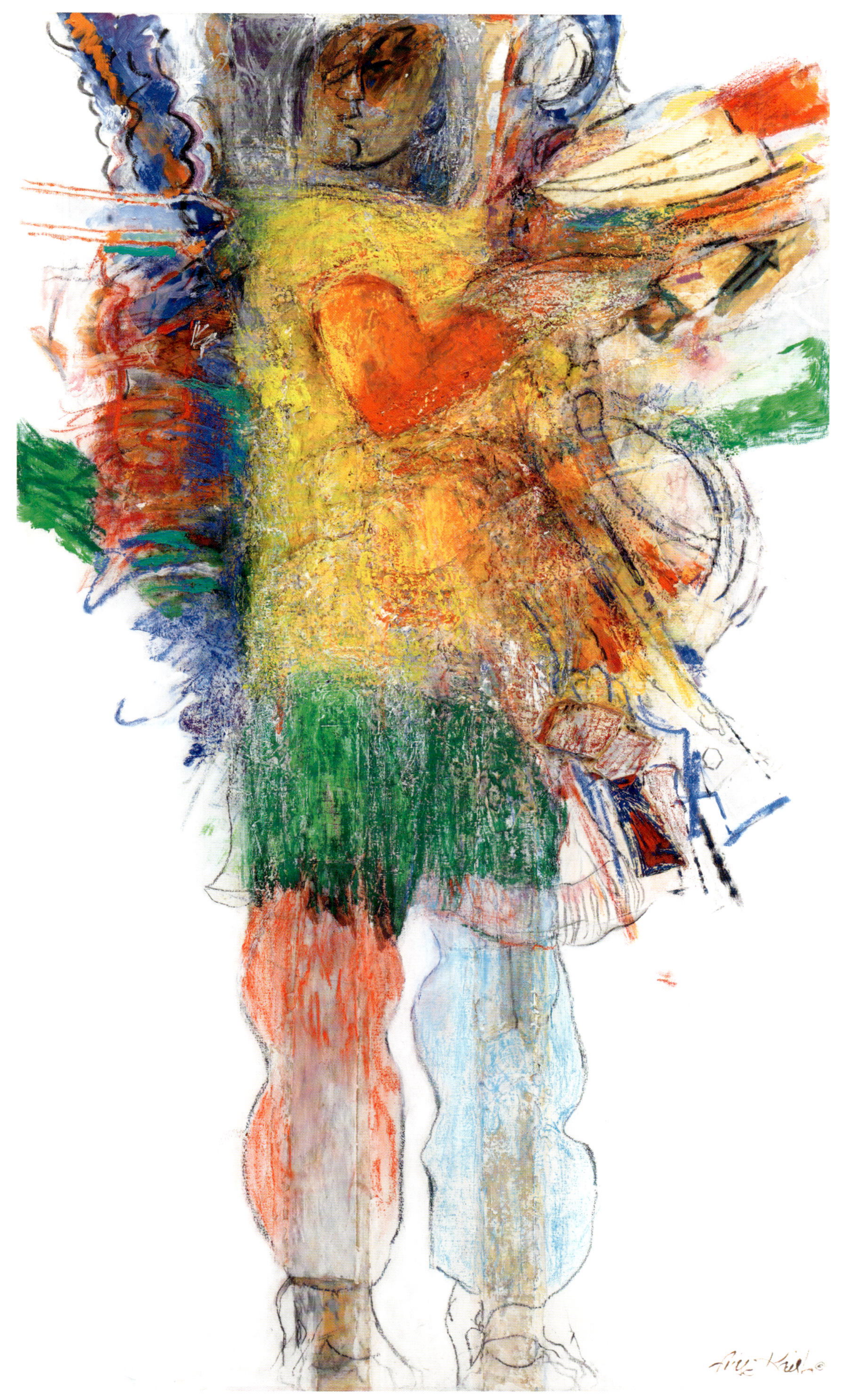

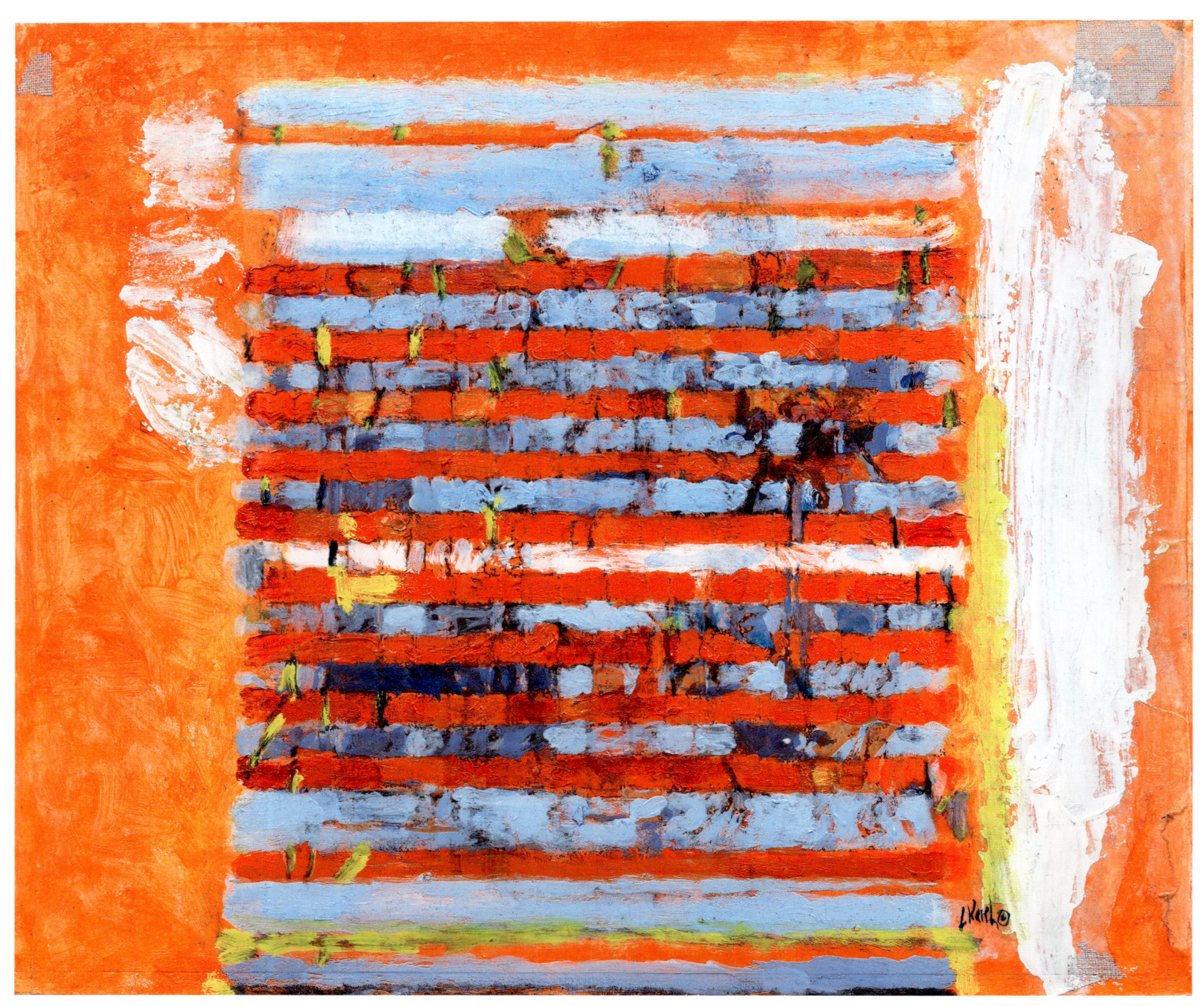

Plate 78
Luise Kaish. *Lovers House B*, 1983–90, collage acrylic on canvas,
11 × 12 ½ in. (27.9 × 31.8 cm)

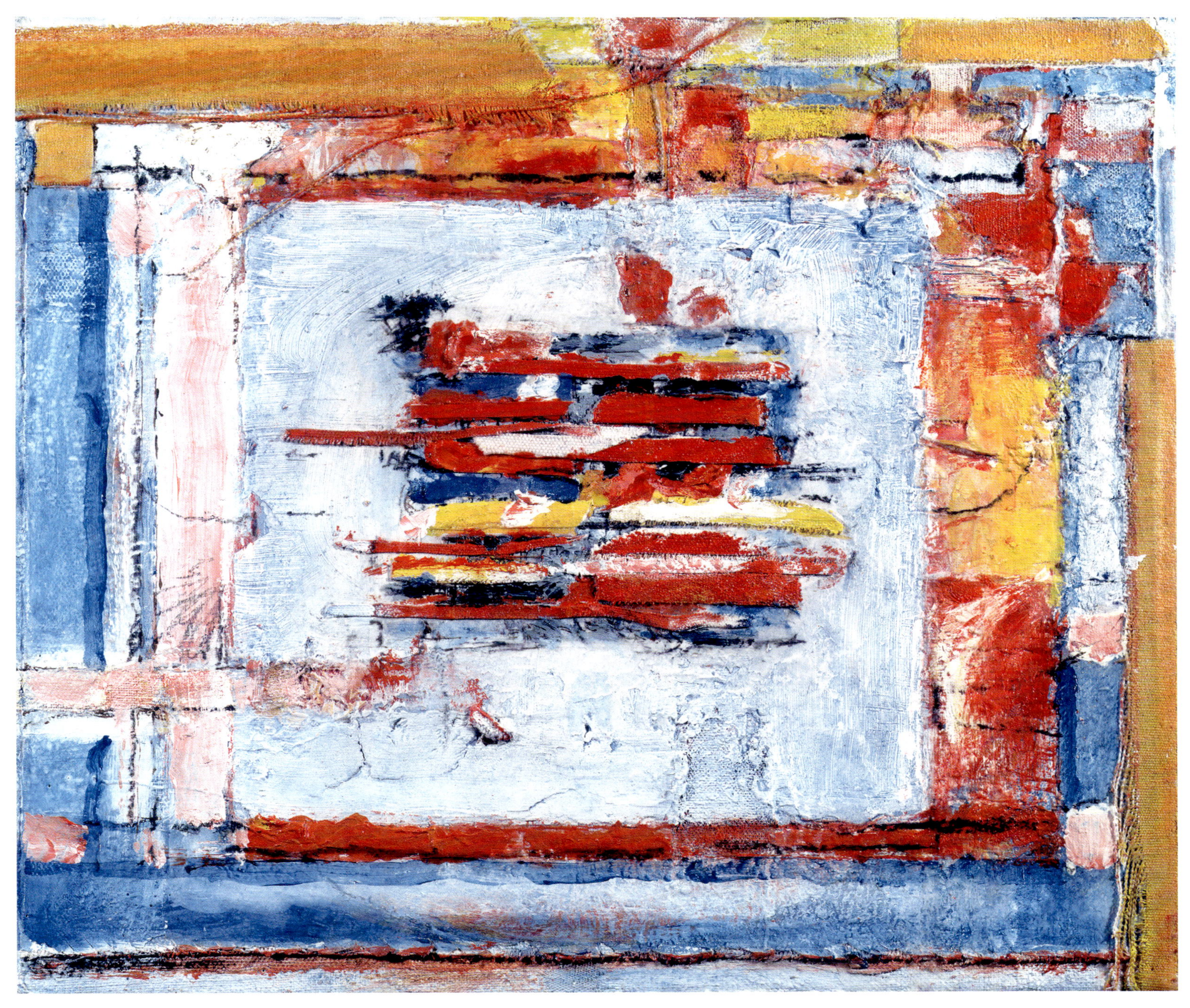

Plate 79
Luise Kaish. *Lovers House V*, circa 1983–90, mixed media on canvas,
11 ½ × 12 ¾ in. (29.2 × 32.4 cm)

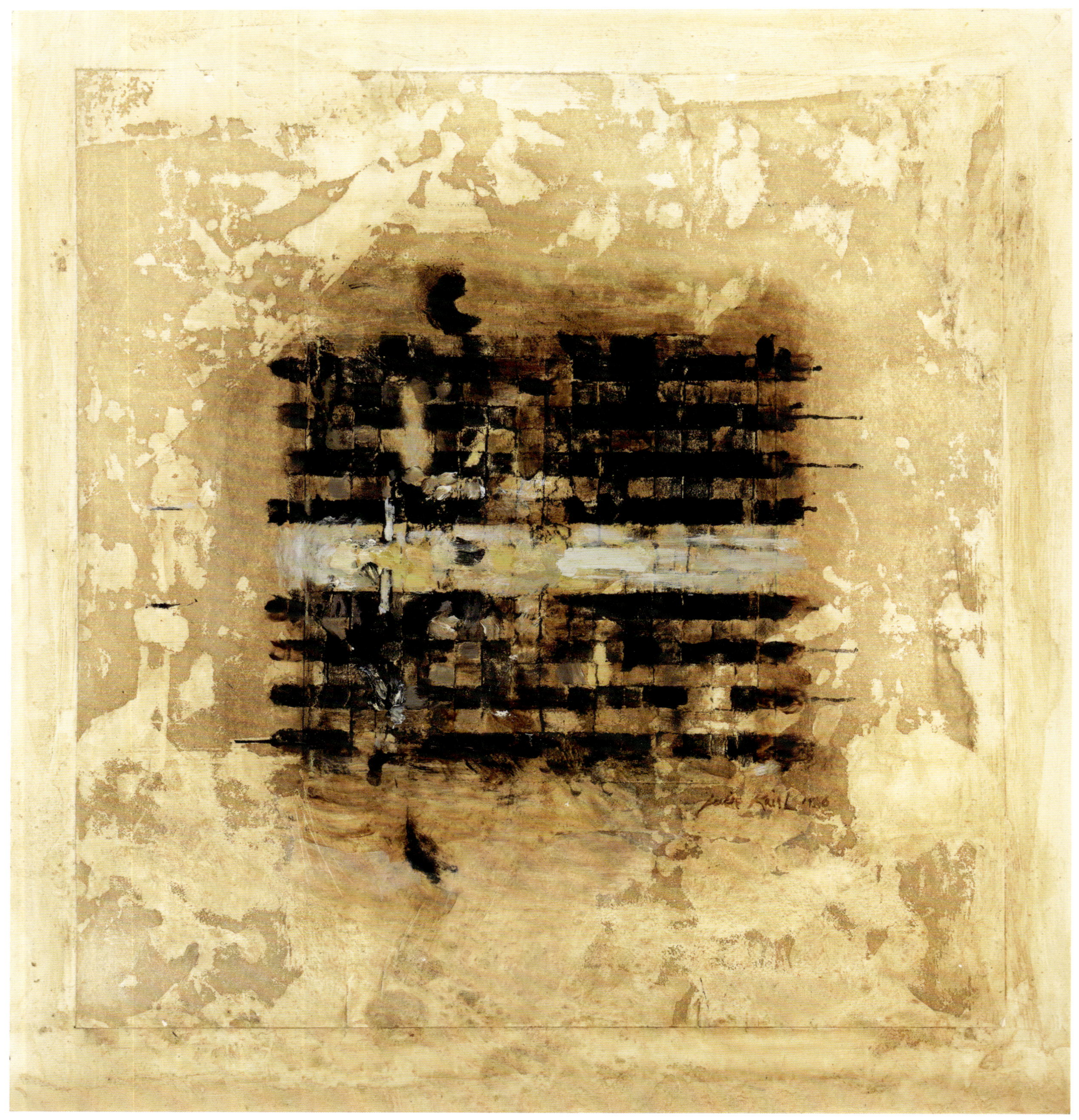

Plate 80
Luise Kaish. *Lovers House VI*, 1983–84, collage, mixed media,
9 ½ × 10 in. (24.1 × 25.4 cm)

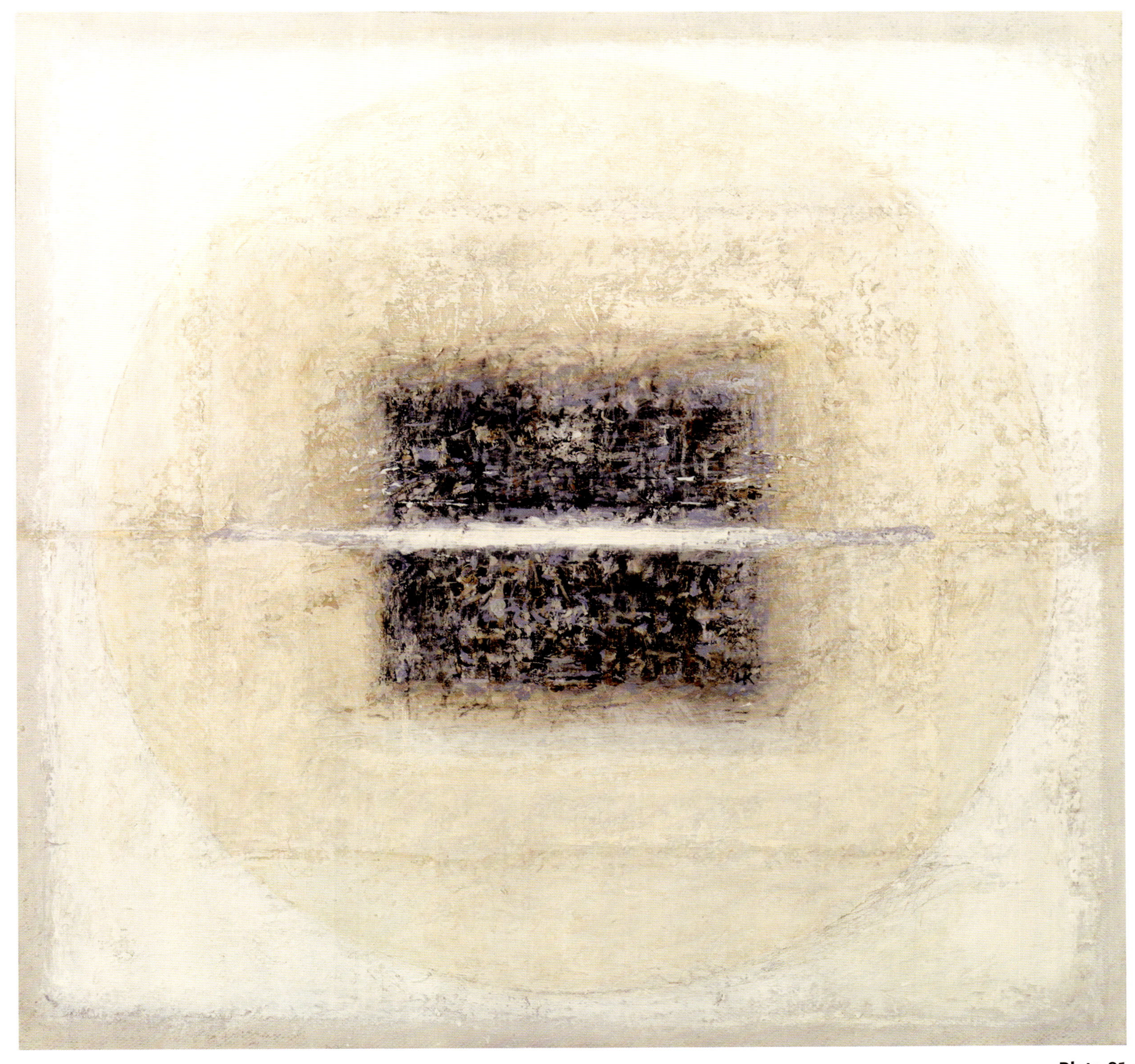

Luise Kaish. *Untitled Lovers House*, 1987, collage, mixed media, 13 × 13 in. (33 × 33 cm)

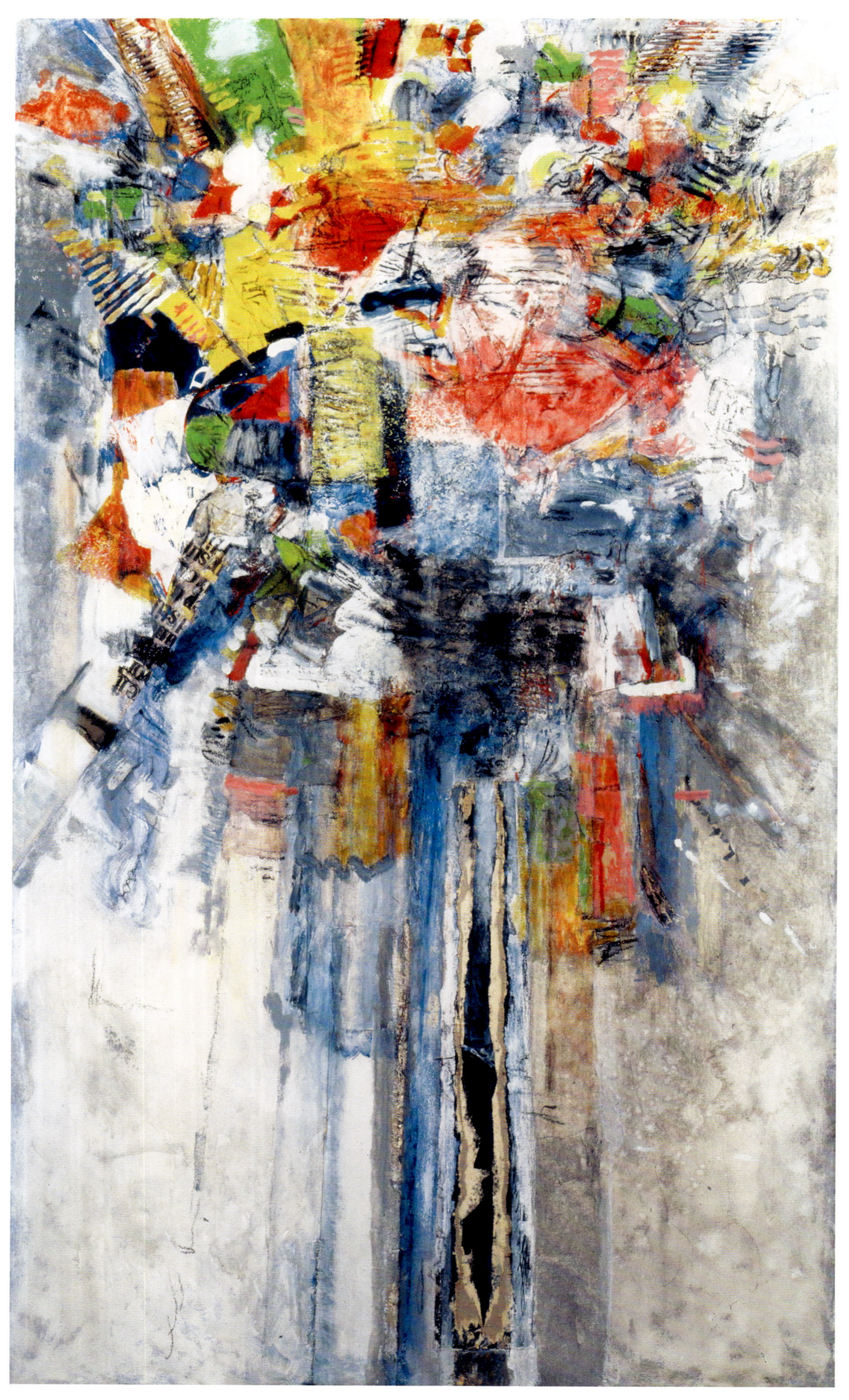

Plate 82
Luise Kaish. *New York II*, 1987,
acrylic on canvas, 57 ½ × 35 in.
(146.1 × 88.9 cm)

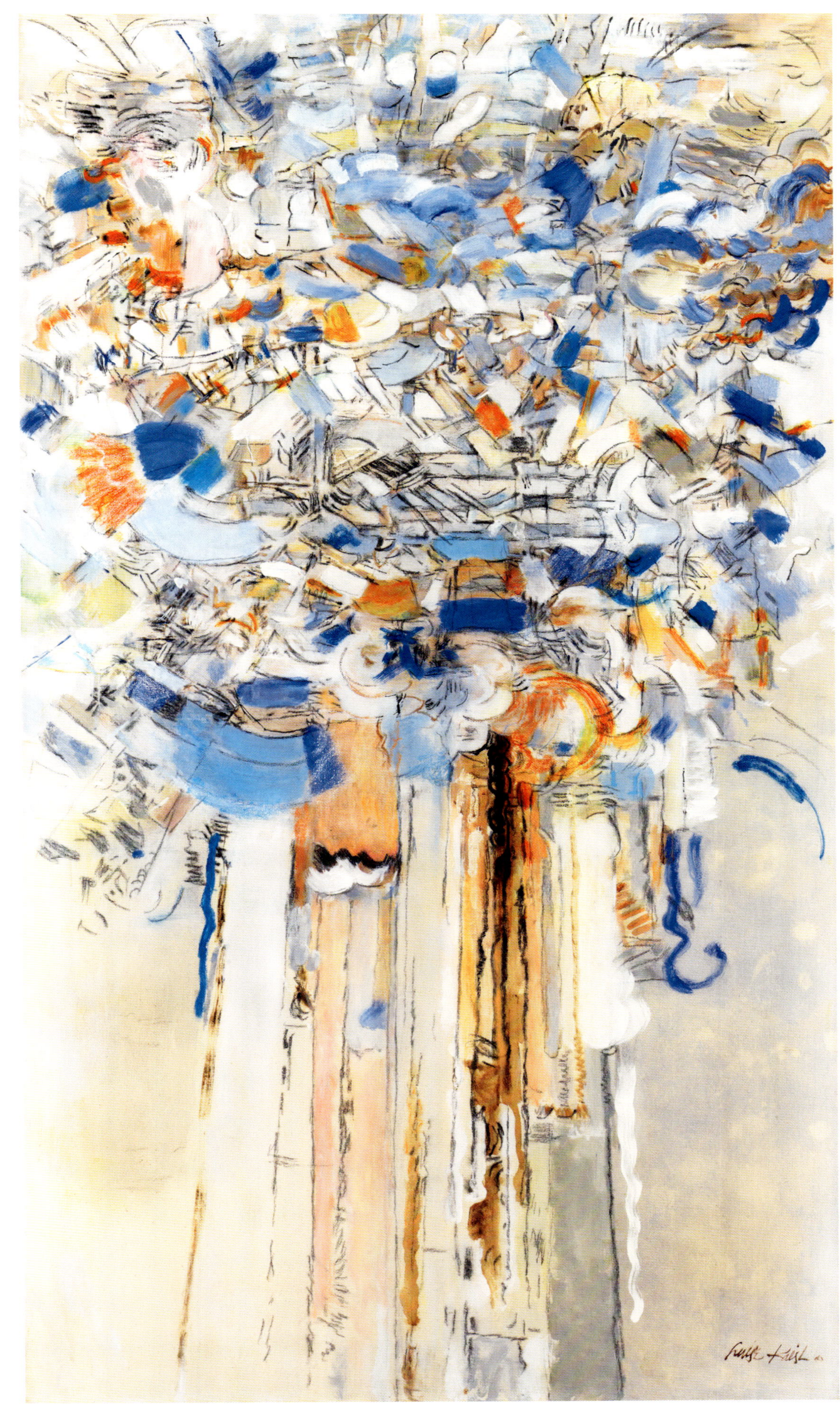

Plate 83
Luise Kaish. *All That Jazz,*
2002, acrylic and charcoal
on canvas, 72 × 41 in.
(182.9 × 104.1 cm)

Landscapes

In the 1990s, until her death in 2013, Luise Kaish moved away from abstraction, producing innumerable land- and skyscapes in watercolor, acrylic, and oil. These works are remarkable in that she began utilizing ultra-bright, Fauve-like colors for the first time in her decades-long career. As she explained in 2012, "I am drawn to painting and color that defy assumptions, cumulative layers, pulsating rhythms and vibrations of color at maximum saturation pervading the works, and alternating strokes that set the color in motion. I use repetition of color and shape to intensify those aspects."[1] Kaish often referred to Claude Monet and William Blake as inspirations for her landscapes. She was inspired, too, by the high skies over the Hudson River, the Hamptons on Long Island, and southern Florida. Her favorite point of inspiration at this time was an off-the-path secluded grove of very old flower trees in Central Park, a place she called her "allée," to which she returned again and again. Her love of nature started during her childhood, when she produced drawings of "the flora and fauna in our garden, the nearby marshlands and ocean, the skies of changing seasons—nature in all its miraculous transformative abundance."[2]

Like the transcendentalists, Kaish had a deep gratitude and appreciation for nature, not only for aesthetic purposes, but also as a tool to observe and understand the structured inner workings of the natural world. Kaish had an explicit desire to have her land- and seascape paintings seen as visualizations of the divine—or manifestations of the sublime. As she explained in 2012, "These days, as I paint from my studio windows, the rising dawn or the turbulent motion filled clouds that sweep the skis on crossing the Hudson, I am reminded of the Transcendentalists and return to the lines of William Wordsworth: the sense of the sublime in the light of setting suns."[3]

Towards the end of her life, while recuperating from various illnesses, she would paint the skies from her studio window, explaining, "as I looked at the skies I was reminded of the story of the poet Schiller who before his death could only see the sky from his bed while he wrote his poetry."[4]

Insightfully, she also said of her landscapes, "I feel that these paintings, which seek to capture the most ephemeral and passing of moments and movements are expressive of the most profound gatherings of my experience."[5] They were for her the culmination of a life's work.

Kaish presented the land- and skyscape paintings in a solo exhibition at the Century Association in 1998, and throughout the 1990s and 2000s at the National Academy of Design, where she was a member. In 2012, the Century Association held a two-person exhibition dedicated to the work of Luise and Morton Kaish. Of Luise's work, Tom Freudenheim asked: "Do the landscapes and skies celebrate Constable's glorying in nature's peace or a Fauvist examination of nature's harsh complexities? But perhaps there are also echoes of late nineteenth-century symbolist meanings lurking in Hodler-like landscapes. Do we see references to early Mondrian trees in wonderful forested vistas, as clues to the layered abstractions toward which she develops her compositions?"[6]

1. Luise Kaish, preparatory notes for talk at the Century Association, 2012, Luise Kaish archives, New York.
2. Ibid.
3. Ibid.
4. Luise Kaish, personal writings, c. 2004, Luise Kaish archives.
5. Ibid.
6. Tom Freudenheim, "Introduction," in *Century Masters, Luise and Morton Kaish, K x 2: II*, exh. cat. (New York: Century Association, 2012), 1–2. The exhibition of the same name was held April 19–May 24, 2012, at the Century Association, New York.

Luise Kaish. *Morning Sullivan's Island* (detail), 1998, (see Plate 88)

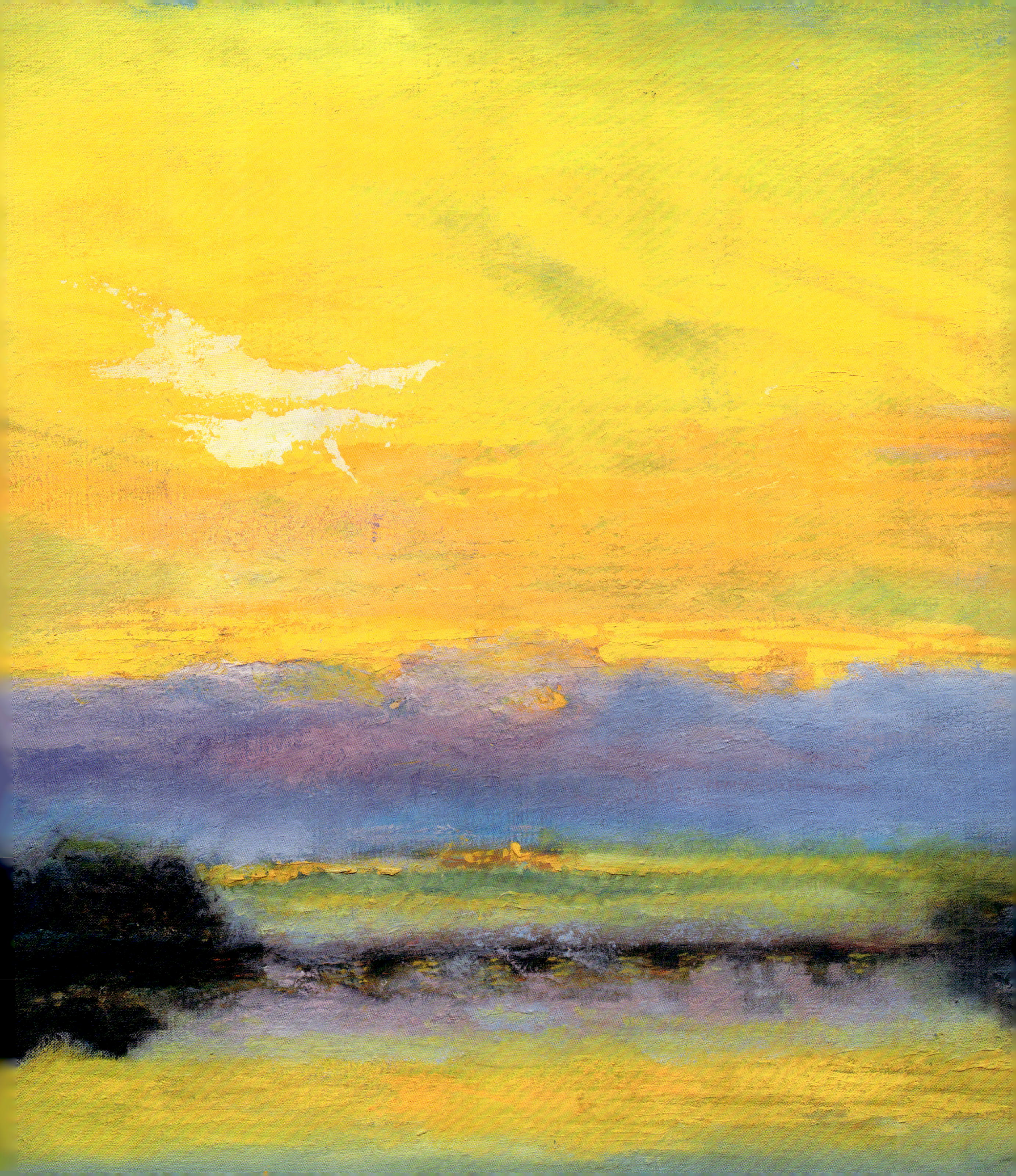

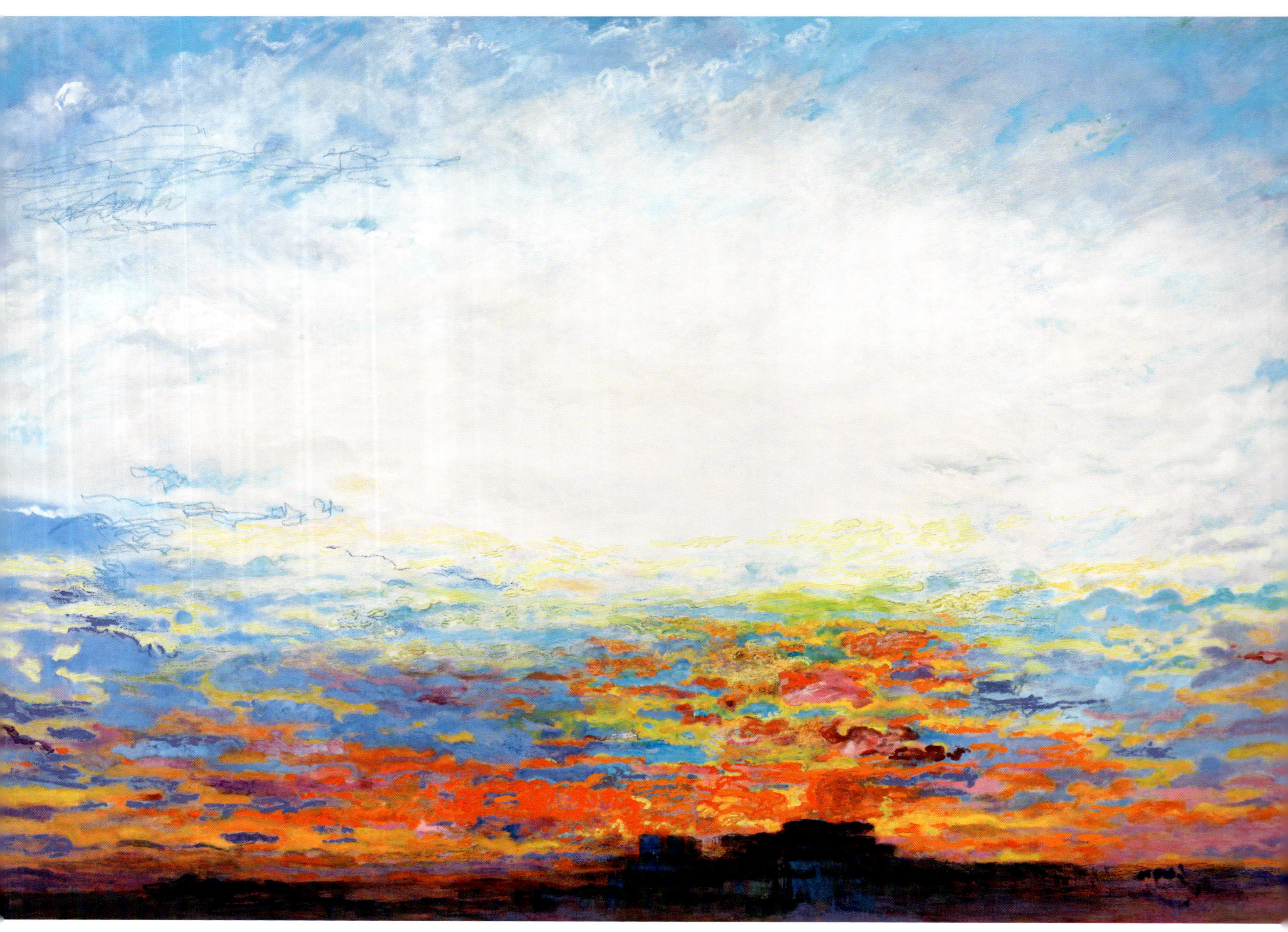

Plate 84
Luise Kaish. *View from the Studio, Rising Sky,* 1993–2004,
oil on canvas, 57 × 82 in. (144.8 × 208.3 cm)

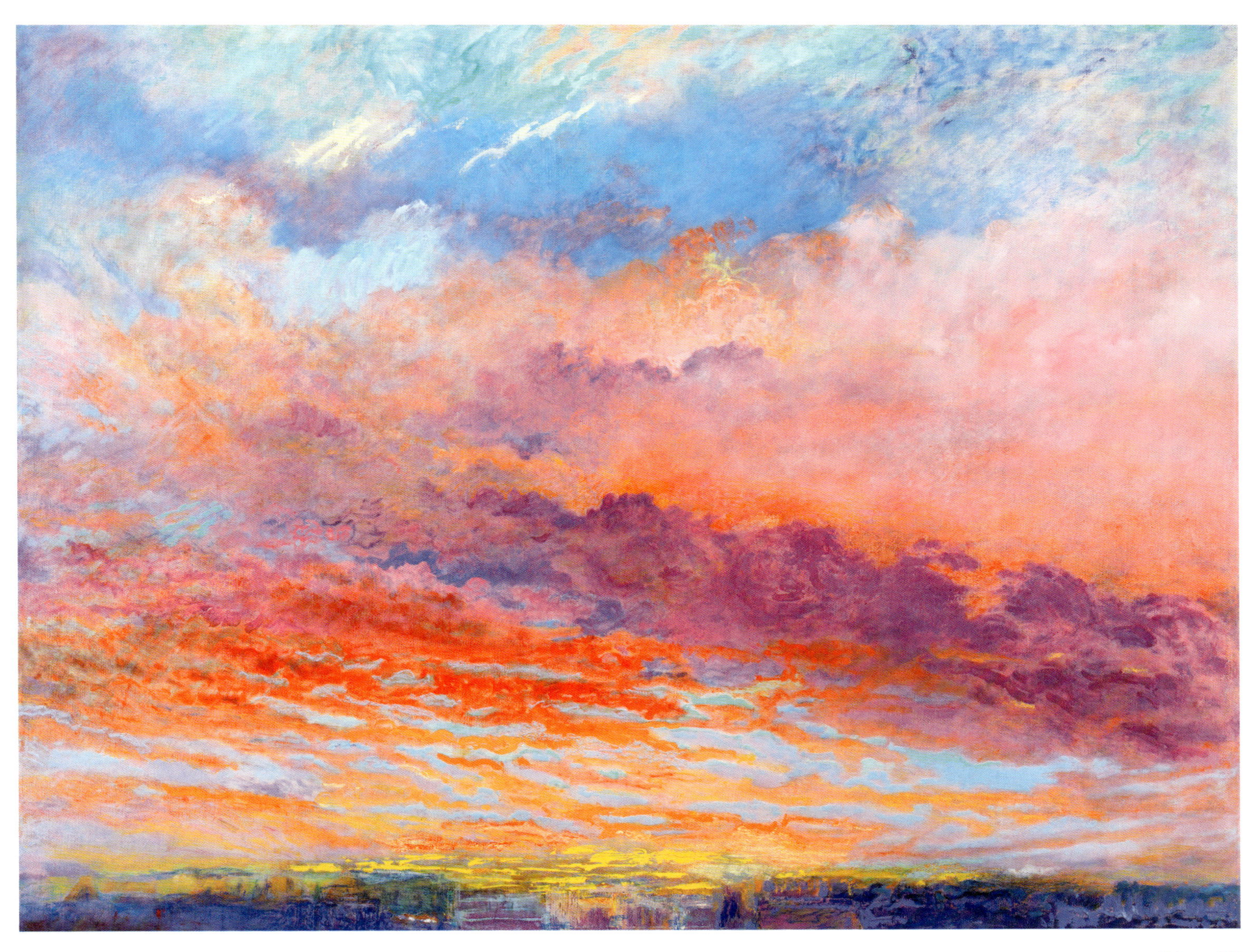

Plate 85
Luise Kaish. *Rising Storm, Spring*, 1998, oil on gesso panel,
40 ½ × 53 in. (102.9 × 134.6 cm)

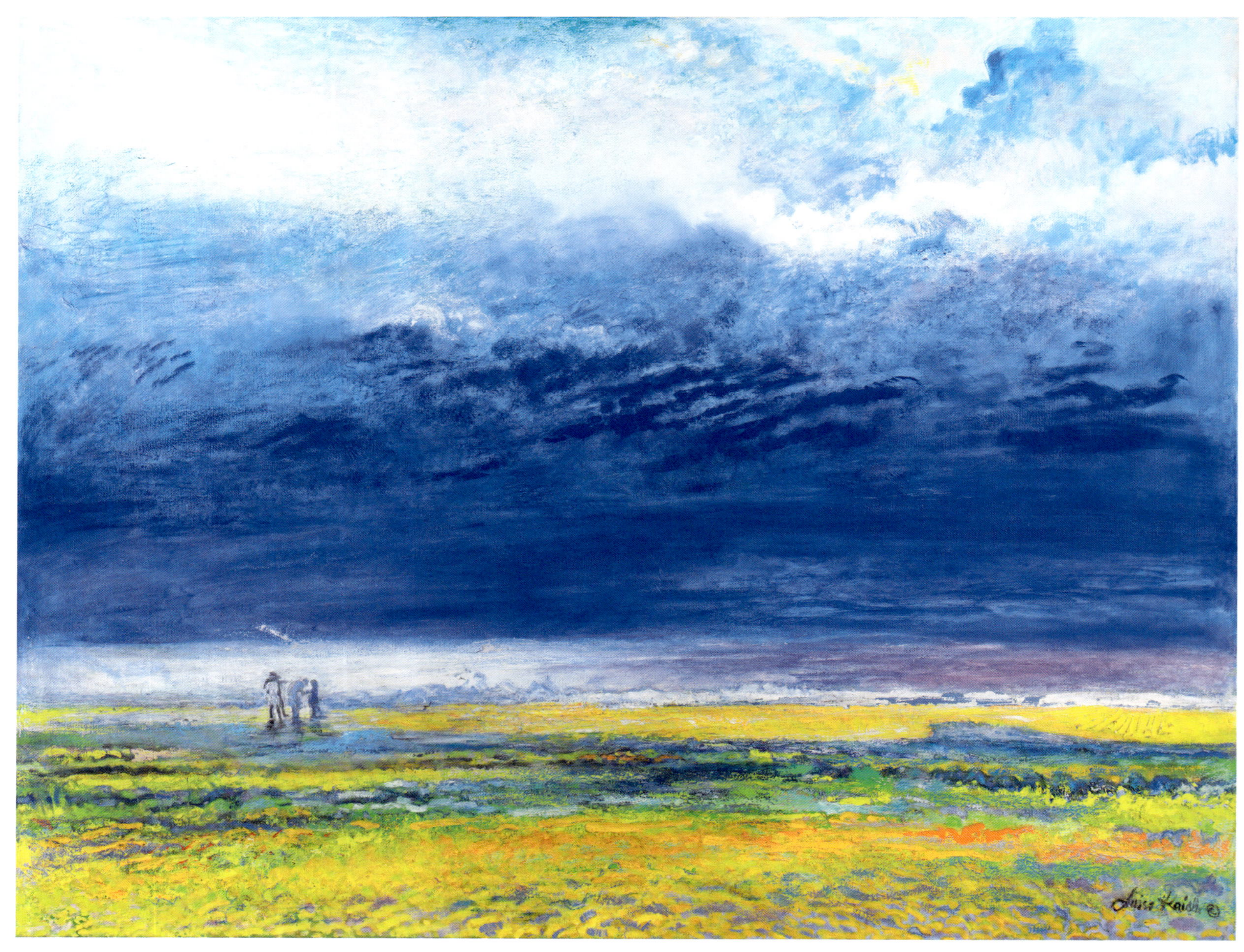

Plate 86
Luise Kaish. *October*, 2004, oil on canvas, 42 × 54 in. (106.7 × 137.2 cm)

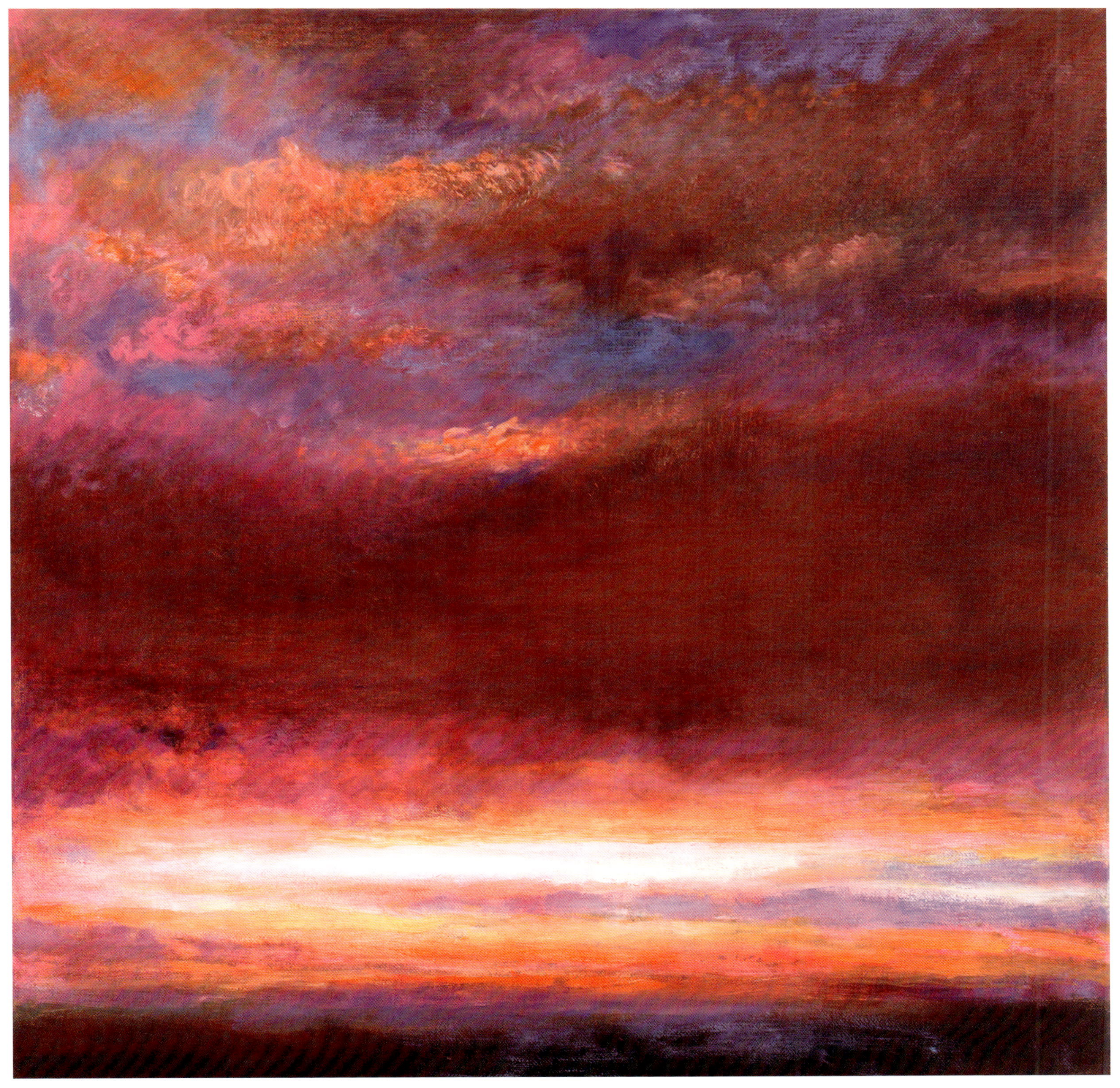

Plate 87
Luise Kaish. *Breaking Light*, circa 1993–98, oil on linen, 16 × 16 in. (40.6 × 40.6 cm)

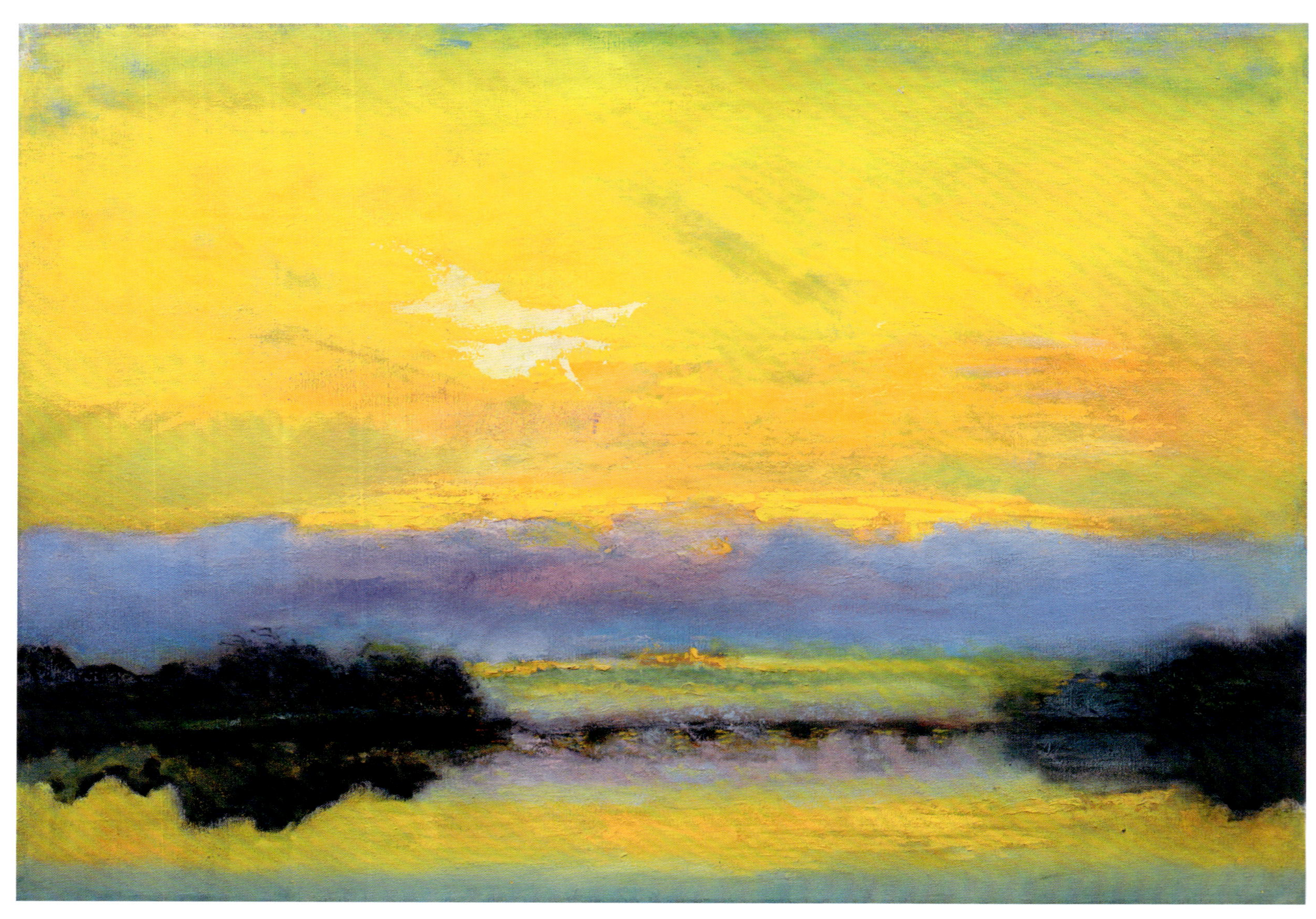

Plate 88
Luise Kaish. *Morning Sullivan's Island*, 1998, oil on canvas,
27 ½ × 39 in. (69.9 × 99.1 cm)

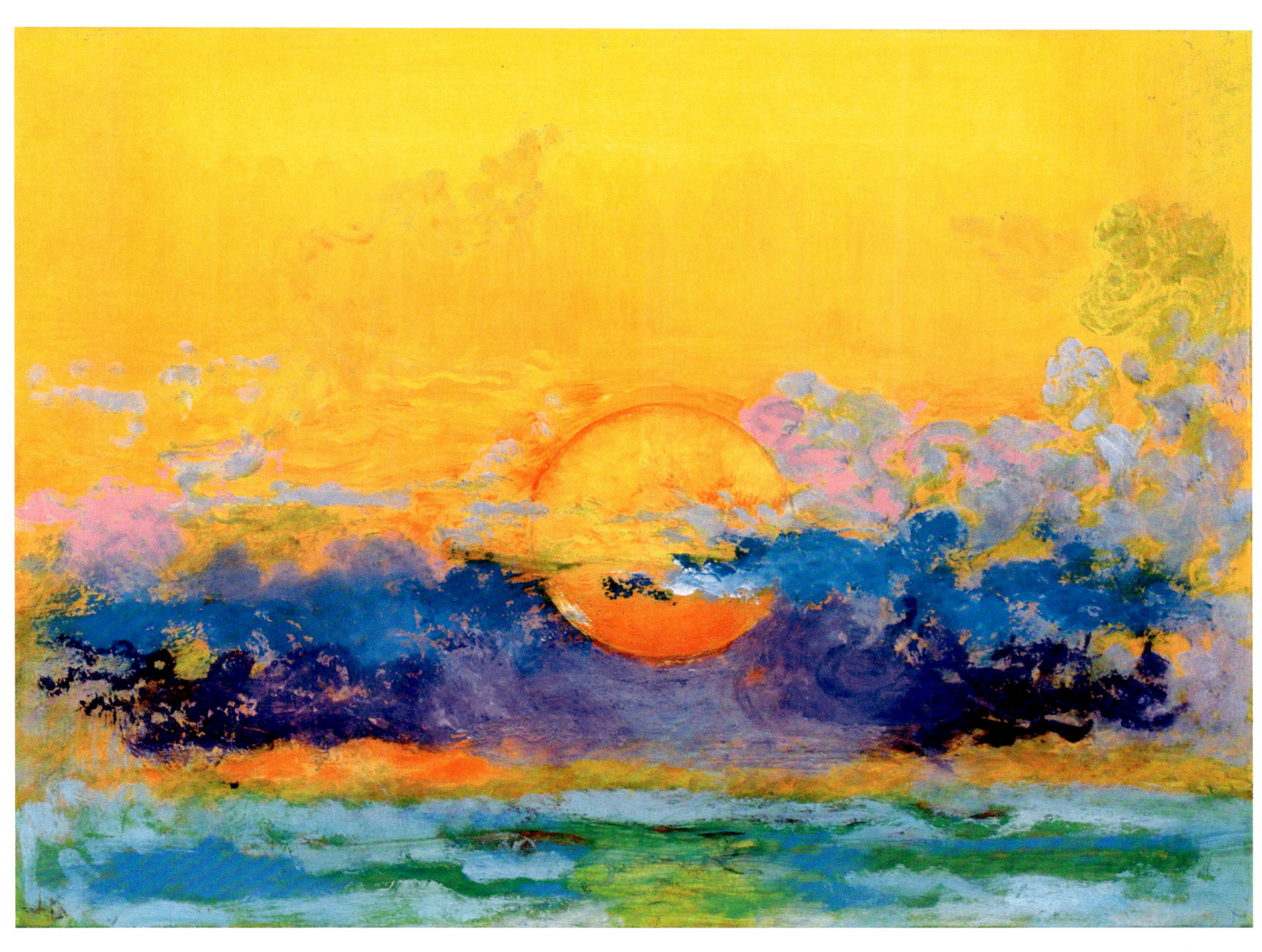

Plate 89
Luise Kaish. *Atlantic 1*, circa 1993–98, oil on linen,
9 × 12 in. (22.9 × 30.5 cm)

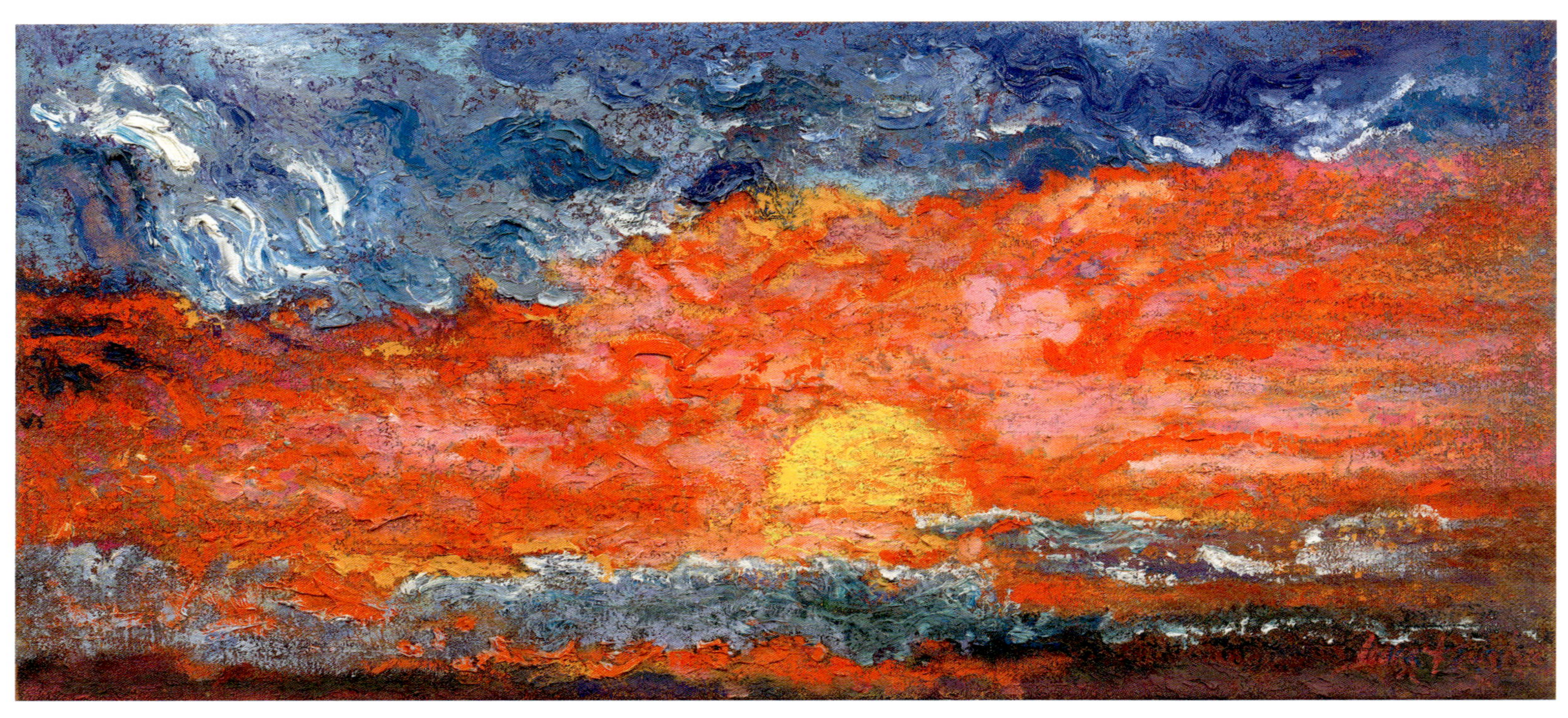

Plate 90
Luise Kaish. *Rising Sun, Sailfish Point*, 1998, oil on linen,
10 × 22 in. (25.4 × 55.9 cm)

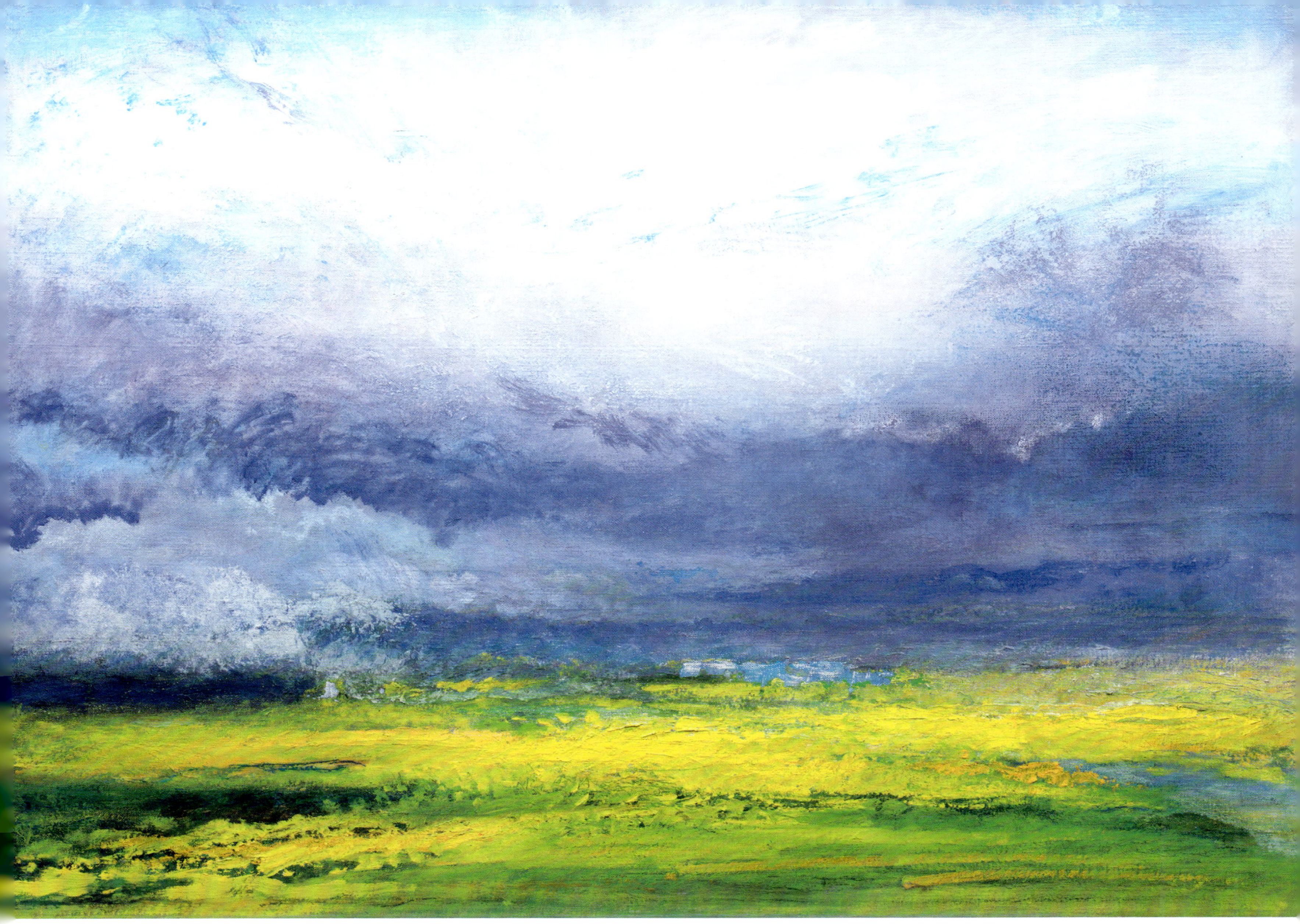

Plate 91
Luise Kaish. *Golden Morning, Mustard Fields*, circa 1993–98,
oil on linen, 20 × 28 in. (50.8 × 71.1 cm)

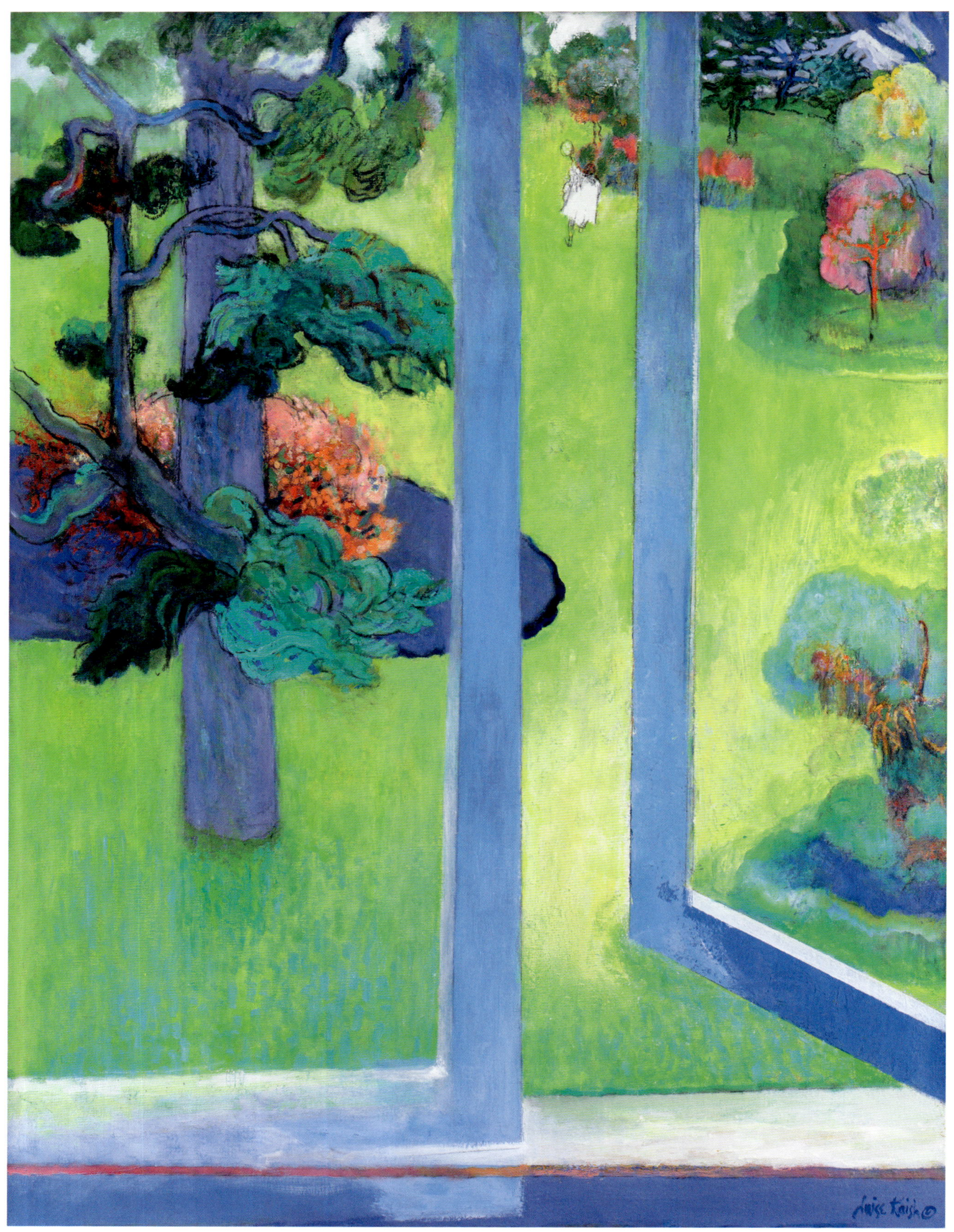

Plate 92

Luise Kaish. *The Butterfly Net, The Priory*, 1998, oil on canvas,
40 × 30 ¼ in. (101.6 × 76.8 cm)

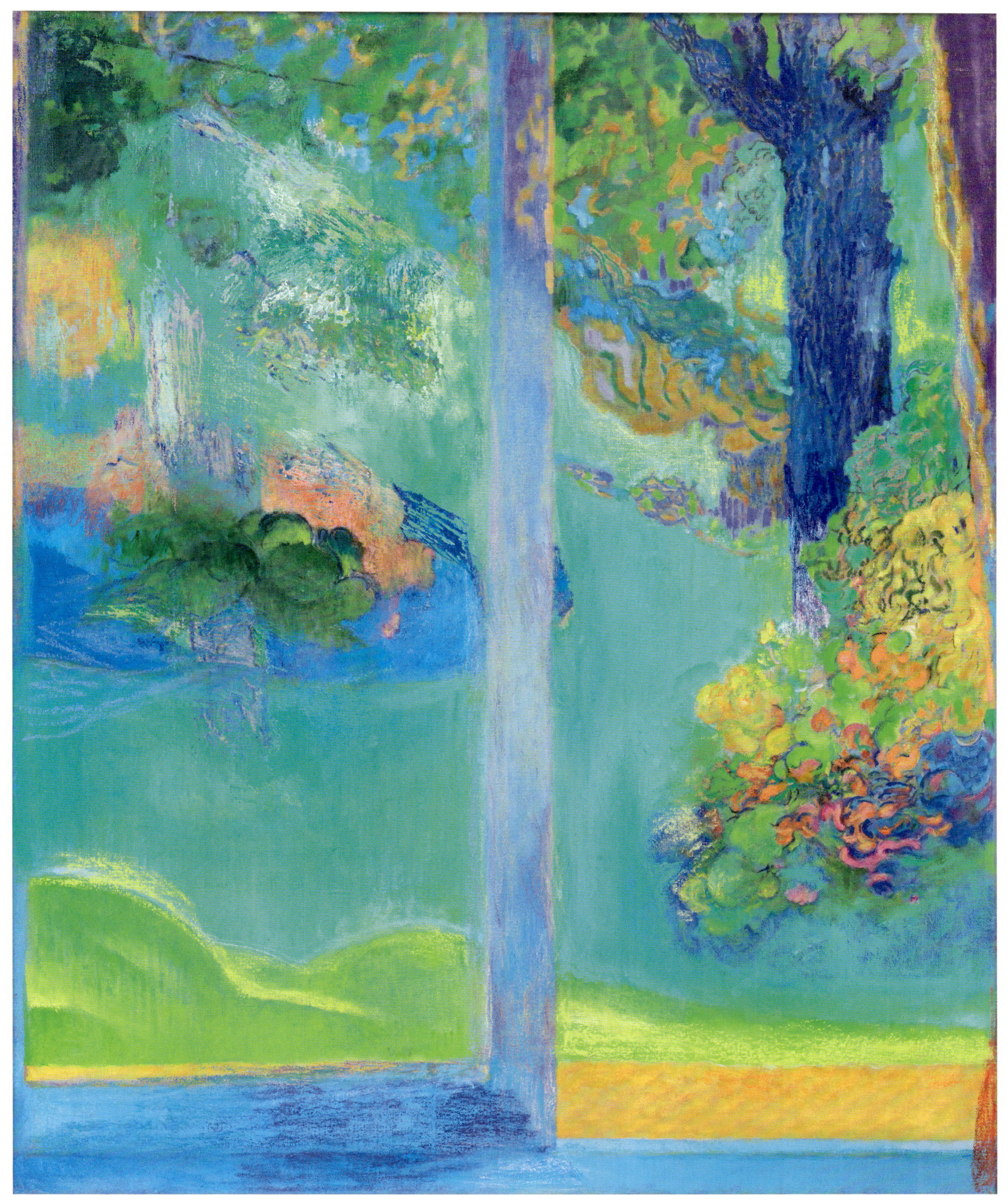

Plate 93
Luise Kaish. *Summer Greens, The Priory III*, circa 1998, oil on linen,
42 × 34 in. (106.7 × 86.4 cm)

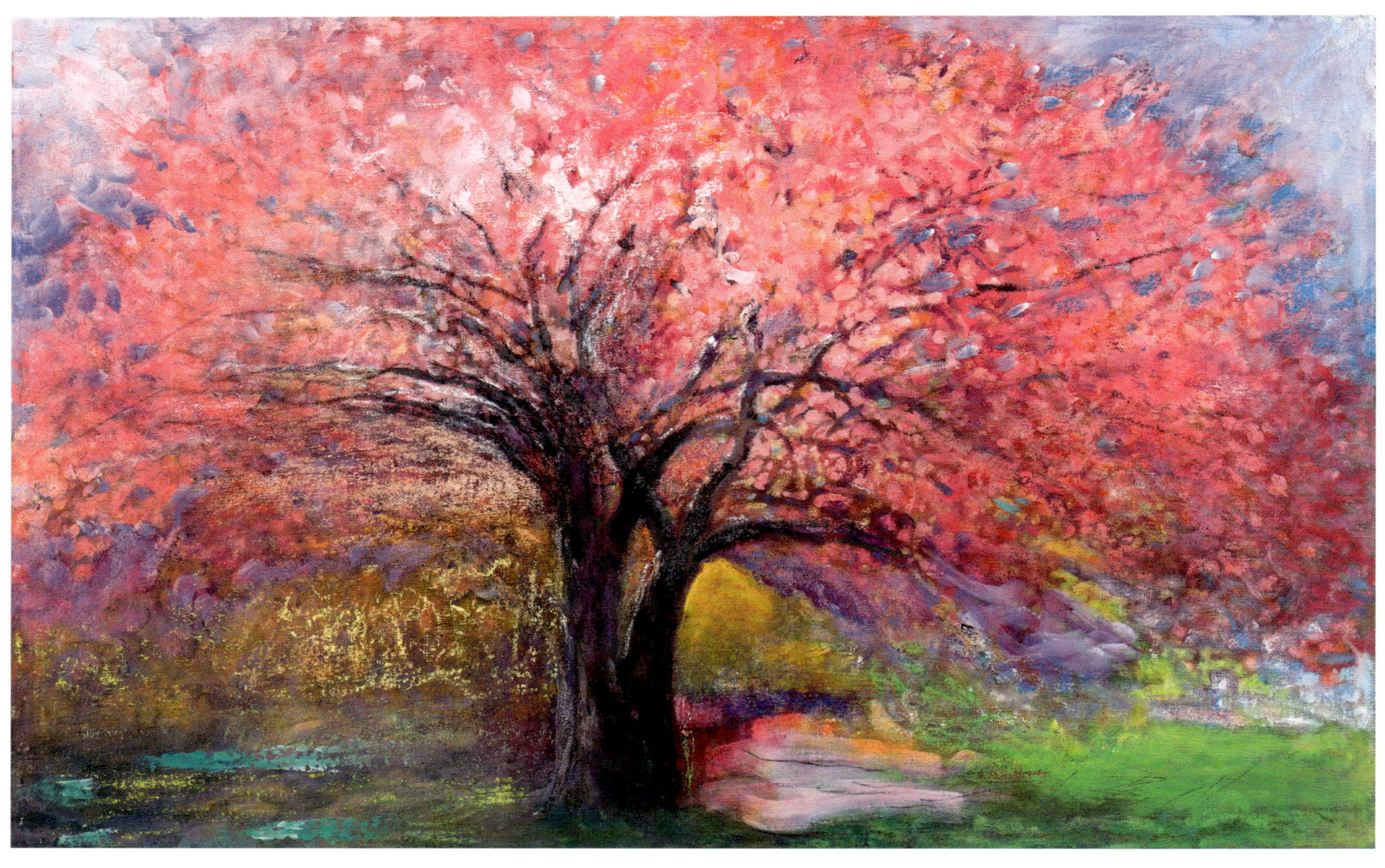

Plate 94
Luise Kaish. *Achingly Beautiful Pink*, 1998, oil on linen,
14 × 22 in. (35.6 × 55.9 cm)

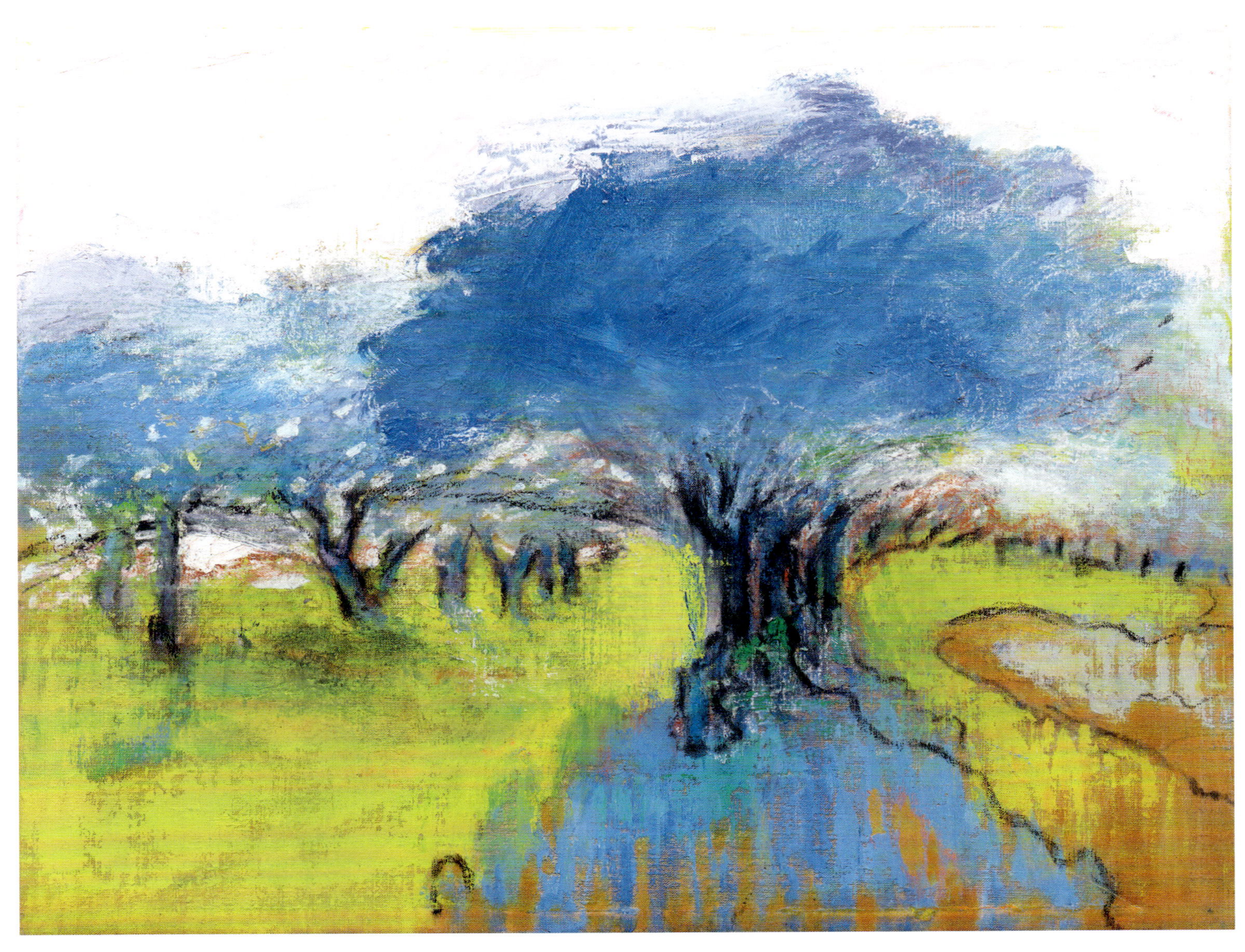

Plate 95
Luise Kaish. *Kensington Blue*, circa 1993–98, oil on linen,
14 × 18 in. (35.6 × 45.7 cm)

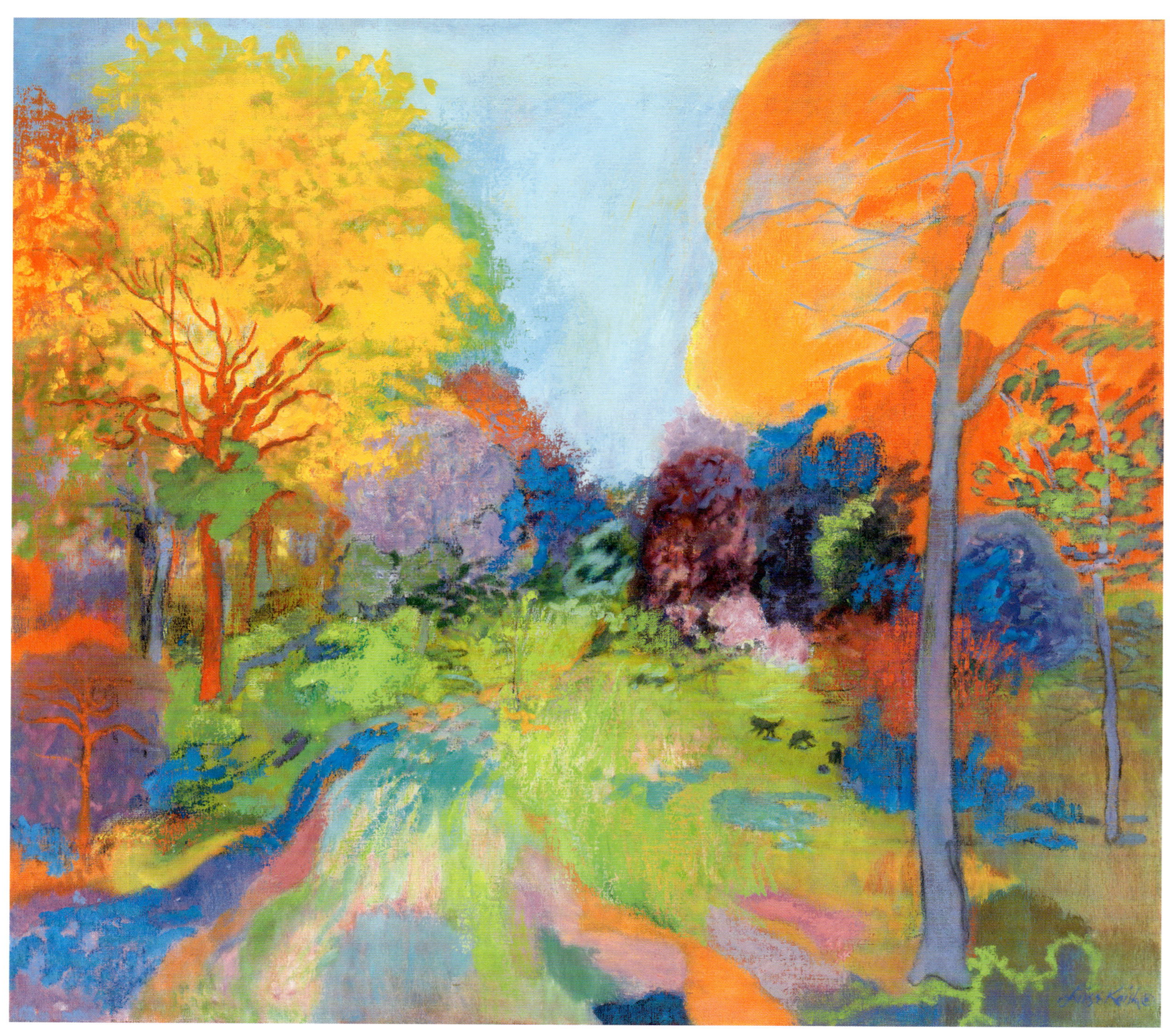

Plate 96
Luise Kaish. *Autumn Glory*, circa 1998, oil on linen,
26 × 28 ½ in. (66 × 72.4 cm)

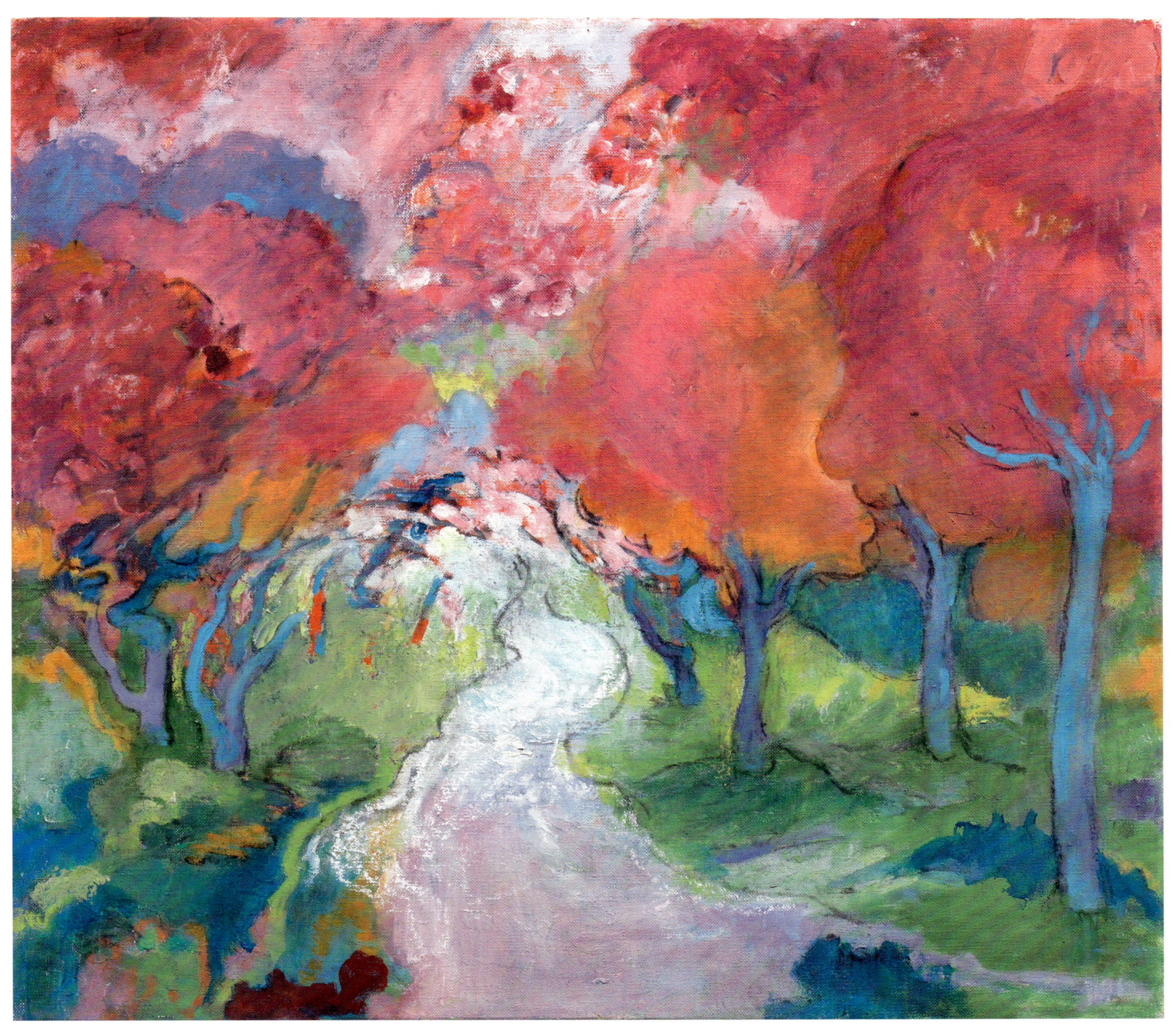

Plate 97
Luise Kaish. *Blossom Allée II*, circa 1993–98, oil on linen,
18 × 20 in. (45.7 × 50.8 cm)

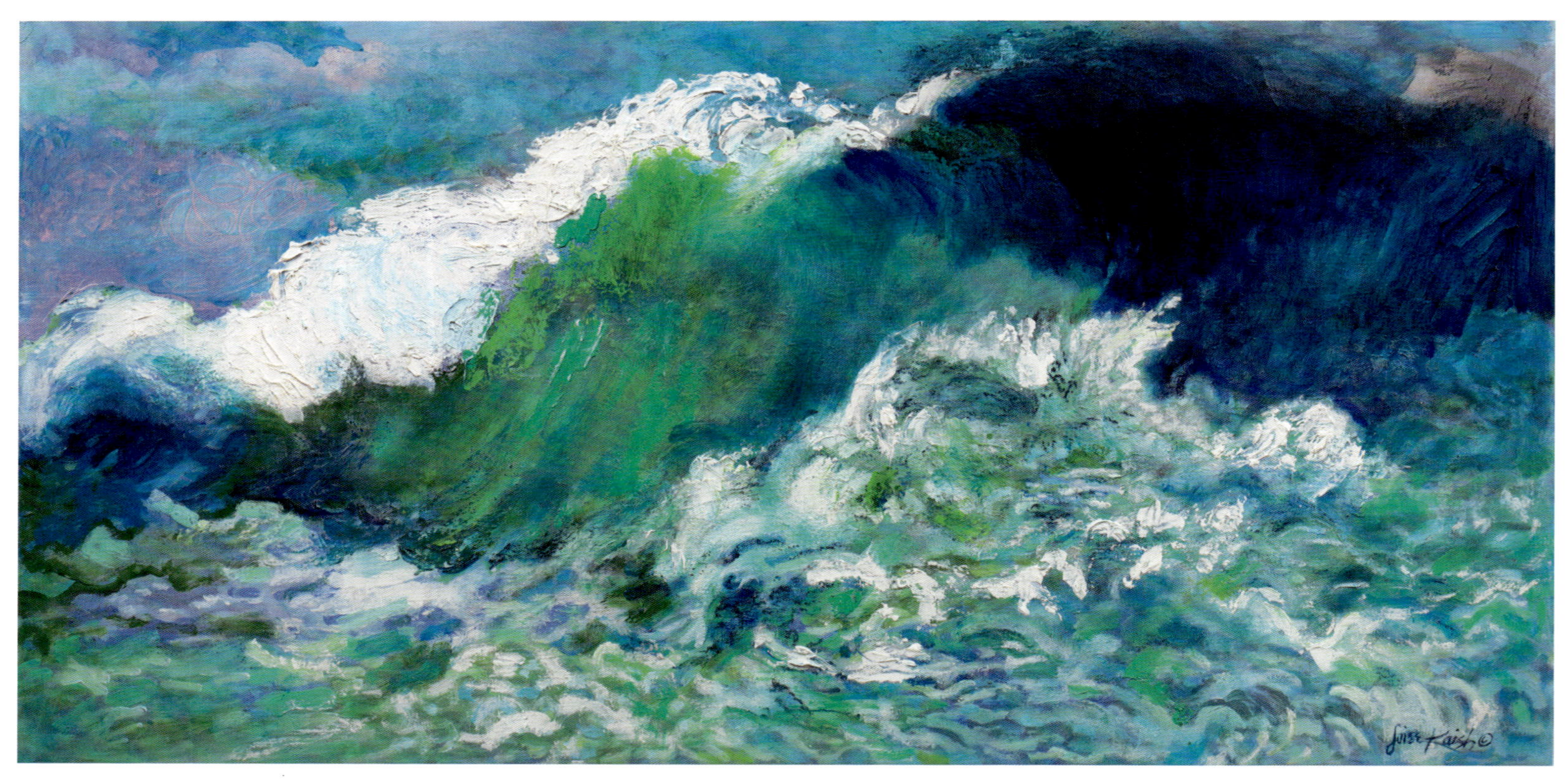

Plate 98
Luise Kaish. *Breaking Waves*, circa 2007–12, oil on linen,
12 × 24 in. (30.5 × 61 cm)

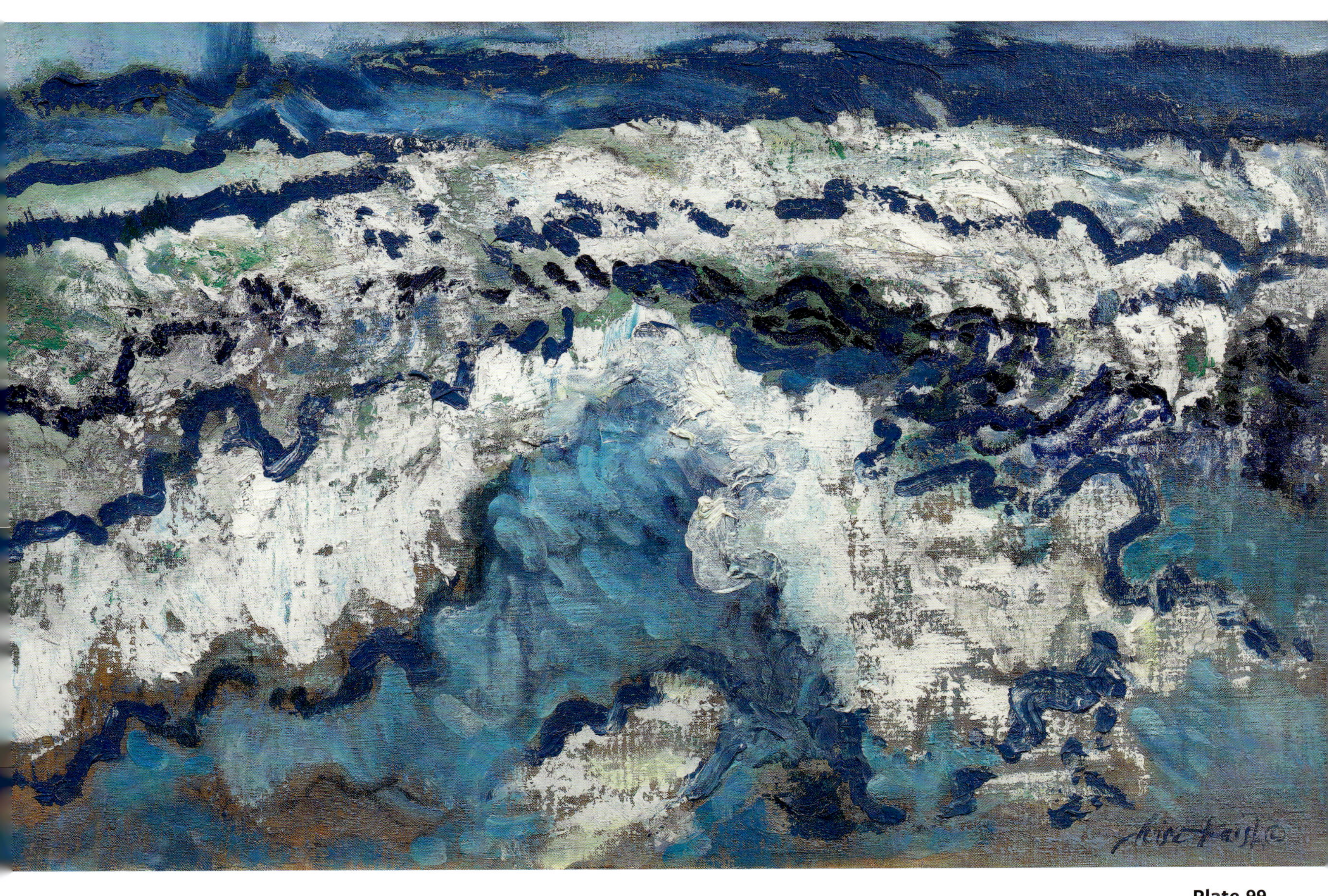

Plate 99
Luise Kaish. *Rising Blue Tide*, circa 2007–11, oil on linen,
12 × 19 in. (30.5 × 48.3 cm)

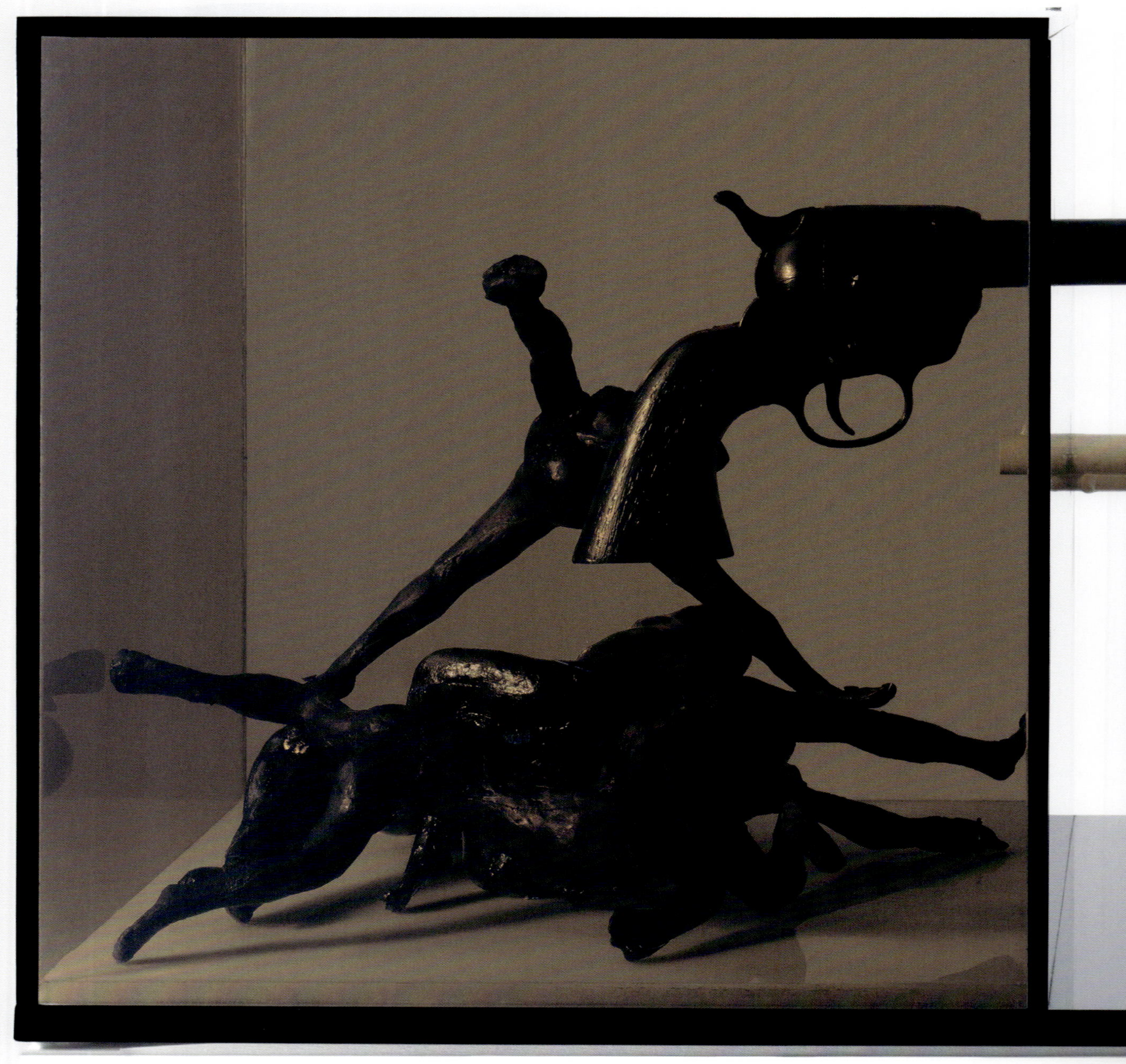

Equation (1967)

In 1967, Kaish was invited to participate in a historically important exhibition at the New School for Social Research called *Protest and Hope: An Exhibition of Contemporary American Art*, which included forty-three American artists whose works addressed the social turbulence of the 1960s—and, most notably, a recent bombing in North Korea. Kaish produced a sculpture specifically for the exhibition, titled *Equation* (1967). It is unique in her oeuvre insofar as it represents a shift in subject matter from religion to

Plate 100
Luise Kaish. *Equation*, 1967, epoxy and plexiglass,
12 × 12 × 27 in. (30.5 × 30.5 × 68.6 cm)

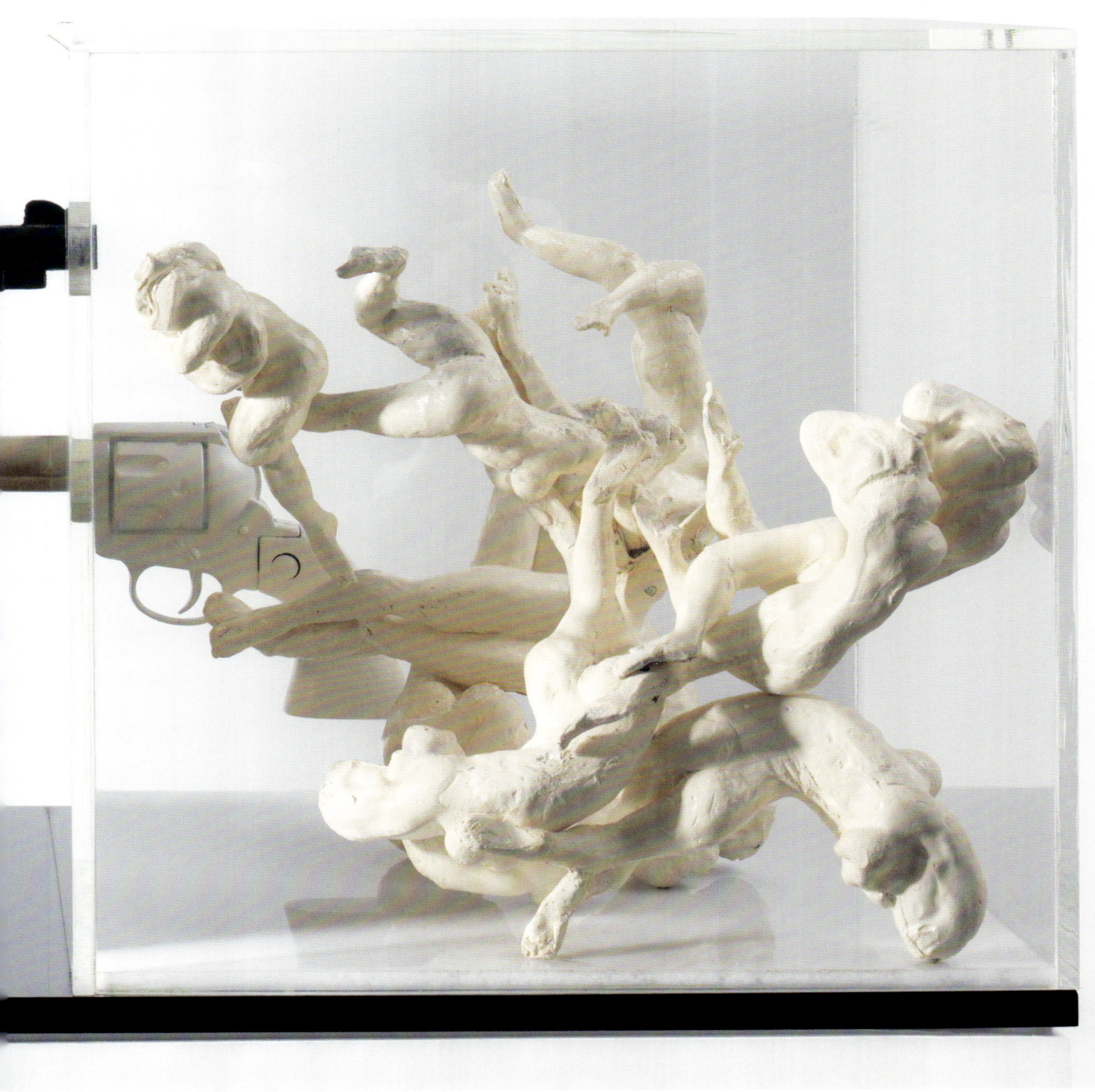

politics. The sculpture comprises two clear plexiglass boxes; in one box sits a cluster of intertwined nudes in white with a white pistol aimed at the second box, within which sits a cluster of black figures and a black pistol aimed at the other box. In an essay about the exhibition, Harold Rosenberg isolated eleven works as the "showpieces" most worthy of consideration—including Kaish's work alongside those by George Segal, Elaine de Kooning, Robert Rauschenberg, Ben Shahn, and Red Grooms.[1]

1.   Harold Rosenberg, "Art of Bad Conscience," *Artworks and Packages*
(Chicago: University of Chicago Press, 1969), 157–70.

Axonometrics (2012)

During World War II, Kaish was employed as a draftsperson at the U.S. naval architectural firm Cox & Stevens, where she worked on plans for the conversion of naval ships to hospital ships. It was there that she learned to produce axonometric projections, helping her to represent the three-dimensional ships in two dimensions. However, unlike a multi-view projection, which depicts only one "side" of an object, the axonometric projections that Kaish produced represented more than one "side" simultaneously. The tools she needed to create these projections included rulers, compasses, T-squares, and drafting pens. The skill set that she developed in her teens was one she would return to again and again throughout her career, notably in her *La Lumière* sculpture (1975–76) but most pointedly in a series of late works called the *Axonometrics* (2012). The series comprises several works on paper and a few small paintings.

In a 2012 lecture at the Century Association, she described her *Axonometrics* as "going for a walk with a line" in reference to a quote by Paul Klee.[1] Indeed, using the same drafting tools as in her youth, Kaish produced abstract axonometric drawings on paper that emphasized geometry, three-dimensionality, movement in space, and, above all, line. The gold, white, and black drawings are covered with quasi-architectural lines, and the surfaces are punctured, pierced, and folded. In the same lecture, Kaish elaborated further: "I am searching for a sense of depth and enigma . . . with an enigmatic presence (figure or structure), floating (surrounded by space), hovering (relating to another presence), embedded (pierced space), or recessive (moving in space)—all revealed and qualified, by light, by color, by structure, by movement, and by line."[2] The resulting drawings are her final works.

Kaish's intention with the *Axonometrics* was to use the drawings as templates for monumental wall pieces. She was aware of twenty-first-century digital fabrication developments and was eager to use the new technology to facilitate the construction of complex works of great scale. She envisioned entire walls of multidimensional bronze and steel, complemented by engraved linear and applied color elements. Although the wall pieces were never realized, the extant works serve as a reminder of Kaish's classic discipline, her confident freedom, and her unwavering drive to push her practice in new and exciting directions.

1. Luise Kaish, "Gallery Talk at the Century Association," Luise Kaish archives. Paraphrased quote from Paul Klee's *Pedagogical Sketchbook*: "A drawing is simply a line going for a walk."
2. Ibid.

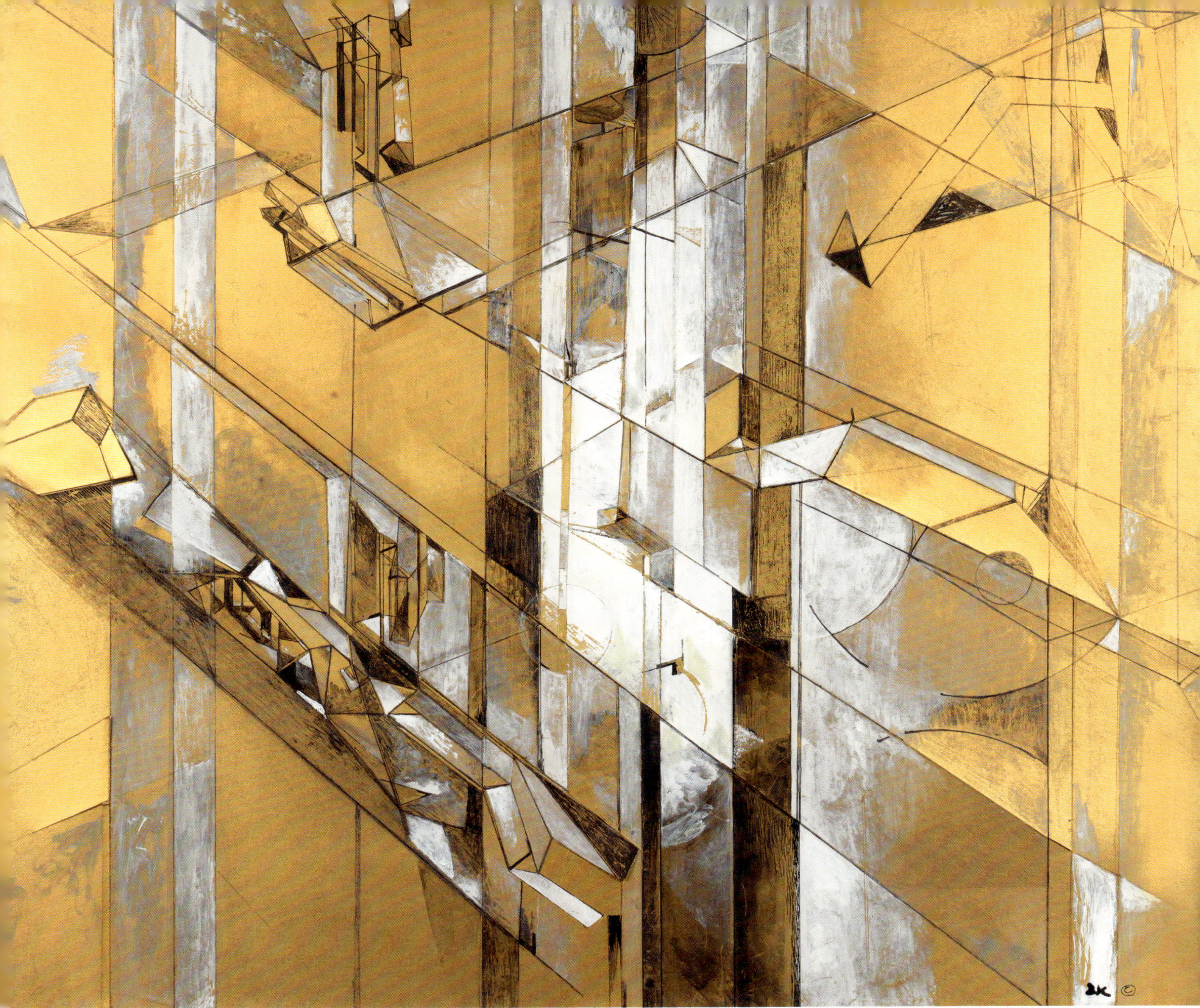

Plate 101
Luise Kaish. *There,* maquette for axonometric bronze relief, 2012,
ink and pigment on gold paper, 22 × 28 in. (55.9 × 71.1 cm)

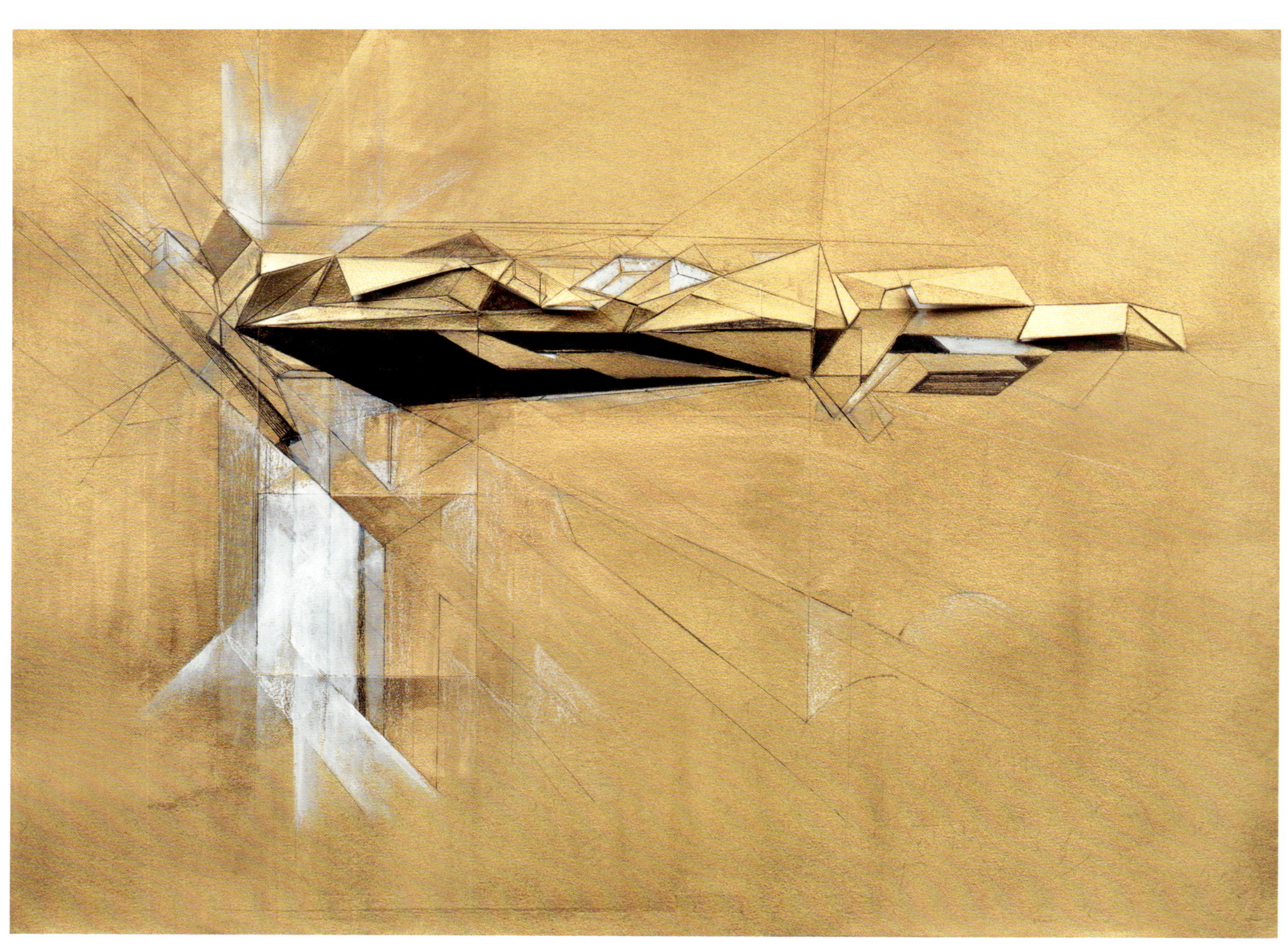

Plate 102

Luise Kaish. *There II,* maquette for axonometric bronze relief, 2012,
ink and pigment on gold paper, 24 ½ × 25 in. (62.2 × 63.5 cm)

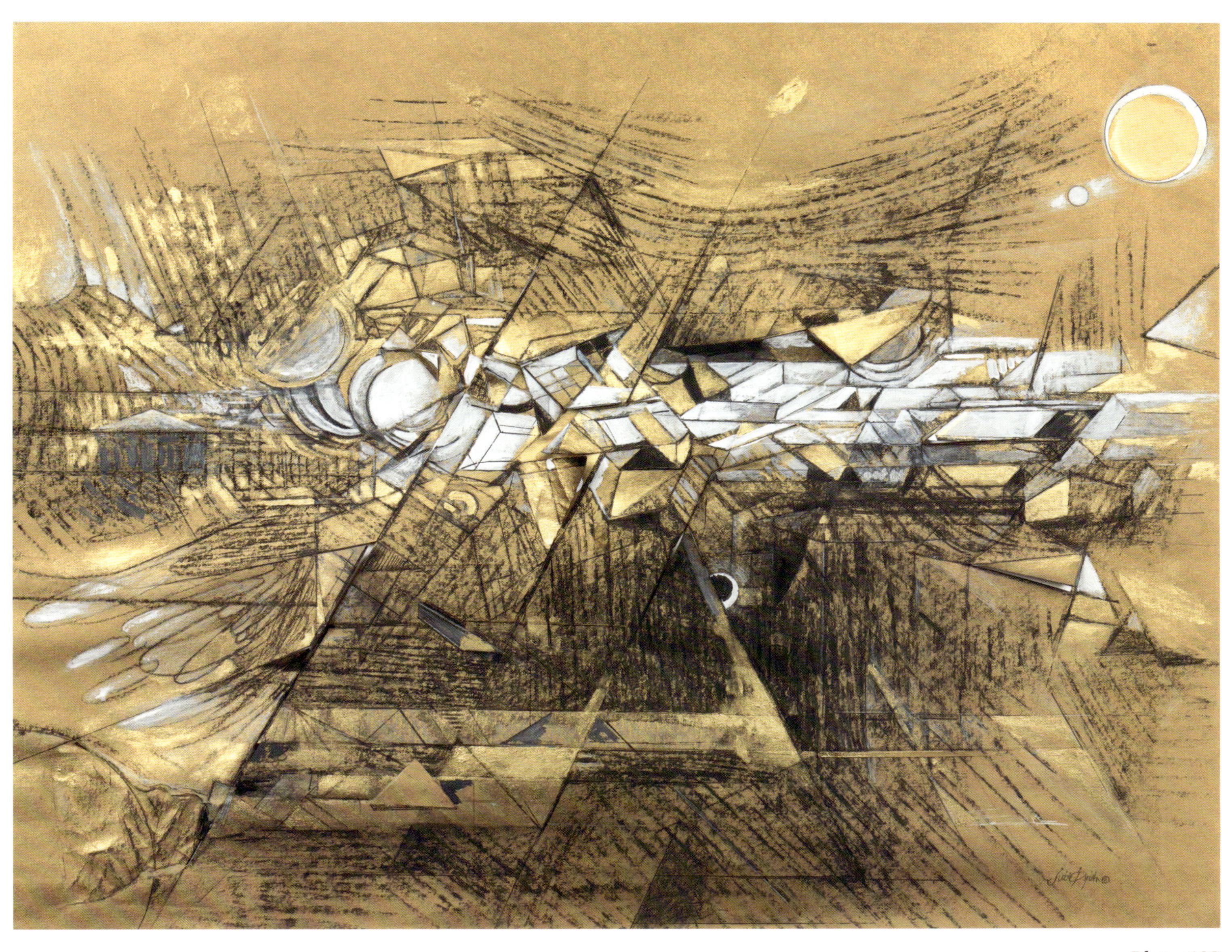

Plate 103
Luise Kaish. *The Wind Is Blowing,* maquette for axonometric bronze relief, 2012, ink and pigment on gold paper, 25 × 30 ½ in. (63.5 × 77.5 cm)

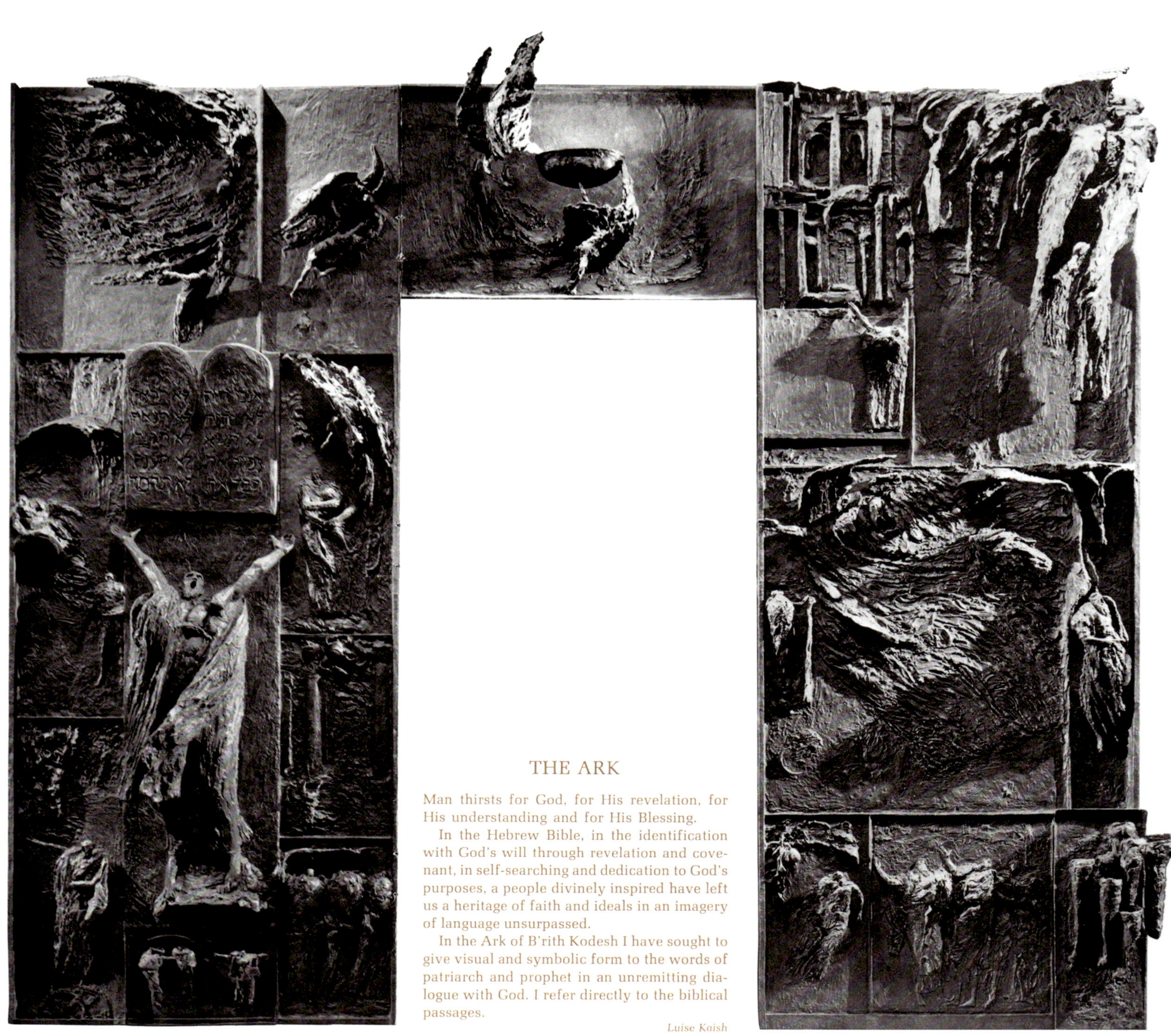

THE ARK

Man thirsts for God, for His revelation, for His understanding and for His Blessing.

In the Hebrew Bible, in the identification with God's will through revelation and covenant, in self-searching and dedication to God's purposes, a people divinely inspired have left us a heritage of faith and ideals in an imagery of language unsurpassed.

In the Ark of B'rith Kodesh I have sought to give visual and symbolic form to the words of patriarch and prophet in an unremitting dialogue with God. I refer directly to the biblical passages.

Luise Kaish

APPENDICES

Appendix A   Biblical excerpts explaining the imagery of Luise Kaish's *The Ark of Revelation*, brochure. Rochester, New York: Temple B'rith Kodesh, 1964. Luise Kaish archives, New York. (see page 226 and Plates 17, 18)

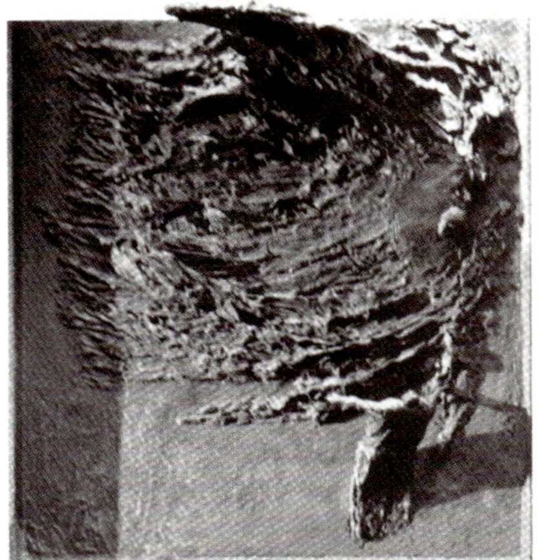

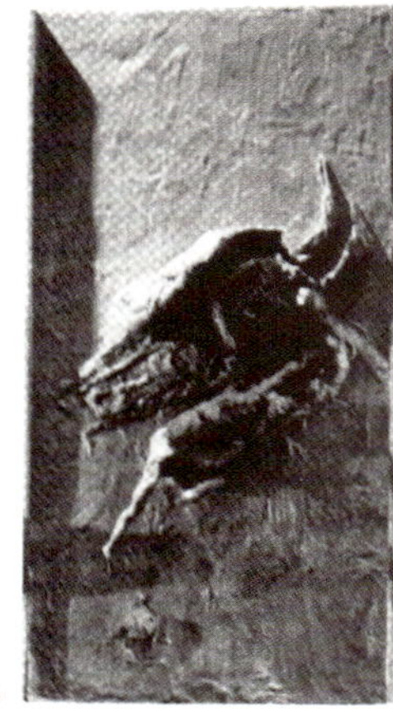

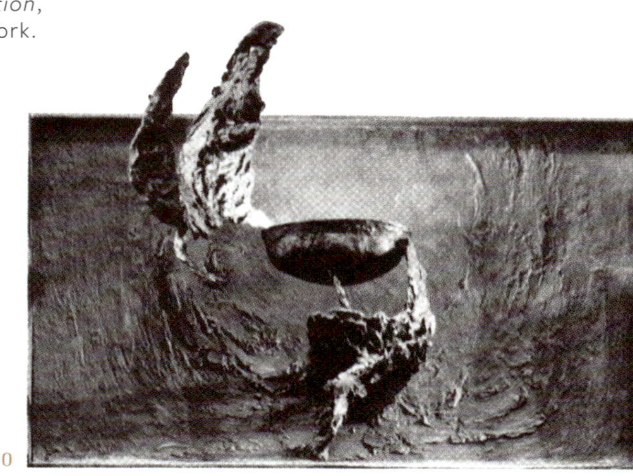

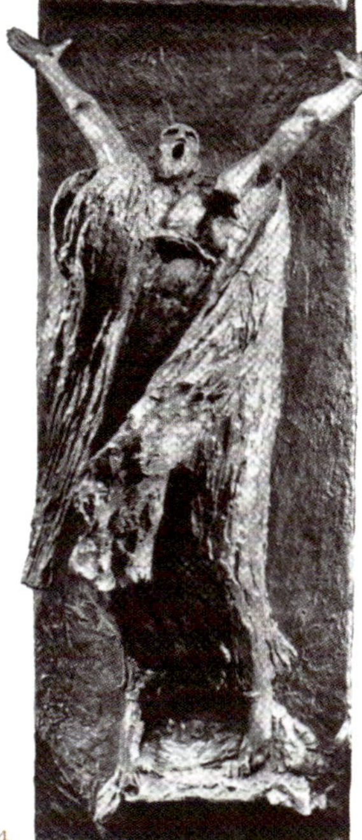

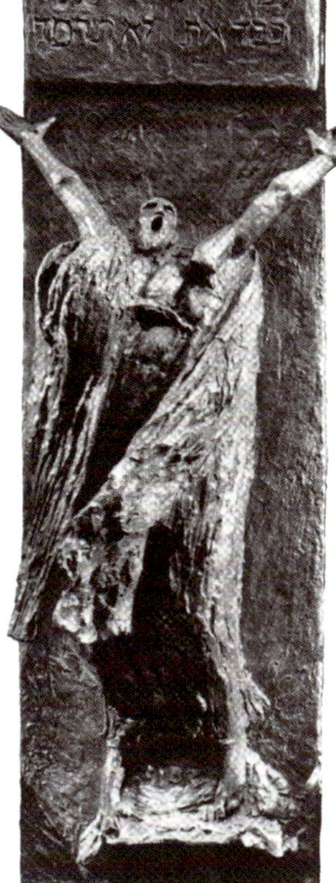

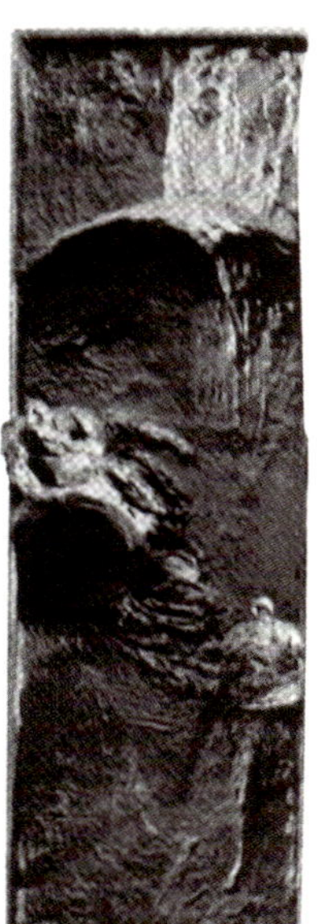

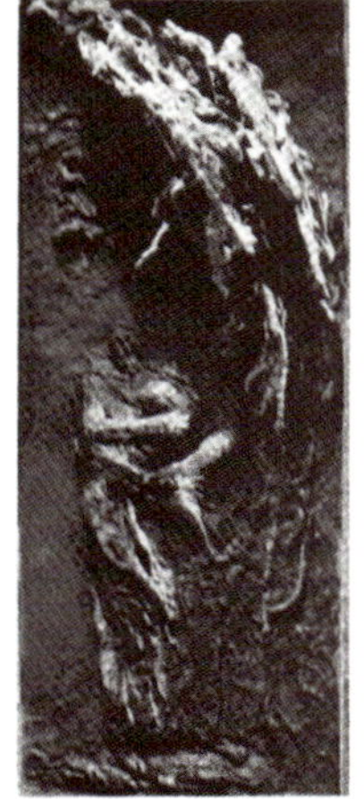

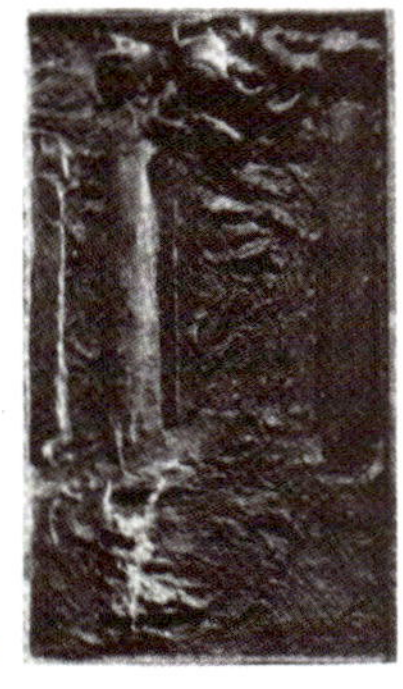

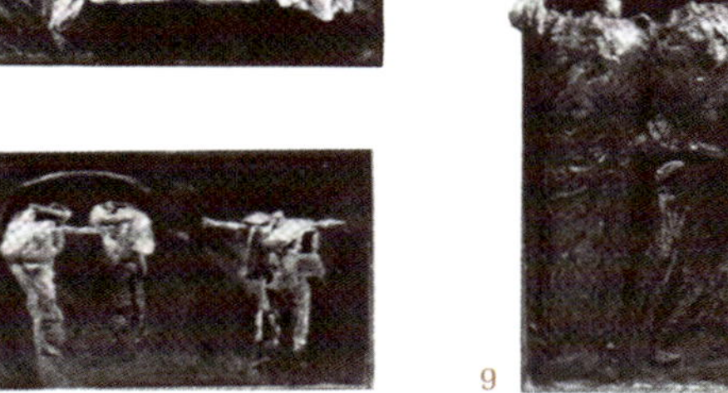

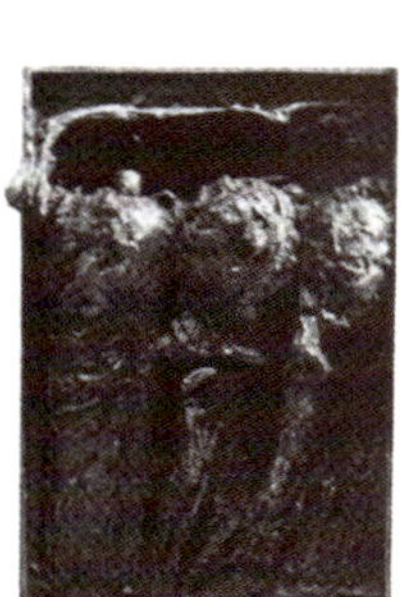

ARK PLAN SHOWING LOCATION OF BIBLICAL EXCERPTS

1
The angel of the Lord appears to stay the hand of Abraham and blesses him . . . "and in thy seed shall all the nations of the earth be blessed; because thou hast hearkened to My voice." *Genesis 22:14-19*

2
Jacob wrestles with the angel and becomes Israel . . . "for I have seen God face to face . . ." *Genesis 32:25-32*

3
God calls to Moses from out of the midst of the burning bush. *Exodus 3:2-7*

4
Moses on Mt. Sinai receives the tablets of stone whereon are the words of the Law as written by the finger of God. *Exodus 24:12*

5
David the psalmist comforts Saul . . . "and the evil spirit departed from him." *First Samuel 16:23*

6
Solomon dedicates the First Temple and . . . "the cloud . . . the glory of the Lord filled the house of the Lord." *First Kings 8:8-12*

7
On Mt. Carmel the fire of the Lord falls and consumes the burnt offering of the prophet Elijah who triumphs over the priests of Baal. *First Kings 18:36-40*

8
Amos, prophet of social justice, is driven from the temple . . . "for the land is not able to bear all his words." *Amos 7:10-12*

9
Exile: "If I forget thee, O Jerusalem." *Psalms 137:1-7*

10
Ner Tamid: . . . "and there will I meet with thee, and I will speak with thee from above the ark-cover, from between the two cherubim which are upon the ark of the testimony . . ." *Exodus 25:18-23*

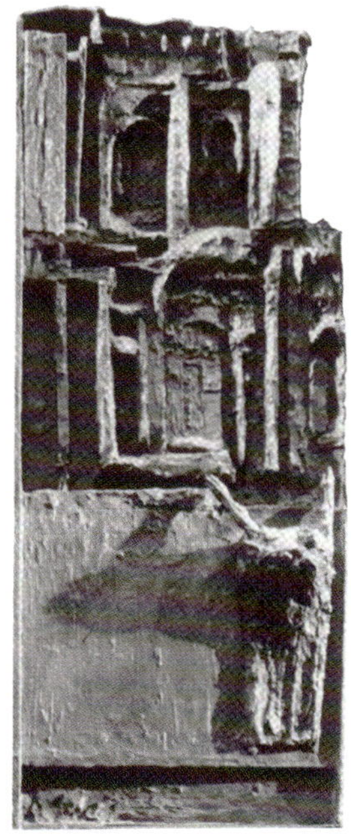

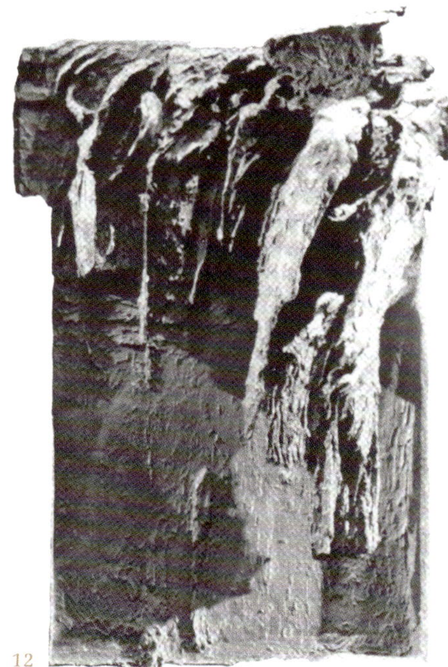

11

12

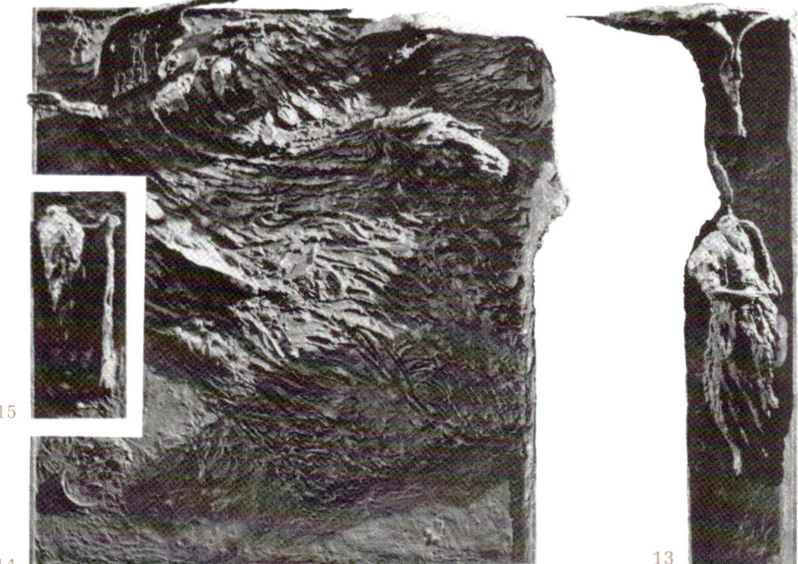

15

14

13

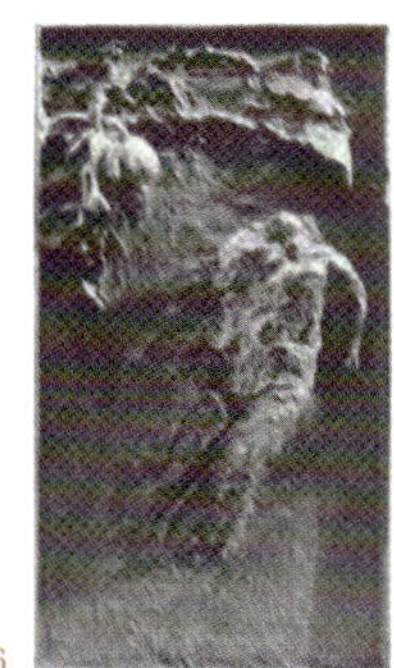

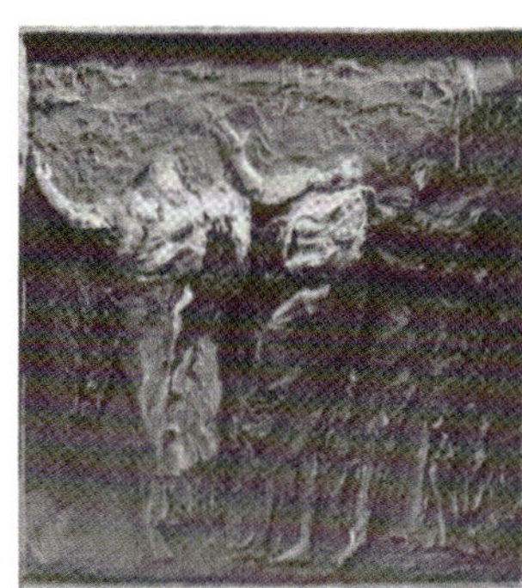

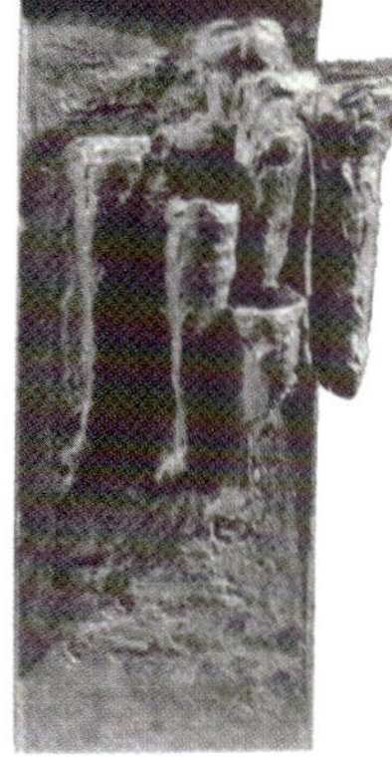

16

17

18

11

The lament of Jeremiah. He forbodes the destruction of Jerusalem: "It may be that they will hearken, and turn every man from his evil way . . ." *Jeremiah 26:2-7*

. . . and foresees the eventual return: "And I will cause them to return to the land that I gave to their fathers, and they shall possess it." *Jeremiah 30:3*

12

The seraphim purify the lips of Isaiah with a glowing coal. "And I heard the voice of the Lord saying: Whom shall I send, and who will go for us: Then I said: Here am I; send me." *Isaiah 6:5-9*

13

Isaiah summons the nation to their mission as "the people of the covenant": "And he said unto me: Thou art my servant, Israel, in whom I will be glorified . . . I will also give thee for a light of the nations, that my salvation may be unto the ends of the earth." *Isaiah 49:1-7*

14

Ezekiel is carried out to prophesy over the Valley of Dry Bones: "Behold, I will cause breath to enter into you, and ye shall live . . . and ye shall know that I am the Lord." *Ezekiel 37:1-3*

15

"And Ezra the priest brought the Torah before the congregation, both men and women, and all that could hear with understanding." *Nehemiah 8:2-4*

16

Jonah sits beneath the gourd "that it might be a shadow over his head, to deliver him from his evil." *Jonah 4:5-11*

17

Nehemiah leads the people in rejoicing after the rebuilding of Jerusalem: "And they said: Let us arise and build. So they strengthened their hands for the good work." *Nehemiah 2:17-18*

18

Menorah: "And thou shalt make a candelabrum . . . make it seven lamps . . ." *Exodus: 25-31*

The Beth Shalom Ark Doors

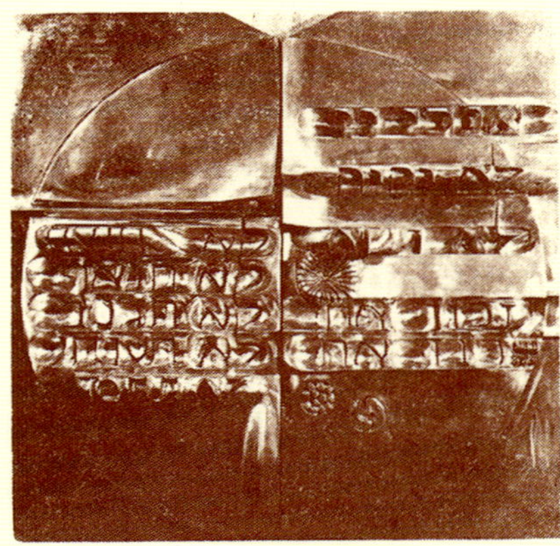

TEMPLE BETH SHALOM

WILMINGTON, DELAWARE

The ark doors and the entire reconstructed Bimah were made possible through the generosity of the late Morris Leibowitz, who passed away on August 13, 1968. This pamphlet is published in his memory.

* * * * *

In accordance with the wishes of the late Morris Leibowitz, the Bimah is dedicated in esteem and friendship to Aaron Finger, Esquire.

THE BETH SHALOM ARK DOORS

THE PROBLEM OF THE ARTIST

Gershon Scholem, the world's greatest scholar in the field of Jewish mysticism, makes the statement, "How can words express an experience for which there is no adequate simile in the finite world?" How can they reveal "a relationship between the Creator and His Creation, between the finite and the infinite?" This is precisely the problem that faces the creative artist.

Luise Kaish is a talented artist, a sensitive and perceptive one. In the execution of the ark doors for Temple Beth Shalom, she has successfully sculptured in bronze a great work of art that combines profundity of thought and impressive artistic vitality.

In daring, bold sculpture, she has given an interpretation of the Ten Commandments based on the medieval, mystic conception of God as En Soph, the Infinite.

GOD AS EN SOPH

The intention of the artist is to communicate to the viewer the larger meaning of the moment at Sinai; not only the revelation of the Ten Commandments, but the profound and enduring meaning seen through the eyes of the mystic. What is that meaning? It is the immediacy of God, His constant Presence, the continuing renewal of His Revelation.

THE MYSTIC'S VIEW OF RELIGION

Institutional Religion has, knowingly or not, created an abyss between God, the Infinite, and man the finite, temporal creature. "Mysticism does not deny or overlook the abyss; on the contrary it begins by realizing its existence, it proceeds to a quest for the secret that will close it in, the hidden path that will span it."

It is on this mystic idea that Luise Kaish has based her powerfully sculptured portrayal. The ark doors are not the conventional design of the Ten Commandments with the Hebrew characters on a flat surface, but a large sphere of burnished bronze, where the sacred characters are carved and etched in bold relief and a group of subtle symbols are similarly carved.

This sphere symbolizes the mystic's concept of God as En Soph, without end, the Absolute Infinity. He is the Creative Will, the First Cause and the Unending Light.

THE SEFIROTH

On the right hand panel which contains the first five commandments, there are seven linear grooves, symbols of the Sefiroth. Mystical speculation has given birth to the conception of the Sefiroth. The world of the Sefiroth is a whole realm of divinity which is present and active in all that exists. There are ten such Sefiroth. They are the ten spheres of divine manifestation in which God emerges from His hidden abode. They are the "mystical crowns of the Holy King," the garments of divinity, the beams of light. They mediate between man, finite and mortal, and God, the En Soph. The seven on the panel are symbols of the seven days of Creation.

These creative acts or powers are symbolized by rays of light (emanations) they are the vital, creative manifestations of God.

THE COMMANDMENTS

The Ten Commandments are always divided into two sections or panels, the first five on one panel represent the commandments between man and God, the second five, between man and man. The commandments themselves have been designed and executed in a highly imaginative style.

The first three commandments are spaced one from the other. Separating the third commandment from the fourth is a circle, sun-like in appearance with multi-grooved lines radiating from the deep center. These, as mentioned above, are the emanations, the rays of light, the creative acts that mediate through the Sefiroth between man and God.

The fourth and fifth commandments are etched close together. These are the commandments honoring one's father and mother, and observing the Sabbath. In the Torah these commandments are always placed together, to indicate a closeness of relationship and meaning (note Lev. 19, 3). Parents are partners with God in the creative process and the Sabbath, the end product of Creation, is God's Sabbath, to be observed by man as God had intended.

The second five commandments on the left hand panel, are deliberately brought together. The first letter, Lamed, of each of the last four commandments, is deeply grooved into the one above. It connotes that each command is closely linked to the other, the violation of one may lead to the violation of the other. Our sages have called attention to the tragic progression of human sinfulness. The sin of covetousness may lead to false testimony, to theft and to murder (as the Rabbis noted in the story of King Ahab and the innocent Naboth and his vineyard.)

The boldness of design, the inscrutable power of the Hebrew lettering are impressive. Some words are deeply grooved and others seem to leap forward in bold relief. "Thou shalt not murder" the fifth command, and "Thou shalt not covet" the tenth, stand forth. Hence, there is a symmetry of design as well as a harmony of thought.

GOD, ISRAEL AND TORAH

Two other symbols must be noted: twelve small circular mounds bound together within a circle. These are the twelve tribes, the people of Israel. Then there is the letter "Yud," the first letter of the ineffable Name of God, deeply carved in a circular disc.

A great religious idea and artistic creativity have been blended together, the vigorous power of an artist which gives visual authenticity to the mystical thought, "God, Israel and Torah are One."

RABBI JACOB KRAFT

THE BIMAH COMMITTEE

ISAAC BUDOVITCH, Chairman

MR. & MRS. ISAAC BUDOVITCH
MR. & MRS. LOUIS J. FINGER
MR. ISADOR GOLDEN
MR. & MRS. RICHARD KANE
MR. & MRS. IRVING MORRIS
MR. & MRS. GEORGE PRESTON
MR. & MRS. BERNARD RAPHAELSON
MR. & MRS. SOL ZALLEA

Appendix B   Rabbi Jacob Kraft. *The Beth Shalom Ark Doors*, brochure. Wilmington, Delaware: Temple Beth Shalom, 1968. Luise Kaish archives, New York. (see plates 21, 22)

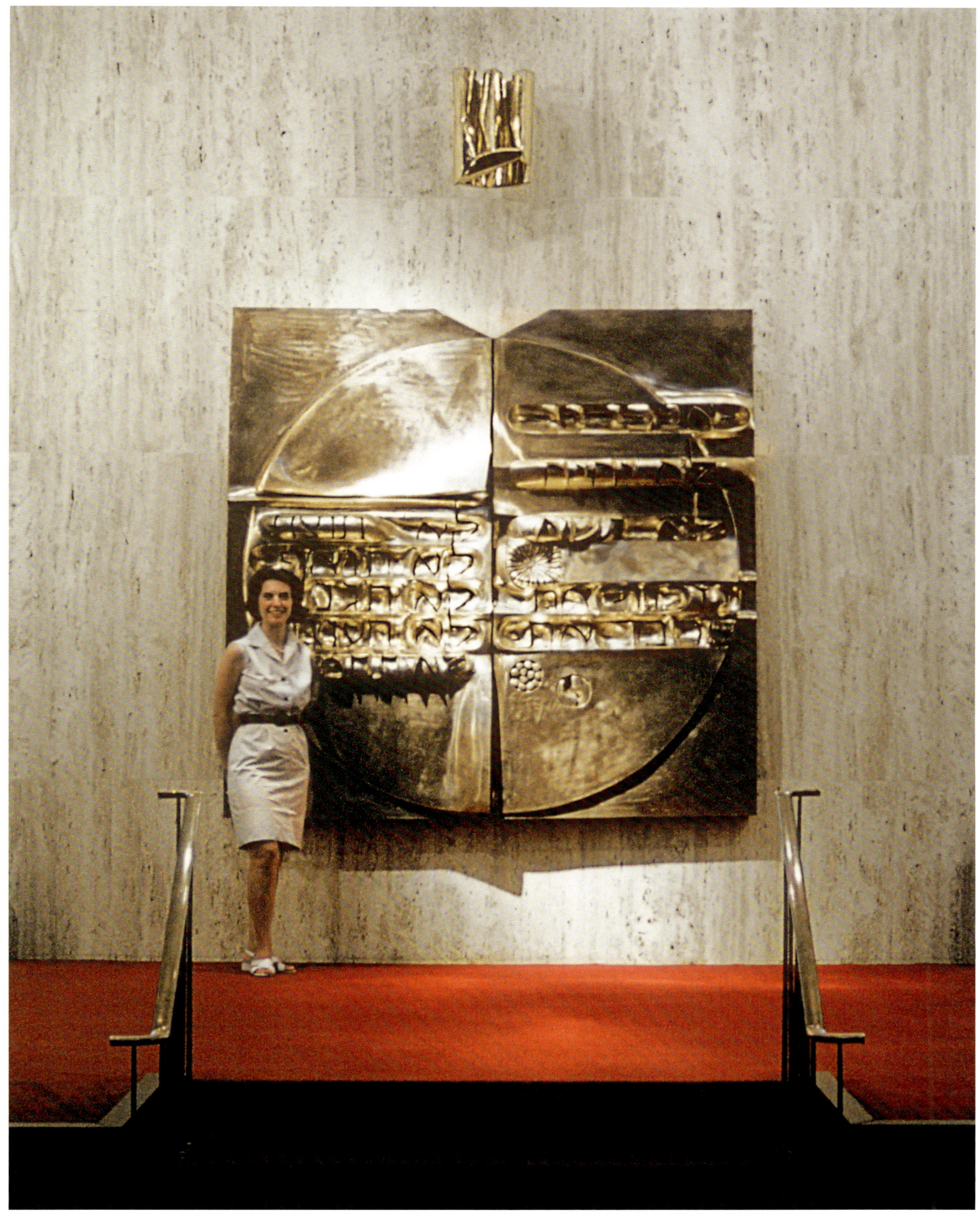

Fig. 66 Luise Kaish with the Beth Shalom Ark Doors, 1968

Appendix C   Luise Kaish. *The Wall of Martyrs*, 1972–74, eight panels, bronze, 4 ¼ × 17 ft. (1.3 × 5.2 m) overall.
Beth El Synagogue Center, New Rochelle, New York (see Plate 27)

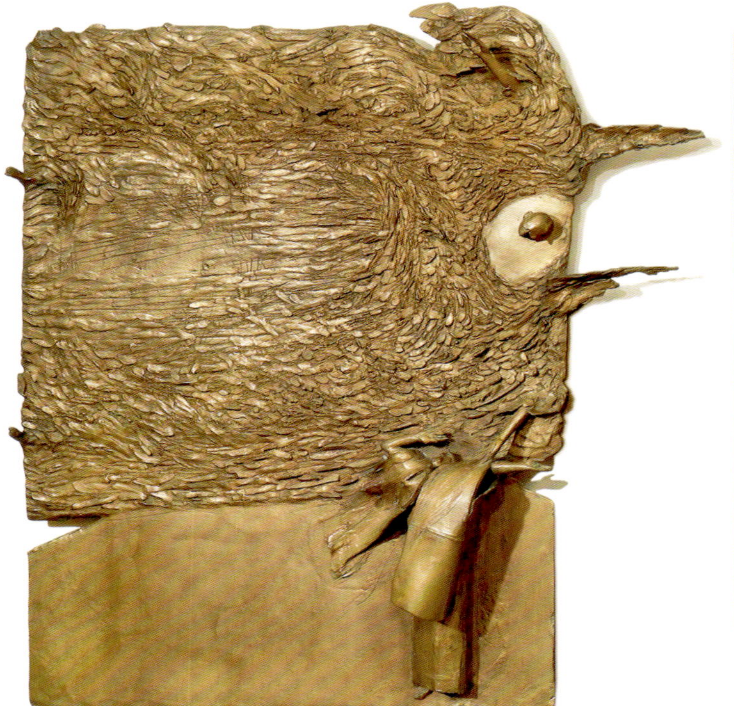

1 The Eternal Martyr

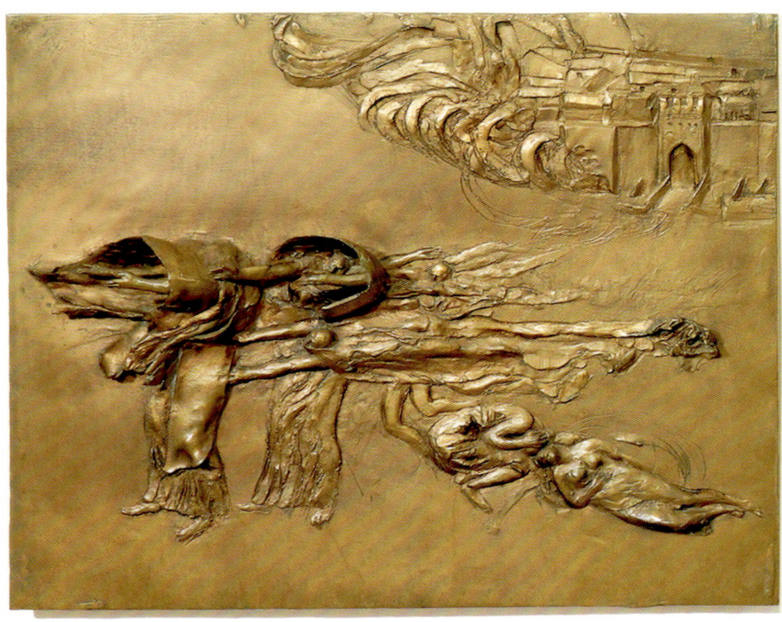

2 The Flight from Jerusalem

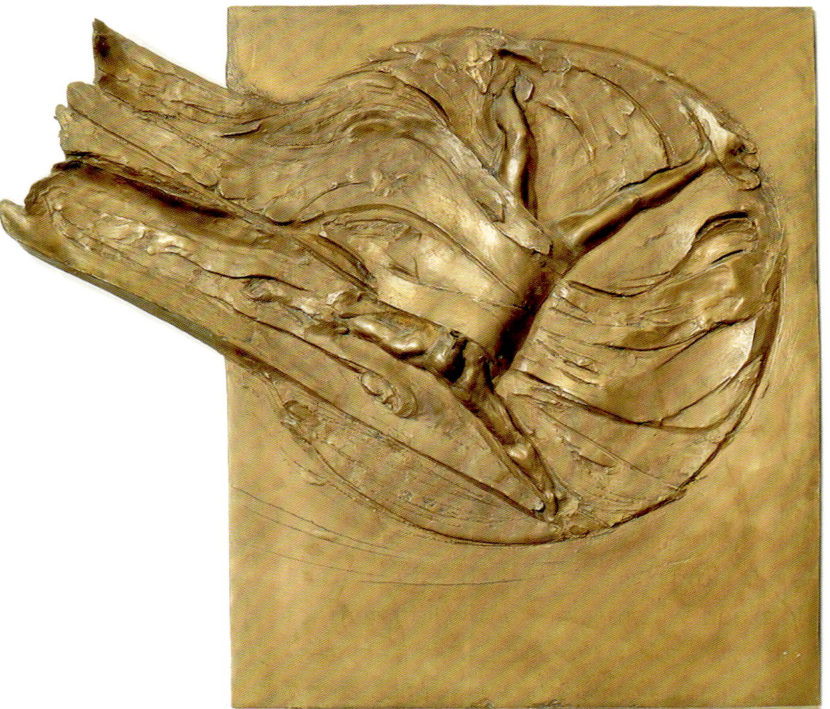

3 The Ten Martyrs

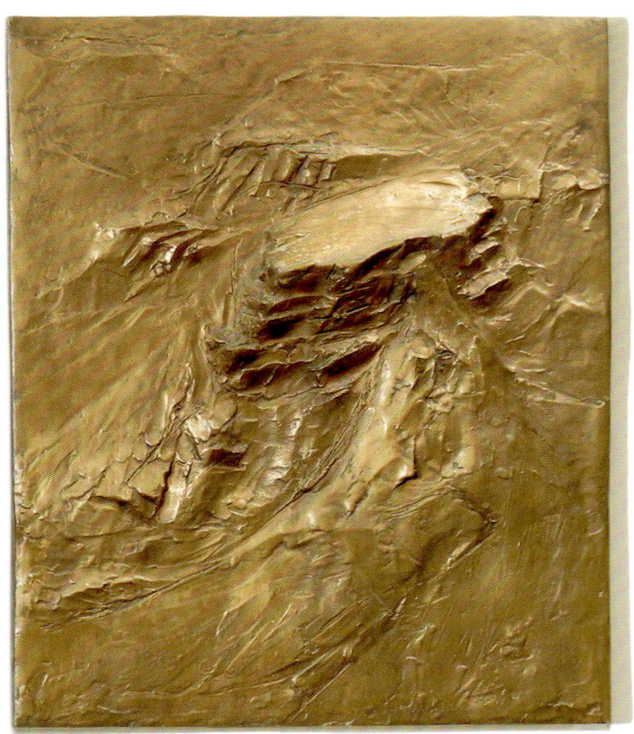

4 Masada

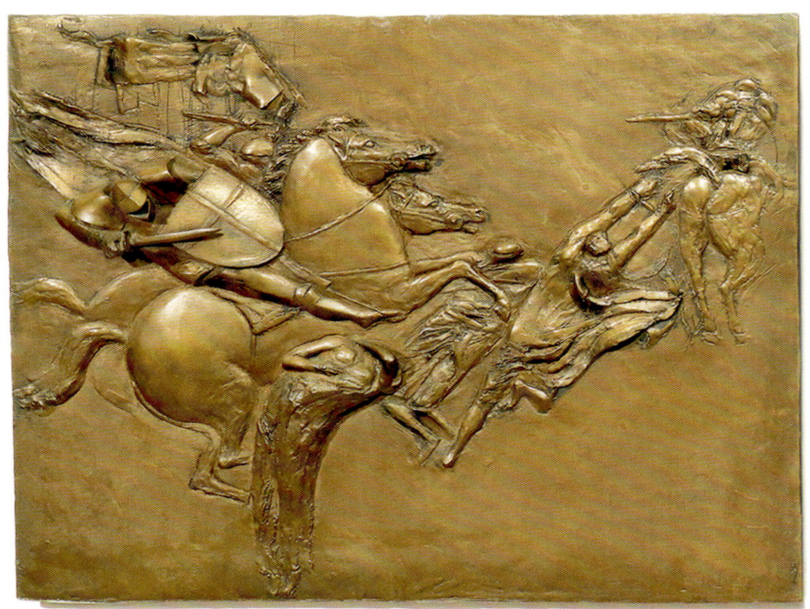

5 The Crusades

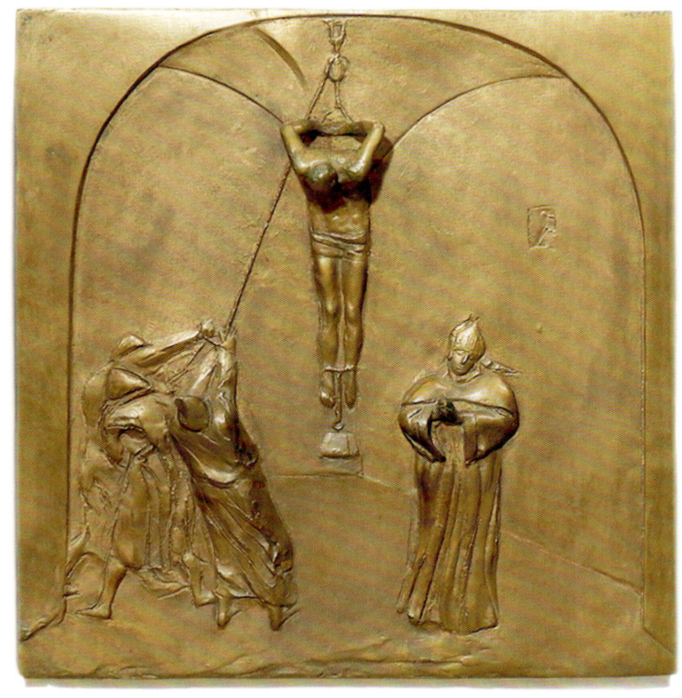

6 The Inquisition

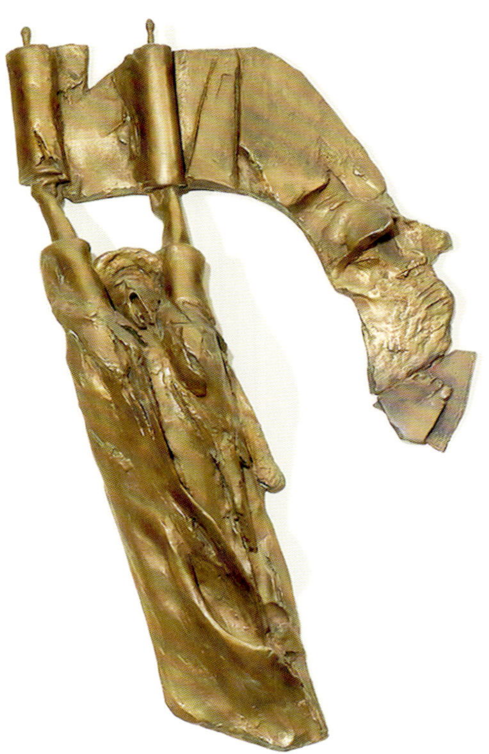

7 The Chmielnitzki

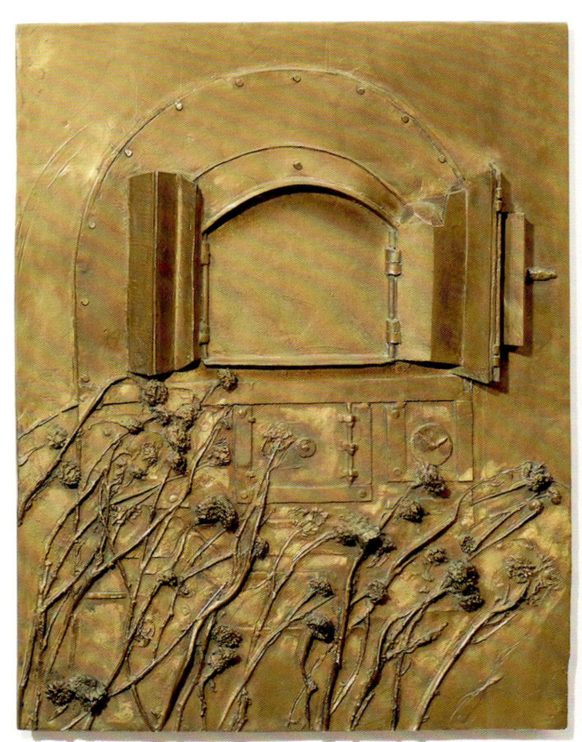

8 The Holocaust

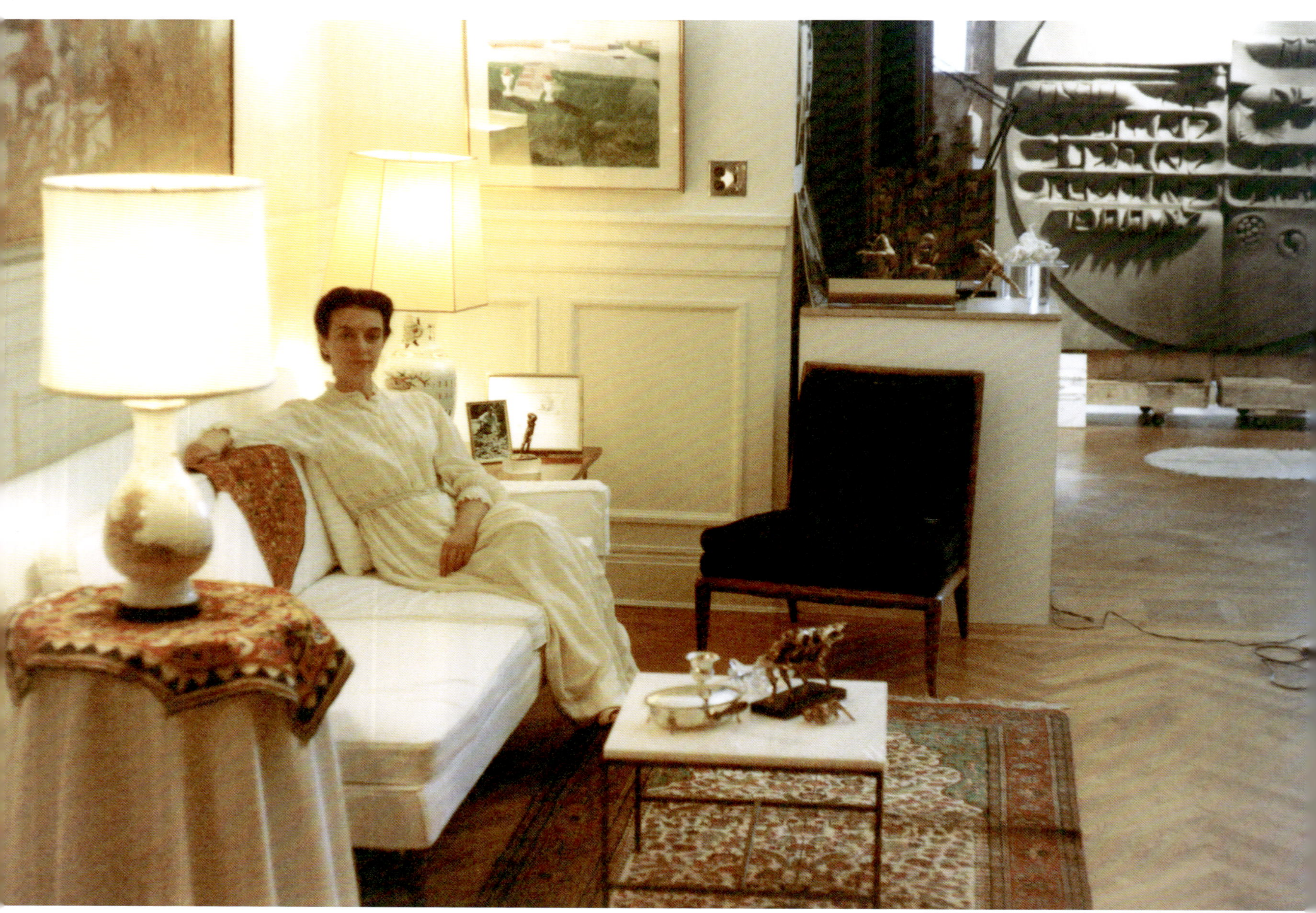

Luise Kaish at ease after a day in the studio, circa 1967

CHRONOLOGY

Jillian Russo

1925

Born in Atlanta, Georgia, on September 8, the middle child of Harry and Elsa Meyers, older sister Ruth (b. 1923), younger brother David (b. 1930) (Fig. 67).

1930–1941

The Meyers family moves to Flushing, Queens. Luise attends grade school at P.S. 32, studies at the Manhattan School of Music, and enrolls in Sunday school at the Flushing Free Synagogue, where broad-minded Rabbi Max Meyer takes his students to visit churches of other denominations. His accepting approach lays the groundwork for her interfaith appreciation and her interest in ecclesiastical art and architecture. At age sixteen she graduates from Bayside High School, where she is art editor of the yearbook and captain of the cheerleaders.

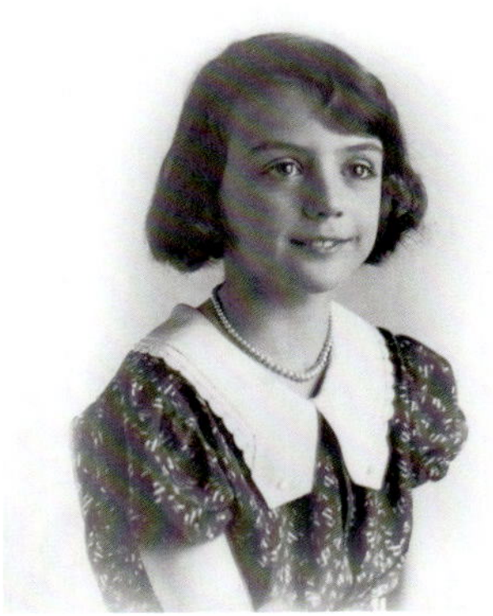

Fig. 67   Luise Meyers, age eight years, 1933

1941–1946

Enrolls in the art education program with a minor in voice at Syracuse University and earns her BFA in 1946. In the winter of 1944, meets painter Morton Kaish, who is a student in the fine arts program, and they become engaged three years later.

1946–1947

Wins a Syracuse University postgraduate fellowship and studies abroad in Mexico. Attends Escuela Nacional de Pintura y Escultura, studying painting with Jesús Guerrero Galván and Alfredo Zalce, and art history with Diego Rivera. Explores lithography at the Taller de Gráfica Popular and intaglio at the Escuela de las Artes del Libro, and creates her first sculptures. Travels throughout Mexico and Guatemala (Fig. 68).

1947

Accepted into the MFA program at Syracuse University, where she studies with renowned Croatian sculptor Ivan Meštrović and is appointed instructor of etching and lithography. Awarded the Everson Museum First Prize in Graphics.

1948

Luise and Morton marry in August at Essex House in New York City (Fig. 69).

1951

Receives MFA from Syracuse. Creates first major commission: the emblematic *Saltine Warrior* statue for the university campus (see Pl. 16). Her sculpture *Mother and Child* is selected for inclusion in *American Sculpture 1951* at the Metropolitan Museum of Art (see Pl. 2). Other artists selected for this juried exhibition include Alexander Calder, José de Creeft, Chaim Gross, Robert Laurent, Paul Manship, and William Zorach (Fig. 70).

Moves to Rochester, New York. Attends services at Temple B'rith Kodesh, where she meets Rabbi Philip Bernstein, who plays a major role in her artistic and spiritual development. Receives the 1951 Jurors Show Award, jointly with Morton, from the Rochester Memorial Art Gallery. Also wins the H. Sullivan Award from the Rochester Memorial Art Gallery, as well as a Louis Comfort Tiffany Foundation Grant. The grant supports the couple's first trip to Europe, including several months in Florence and travel by car

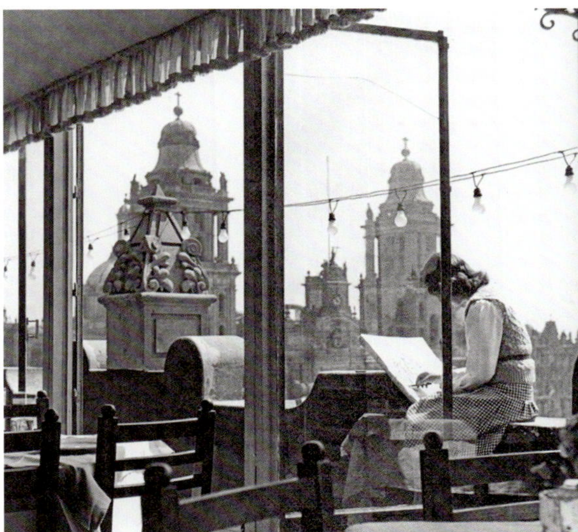

Fig. 68   Luise in Mexico, circa 1946–47

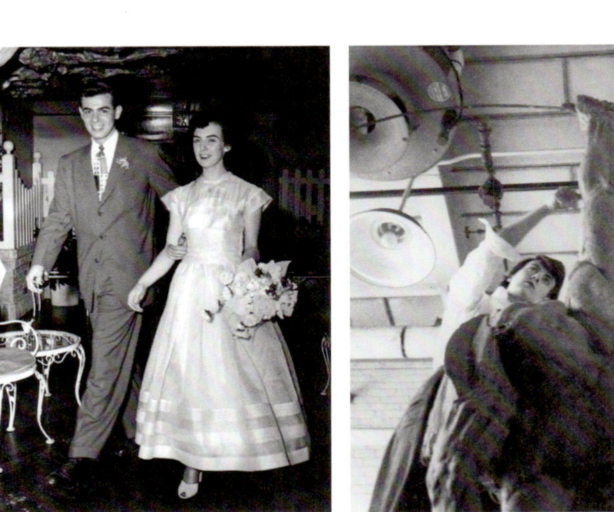

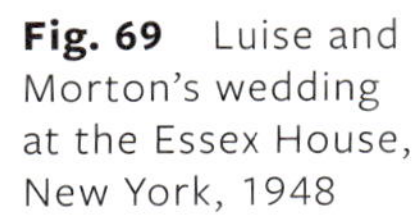

Fig. 69   Luise and Morton's wedding at the Essex House, New York, 1948

Fig. 70   Luise at work on the *Saltine Warrior*, Syracuse University, Syracuse, New York, 1951

through northern Italy, Belgium, Switzerland, southern France, and Spain (Fig. 71).

1952
Begins working at the Sculpture Center in Queens, New York, alongside a group of four other women, including Katherine Nash, Dorothy Robbins, Barbara Lekberg, and Lin Emery, who are all experimenting with welding.

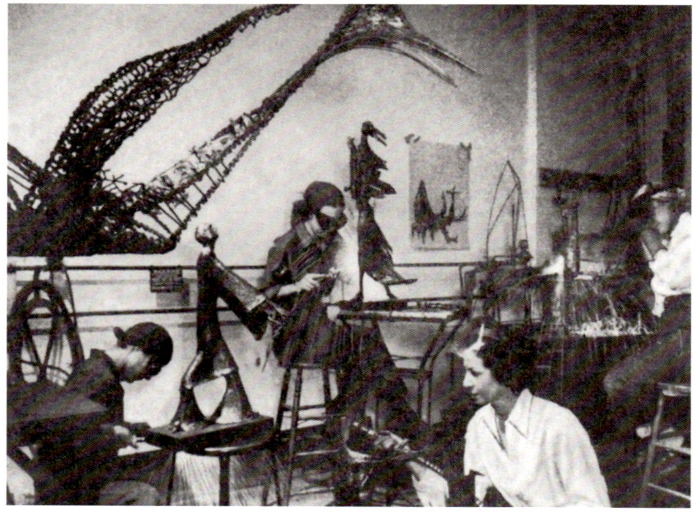

Fig. 72 Luise welding with colleagues at the Sculpture Center, New York, 1953

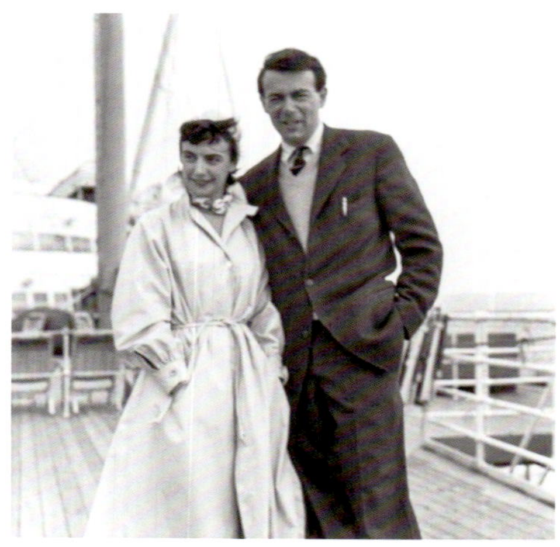

Fig. 71 Luise and Morton's first trip to Europe on the SS *NIEUW Amsterdam*, 1951

1955
Exhibits in a two-person show with sculptor William Muir at the Sculpture Center. Among the works on view are *Desert Specter* and *And Behold A Ladder*, which reflect the influence of the Western desert landscape, as well as a series of small sculptures of children at play.

Fig. 73 Luise on her national park tour, 1954

1956–1957
Second trip to Europe with Morton. The couple rents an apartment near the Trevi Fountain in Rome. Attends services at the Great Synagogue of Rome, which inspires a series of religious figures and prophets. Rabbi Philip Bernstein admires these works during a visit to her Rome studio and suggests a collaboration with architect Pietro Belluschi on the new Temple B'rith Kodesh in Rochester, New York. Travels to Egypt, Greece, Dachau, and Normandy.

1953
Exhibits in *Women Welders* at the Sculpture Center, alongside Ilse Erythropel, Priscilla Pattison, Katherine Nash, Dorothy Robbins, Barbara Lekberg, Lin Emery, and Ruth Vodicka (Fig. 72).

1954
Travels for four months throughout the Western United States, visiting the national parks with Morton (Fig. 73). The couple is featured in the joint exhibition *Paintings and Sculpture by Mort and Luise Kaish* at the Rochester Memorial Art Gallery.

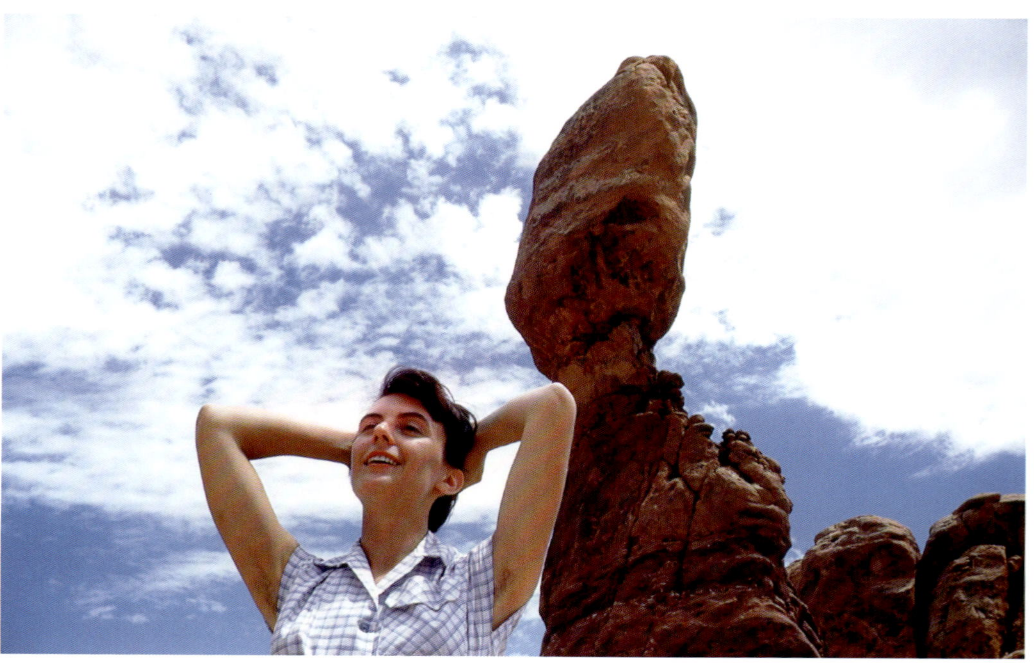

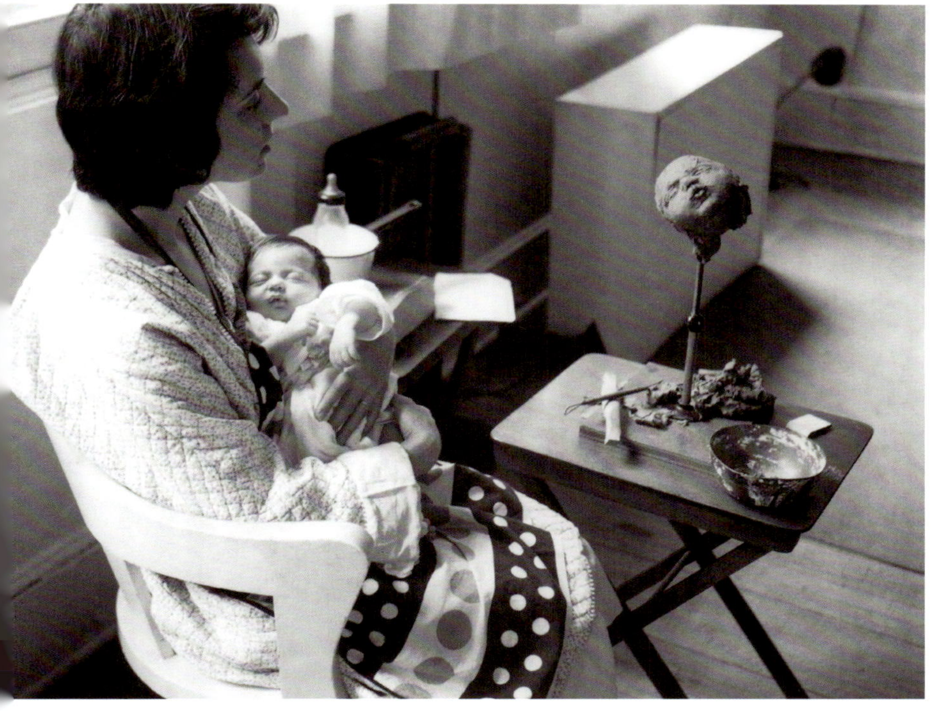

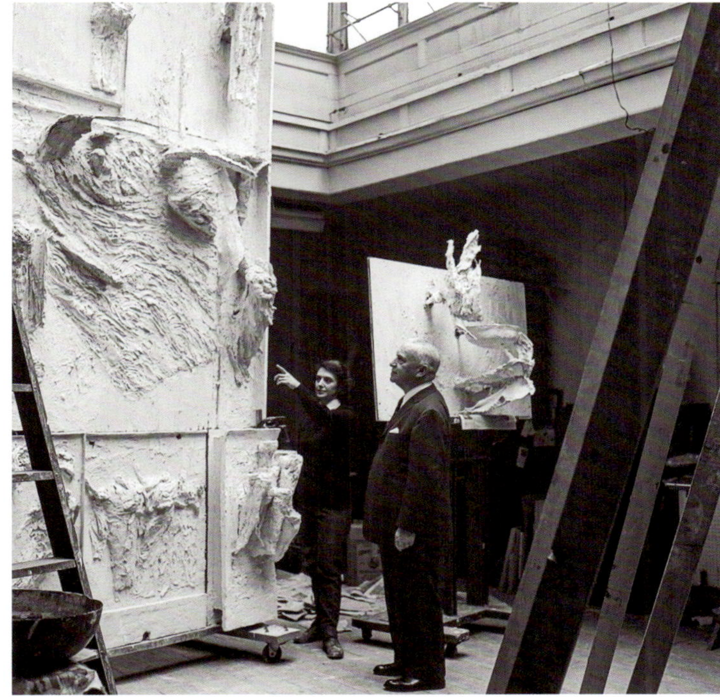

Fig. 74 Luise with her daughter Melissa, 1961

Fig. 75 Rabbi Bernstein visits Luise's MacDougal Street studio, circa 1962

1958

Returns to New York and moves into a skylit loft studio on MacDougal Street in Greenwich Village. The studio is located above the Rienzi coffee shop, where Allen Ginsberg reads poetry, and a few blocks away from the Cedar Tavern, Hans Hofmann's art school, and Larry Rivers's studio. Exhibits in first solo show at the Sculpture Center and receives critical acclaim from Robert Dash and Irving Sandler.

1959

Receives a John Simon Guggenheim Memorial Foundation Fellowship. Exhibits in *Contemporary American Painting and Sculpture* at the Krannert Art Museum, University of Illinois at Champaign, and alongside Ruth Asawa, John Chamberlain, Dorothy Dehner, Jacques Lipchitz, George Rickey, and David Smith in MoMA's multivenue exhibition *Recent Sculpture U.S.A.*, which is curated by James Thrall Soby. The exhibition travels to the Denver Art Museum, Los Angeles County Museum of Art, City Art Museum of Saint Louis, and the Museum of Fine Arts, Boston.

1960–1961

Awarded the sculptural commission for Temple B'rith Kodesh and selects the theme of *The Ark of Revelation* (see Pls. 17, 18). Daughter Melissa is born on May 4, 1961 (Fig. 74).

1964

The Ark of Revelation is installed and dedicated in March. The *Rochester Times-Union* describes it as "one of the great examples of ecclesiastical art in America."[1] Travels to Portugal in the summer. Studies Manueline architecture, visits the local bronze-casting facilities, and creates landscape sketches (Fig. 75).

1962–1966

Participates in a series of prestigious group exhibitions, including the *Whitney Museum of American Art Annual Exhibition 1962*, alongside Louise Nevelson, Isamu Noguchi, and Marisol; the *Whitney Museum of American Art 1964 Annual Exhibition of Contemporary American Sculpture*, alongside Bruce Conner, Joseph Cornell, Claire Falkenstein, David Hare, and Edward Kienholz; and the historical exhibition *Women Artists of America, 1707–1964*, at the Newark Museum.

1966

Commissioned by architect Richard Chalfant to design the altar for Temple Beth Shalom in Wilmington, Delaware (see Pls. 21, 22).

1965–1967

Creates the sculpture *Christ in Glory* and a tabernacle for the altar of the Holy Trinity Mission Seminary Church in Silver Spring, Maryland, which is commissioned by architect James T. Canizaro (Fig. 76; see Pls. 19, 20).

1967

Participates in the *Protest and Hope* exhibition at the New School Art Center along with Elaine de Kooning, Red Grooms, and George Segal. The exhibition garners positive reviews from critics Emily Genauer and Harold Rosenberg.

1968

Completes a non-figurative commission for Temple Beth Shalom. *Luise Kaish, Recent Sculpture*, curated by Phillip Bruno, opens at Staempfli Gallery, New York (Fig. 77). During the summer, spends two months drawing and painting in East Hampton, where she meets Lee Krasner, Conrad Marca-Relli, and art critic Clement Greenberg.

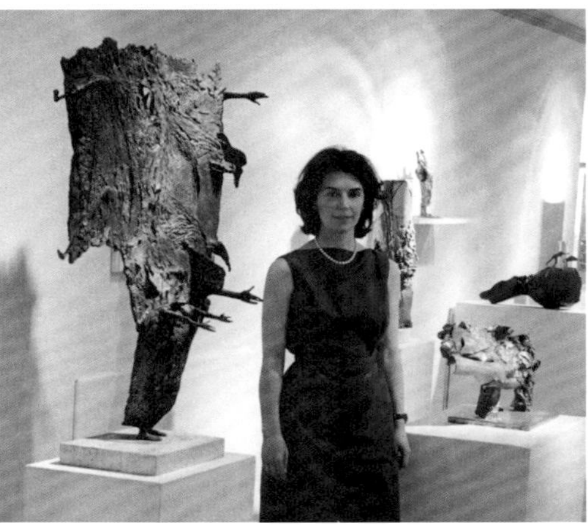

Fig. 77 Opening at Staempfli Gallery, New York, 1968

1970

Awarded the Prix de Rome for Sculpture at the American Academy in Rome as well as the Augustus Saint-Gaudens Fellowship. The most influential studio visits are from Philip Guston, Harold Clurman, and Buckminster Fuller. Begins work on the *Voyages* and *Spheres* sculpture series. Also meets artists Charles Perry, Jack Zajac, Varujan Boghosian, Dimitri Hadzi, and Susan Smyly (Fig. 78).

1972

Exhibits the *Voyages* and *Spheres* series in *Luise Kaish: Recent Sculpture* at the American Academy in Rome and *K x 2: Luise Kaish Sculture, Morton Kaish Pitture / K x 2: Paintings by Morton Kaish, Sculpture by Luise Kaish* at the American Embassy in Rome. Begins work on a commission for *The Wall of Martyrs*, a large-scale, eight-panel bronze sculpture commemorating Jewish martyrdom throughout history, for the Beth El Synagogue Center in New Rochelle (see Pl. 27; Appendix C). Travels to Turkey, Istanbul, Israel, Tunisia, and Sicily. Exhibits in *American Women: Twentieth Century* at the Lakeview Center for the Arts and Sciences, Peoria, Illinois, alongside Ruth Asawa, Lynda Benglis, Lee Bontecou, Louise Bourgeois, Judy Chicago, Helen Frankenthaler, Grace Hartigan, and Marisol.

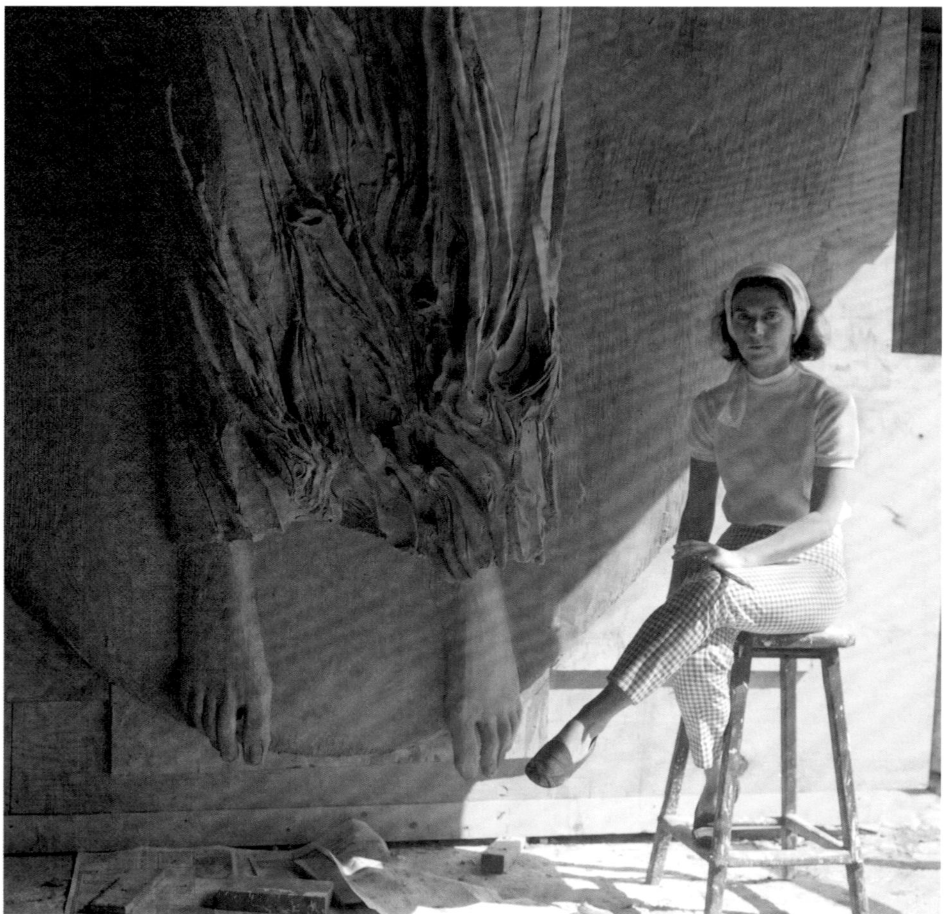

Fig. 76 Taking a break at Modern Art Foundry during preparation for the casting of *Christ in Glory*, circa 1965–67

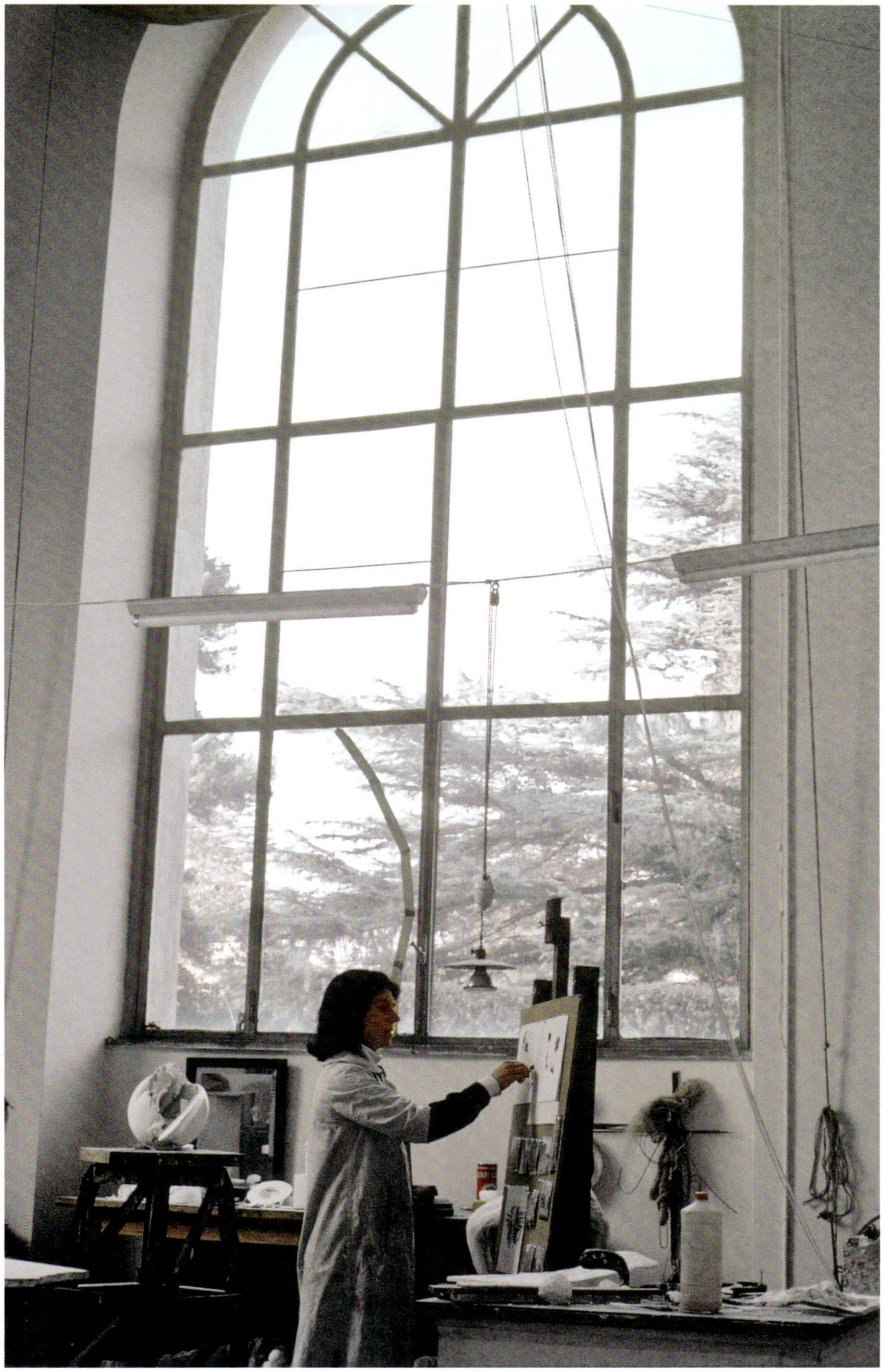

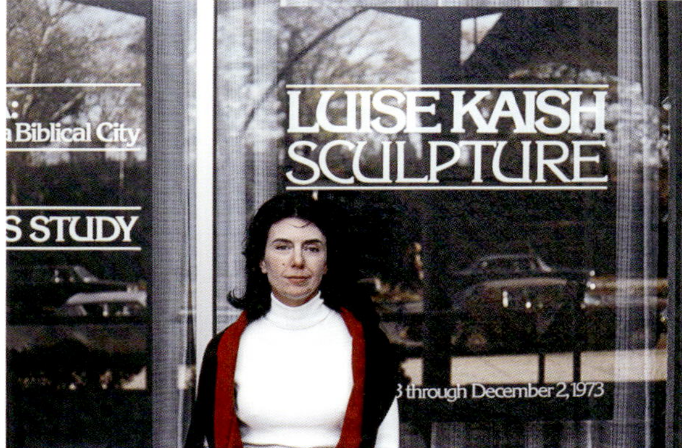

Fig. 79 Luise at her opening of her retrospective at the Jewish Museum, New York, 1973

1973

Luise Kaish Sculpture, a retrospective exhibition of more than eighty works, opens at the Jewish Museum (Fig. 79). Invited to be a panelist at the American Jewish Congress in Jerusalem. She is the only speaker representing the visual arts alongside other cultural luminaries including American-Israeli poet Shirley Kaufman, conductor and composer Hugo Weisgall, rabbi and author Chaim Potok, and novelist Herbert Gold.

Appointed to the board of trustees of the American Academy in Rome. Serves in the position until 1981 and is one of only a few women on the board. Other members of the academy's board of trustees (or the fine arts advisory panel for sculpture) during this time include Edward Larrabee Barnes, Walker Cain, Adele Chatfield-Taylor, Philip Guston, Susan Morse Hilles, Jasper Johns, J. Russell Lynes Jr., Philip Johnson, Claes Oldenburg, George Segal, James Johnson Sweeney, and Jack Tworkov.

1973–1974

Completes commissions *Eternal Light* for Hebrew Union College, Jerusalem (see Pl. 28); *Menorah and Eternal Light* for Temple B'nai Abraham, New Jersey (see Pls. 23–26); and *Four Editions: Twelve Tribes, Moses, Menorah, Shabbat*, for the Jewish Museum, New York.

Fig. 78 Luise in her studio at the American Academy in Rome, 1972

1974

Receives a joint residency with Morton at Dartmouth College. In addition to spending time in the studio, works with students and prepares the exhibition *Luise Kaish, Morton Kaish: Artists-in-Residence*.

1974–1975

Commissioned by art patron and philanthropist Vera List to create a memorial to the Holocaust for the Jewish Museum, which will be installed in its Fifth Avenue entrance from 1975 to 1993 (Fig. 80; see Pl. 29).

1975

Awarded a joint summer residency with Morton at the MacDowell Colony in Peterborough, New Hampshire. Meets printmakers Clare Romano and John Ross and poets Rachal Hadas and Peter Viereck. Begins experimenting with collage using charred canvas, creating the first works in her *Burntworks* series.

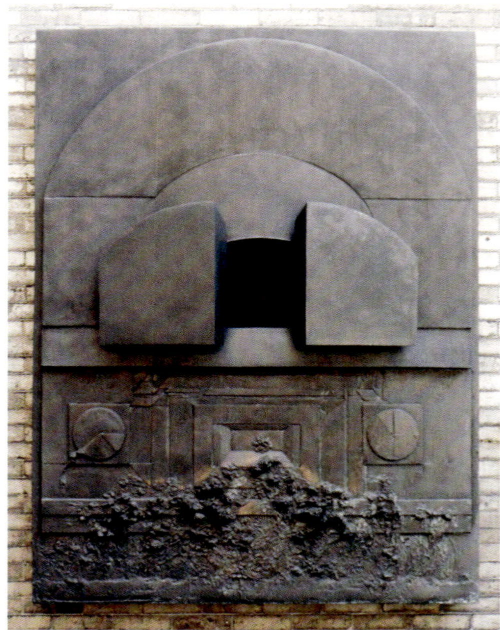

Fig. 80 Luise Kaish, *Holocaust Memorial*, 1975, Jewish Museum, New York (see Plate 29)

1975–1976

Creates *La Lumière*, a monumental mobile orb made of highly reflective silicon bronze, commissioned by Michel and Mary Ann Fribourg for Continental Grain Company's New York corporate offices (see Pl. 57).

1979

With the support of grants from the Ford Foundation and Batelle Seminars and Study Programs, Luise and Morton are awarded visiting artist positions at the University of Washington, Seattle. In the summer they travel to Alaska, where a flight over the glaciers inspires the next series of collages.

1980–1986

Appointed professor and chair of the Division of Painting and Sculpture at Columbia University. Establishes a gallery to exhibit student work, modernizes the studios, and invites distinguished visiting artists Lee Krasner, Alice Neel, Charles and Ray Eames, Sean Scully, and Laurie Anderson. A popular professor, Luise facilitates dialogue between sculptors and painters, encouraging students to work in both mediums.

1981

Luise Kaish: Recent Collages opens at Staempfli Gallery, New York. The exhibition features the new *Burntworks* series, some of which incorporate vivid colors. The Metropolitan Museum of Art acquires one of the works, *H.H.H* (see Pl. 71), for its permanent collection.

1984

A second collage solo exhibition, *Luise Kaish: New Work*, opens at Staempfli Gallery. It introduces earth-toned, mixed-media paintings inspired by the 1979 Alaska trip. Travels to Thailand and visits the major architectural monuments in Bangkok and Ayutthaya.

1985

Travels to Kyoto and Tokyo, where she visits with local artists and architects, and views major works of Japanese art. Luise and Morton are invited to be artists-in-residence at the University of Haifa, Israel, with the support of a grant from the U.S. Information Service of the United States Embassy. They travel to kibbutzim and to Arab villages, spend a week in Miskenot Sha'ananim, and exhibit their work at the university gallery in Haifa and in Jerusalem at the United States Information Office.

1987–89

Travels to Paris to formulate an undergraduate exchange program for painting and sculpture students between Columbia University and the École des Beaux-Arts. Visits London in May 1987 and December 1988, where she studies the Turner collection at Tate Britain.

1988

Exhibits new mixed-media paintings, which combine dynamic, bright colors and expressive brushwork with collage elements and geometric forms, in *Luise Kaish: New Paintings* at Staempfli Gallery.

1989

Honored with the George Arents Pioneer Medal, Syracuse University's highest alumni honor. Becomes one of the first women to be elected to the Century Association in New York.

1990

The solo exhibition *Luise Kaish* opens at the University of Arkansas Fine Arts Center Gallery in Fayetteville, Arkansas.

1993

Named professor emerita in the Faculty of Art at Columbia University, and trustee emerita at the American Academy in Rome.

1993–1998

Focuses primarily on landscape painting. She is drawn to a remote area of Central Park with a grove of cherry blossom trees, which she visits repeatedly and nicknames her "allée." Other locations that became inspirations for their natural beauty include Riverside Park and the Hudson River as seen from her studio in New York, as well as Sailfish Point in Palm Beach,

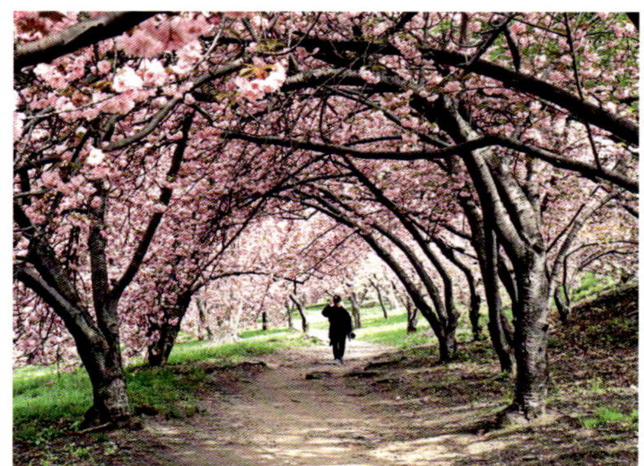

Fig. 81 Luise's "allée," Central Park, New York

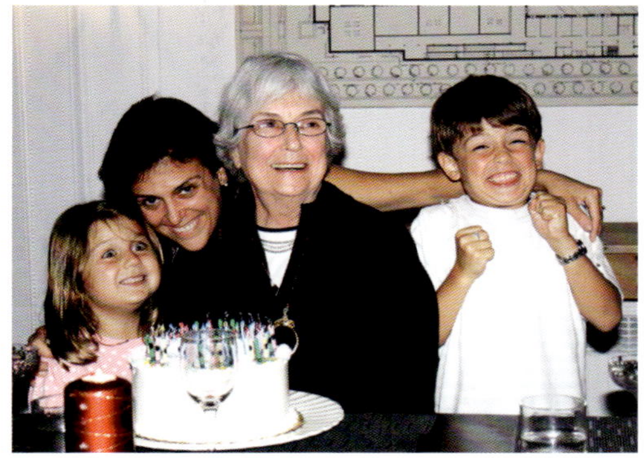

Fig. 82 Luise with her daughter and grandchildren

Florida, and Sullivan's Island, North Carolina, where she and Morton spent time during the winter months (Fig. 81).

1997–2009
Participates in National Academy of Design annual exhibitions.

1998
The solo exhibition *The Colors of Seasons*, featuring her the landscape series, opens at the Century Association. In a brief opening statement to the exhibition, Luise emphasizes the emotive properties of color: "The poetics of color sound remembrance, shape memory, feeling, sequence events, the absurd. Color reveals a pathway to our hidden worlds beyond reserve."[2]

That same year, her work is also included in *Contemporary Artists Welcome the New Year— The Jewish Museum Graphic Commission*.

1998–2001
First grandchild, Robert Dorfman, is born on February 28, 1998. Three years later, her second grandchild, Kathryn Dorfman, is born on June 14, 2001 (Fig. 82).

2004–2009
Luise and Morton spend summers in East Hampton, where she creates a series of seascapes depicting the dynamic movement of waves and the shoreline at Main and Georgica Beaches.

2009–2010
Exhibits in *From Maquette to Monument* at the Century Association, which chronicles her creation of *The Ark of Revelation* through sixteen photographs she took at her studio, the bronze foundry, and Temple B'rith Kodesh in Rochester. In 2010, fifteen of the photographs are shown in a solo exhibition at B'rith Kodesh and subsequently become a permanent installation. The exhibition coincides with the Philip Bernstein commemorative Shabbat service, at which Luise delivers a lecture on the genesis and development of the *Ark*.

2009–2012
Creates a series of four axonometric drawings, which are conceived as conceptual studies for architectural-sized relief sculptures. Constructed of gold paper, gold paint, and ink, these gem-like pieces are defined by bold, geometric lines, foregrounding her masterful drawing skills. The lines are scored in places so that the paper lifts, giving the works a collage-like three-dimensionality.

2012
Exhibits with Morton for the last time in the *Century Masters, Luise and Morton Kaish, K x 2: II* at the Century Association (Fig. 83).

2013
Dies March 7, 2013, at age eighty-seven. She requests her ashes be launched into deep space.

Endnotes

1. Virginia J. Smith, "A Masterpiece of Art: B'rith Kodesh Ark Great Sculpture in Bronze." *Rochester Times-Union*, March 26, 1964, 12A.
2. Luise Kaish, Exhibition Statement for *The Colors of Seasons*, April 1998.

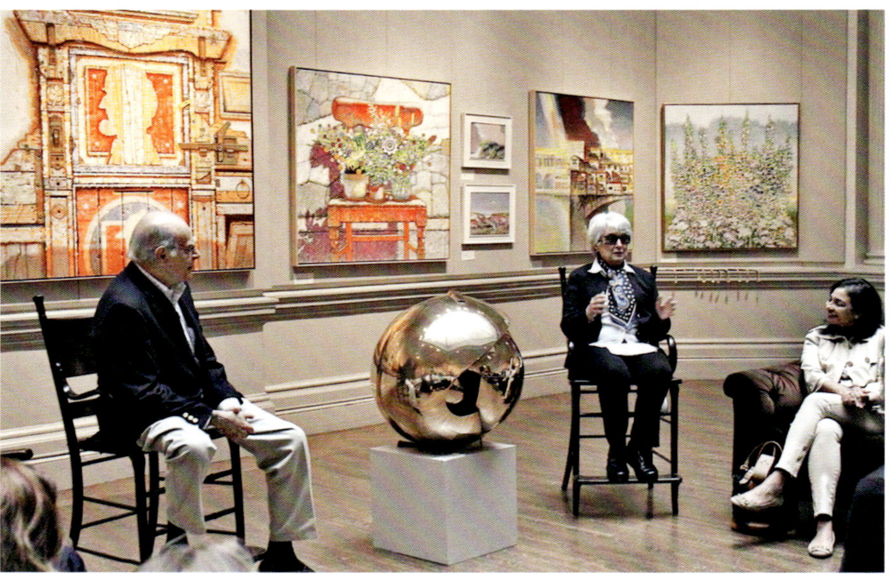

Fig. 83 Luise and Morton at the *Century Masters* exhibition, Century Association, New York, 2012

EXHIBITION HISTORY

Jillian Russo and Andrea Lynn Kutsenkow

1940s

Twenty-Second Annual Exhibition of the Associated Artists of Syracuse, circa late 1940s. Syracuse Museum of Fine Arts, Syracuse University, New York.

1950s
Solo Exhibitions
Sculpture by Luise Kaish, 1954. Memorial Art Gallery, University of Rochester, New York.

Paintings and Sculpture by Mort and Luise Kaish, Fall 1954. Memorial Art Gallery, University of Rochester, New York.

Luise Kaish, March 24–April 11, 1958. Sculpture Center, New York. Exh. cat. New York: Sculpture Center, 1958.

Group Exhibitions
Rochester Finger Lakes Exhibition, circa May 4–26, 1951. Memorial Art Gallery, University of Rochester, New York.

American Sculpture 1951: A National Competitive Exhibition, December 7, 1951–February 24, 1952. Metropolitan Museum of Art, New York. Exh. cat. by Robert Beverly Hale. New York: Metropolitan Museum of Art, 1951.

Exhibit of Sculpture, February 13–29, 1952. Grover Cronin Compass Room, Sculpture Center, New York. Exh. cat. by Dorothea Denslow. New York: Sculpture Center, 1952.

Women Welders, November 1–20, 1953. Sculpture Center, New York. Exh. cat. by Sahl Swarz. New York: Sculpture Center, 1953.

Annual Exhibition of Painting and Sculpture, 1953. Pennsylvania Academy of the Fine Arts, Philadelphia, Pennsylvania. Exh. cat. ed. Peter Hastings Falk. *The Annual Exhibition Record of the Pennsylvania Academy of the Fine Arts: Volume III, 1914–1968*. Madison: Sound View Press, 1989.

Steel, Iron and Men, 1954. Birmingham Museum, Alabama.

Sculpture '54: A Selection of Contemporary Works in Bronze, Wood, Stone, Terra Cotta, Steel, Plastic and Mosaic, December 13, 1954–January 22, 1955. Sculpture Center, New York.

The New Decade: Thirty-Five American Painters and Sculptors, 1955. Whitney Museum of American Art, New York.

Carvings Muir, Weldings Kaish, February 28–March 18, 1955. Sculpture Center, New York. Exh. cat. by Sahl Swarz. New York: Sculpture Center, 1955.

Seventh Annual Emily Lowe Award Competition Winners, December 1955. Lowe Award Room, Ward Eggleston Galleries, New York.

Spring '56, April 15–May 13, 1956. Sculpture Center, New York. Exh. cat. by Dorothea Denslow and Sahl Swarz. New York: Sculpture Center, 1956.

Exhibition of Jewish Art: Bronzes by Luise Kaish; Etchings, Lithographs by Morton Kaish, January 9–February 2, 1958. Memorial Art Gallery, University of Rochester, New York.

Audubon Artists Sixteenth Annual Exhibition: Oils, Watercolors, Pastels, Casein Paintings, Graphics, Sculpture, January 16–February 2, 1958. National Academy Galleries, New York. Exh. cat. New York: National Academy of Design, 1958.

I. Biennale Christlicher Kunst der Gegenwart, 1958. America House, Munich, Germany. Traveled to the German–American Institute, Mannheim, Germany; America House, Berlin, Germany; and Oratorien des Domes, Salzburg, Austria.

Contemporary Sculpture, 1958. Staten Island Museum, New York.

Audubon Artists Seventeenth Annual Exhibition, January 14–February 1, 1959. National Academy Galleries, New York.

Contemporary American Painting and Sculpture, 1959. Krannert Art Museum, University of Illinois, Champaign-Urbana, Illinois. Exh. cat. Champaign: Krannert Art Museum, 1959.

Recent Sculpture U.S.A., May 13–August 16, 1959. Museum of Modern Art, New York. Exhibition traveled to Denver Art Museum, Colorado; Los Angeles County Museum, California; City Art Museum of St. Louis, Missouri; Museum of Fine Arts, Boston, Massachusetts. Exh. cat. by Walter Bareiss and James Thrall Soby. New York: Museum of Modern Art, 1959.

Summer Exhibit of Permanent Collection, Summer 1959. Memorial Art Gallery, University of Rochester, New York.

Sculpture by Thirty-One Artists, 1959. Philadelphia Art Alliance, Pennsylvania.

Autumn of Our Thirty-First Year, October 25–November 11, 1959. Sculpture Center, New York. Exh. cat. New York: Sculpture Center, 1959.

1960s
Solo Exhibitions
Luise Kaish, Recent Sculpture, April 23–May 11, 1968. Staempfli Gallery, New York.

Sculpture and Drawings by Luise Kaish: Studies and Maquettes for Commissioned Sculpture and Independent Works on Old Testament Themes, January 9–February 23, 1969. Saint Paul Art Center, Minnesota.

Group Exhibitions
The Sculptors Guild Annual Exhibition, 1960. Lever House, New York.

National Exhibition of Painting, Graphics, and Sculpture, 1960. National Council of Churches, Civic Auditorium, San Francisco, California.

Audubon Artists Eighteenth Annual Exhibition: Oil, Sculpture, Watercolor, Casein, Graphic, January 21–February 7, 1960. National Academy Galleries, New York. Exh. cat. New York: National Academy of Design, 1960.

Exhibition of Works by Contemporary American Artists, March 10–March 26, 1961. Academy Art Gallery, National Academy of Arts and Letters, New York.

Contemporary American Painting and Sculpture, February 26–April 2, 1961. Krannert Art Museum, University of Illinois, Champaign-Urbana, Illinois. Exh. cat. Champaign: Krannert Art Museum, 1961.

Autumn of Our Thirty-Third Year, September 17–October 12, 1961. Sculpture Center, New York. Exh. cat. New York: Sculpture Center, 1961.

Women Artists in America Today, April 10–30, 1962. Dwight Art Memorial, Mount Holyoke College, South Hadley, Massachusetts.

Gallery Group Summer '62: Paintings, Sculpture, Drawings, Gravure, Summer 1962. Schuman Gallery, Rochester, New York.

Whitney Museum of American Art Annual Exhibition 1962: Contemporary Sculpture and Drawings, December 12, 1962–February 3, 1963. Whitney Museum of American Art, New York. Exh. cat. New York: Whitney Museum of American Art, 1962.

Annual Exhibition of Painting and Sculpture, 1962. Pennsylvania Academy of the Fine Arts, Philadelphia, Pennsylvania.

Fifth Annual Exhibition, Fall 1963. Lever House Lobby, Sculptors Guild, New York.

Eleventh Exhibition of Contemporary American Painting and Sculpture 1963, March 2–April 7, 1963. Krannert Art Museum, College of Fine and Applied Arts, University of Illinois, Champaign-Urbana, Illinois. Exh. cat. Urbana: University of Illinois Press, 1963.

An Exhibition of Original Art Commissioned by the Container Corporation of America, 1936–1963, Fall 1963, Time-Life Building, New York. Exh. cat. New York: Container Corporation of America, 1963.

The Fourteenth Christocentric Arts Festival: An Invitational Exhibition of Contemporary Christian Liturgical Art, March 8–22, 1964. Lewis Gallery, Newman Foundation, University of Illinois, Champaign-Urbana, Illinois. Exh. cat. by Father Joseph B. Mackowiak. Champaign: Newman Foundation, 1964.

National Association of Women Artists 1964 Annual Exhibition, May 7–24, 1964. Galleries of the National Academy of Design, New York. Exh. cat. New York: National Academy of Design, 1964.

HTAL Invited Painting and Sculpture Exhibition, November 21, 1964–January 3, 1965. Heckscher Museum of Art, Huntington, New York.

Whitney Museum of American Art 1964 Annual Exhibition of Contemporary American Sculpture, December 9, 1964–January 31, 1965. Whitney Museum of American Art, New York. Exh. cat. New York: Whitney Museum of American Art, 1964.

Annual Exhibition of Painting and Sculpture, 1964. Pennsylvania Academy of the Fine Arts, Philadelphia, Pennsylvania.

Religious Art from Byzantium to Chagall, December 13, 1964–January 10, 1965. Buffalo Fine Arts Academy and Albright-Knox Art Gallery, Buffalo, New York. Exh. cat. Buffalo: Albright-Knox Art Gallery, 1964.

Women Artists of America, 1707–1964, April 2–May 16, 1965. Newark Museum, New Jersey.

The Josephine and Phillip A. Bruno Collection, 1965. Finch College Museum of Art, New York.

Sculpture from the Albert A. List Family Collection, 1965. New School for Social Research, New York.

Art in the Residence of the American Ambassador, 1965. United States Department of State, Athens, Greece.

The Fifteenth Christocentric Arts Festival: An Invitational Exhibition of Contemporary Christian Liturgical Art, March 20–April 3, 1966. Lewis Gallery, Newman Foundation, University of Illinois, Champaign-Urbana, Illinois.

Contemporary Americans, February 12–March 13, 1966. Arkansas Art Center Galleries, Little Rock, Arkansas.

Har Zion Temple Art Exhibition on Jewish and Biblical Themes, April 17–26, 1966. Har Zion Temple, Philadelphia, Pennsylvania.

Contemporary Art from the Synagogue, June–August, 1966. Jewish Museum, New York.

Sculpture 1966: The Sculptors Guild Annual Exhibition, October 23–November 20, 1966. Lever House, New York. Exh. cat by William Talbot. New York: Sculptors Guild, 1966.

Religious Art, 1966. Champion International Building, Plywood, New York.

Protest and Hope: An Exhibition of Contemporary American Art, October 24–December 2, 1967. Wollman Hall, New School Art Center, New York. Exh. cat. New York: New School for Social Research, 1967.

Drawings by Painters and Sculptors, 1967. New School Art Center, New School for Social Research, New York.

Contemporary American Painting and Sculpture, 1969. Krannert Art Museum, University of Illinois, Champaign-Urbana, Illinois.

Second Flint Invitational: A Second Invitational Exhibition of Contemporary Painting and Sculpture, October 25–December 25, 1969. Flint Institute of Arts in the De Waters Art Center, Flint, Michigan. Exh. cat. Flint: Flint Institute of Arts, 1969.

American Drawings of the Sixties: A Selection, November 11, 1969–January 10, 1970. New School Art Center, New School for Social Research, New York. Exh. cat. New York: New School Art Center, 1969.

1970s
Solo Exhibitions
Luise Kaish: Recent Sculpture, 1972. American Academy in Rome, Italy. Exh. cat. Rome: American Academy in Rome, 1972.

Luise Kaish Sculpture (retrospective), October 2–December 2, 1973. Jewish Museum, New York. Exh. cat. by Avram Kampf. New York: Jewish Museum, 1973.

Group Exhibitions
K x 2: Luise Kaish Sculture, Morton Kaish Pitture / K x 2: Paintings by Morton Kaish, Sculpture by Luise Kaish, December 5, 1972–January 5, 1973. United States Information Service, American Embassy in Rome, Italy. Exh. cat. Rome: American Embassy in Rome, 1972.

Luise Kaish, Morton Kaish: Artists-in-Residence, August 2–September 3, 1974. Jaffe–Friede and Strauss Galleries, Hopkins Center, Dartmouth College, Hanover, New Hampshire. Exh. cat. by Matthew Wysocki. Hanover: Dartmouth College, 1974.

Luise and Morton Kaish: Sculpture and Art, 1976. Lowe–Levinson Art Gallery, Temple Beth Shalom, Miami Beach, Florida.

Sculpture in the Spring, April 4–May 3, 1970. Museum of Art, University of Connecticut, Storrs, Connecticut.

Louise [sic] *Kaish, John Matt, Robert Strini*, through June 30, 1972. American Academy in Rome, Italy.

American Women: Twentieth Century, September 15–October 29, 1972. Lakeview Center for the Arts and Sciences, Peoria, Illinois. Exh. cat. by Ida Kohlmeyer and Lowell Adams. Peoria: Lakeview Center for the Arts and Sciences, 1972.

An Exhibition of Contemporary Painting and Sculpture, March 16–April 15, 1973. Academy Art Gallery, American Academy of Arts and Letters, New York.

Sculpture from the Collection of the Memorial Art Gallery, August 1–31, 1973. Lincoln First Bank, Rochester, New York.

American Art in Upstate New York: Drawings, Watercolors and Small Sculpture from Public Collections in Albany, Buffalo, Ithaca, Rochester, Syracuse and Utica, July 12–August 25, 1974. Traveled to Memorial Art Gallery, University of Rochester, New York; Herbert F. Johnson Museum of Art, Cornell University, Ithaca, New York; Everson Museum of Art, Syracuse, New York; Munson-Williams-Proctor Institute, Utica, New York; and Albany Institute of History and Art, New York.

The Sculptors Guild Annual Exhibition, 1974. Lever House, New York.

Staempfli in L.A., October 13–November 1, 1975. Ankrum Gallery, Los Angeles, California. Exh. cat. by Joan Ankrum and William Challee. Los Angeles: Ankrum Gallery, 1975.

Jewish Experience in the Art of the Twentieth Century, October 16, 1975–January 25, 1976. Jewish Museum, New York. Exh. cat. by Avram Kampf. New York: Jewish Museum, New York, 1975.

Bicentennial Festival of Arts: The Creative American Jew, May 22–27, 1976. Jewish Community Center, Wilmington, Delaware. Exh. cat. Wilmington: Jewish Community Center, 1976.

The Sculptors Guild Annual Exhibition, October 22–November 18, 1976. Lever House, New York.

The Sculptors Guild Annual Exhibition, October 26–November 17, 1977. Lever House, New York.

Fiftieth Anniversary Benefit Exhibition, January 22–February 22, 1978. Sculpture Center, New York.

Alumni Artists' Exhibition / 1979, January 23–February 23, 1979. Lubin House Gallery, Syracuse University, New York.

West '79 / The Law: An Exhibition of Contemporary Art Reflecting Aspects of the Law, March 29–May 11, 1979. Minnesota Museum of Art / Community Gallery, Saint Paul, Minnesota. Exh. cat. by Gerard L. Cafesjian and William E. Woolfenden. Saint Paul: Minnesota Museum of Art, 1979.

The Sculptors Guild Annual Exhibition, 1979. Lever House, New York.

1980s
Solo Exhibitions
Luise Kaish: Recent Collages, November 10–December 5, 1981. Staempfli Gallery, New York. Exh. cat. New York: Staempfli Gallery, 1981.

Luise Kaish: New Work, October 9–November 3, 1984. Staempfli Gallery, New York. Exh. cat. New York: Staempfli Gallery, 1984.

Luise Kaish: New Paintings, March 1–26, 1988. Staempfli Gallery, New York. Exh. cat. New York: Staempfli Gallery, 1988.

Group Exhibitions
Nineteenth and Twentieth Century Women Artists, October 1983. Susan Blanchard Gallery, New York.

Art, Design and the Modern Corporation: The Collection of Container Corporation of America, October 18, 1985–January 12, 1986. National Museum of American Art, Washington, D.C. Touring exhibition. Exh. cat. by Neil Harris and Martina Roundabush Norelli. Washington, D.C.: Smithsonian Institution Press, 1985.

Marsha Pels, Richard Merkin, Sol LeWitt, Luise Kaish, February 1986. Lubin House Gallery, Syracuse University, New York.

Sculpture, December 9, 1986–January 10, 1987. Staempfli Gallery, New York.

Luise Kaish, Paintings; Morton Kaish, Monotypes, April 30–May 28, 1988. Oxford Gallery, Rochester, New York.

The Art of Drawing VI, December 12, 1989–January 13, 1990. Staempfli Gallery, New York, New York.

1990s
Solo Exhibitions
Luise Kaish, October 29–November 23, 1990. Fine Arts Center Gallery, University of Arkansas, Fayetteville, Arkansas.

The Colors of Seasons, April 21–May 22, 1998. President's Room, Century Association, New York.

Group Exhibitions
An Exhibition by Faculty of the Visual Arts, September 16–October 31, 1992. Miriam and Ira D. Wallach Art Gallery, Schermerhorn Hall, Columbia University, New York.

Works by New Artist Members: C. Sperry Andrews, Anne Blodgett, Russell Connor, Neil Estern, Luise Kaish, Robert Kipniss, Henry Wolf, June 1–July 2, 1993. Gallery of the Century Association, New York.

Recent Acquisitions: Works on Paper by Women Artists, May 5–August 13, 1995. Memorial Art Gallery, University of Rochester, New York.

National Academy Museum and School of Fine Art 172nd Annual Exhibition, 1997. National Academy Museum and School of Fine Art, New York. Exh. cat. by David B. Dearinger. New York: National Academy Museum and School of Fine Art, 1997.

Contemporary Artists Welcome the New Year— The Jewish Museum Graphic Commission, March 8–May 10, 1998. Jewish Museum, New York.

National Academy Museum and School of Fine Art 174th Annual Exhibition, March 17–April 25, 1999. National Academy Museum and School of Fine Art, New York. Exh. cat. New York: National Academy Museum and School of Fine Art, 1999.

2000s
Solo Exhibitions
From Maquette to Monument, October 2010. Temple B'rith Kodesh, Rochester, New York.

Group Exhibitions
National Academy Museum and School of Fine Art 175th Annual Exhibition, February 9–March 26, 2000. National Academy Museum and School of Fine Art, New York. Exh. cat. New York: National Academy Museum and School of Fine Art, 2000.

National Academy Museum and School of Fine Art 176th Annual Exhibition, May 22–June 24, 2001. National Academy Museum and School of Fine Art, New York. Exh. cat. New York: National Academy Museum and School of Fine Art, 2001.

National Academy Museum and School of Fine Art 178th Annual Exhibition, May 2–June 15, 2003. National Academy Museum and School of Fine Art, New York. Exh. cat. New York: National Academy Museum and School of Fine Art, 2003.

A Fine Line: Drawings by National Academicians, September 7, 2003–January 4, 2004. National Academy Museum and School of Fine Art, New York.

Realism Now: Traditions and Departures— Mentors and Protégés, Part II, May 15–July 17, 2004. Vose Contemporary: A Division of the Vose Galleries of Boston, Massachusetts. Exh. cat. by John D. O'Hern., Nancy Allyn Jarzombek, and Marcia L. Vose. Boston: Vose Galleries of Boston, 2004.

Disegno: The 180th Annual Exhibition, May 25–July 3, 2005. National Academy Museum and School of Fine Art, New York. Exh. cat by Nancy Malloy. New York: National Academy Museum and School of Fine Art, 2005.

The 182nd Annual Exhibition of Contemporary American Art, May 16–June 24, 2007. National Academy Museum and School of Fine Art, New York.

Crate 1 of 2: Paintings and Sculptures from the Collection at the Minnesota Museum of American Art, June 13–August 28, 2008. Minnesota Museum of American Art, Saint Paul, Minnesota.

The 184th Annual Exhibition of Contemporary American Art, April 16–June 10, 2009. National Academy Museum and School of Fine Art, New York.

From Maquette to Monument, 2009. Century Association, New York.

2010s
Group Exhibitions
Century Masters: Luise and Morton Kaish, K x 2: II, April 19–May 24, 2012. Century Association, New York. Exh. cat. by Tom L. Freudenheim and Donald Holden. New York: Century Association, 2012.

In Residence: Contemporary Artists at Dartmouth, January 18–July 6, 2014. Hood Museum of Art, Dartmouth College, Hanover, New Hampshire. Exh. cat. by Michael R. Taylor and Gerald Auten. Hanover: Hood Museum of Art, 2014.

Women Artists of the Century: Celebrating 30 Years, October 24–November 26, 2019. Century Association, New York.

SELECTED BIBLIOGRAPHY

Jillian Russo and Andrea Lynn Kutsenkow

Exhibition Catalogues

An Exhibition of Original Art Commissioned by the Container Corporation of America, 1936–1963. New York: Container Corporation of America, 1963.

Ankrum, Joan, and William Challee. *Staempfli in L.A.*, October 13–November 1, 1975. Ankrum Gallery, Los Angeles, California, 1975.

Audubon Artists Sixteenth Annual Exhibition: Oils, Watercolors, Pastels, Casein Paintings, Graphics, Sculpture, January 16–February 2, 1958. New York: National Academy of Design, 1958.

Audubon Artists Eighteenth Annual Exhibition: Oil, Sculpture, Watercolor, Casein, Graphic, January 21–February 7, 1960. New York: National Academy of Design, 1960.

Autumn of Our Thirty-First Year, October 25–November 11, 1959. New York: Sculpture Center, 1959.

Autumn of Our Thirty-Third Year, September 17–October 12, 1961. New York: Sculpture Center, 1961.

Bareiss, Walter, and James Thrall Soby. *Recent Sculpture U.S.A.*, May 13–August 16, 1959. New York: Museum of Modern Art, 1959.

Cafesjian, Gerard L., and William E. Woolfenden. *West '79 / The Law: An Exhibition of Contemporary Art Reflecting Aspects of the Law*, March 29–May 11, 1979. Saint Paul: Minnesota Museum of Art, 1979.

Contemporary American Painting and Sculpture, 1959. Champaign, Illinois: Krannert Art Museum, 1959.

Contemporary American Painting and Sculpture, February 26–April 2, 1961. Champaign, Illinois: Krannert Art Museum, 1961.

Dearinger, David B. *The National Academy Museum and School of Fine Art 172nd Annual Exhibition*, 1997. New York: National Academy Museum and School of Fine Art, 1997.

Denslow, Dorothea. *Exhibit of Sculpture*, February 13–29, 1952. New York: Sculpture Center, 1952.

Denslow, Dorothea, and Sahl Swarz. *Spring '56*, April 15–May 13, 1956. New York: Sculpture Center, 1956.

Falk, Peter Hastings, ed. *The Annual Exhibition Record of the Pennsylvania Academy of the Fine Arts: Volume III, 1914–1968*. Madison, Connecticut: Sound View Press, 1989.

Freudenheim, Tom L., and Donald Holden. *Century Masters, Luise and Morton Kaish, K x 2: II*, April 19–May 24, 2012. New York: Century Association, 2012.

Eleventh Exhibition of Contemporary American Painting and Sculpture 1963, March 2–April 7, 1963, Krannert Art Museum. Urbana: University of Illinois Press, 1963.

Hale, Robert Beverly. *American Sculpture 1951: A National Competitive Exhibition*, December 7, 1951–February 24, 1952. New York: Metropolitan Museum of Art, 1951.

K x 2: Luise Kaish Sculpture, Morton Kaish Pitture / K x 2, Paintings by Morton Kaish, Sculpture by Luise Kaish, December 5, 1972–January 5, 1973. Rome: American Embassy in Rome, 1972.

Kampf, Avram. *Luise Kaish Sculpture* (retrospective), October 2–December 2, 1973. New York: Jewish Museum, 1973.

Kampf, Avram. *Jewish Experience in the Art of the Twentieth Century*, October 16, 1975–January 25, 1976. New York: Jewish Museum, 1975.

Kohlmeyer, Ida, and Lowell Adams. *American Women: Twentieth Century*. Peoria, Illinois: Lakeview Center for the Arts and Sciences, 1972.

Luise Kaish, March 24–April 11, 1958. New York: Sculpture Center, 1958.

Luise Kaish: Recent Sculpture, 1972. Rome: American Academy in Rome, 1972.

Luise Kaish: Recent Collages, November 10–December 5, 1981. New York: Staempfli Gallery, 1981.

Luise Kaish: New Work, October 9–November 3, 1984. New York: Staempfli Gallery, 1984.

Luise Kaish: New Paintings, March 1–26, 1988. New York: Staempfli Gallery, 1988.

Mackowiak, Father Joseph B. *The Fourteenth Christocentric Arts Festival: An Invitational Exhibition of Contemporary Christian Liturgical Art*, March 8–22, 1964. Lewis Gallery, Newman Foundation, University of Illinois. Champaign: Newman Foundation, 1964.

Malloy, Nancy. *Disegno: The 180th Annual Exhibition*, May 25–July 3, 2005. New York: National Academy Museum and School of Fine Art, 2005.

National Association of Women Artists 1964 Annual Exhibition, May 7–24, 1964. New York: National Academy of Design, 1964.

National Academy Museum and School of Fine Art 174th Annual Exhibition, March 17–April 25, 1999. New York: National Academy Museum and School of Fine Art, 1999.

National Academy Museum and School of Fine Art 175th Annual Exhibition, February 9–March 26, 2000. New York: National Academy Museum and School of Fine Art, 2000.

National Academy Museum and School of Fine Art 176th Annual Exhibition, May 22–June 24, 2001. New York: National Academy Museum and School of Fine Art, 2001.

National Academy Museum and School of Fine Art 178th Annual Exhibition, May 2–June 15, 2003. New York: National Academy Museum and School of Fine Art, 2003.

O'Hern, John D., Nancy Allyn Jarzombek, and Marcia L. Vose. *Realism Now: Traditions and Departures—Mentors and Protégés, Part II*, May 15–July 17, 2004. Boston: Vose Galleries of Boston, 2004.

Protest and Hope: An Exhibition of Contemporary American Art, October 24–December 2, 1967, Wollman Hall, New School Art Center. New York: New School for Social Research, 1967.

American Drawings of the Sixties: A Selection, November 11, 1969–January 10, 1970. New York: New School Art Center, 1969.

Religious Art from Byzantium to Chagall, December 13, 1964–January 10, 1965. Buffalo, New York: Albright-Knox Art Gallery, 1964.

Second Flint Invitational: A Second Invitational Exhibition of Contemporary Painting and Sculpture, October 25–December 25, 1969. Flint, Michigan: Flint Institute of Arts, 1969.

Swarz, Sahl. *Women Welders*, November 1–20, 1953. New York: Sculpture Center, 1953.

Swarz, Sahl. *Carvings Muir, Weldings Kaish*, February 28–March 18, 1955. New York: Sculpture Center, 1955.

Talbot, William. *Sculpture 1966: The Sculptors Guild Annual Exhibition*, October 23–November 20, 1966, Lever House, New York. New York: Sculptors Guild, 1966.

Taylor, Michael R., and Gerald Auten. *In Residence: Contemporary Artists at Dartmouth*, January 18–July 6, 2014. Hanover, New Hampshire: Hood Museum of Art, 2014.

Whitney Museum of American Art Annual Exhibition 1962: Contemporary Sculpture and Drawings, December 12, 1962–February 3, 1963. New York: Whitney Museum of American Art, 1962.

Whitney Museum of American Art 1964 Annual Exhibition of Contemporary American Sculpture, December 9, 1964–January 31, 1965. New York: Whitney Museum of American Art, 1964.

Books

Baigell, Matthew. *Jewish Art in America: An Introduction*. Lanham, Maryland: Rowman & Littlefield, 2007.

Brommer, Gerald F. *Wire Sculpture and Other Three-Dimensional Construction*. Worcester, Massachusetts: Davis Publications, 1968.

Eisenstadt, Peter. *Affirming the Covenant: A History of Temple B'rith Kodesh, Rochester, New York, 1848–1998*. Rochester: Temple B'rith Kodesh, 1999.

Frascina, Francis. *Art, Politics and Dissent: Aspects of the Art Left in Sixties America*. Manchester, UK, and New York: Manchester University Press, 1999.

Gruber, Samuel D. *American Synagogues: A Century of Architecture and Jewish Community*. New York: Rizzoli International Publications, 2003.

Hayes, Bartlett. *Tradition Becomes Innovation: Modern Religious Architecture in America*. New York: Pilgrim Press, 1983.

Heller, Jules, and Nancy G. Heller, eds. *North American Women Artists of the Twentieth Century: A Biographical Dictionary*. New York and London: Garland Publishing, 1995.

Kampf, Avram. *Jewish Experience in the Art of the Twentieth Century*. South Hadley, Massachusetts: Bergin & Garvey, 1984.

Leighton, Josephine. *1959 and 1960 Reports of the Secretary General and of the Treasurer*. New York: John Simon Guggenheim Memorial Foundation, 1961.

Lipsey, Roger. *An Art of Our Own: The Spiritual in Twentieth Century Art*. Boston: Shambhala Publications, 1988.

Rajtar, Steve, and Frances Elizabeth Franks. *War Monuments, Museums, and Library Collections of Twentieth Century Conflicts: A Directory of United States Sites*. Jefferson, North Carolina: McFarland & Company, 2002.

Rosen, Aaron, ed. *Religion and Art in the Heart of Modern Manhattan: St. Peter's Church and the Louise Nevelson Chapel*. New York: Routledge, 2017.

Roukes, Nicholas. "Technique Experiment 19: Explore Canvas Collage." In *Acrylics Bold and New*, 134–135. New York: Watson-Guptill, 1986.

Rubinstein, Charlotte Streifer. *American Women Sculptors: A History of Women Working in Three Dimensions*. Boston: G. K. Hall & Co., 1990.

Schmeckebier, Alexandra K., ed. *The Syracuse University Collection—1964—Painting, Drawing, Sculpture*. New York: School of Art of Syracuse University, 1964.

Watson-Jones, Virginia. *Contemporary American Women Sculptors*. Phoenix: Oryx Press, 1986.

Articles

"$1,500,000 Guggenheim Fellowships Given to 321." *New York Herald Tribune*, April 20, 1959, A4.

"A Celebration of Henry Moore." *Columbia University Record* 8, no. 30 (May 27, 1983): front page.

"A Major Synagogue by Belluschi." *Architectural Record*, November 1963, 143–48.

Ashston, Dore. "Art: Coptic Mysteries," *New York Times*, March 27, 1958, 30.

"Art Tour: The Galleries—A Critical Guide." *New York Herald Tribune*, October 26, 1963.

"Art: Recent Sculpture." *New York Times*, May 13, 1959, 34.

"Artists from New York." *Derry Journal*, July 22, 1977, 10; September 30, 1977, 26–27.

Bashman, Howard J. "Panel Members Predict Topics." *Columbia Daily Spectator*, February 7, 1984, 1–2.

Batkin, Stanley Irving. "Wall of Martyrs." In *Let Them Make Me A Sanctuary: A Contemporary American Synagogue Inspired by the Art of Ancient Israel*, 66–72. New York: Behrman House, 1978.

Barry, Pat. "About Women: Post Office Stone Pays Sculptor Dividends," *Democrat and Chronicle* (Rochester), May 30, 1951, 7.

"Beth El Invites Public to view Wall of Martyrs." *Gannet Westchester Newspapers*, April 19, 1979, A4.

"Beth El's 'Wall of Martyrs' is Ready for Showing." *Standard-Star* (New Rochelle), October 1, 1973, 10.

"Bronze Frieze for Synagogue Depicts Jewish Martyrdom." *American Examiner–Jewish Week*, November 9, 1974, 10.

Burrows, Carlyle. "Art Shows: Two Sculptors." *New York Herald*, March 13, 1955, E15.

Burrows, Carlyle. "Audubon Artists Exhibit Will Be Open Tomorrow." *New York Herald Tribune*, January 14, 1959, 13.

Canaday, John. "10 Studio Exhibitions Are Summarized." *New York Times*, April 27, 1968, 35.

Chayat, Sherry. "Art: Kaishes Take Different Paths Beyond Reality." *Rochester Herald Journal*, Summer 1988, 22.

Chirello, Steve. "Sculpture Court Dedication Set." *Syracuse Record* 22, no. 12 (October 28, 1991): front page.

Coates, Robert M. "The Art Galleries: Whither, Whither?" *New Yorker*, December 19, 1964, 152–55.

Coates, Robert M. "The Art World: Anniversary," *New Yorker*, November 5, 1966, 150–56.

Dash, Robert W. "Luise Kaish." *Arts Magazine* 32 no. 7 (April 1958): 63.

Devree, Howard. "Welded Sculpture." *New York Times*, November 8, 1953, X11.

Devree, Howard. "About Art and Artists: Spanish Themes Shown at Wildenstein's—Gallery Uncorks Sketches in Wine." *New York Times*, December 7, 1955, 36.

Devree, Howard. "About Art and Artists: Sculpture Center Has a Lively Annual Show." *New York Times*, April 21, 1956, 20.

Devree, Howard. "Art: An Eventful Week: Other Recent Work." *New York Times*, April 22, 1956, 121.

Devree, Howard. "Sculpture Today: Museum Opens Contemporary Survey—Early Work by Jaques Villon." *New York Times*, May 17, 1959, 16.

"Discover 'La Lumiere.'" *Continews*, Spring 1978, front cover, 4, 5.

Edelstein, Andy. "Book Glorifies Synagogue; Author Sees More Buildings California and Florida." *Jewish Week–American Examiner*, week of August 5, 1979, 13.

"Emeriti Faculty Fill Their Calendars with Travel, Study and Teaching." *Columbia University Record* 19, no. 15 (January 28, 1994): 7.

"Fellows in the News: Visual Artists." [*MacDowell*] *Colony Newsletter* 7, no. 1 (Winter 1977–78): back page.

"From the Ancient to Today." *The Bookshelf*, March–April 1959, front cover.

"Gallery Openings, Museum Exhibitions." *New York Times*, January 28, 1962, 100.

Geffen, David. "Spiritual Grandeur." *Jerusalem Post Magazine*, January 30, 1981, 13.

Genauer, Emily. "Art: Groups and Solos: Beatnik Sculpture in Big Museum Show." *New York Herald Tribune*, May 17, 1959.

Genauer, Emily. "On the Arts: The Violent Strain in Modern Art." *Newsday*, June 15, 1968, 35.

Genauer, Emily. "Sculpture Center Show." *New York Herald Tribune*, April 22, 1956, F13.

Genauer, Emily. "Art Exhibition Notes." *New York Herald Tribune*, March 29, 1958, 11.

Gerrit, Henry. "Luise Kaish: A Lyrical Essay." *Arts Magazine* 62, no. 7 (March 1988): 86–88.

Gerrit, Henry. "New York Reviews: Luise Kaish." *Arts Magazine* 59, no. 1 (February 1985): 151–53.

Gruen, John. "Sculptors Guild Exhibit." *New York Herald Tribune*, October 22, 1963.

Grossman, Emery. "Interview with Luise Kaish, Sculptor." *Temple Israel Light* 8, no. 3 (November–December 1966): 6–8.

"Guggenheim Fund Grants $1,500,000." *New York Times*, April 20, 1959, 23.

"Historic Moment." *Democrat and Chronicle* (Rochester) [Cf. Barry, Pat], April 4, 1964, 4.

"It Suits the Millers to Lop-Sided T." *Canadian Homes*, July 1961, 32–22.

"Jewish History a Reality." *Standard-Star* (New Rochelle), November 4, 1974.

"John Chancellor Visits Lubin House." *Syracuse Record*, January 14, 1991.

Kaish, Luise. "'The Wall of the Martyrs': The Artist Views Her Work." *Beth El Bulletin*, October 1974, 5, 13–14.

Kaish, Morton. "The Century Memorials: Luise Clayborn Kaish (1925–2013)." In *The Century Yearbook 2014*, 355. New York: Century Association, 2014.

Kalvaitis, Julia. "A Collective Portrait of Ivan Meštrović and His Students: The Syracuse Years, 1947–1955." Master's Thesis, Syracuse University, New York, 1998, 88–89, 118, 176.

Kampf, Avram. "Artwork in the Prayer Hall: Temple B'rith Kodesh, Rochester, New York." In *Contemporary Synagogue Art: Developments in the United States, 1945–1965*, 227–30. New York: Union of American Hebrew Congregation, 1966.

Kelley, Mary Lou. "Kaishes Find Dartmouth Fruitful." *Christian Science Monitor*, August 23, 1974, 4E.

Larue, Arlene C., ed. "Sketching . . . " *Syracuse Herald America*, August 14, 1949, front cover.

Levin, Gail. "Jewish American Artists: Whom Does That Include?" *Journal of Modern Jewish Studies* 9, no. 3 (2010): 422.

Lipsey, Roger. "Luise Kaish's Small Worlds." *Arts Magazine* 56, no. 3 (November 1981), 158–60.

"Luise Kaish." *Acier Stahl Steel* 32 (May 1967): 20.

Mandeville, Linda. "A View of Her Own: Artist Luise Kaish." *Columbia Magazine*, February 1985, 19–23.

"Marriage of Styles: Luise & Morton Kaish, We're in the Kaishes' Picture." *Syracuse University Magazine* 5, no. 3 (March 1989): back cover.

Martin, Richard. "Luise Kaish." *Arts Magazine* 59, no. 2 (October 1984): 11.

Mulligan, Charles L. "In the Art Galleries: Luise Kaish of Flushing." *New York Post*, December 25, 1955, 12M.

Naltchayan, Harry. "Ecstasy." *Washington Post*, August, 5, 1967, D13.

"New York Headquarters." *Continews*, Spring 1978, 9, 13.

Odenhausen. "Stahlskulpturen von Luise Kaish." *Acier Stahl Steel* 28 (April 1963): 193–94.

"Presidential Commission to Study Future of Columbia." *Columbia University Record* 9, no. 20 (February 17, 1984): 1, 8.

Preston, Stuart. "Art: Another Museum; Early American Works Will Be Exhibited." *New York Times*, September 27, 1963, 26.

"Religious Arts Exhibit—1975 San Antonio Conference." *Faith & Form VIII* (Fall 1975): 8.

Robertson, Nan. "Dean of the Arts School at Columbia Is Leaving." *New York Times*, October 3, 1986, C16.

Rosenberg, Harold. "The Art World: Jews in Art." *The New Yorker*, December 22, 1975, 64–68.

Russell, John. "Art People." *New York Times*, Friday, June 6, 1980, T17.

Sandler, Irving. "Luise Kaish." *Art News* 57, no. 2 (April 1958): 18.

Schetterer, June. "Jews' History Told in Bronze." *Standard-Star* (New Rochelle), October 31, 1974, 3.

Schloss, Edith. "Around European Galleries." *International Herald Tribune*, June 24–25, 1972, 7.

Schoen, Myron E. "A Symbol of Judaism's Sacred Mission." *American Judaism* (Fall 1964): 26.

"Sculptor Named." *Playground Daily News* (Fort Walton Beach, Florida), July 17, 1980.

"Sculptresses Turn to Welder's Torch." *New York Times*, November 7, 1953, 23.

"Sculpture Court Becomes a Reality." *Syracuse University College of Visual & Performing Arts Alumni Newsletter* 7, no. 1 (Spring 1992): 10–11.

Smith, Virginia J. "A Masterpiece of Art: B'rith Kodesh Ark Great Sculpture in Bronze." *Rochester Times-Union*, March 26, 1964, 12A.

Smith, Virginia Jeffrey. "Gallery Showing Kaish Work." *Rochester Times-Union*, October 14, 1954, 38.

Smolko, Nona. "A Superfine Design: Architect Richard Chalfant Delights in Showing Off His Showplace." *Delaware Today*, July 1987, 118–20.

Sorkin, Jenni, and Linda Theung. "Selected Chronology of All-Women Group Exhibitions, 1943–83." In *WACK! Art and the Feminist Revolution*, n.p. Exh. cat. Cambridge and London: MIT Press, 2007.

"Statue Unveiled." *Post Standard* (Syracuse), June 4, 1951, front cover.

"Summer '85 Art Workshops." *Inside University of Haifa*, no. 7 (Summer/Fall 1985): 14.

Tatham, David. "Ivan Meštrović in Syracuse, 1947–1955." *Syracuse University Library Associates Courier* 32 (1997): 5–24.

Tsutakawa, Mayumi. "Arts and Entertainment: New York Beckons Kaish and Kaish." *Seattle Times*, July 24, 1979, D6.

Walrath, Jean. "Jewish Artists Stimulating in Exhibit." *Democrat and Chronicle* (Rochester), January 19, 1958, 6E.

PHOTO CREDITS

Walrath, Jean. "New Temple Menorah is Kaish Sculpture," *Democrat and Chronicle* (Rochester), January 3, 1960, 10D.

"Women Artists to Exhibit Work." *New York Times*, March 4, 1962, 62.

Werner, Alfred. "Book Reviews." *Jewish Social Studies* (1966): 124.

Werner, Alfred. "Jewish Women in the Fine Arts." *Pioneer Women* (November–December 1978): 13–15, 18.

Werner, Alfred. "Views and Visions." *Jewish News*, October 6, 1967, 12, 28.

Whiteman, Brenda. "Arents Pioneer Medal: Luise Kaish." *Syracuse Record* 19, no. 34 (May 30, 1989): 4.

Willard, Charlotte. "In the Art Galleries: A Bloom in the Wasteland: Luise Kaish." *New York Post*, May 11, 1968, 50.

Young, James E., Deborah Dash Moore, and Nurith Gertz, eds. "Visual Culture." In *The Posen Library of Jewish Culture and Civilization*, vol. 10, *1973–2005*, 517. New Haven and London: Yale University Press; Lucerne: The Posen Foundation, 2012.

INDEX

ACKNOWLEDGMENTS

There are many people who helped make this book happen. The Kaish Family Art Project is profoundly grateful to Maura Reilly, the editor and champion of this book, which has come to fruition through her vision and perseverance. For their outstanding and thoughtful contributions to this volume, we thank the authors, Daniel Belasco, Samuel Gruber, Eleanor Heartney, Norman Kleeblatt, Gail Levin, Roger Lipsey, and Vanja Malloy. Thanks also to Jillian Russo, who wrote the chronology, bibliography, and exhibition history, and to Andrea Kutsenkow, who diligently pre-processed Luise's archival records and contributed to the bibliography and exhibition history. From the very beginning of this project, Sarah McCollum Williams made invaluable contributions to all aspects of research and worked closely with the authors. This project would not have been possible without the dedication and knowledge of Luise's husband, Morton, and her daughter, Melissa. Their journey began by documenting Luise's work, with the generous guidance of Joan Jeffri, and continued with the creation of a comprehensive oral history, spearheaded by Liza Zapol.

For their contributions to the visual impact of the book, we thank Kat Kiernan, who oversaw the book layout production, secured reproduction rights, and arranged photography of Luise's major commissions; Elisabeth Foulkes, who, with her unfailingly professional touch, managed all aspects of digital reproduction; Susie Carter, who seamlessly organized photo shoots; Gerard D'Albon, who assisted with photography, photo editing, and innovative design concepts; and Carolyn Bost, who gave steadfast support in daily operations.

A special thanks to Jeffrey Spring and his sister Mary Jo of Modern Art Foundry for their unflagging generosity and patience providing us with invaluable oral history as well as tutelage in the intricacies of bronze casting and restoration. For three generations, the Spring family worked alongside Luise to realize her daring monumental commissions. Many thanks also to Bruce Gitlin of Milgo Bufkin, who was integral to the realization of Luise's major commissions using innovative fabrication techniques, and generously provided oral history for the book.

The staff and leadership of institutions where Luise's major commissions are installed were tremendously helpful with the research and coordination of photography for the works, providing access and sharing historical knowledge. We would like to thank Domenic Iacono and Emily Dittman, Syracuse University Art Galleries, for their guidance on the book in its preliminary stages, and for Emily's assistance with photography and research (*Saltine Warrior*); Rabbi Peter Stein (*The Ark of Revelation*); Brother Steven Vesely, S.T. (*Christ in Glory*); Rabbi Michael Beals and Debbie Kraft Harris (*The Beth Shalom Ark Doors*); Erica Leventhal, Beth El Synagogue Center (*The Wall of Martyrs*); Gail Milchman, Temple B'nai Abraham (*Menorah, Eternal Light*); Rabbi Naamah Kelman, Hebrew Union College, and Dina Recanati and Shlomit Molho, for facilitating photography in Jerusalem (*Eternal Light*); and MaryAnn Fribourg and Continental Grain Corporation (*La Lumière*). For their early strategic vision we thank Adam Chinn, Christy MacLear, and Allan Schwartzman. We are grateful to John Stomberg, Juliette Bianco, and Katherine Hart of the Hood Museum of Art, Dartmouth College, for their insights and encouragement.

Dan Giles, Managing Director at D Giles Limited, believed in this project from the start; we thank you and all your dedicated colleagues who shepherded it through to completion, including Allison McCormick, Louise Ramsay, Louise Parfitt, and Harry Ault.

Finally, we wish to acknowledge Morton Kaish for over seven decades of remarkable photographs of Luise at work.

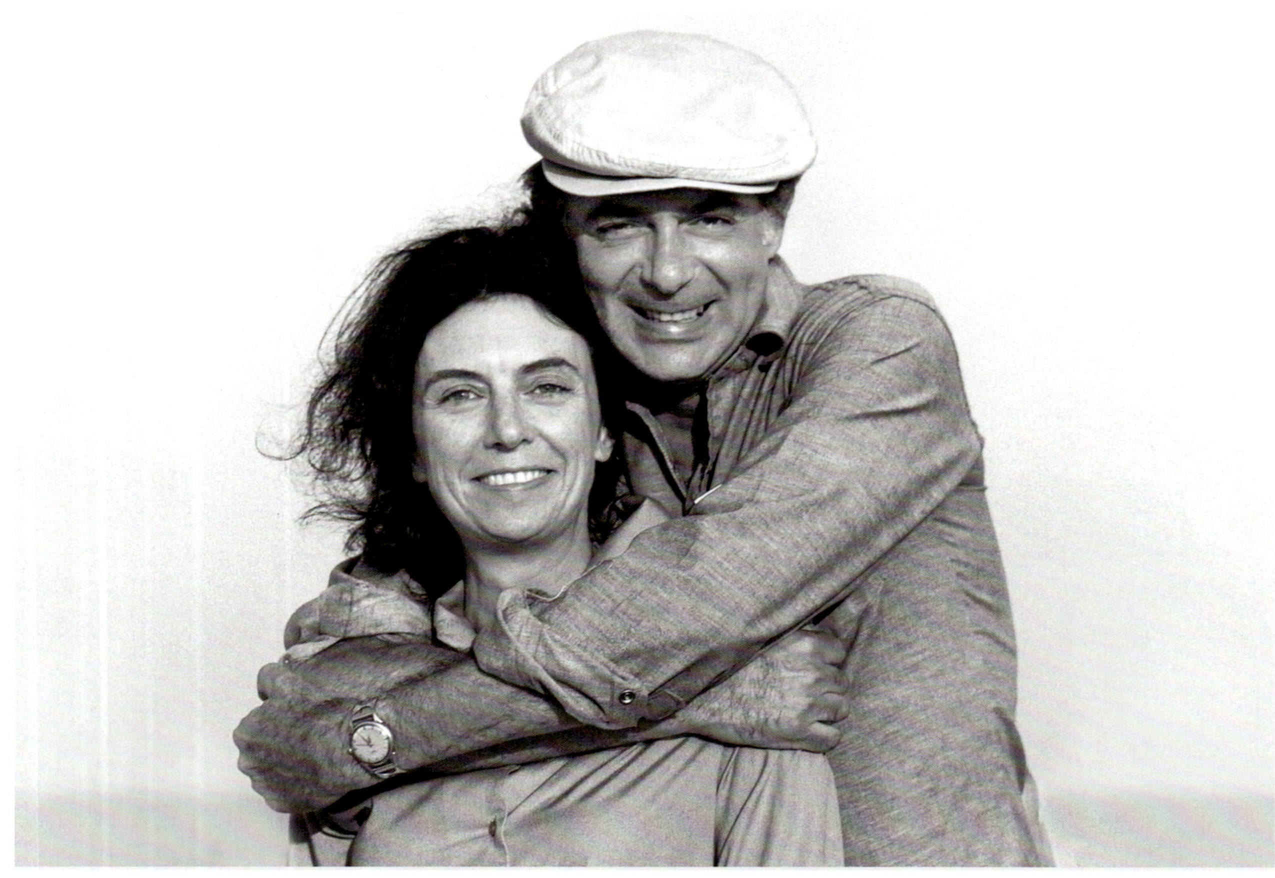

The sky was purple, snow falling softly the night we met.

Students skating on an ice pond in upstate New York.

I thought her more beautiful than anyone I'd ever known.

In time, I learned she came from a long line of techies—by way of
New Orleans, Atlanta, and Cripple Creek. People who made things.

Including a grandfather who had figured out a way to move
coal barges down the Ohio River, and a father who invented a
World War II device to eject wounded Air Force pilots from
their doomed planes.

When I asked her to marry me, she said, "There's really so much
waiting to do. You have to know, if it's the white picket fence you're
looking for, I'm not the girl for you."

Years later, she would recall a split second's pause. Then I said,
"Okay, let's do it all." And we did.

Morton Kaish